Jacques Mordal

Twenty-Five Centuries of Sea Warfare

Translated by Len Ortzen
With drawings and maps by Michel Fontaine

Futura Publications Limited
Futura Book

A Futura Book

First published in Great Britain in 1965
by Souvenir Press Limited, and simultaneously
in Canada by The Ryerson Press, Toronto 2,
Canada

First published in France in 1959
by Editions Robert Laffont under the title
25 *Siècles de Guerre sur Mer*

First Futura Publications edition 1976

ISBN 0 8600 7303 3
Printed in Great Britain by
Hazell Watson & Viney Ltd
Aylesbury, Bucks

Futura Publications Limited
Warner Road, London SE5

CONTENTS

v

PART TWO

Great Battles in World War Two

ILLUSTRATIONS

(between pages 204 and 205)

*Acknowledgments and thanks are due to the National Maritime
Museum and the Imperial War Museum for permission to use
photographs appearing in this book*

DRAWINGS AND MAPS

PREFACE

FROM the day when Cain killed Abel, men have gone on fighting; first on land, then at sea, as soon as they discovered that a hollowed-out tree-trunk made an excellent boat; and finally in the air, when they had learnt to fly. They have fought with sticks, slings, arrows, and cannon-balls; and are now prepared with guided missiles and nuclear bombs. But what matters more than the weapons are the men who use them. For, scourge though war may be, it is not made up only of ruin and suffering. It also brings out the finest human qualities, and stimulates the intellect, imagination, and powers of decision. War is never clear-cut, and battles whose issue would seem certain are often swayed by those imponderables which are called luck by some people and chance by others; so that a desperate situation is retrieved at the last moment, or a victory within grasp is snatched away.

Uncertain as are the fortunes of war on land, they are more so on the seas. Naval combat has retained its particular character, in spite of improvements in technique and the introduction of new weapons. The state of the elements and the condition of his material have a greater determining influence upon the seaman than upon any other fighter, yet he has possibilities of manoeuvre unknown in any other sphere of warfare, which he can utilize to the utmost if he has the will and the intelligence.

There have been immense changes since the time of the primitive canoe to the 65,000-ton armour-plated monsters of the Japanese in the war in the Pacific. But the tenets of sea warfare have not changed so much between the time when the Battle of Actium decided the fate of the Roman world and the Normandy Invasion that of Europe; both bore out the unchallengeable rule that "victory comes from the sea". New methods and new weapons, but the sea remains, hard on those who do not know it well, kindly to those at home on it, giving scope to initiative, stratagem, and surprise manoeuvres. While victory on land usually goes to the larger army or the better equipped, at sea the issue of a battle is less often determined by strength. Naval warfare has always contained an element of chance, and will probably continue to do so, whatever new weapons are invented. Harsher and more pitiless than land warfare—nowadays, a warship does not surrender!— sea warfare, nevertheless, still has something chivalrous about it. The guns fire on a vessel, not at men. Once the enemy ship is destroyed, its sailors become men in peril whom the law of the sea demands should be rescued even at the risk of one's own safety.

Sea battles are not fought to conquer thousands of square miles of salt water, but to gain mastery of the seas, to sail them without let or hindrance and forbid them to the enemy. Though nowadays the mastery is not complete without control of the skies.

In olden days pirates laid in wait on the main sea-routes like high-waymen, to capture or sink merchant ships. In our time, that danger in wartime usually comes from submarines or aircraft, and the protection of its merchant shipping is one of the prime concerns of a power at war.

In the seventeenth century a French admiral, Jean Bart, with only five frigates kept more than fifty English and Dutch warships at sea. In present times, a *Bismarck* has merely to show itself in the Atlantic for half the British fleet to go into action. The battle for the seas has changed in aspect but its principles remain the same, and are always likely to as long as the transport plane does not oust the cargo-boat. And as it took twenty-two tons of petrol to transport one ton of freight by airlift, at the time of the Korean War, the change does not seem likely!

Even in this age of nuclear warfare, it is still naval power which basically provides the most efficient deterrent to Soviet inter-continental missiles; the Allied aircraft-carriers, in spite of their apparent vulnerability, and the nuclear-powered Polaris submarines form the best bases for firing guided missiles. Having a range of eight hundred miles a day, the nuclear submarine can emerge at some unexpected point within reach of an enemy target, fire its missiles, and disappear again into the ocean fastness.

In spite of the great advances in mechanization and the development of scientific weapons, the role of the seaman is still as important as in the days of the sailing-ship. Although a flotilla commander does not now lead his men to board an enemy craft, and although he has radar and Asdic to give him a far greater picture of the scene of action than ever Nelson had with his spy-glass, the final decision, nevertheless, still rests with him, with the interpretation he gives to the information provided, and the use he makes of the means at his disposal. Each member of a warship's company, from the captain to the youngest seaman, has a definite job to do. To have his squadron or fleet in the right place at the right time, with the right equipment, and to seize an opportunity—that is the commander's role. To fight the ship and keep her in action, to save her from a dangerous situation—that is the role of the captain and crew.

The object of this book is to show how, from the earliest days, sea-men have carried out those missions on celebrated occasions when the fate of kingdoms or empires has been at stake. I have tried not so much to follow the evolution of naval warfare and its influence on the course of history, as to help the reader follow the action of these heroic combats, and realize to what noble heights men can rise when backed by sound experience and tactics.

It seemed to me that the interest of these different battles would be increased if the political and historical context of each were given some mention. But this book is not intended to be a comprehensive history of sea warfare. Many of the great naval battles are here described, but it has not been possible to deal with them all. On the other hand, some minor engagements are included because of their exceptional circumstances, or because of the outstanding qualities of the men who distinguished themselves.

PART ONE

In the Time of Oars and Sail

THE NAVAL BATTLES OF ANTIQUITY

From Sesostris to Xerxes—Salamis, the first naval battle in history (480 B.C.) —the sea-power of Carthage—birth of the Roman Navy—Caius Duilius and his secret weapons—the naval battles of the Punic Wars—Archimedes at Syracuse—the Mediterranean becomes a Roman lake—Antony and Cleopatra— the amazing Battle of Actium (31 B.C.).

IN the years 483–2 B.C. the great subject of conversation in Athens was the sensational discovery of a rich vein of silver in the mines of Laurium. The Athenians had already extracted more than a hundred talents of the precious metal. What was to be done with all this wealth? The city's finances were prosperous, so some of the people were of the opinion that it should be shared out. But Themistocles intervened and advised his fellow-citizens to forgo the benefits in view and to use the money for building a fleet of warships. The Athenians were in fact having trouble with Aegina, an island some twenty miles to the south, where the people had taken to piracy. The advice was followed, and orders were given for the building of a hundred triremes—galleys with three banks of oars.

This was the birth of the Athenian Navy, which three years later saved Greece by its victory off Salamis, in the first naval battle known to us in some detail.

The ancients, particularly the peoples living on the shores of the Mediterranean, had of course learnt how to handle boats long before the fifth century B.C. Without going back so far as Noah, whose Ark can be considered the ancestor of the floating townships of today, a Phoenician named Onous is credited with being the first to have thought of lopping the branches from a tree-trunk for it to carry him across the water. Just when this occurred is far from certain, as it is not even known in which century his compatriot Sanchoniathon, who attributed him with the discovery, actually lived. Some authorities place him as early as the twenty-first century B.C., others only in the thirteenth.

In any case, there is no doubt that the Greeks—reputed to be the earliest sailors in history, after the Phoenicians—had learnt how to build boats, if only for the Trojan War, which took place about the year 1270 B.C. The Egyptians, though, had crossed the seas much earlier than that, and to them are due the first examples of boat-building in the ancient world, from primitive canoes made by splitting a giant reed down the middle to slender boats of plaited bulrushes or of reeds covered with papyrus. In the time of Sesostris, at the latter part of the sixteenth century B.C., the first long rowing-boats were seen on the Nile; a short time after, they had a platform added at both ends for carrying fighting-men. Such were the earliest warships, and there was little real change between them and the galleys which sailed the seas for the next three thousand years. The last naval battle in which galleys took part was on July 9th, 1790, in the Baltic; and there were still some in service during the Russo–Swedish War of 1809. This record of continuity is unlikely to be broken by the cruiser or the battleship, condemned as out-of-date before reaching their first centenary, nor by the bomber, superseded by the guided missile after an even shorter life.

The galley, rigged with mast and sail, held the mastery of the Mediterranean for tens of centuries. It depended almost entirely on its rowers, though, especially when engaged in battle; the sails were only used to make course when the wind was favourable.

The danger from the Aeginian islanders, that Themistocles had brandished before his fellow-citizens to arouse their interest in sea-power, was really of small importance compared with the threat from the Persians. Xerxes was then at the height of his power, and had attacked Greece on several occasions. He possessed a fine fleet but had poor crews; and the sea was not always helpful to his enterprises—as is well known, he once had the waves whipped to punish them for dispersing his fleet by storm. He needed his ships as support for his invading army. The Persian soldiers could cross the Hellespont and march down the coast of Thrace and Macedonia, but their supplies and equipment had to be transported by sea. These supply vessels had been scattered by a sudden storm when off Mount Athos, during the expedition of 492 B.C., and the invading troops were forced to turn back because of lack of supplies. The next attempt, in 490, had been repulsed by Miltiades at the famous Battle of Marathon. The Athenians then thought themselves safe, but Themistocles realized that this victory over the Persians was not the end of the affair, that it would only lead to a greater conflict. And then what would happen? "You cannot succeed in holding off that vast army by land," he told the Athenians. "What is needed, is to cut its food supplies by destroying the fleet. Faced with famine, it will be obliged to turn back. That is your only hope."

Now at that time the Athenians had only about fifty galleys. The war against the Aeginians provided an excellent opportunity to increase

he number of units without giving Xerxes cause to declare that it was
an act of aggression. The newly discovered silver-mine would provide
he necessary money. Work was begun, and in less than three years the
Athenians built the hundred triremes with the hundred talents of silver,
and another hundred ships as well, paid for by the production of the older
mines of Laurium.

The Athenian galley was even then a vessel of some considerable size.
It had a complement of five officers, including the captain or trierarch,

A Greek galley

and the pilot, with the three banks of oars manned by 174 rowers, who
were also required to help the crew—few in number—in handling the
sails and working the ship. The actual fighting-men carried usually
consisted of four Cretan archers and fourteen hoplites—heavily-armed
foot-soldiers.

Xerxes, as Themistocles had anticipated, soon sent another army into
Greece, and of a size that made the previous expeditions seem little more
than reconnaissance forces. In the spring of 480 B.C. the Persian King
had assembled an army of 180,000 in Asia Minor; this huge force
crossed the Bosphorus on two bridges of boats, and then followed the
route of previous invaders down the coast of Macedonia. It was supported by a fleet which, according to Herodotus, comprised 1,207 galleys
carrying more than 200,000 men. Xerxes, learning from his disaster
in 492, had taken large-scale measures and cut a canal across the base
of the Mount Athos peninsula, deep enough for his largest vessels, and
so the most dangerous waters for his fleet were avoided.

Themistocles, who was chosen as commander-in-chief by his fellow-
countrymen when the invading forces drew near, wanted to send the

Greek fleet to meet the Persian as far up the coast as possible. Unfortunately, he had to deal with a coalition of small city-states that were very difficult to control. Sparta and Athens were admittedly the most powerful, but all the others had a voice in the matter. There was much discussion but less action. Meanwhile, Xerxes was continuing his advance. The heroic sacrifice of Leonidas at Thermopylae delayed but did not halt it. Plundering and sacking everything in their path the Persians were soon in sight of Athens. Only then was Themistocles able to obtain the general mobilization that he had been urging; the Greeks took up their arms and manned their ships.

Athens had almost three hundred galleys, many more than Sparta whose men were better soldiers than sailors. The command of the allied fleet should therefore have gone to Themistocles, who wanted to engage the enemy at the entrance to the gulf of Athens. But a matter of age caused the command to go to a Spartan, Eurybiades, who favoured a withdrawal to the Isthmus of Corinth. Themistocles had great difficulty in getting his plan accepted, but finally obtained agreement for the fleet to take up a defensive position at the head of the narrow straits separating the island of Salamis from the mainland, not far from the Piraeus and the Bay of Phalerum, which was then the port of Athens.

Fortunately for the Greeks, the elements had already helped to reduce the size of the enemy fleet; nearly four hundred of its ships had been destroyed by gales or by being driven ashore, and only nine hundred arrived and anchored in the Bay of Phalerum. Nevertheless, the war seemed lost for the Greeks. Athens had fallen, its remaining inhabitants had fled, and the victor was considering a diversionary attack on the island of Cythera to draw the Spartan army towards the southern end of the Peloponnese. However, Xerxes dropped this idea, as the situation among the Greeks had in the meantime taken a sudden turn. The Athenians were deeply disturbed by the sack of their city and the men from the Peloponnese were anxious about the fate of their home towns; there was again talk of withdrawing to the Isthmus of Corinth. Themistocles saw the danger and conceived a stratagem. By use of a double-agent, he let Xerxes believe that the Greeks were about to turn and flee and that the Persians would do well to attack at once, gaining advantage from the confusion among the Greek Fleet and preventing its joining up with the land forces.

Xerxes fell into the trap; against the advice of Artemisia, the wise and fearless Queen of Halicarnassus, who had constantly warned him that the Greeks were the more experienced sailors, he sent his ships into battle. His first move was to order two or three hundred galleys to make for the south of the island of Salamis, with the object of cutting the enemy's retreat. Themistocles could ask for nothing better; Xerxes thus reduced his superior strength still further, leaving himself with six hundred vessels against the three hundred and eighty of the Greeks. The margin was again narrowed by the clever tactics of Themistocles, for he drew up his fleet in narrow waters and thus prevented the Persians attacking in full force at one time.

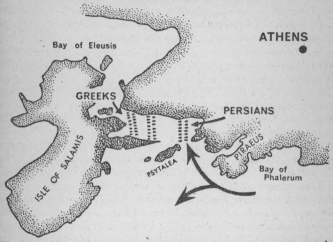

The Battle of Salamis, 480 B.C. (from Potter's *The United States and World Sea Power*)

Another advantage resulting from Xerxes's decision to blockade the waters to the south-west of Salamis was that the morale of the Greeks had risen and their hesitations had vanished. Their retreat was now cut, debate was pointless, the only thing left to do was to fight. Eurybiades allowed Themistocles to complete his plan of taking up a defensive position in the narrow straits where the large Persian ships could only advance in line abreast a few at a time. Moreover, Themistocles—who knew his home waters perfectly—counselled his captains to take no action until the wind had risen, the wind which always gets up in that channel at the same hour of the day. It would have little effect upon the Greek ships, which were low in the water, but would greatly inconvenience the Persians', whose prow and deck stood much higher.

The plan worked perfectly! Hampered by their own numbers, buffeted by the wind, and entangled one with the other, the Persians were forced to advance in line ahead against the solid front of the Greek Fleet. The poet Aeschylus, who took part in the action, wrote that the hoplites and archers did wonders and soon threw the enemy into confusion. The Persians found it almost impossible to manoeuvre their heavy vessels in those narrow waters and against the wind, and broke off the action. Xerxes, who had watched the course of the battle from a throne set upon the shore, knew by evening how great was the havoc caused to his fleet.

His ally Artemisia alone distinguised herself, disengaging from the confused fighting by audaciously flying a Greek banner and attacking a Persian ship—that of King Clamasithymus, whom she particularly disliked—and sending it to the bottom. Her idea of a team spirit was obviously peculiar, but at that period one could not expect too much; Cleopatra's conduct at the Battle of Actium, as will be seen later, was just as odd. In any case, Xerxes did not seem to hold it against her, and his only comment was that during the battle the men had acted like women, and the women had shown the courage of heroes! As for the Greeks, they were completely taken in by her ruse; believing Artemisia's ship to be one of their own, they let her slip away unmolested.[1]

The Greeks were saved by this naval victory, and had lost only forty or so ships against the Persians' two hundred, excluding the latter's ships captured by the Greeks. And they owed their safety to Themistocles, who had realized that the most powerful army is dependent upon its lines of communication, and that when its supplies come by sea a naval disaster can settle the issue. The Greek victory at Salamis was followed up a year later and completed by the destruction of the remnants of Xerxes's fleet off Mycale, a headland of Asia Minor.

Carthage was destined by its dominating central position to become a great sea-power, but as the Carthaginians extended their influence they clashed with the other nations engaged in the sea trade of the Mediterranean. At the time of the Battle of Salamis they had supported the Persian cause and attacked the Greek colonies in Sicily; their ships suffered a defeat off Himera, on the northern coast, the very day—it is believed—that Xerxes saw his own fleet routed.

Many generations passed before Carthage was able to wrest the mastery of the Mediterranean from Athens. Greece was then weakened by internal strife, by the Peloponnesian War, and the invasions of Alexander the Great; gradually, Rome took over the task of defending Mediter-

---

[1] Artemisia knew more than one trick. At the siege of Latmus in Asia Minor, that same year, she organized a religious ceremony with music and many acolytes in a wood sacred to the Great Mother of the Gods, just outside the besieged town. Its defenders were drawn by curiosity to the scene of the ceremony, leaving the way clear for Artemisia's soldiers to emerge from hiding and make the people of Latmus pay dearly for the festival they had gone to admire.

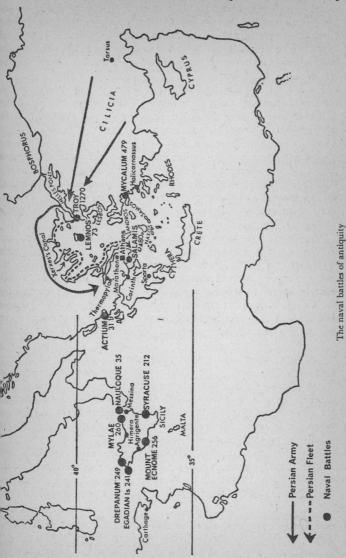

The naval battles of antiquity

— Persian Army
- - - Persian Fleet
● Naval Battles

ranean civilization. Yet at the outbreak of the Punic Wars in 264 B.C. the power of Rome depended almost entirely on her legions. She had no navy, and at most could only oppose the great quinqueremes of the Carthaginians with modest triremes built and manned by her Greek allies. Nothing could stop the enemy destroying the Romans' sea communications and increasing the attacks on the Italian coast. It was a time when the Carthaginians were able to boast of preventing the Romans from even bathing on their own beaches!

However, far from despairing, the Romans determined to do everything possible to meet the enemy, even in the element where he seemed unbeatable. They began by building galleys similar to enemy ships that had been driven ashore on the Italian coast, and in a surprisingly short time had a fleet of a hundred galleys with five banks of oars and a score of triremes; command of it was given to the consul Caius Duilius. This was in 260 B.C., and the war against Carthage was four years old. Duilius soon realized that it is one thing to build ships and quite another to train crews, and that unless some new weapon were discovered his apprentice sailors would stand little chance against the far more experienced Carthaginians. So he invented the grappling-iron, and this secret weapon of the time brought victory to the Romans in the first sea battle in their history.

The clash occurred off Mylae, on the north coast of Sicily. A fleet of one hundred and twenty-five Carthaginian galleys sighted a force of Roman ships slightly superior in number, and turned eagerly to the attack expecting a quick and easy victory; thirty of their galleys left the main body and swooped down upon the Roman Fleet. But at the first shock a number of gangways were slid swiftly across from the stems of Roman ships and hooked securely to the decks of the enemy. Before they had time to realize what was happening, the crews of the leading Carthaginian ships were overwhelmed by Roman legionaries, who swarmed across these devilish gangways and put the enemy to the sword.

The crews of the main wave of Carthaginian ships were aware that something unusual was happening and that the forepart of the Roman galleys was best avoided; so they endeavoured to attack aft or amidships. But they were now at a numerical disadvantage, and many were captured; the remainder lost heart and abandoned the action.

Great was the joy in Rome. Duilius was accorded a triumph, and was given the signal privilege of "an escort of musicians and torch-bearers when returning from dining with friends". The Italian Navy has remembered this first sea-captain, whose initial action was so strikingly effective, for one of its cruisers in commission at the beginning of the Second World War was called the *C. Duilio*.

The Romans did not stop at that first victory; four years later, within sight of Mount Ecnome on the south coast of Sicily, they again had great success with their grapples. A fleet of two hundred and fifty Roman galleys under the command of two consuls, Regulus and Nanlius, was escorting some transport ships from Messina when about an equal number of Carthaginian galleys, led by the celebrated Hamilcar, hove in sight and advanced to the attack. But the Romans inflicted such a defeat that they were able with impunity to carry the war to North African soil.

In 249 B.C. the consul Appius Claudius Pulcher was less fortunate at Drepanum—the present-day Trapani. He took his fleet up one of the channels, thinking to catch the Carthaginians at anchor and bring off the grappling trick in the narrow waters. But the Punic admiral was not to be trapped so easily; he got his ships under way and reached the open sea by the other channel. Claudius was imprudent enough to follow him; the Carthaginians were in their element in open waters, they avoided being grappled, and their skilful manoeuvring won them the day. Ninety-three ships and twenty thousand Roman soldiers fell into their hands. But then had not Claudius—as was pointed out to him when he got back to Rome—made the great mistake of going into action against the signs of the oracles? He had been informed that the sacred chickens were refusing to eat. "Throw them into the sea," he had replied. "If they don't want to eat, they can drink, then." This sacrilegious remark nearly cost him his life; all the influence of highly placed friends, not to mention his sister, a vestal virgin, was needed for him to escape with a heavy fine.

Not long afterwards, another disaster—due to a storm this time—brought the loss of a hundred ships. But the Romans did not give way to despair. They began at once to rebuild their fleet, and crews were trained more thoroughly. Carthage, on the other hand, was content to rest on her laurels. When news of the Roman rearming reached Hannon, the Carthaginian naval commander, his crews were rusty from long idleness in harbour. The Roman Fleet awaited him off the western point of Sicily, in the neighbourhood of the Egadian islands, not far from the scene of the disastrous action of 249 B.C. Hannon's ships came up from the west with the wind astern, hoping to smash and scatter the Romans without too much loss. But he no longer had to do with 'prentice crews. His opposite number, the consul Lutatius Catulius, was an experienced seaman, and the fleet he commanded was vastly superior to its predecessors. It held the attack of the Carthaginians, sank fifty of their ships and captured seventy. Hamilcar evacuated Sicily in disgust. (In the spring of 241 B.C.)

It would have been better for the unfortunate Hannon if he had not returned to Carthage. Luckless commanders were not treated gently there. Less fortunate than Claudius had been, he was condemned to death and crucified.[1]

So the Mediterranean became a Roman lake. When the Second Punic War began, Carthage had still not rebuilt her fleet and was at a strategical disadvantage; in spite of Hannibal's great victories on land, by the Trebia, by Lake Trasimene, and at Cannes, the war ended disastrously for Carthage. In 202 B.C. the Romans were able to invade North Africa because of their command of the seas

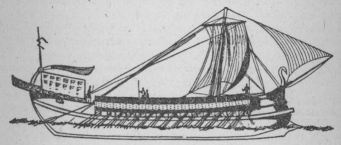

Reconstruction of a Roman trireme

Syracuse had revolted against the Romans earlier in the war, in 212. A strong combined force commanded by the consul Marcellus besieged the town by land and sea. This siege, which lasted for three years, is famous for the part played by Archimedes. He is credited with the invention of a number of extraordinary devices to destroy the Roman ships; massive beams heavily weighted with stones were dropped on galleys under the sea-walls, to stave in their decks, and a kind of great iron hand or grab worked by a chain tried to lift ships by the stern and then break them by letting them fall into the water. But Archimedes's most famous invention during the siege was a huge parabolic mirror with which he managed to set fire to some of the enemy ships by reflecting the sun's rays upon them. In spite of all the damage he inflicted on the Romans, Marcellus wanted the life of the great scientist to be spared. But when the town eventually fell, Archimedes was killed in his workroom by a Roman soldier, unaware of his identity, because he was absorbed in a geometrical problem traced out on the sand and refused to leave until he had solved it.

[1] This was not the Hannon who is celebrated for his voyage round Africa, which took place in 480 B.C.

The Romans met with no opposition in the western Mediterranean after the fall of Carthage, and gradually extended their control towards the eastern shores. In 191 B.C. Livius Salinator, with a hundred large ships under his command, defeated a force of eighty Syrian galleys led by Polyxenidas, admiral of Antiochus the Great, off the coast of Cilicia. Twenty-three of the Syrian vessels were boarded and captured, and the rest fled. In the following year Polyxenidas was again defeated by a Roman fleet, commanded by Emilius, who captured thirteen of his ships and burnt twenty-nine. Another great victory was won by the Romans in the Aegean a hundred years later, when the famous Lucullus first defeated Mithridates on land and then surprised his fleet off Lemnos, capturing twenty-two ships.

Rome's power knew no limits. The only way to find a worthy enemy at sea seemed to be for the Roman Navy to fight between itself! And that in fact was what did happen at Actium in 31 B.C.

There can be few other instances of such peculiar psychological circumstances leading up to a battle as in the case of this famous action in which Octavian—later the first Roman Emperor, Augustus—was victorious over the combined fleets of his rival, Mark Antony, and the latter's mistress, Cleopatra, Queen of Egypt.

The situation was extremely intricate. Antony had been an associate of Julius Caesar and had crossed the Rubicon with him, then been chosen by Caesar to share the consulship; but Antony had nevertheless helped to plot the murder of the dictator, if Plutarch is to be believed, in order to seize absolute power for himself. However, there were rivals; first and foremost, Octavian, Caesar's grand-nephew and adoptive son, who in spite of his youth—he was only eighteen at the time—had no intention of being deprived of his inheritance. Then there was the beautiful Cleopatra, whom Caesar had set more securely upon the throne of Egypt and who was intriguing to conquer Rome for Caesarion, her son by Caesar. ... In short, much plotting went on for three years, with Antony and Octavian constantly quarrelling and becoming reconciled again.

"If Cleopatra's nose had been a little shorter ..." Octavian might never have triumphed if Antony had not fallen madly in love with the Queen of Egypt when she visited him at Tarsus. For her, Antony divorced his first wife, Fulvia, although she was strongly supporting his cause in Rome, and then abandoned his second, Octavia, his rival's sister, whom he had married to seal a temporary reconciliation; and had also given up some of the Eastern provinces which had been his share of the Roman Republic's possessions.

These various indulgences and desertions were to be his ruin. Rome eagerly embraced Octavian's cause and declared war on Cleopatra and on Antony, with whom she had taken refuge.

Antony had raised a very strong force in the Eastern provinces he controlled—a fleet of about 500 galleys with two to ten banks of oars, and an army of 200,000 foot-soldiers and 12,000 cavalry. Octavian's fleet was only half the strength of Antony's, he had but 80,000 soldiers, though 12,000 cavalry too. Antony also had the benefit of all the Egyptian forces, which Cleopatra had placed under his command; but this had disadvantages, for the Romans were making war on Cleopatra rather than on Antony, and if she had returned to Egypt matters might have been arranged. However, Antony was strong enough on land to stand firm and await the attack of Octavian's legions. He was much less sure of his chances at sea, where his superiority in numbers was offset by the greater skill of the Roman sailors, who had shown their mettle a few years previously during the campaign against Sextus Pompey.[1]

Cleopatra, however, wanted her lover to fight the battle at sea, and because of her urgings he disposed his fleet off Actium, the southern peninsula at the entrance to the Ambracian Gulf, on the Ionian coast of Greece.[2]

Antony had little faith in the fleet as such. There was a dearth of good sailors; he burnt his worst ships to prevent their falling intact into enemy hands, and made up the crews of the others with legionaries who had fought only on land. He placed his hopes chiefly in the seventy Egyptian ships commanded by Cleopatra in person, which were much better manned than his own. He had in fact no intention of engaging in a real sea-fight. To his mind, the heavy vessels anchored in the mouth of the gulf and chained together constituted a floating fortress—and an impregnable one, he hoped. Many naval commanders after him were to learn the cost of ignoring the essential character of sea warfare—mobility and freedom to manoeuvre.

Octavian's fleet crossed the Ionian Sea and reached Epirus before Antony had time to complete his defences. The latter's destruction of some of his ships had greatly reduced his superiority in numbers; and his opponents were not only more experienced on water but also had

[1] A campaign notable for the sea-fight off Nauloque, on the north coast of Sicily, in waters where Duilius had been victorious during the Punic wars. The Battle of Nauloque took place in 35 B.C., four years before Actium, and by skilful use of grapples Octavian's fleet completely crushed that of Sextus Pompey, only 17 of the latter's 300 ships managing to escape.

[2] Cleopatra thought that a naval battle would enable her to disengage her forces more easily if things went badly. When she withdrew, there was no longer any reason for the fighting to continue; but her departure was more like a flight, and—as will be seen—led to Antony's unpardonable action of abandoning his men to follow her.

another new weapon, the harpoon, which proved as revolutionary as the grapple had been. It was an invention of Agrippa, Octavian's chief lieutenant and one of the best naval commanders of the time, as the course of the battle was to show.

The object of the harpoon was similar to that of the grapple. This primitive weapon, a heavy log with a steel beak, was shot by catapult

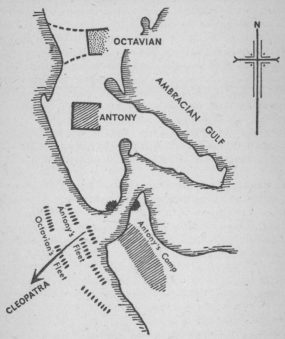

The Battle of Actium, 31 B.C.

deep into the side of an enemy ship, then the attached hawser was pulled in, bringing the enemy vessel close enough to be boarded—and at hand-to-hand fighting the Roman legionary had no superior. These technical advances, coupled with the greater experience of the Roman crews, left Antony's hardened comrades-in-arms without illusions as to the likely outcome of the battle. "Leave the fighting at sea to the Phoenicians and the Egyptians," they said to him. "They're more used to it. And let us who are better at fighting on firm land win or die there."

But it was the smiles or frowns of his mistress that mattered to Antony now, not the rules of warfare; and Cleopatra, consciously or not, was to lead him to his ruin.

The sea was so rough for three days following Octavian's arrival that no action was possible. On the fourth day the weather began to improve, and by the fifth the sea was calm again. The battle to decide the fate of Rome was joined within sight of the troops of both sides, standing idly on either shore of the gulf.

Antony had ordered his ships' captains to await the enemy attack, for their heavy vessels would be endangered by the reefs and shallows farther out; Octavian was thereby deprived of the advantage he hoped to have from his ships of small draught and the skill of their crews. Until late morning the two fleets observed each other without budging from their positions. But at about noon a breeze rose from the sea; Antony's men began to show signs of impatience, eager to prove their worth. Those on the left wing could stand the inactivity no longer, and shot out of line towards the enemy, hoping to overwhelm him with their taller ships. Octavian at once grasped his opportunity. He withdrew his right wing towards the open sea, where his light craft could manoeuvre better than Antony's, which were further handicapped by their lack of real sailors. The stratagem was completely successful. Octavian's ships, suddenly changing course, bore down on the enemy, grappling and boarding them. The fight was little different from what it would have been on land, the Roman legionaries on both sides hacking at each other with pikes and swords, hurling fire-brands and burning pitch on to their opponents' decks.

Meanwhile Agrippa, who commanded the left wing of Octavian's fleet, was carrying out the manoeuvre that won the day; bearing down on the enemy's right he obliged the opposing commander, Publicola, to swing his ships round to avoid being outflanked. This was fatal for the latter, who thus became separated from the rest of Antony's fleet, and before long there was dangerous confusion on that wing.

The issue was still in doubt, however, when Cleopatra made a signal to her ships which were not yet engaged. The Egyptians were at once seen to hoist their sails and pass through the line of battle, creating even more confusion. It was thought that Cleopatra would tack and return to the assault. Not at all; with a good wind in their sails, her ships set course for the Peloponnese. Neither Octavian's nor Antony's forces could believe their eyes at this sudden flight. But the greatest surprise was when Antony himself, unable to understand his beloved's action, jumped into a fast galley and sped after her, leaving his forces to their fate. Five of Octavian's galleys gave chase, but he succeeded in overhauling and joining Cleopatra's ship—she refused to let him aboard at first—and sailed away in dishonour.

Most of Antony's fleet fought on, unaware that their leaders' desertion made the struggle pointless. The light was fading before they gave in, exhausted by the fighting and impeded by the strong wind, which was blowing up for a gale. Three hundred of their ships fell into Octavian's hands. Five thousand men had lost their lives in the battle, which had been caused in the main by the jealousy of two women, Octavia and Cleopatra. But it enabled Octavian, with his one great rival out of the way, to rise to supreme power and bring about the splendid Augustan age of the Roman Empire. While the accursed lovers, Antony and Cleopatra, met their death a year after Actium—an inevitable and logical conclusion to their wretched adventure.

Neither of the opposing commanders-in-chief at Actium was a sailor. Each owed his past victories on land, in nearly every case, to the skill of his lieutenants. There can be no doubt that Agrippa's stratagem had a decisive effect in Octavian's favour. The experience of the Roman sailors and the unexpected action of Cleopatra did the rest.

II

THE COMING OF THE NORMANS

The Romans in Britain—invasions by Angles, Saxons, and Danes—the Norsemen raid the French coast—Paris attacked by river—William the Conqueror and his invasion fleet—a masterly amphibious operation.

IT was not until early in the Christian era that sea warfare, previously confined to the Mediterranean, began to develop in the waters round Britain. There were probably fights between Norsemen before then, in the North Sea and the Baltic, but no account has come down to us; whereas Julius Caesar's *De Bello Gallico*, his account of the wars in Gaul and his invasions of southern Britain, mentions for the first time places that were to be heard of in history again and again in connection with epic naval battles. Long before Caesar, however, the Greeks had acquired some scanty knowledge of these misty islands. The first voyage of which there is an actual record was that undertaken about 324 B.C. by the Greek mathematician and explorer, Pytheas. Setting out from Massilia (Marseilles), he and his companions sailed round the Iberian peninsula and along the Gallic coast to Brittany, and thence up the Channel to Kent and across to the Scandinavian coast—perhaps even to Iceland.[1] He was astonished to discover that "the barbarians of the north" enjoyed a degree of civilization comparable to that of his compatriots, and were by no means inferior to Phoenician sailors, who had visited these islands earlier. Long before the first invasion attempt by Julius Caesar, the ancient Britons—the Picts and Scots—had probably begun to trade with tribes on the Continent, which they could see across the Straits on a clear day. What is certain is that the victorious Romans did not long hesitate after reaching the water obstacle on the northern coast of Gaul; from the headland, now known as Cape Griz Nez, they must have been tantalized by the sight of the white cliffs opposite. Caesar soon set up ship-building yards at Boulogne, and the harbour was a scene of busy activity throughout his pro-consulship.

He had many opportunities of observing the native sailors and their craft. The ships were stoutly built with seasoned oak-timbers, their prows stood high above the water, and their sails were of coarse leather; they

---

[1] Pytheas described a land that he called Thule, six days sail from Albion. Opinions are divided as to whether it was Iceland or Jutland, although there is little resemblance between the two.

were better able than his own to resist the rough seas and gales of the
Channel. The Roman galleys, more used to the calm and tideless sea
of the Mediterranean, had the advantage in fine weather; but as soon
as the wind rose, superiority was with the northerners. Moreover,
the high counters of their vessels made it impossible for the Romans to
ply the usual missile weapons with any hope of success, and severely
hampered those boarding tactics which, ever since the battle of Mylae,
had been favoured by the Romans.

A large drakkar crossing to England with men and horses (*from the Bayeux Tapestry*)

After five centuries occupation of Britain and Gaul, the Roman legions
were withdrawn to defend Italy against the threatening invasion of the
Goths. One of the few naval battles in the Mediterranean recorded at
this period took place in 551, off the town of Sinnigallia on the Adriatic
coast, between a Roman fleet and that of Totila, chief of the Goths.
Formidable though they were on land, the Goths proved much less
so on water. The Romans boarded the enemy, and in hand-to-hand
fighting soon cleared the decks, most of the Goths perishing by the sword
or by drowning.

Britain, meanwhile, left undefended and an easy prey, was slowly
but steadily coming under the sway of successive waves of migrants,
sailing in from the Scandinavian and German shores. First over the
seas came the Saxons, in 449, only a year after the Roman evacuation;
their chief concern was to establish trading settlements. But they were
followed by more dreaded invaders, the Angles, who crossed from the
Baltic in 582 under the leadership of their King Ida. It was the first
organized expedition from overseas since the time of Caesar, and no

peaceful one either; landing from sixty ships at the mouth of the Tyne, they advanced inland, ravaging the country and driving the original inhabitants towards the west. Many of the Britons who escaped capture or death crossed the Channel and settled in the Gaulish coastal area of Armorica, now known as Brittany. It was from this stock that there arose a race of hardy seamen destined to rank among the English shipman's most bitter foes.

The Anglo-Saxon invaders fought over Britain for the next three hundred years. The country was eventually divided into seven kingdoms, until Egbert, King of Wessex (800–836), proved himself the strongest and laid the basis of English unity. But then the predatory Norsemen came on the scene, and it was the turn of the invaders to undergo invasion!

The Scandinavians had always been sea-rovers, through necessity as much as by inclination; they drew their subsistence from the sea, they scoured it, lived and died on it. The title of "Sea-king" given to the leaders of their bands was as greatly prized as the highest orders of nobility in other lands at a later period. There were so many fighting-men continually at sea that at the beginning of the ninth century "the number of Danes roving the seas was much greater than those remaining on land".[1]

These hordes came to grips among themselves now and again, as might be expected. The old sagas tell of a great sea-battle at Bravalla off the coast of "Scania" about the year 735. All the sea-kings, all the freebooting Norsemen took part; more than a thousand sail were present, so it is said. The fighting continued on the shore, and some of the fiercest struggles were those in which women-warriors took part—the Skoldmeyars, as they were called, or Buckler-Virgins, similar to the Amazons of antiquity.

Before long the Norsemen were ranging across the North Sea in their drakkars—sailing-craft with a high prow and shaped like a dragon—which they handled with great skill. Their favourite tactics were to lie in wait in small bays near the mouth of a river, and to pounce on craft putting to sea—hence their name of Viking, from *vik*, meaning "bay" in Norwegian.

Their raids were solely for the purpose of pillage, each band being led by its "sea-king", though he took no greater share of the plunder than any of his men. But the raiding bands gradually joined forces, and in 787 an organized descent was made on the Wessex coast; a few years later, in 794, Northumbria was invaded. The Anglo-Saxons were

[1] *History of the Norsemen*, by Henry Wheaton.

overwhelmed and forced to retreat westwards, just as they themselves had chased out the Celts two centuries earlier.

In the latter part of the ninth century, one of the more notorious sea-kings, Ragnar Lodbrok, built two ships larger than any seen before in order to lead a strong raiding force. The weather turned against him, however, and he was forced to return to his base. Nothing daunted, he set sail again and reached the Northumbrian coast, but his ship was driven ashore and wrecked. He led his men inland, burning and plundering as they went, until Ella, King of Northumbria, captured him and had him cast into a cell filled with poisonous snakes.

The news of this horrible death roused the wrath of the Danes and incited them to increase their raiding expeditions. In 867 Ragnar's sons made a landing on the East coast and captured York, then gained possession of the whole of Northumbria. They avenged their father by having Ella put to death with even greater cruelty; his chest was torn open with red-hot irons and his lungs were ripped from his living body.

During the Roman occupation the Celts had not been concerned with the defence of their shores; and the Anglo-Saxons had given but little more thought to the matter. Their different Kingdoms were entirely without plans for co-operation and mutual support in times of stress, so a combined fleet was impossible until there was some kind of national solidarity. This was brought about by Alfred the Great, when he succeeded to the leadership of the West Saxons in 872. He recognized that the only way to secure a lasting peace for the country was to meet and overthrow the Norse invaders before they could effect a landing; and it was not long before there were flotillas manned and ready at various points round the coast. Alfred's far-sighted measures were rewarded with success, and he managed to stem the Danish inroads; but he was unable to expel the newcomers who had already established themselves in strength. However, he managed to limit their expansion and fix their boundaries by treaty.

The Norsemen were then obliged to turn their attention elsewhere, and began to penetrate more deeply into France. They had already made several incursions into western Europe, but their first major raid ended in disaster. Sailing up the Meuse, they had been attacked by the Franks on their return and had lost all their loot. This had occurred at the beginning of the sixth century. During the reign of Charlemagne they harassed the west coast of France, but at the break-up of the Empire they went marauding all round Europe, from the Elbe to the Guadalquivir, laying waste to Seville in 827.

These expeditions, however, can hardly be classed as sea battles; the Norsemen were unrivalled on water, where their worst enemies were wind and weather. They kept to the coasts as much as possible, swooping into estuaries and rivers to raid inland. Their craft were very light, so frail in appearance that it is difficult to imagine them among the dangerous waters of the Frisian islands or in the reef-ridden channels between Ushant and the mainland, or meeting the gales in the Bay of Biscay. But they were intended to go everywhere; when a river became too shallow, or progress was impeded by a barrage of trees or some such defence-work, the Norse warriors manhandled their vessels to pass round the obstruction. These invaders in search of plunder were thus likely to appear in the most unexpected places. In 843 a fleet making for France divided to carry out two raids; one half rounded the coast of Brittany to attack Nantes, while the other, led by Ragenar, forced its way up the Seine, sacked Rouen, and continued to Paris, burning and plundering on the way. The fortified Ile de la Cité resisted their attacks, but they looted the abbey of St. Germain-des Prés on the south bank and then swept upstream as far as Melun. Charles the Bald had to pay a heavy bribe to be left in peace.

But that was little compared with what was to follow! Frustrated by King Alfred's resolute attitude, the Danes in England joined forces with their cousins in Jutland and the Frisian islands to form a great array under the orders of the notorious Hasting (known also as Siegfried or Sigefroy). This fleet of 700 sail, carrying 30,000 warriors, arrived within sight of the walls of Paris on November 24th, 885.

The French capital was contained chiefly on the Ile de la Cité in those days, with a settlement on either bank of the river. Its defenders, under the leadership of Count Eudes and Bishop Gosselin, held out for a whole year. The besiegers assailed them with every weapon of war invented since the time of the Romans. Vessels were set on fire and directed against the bridges; but before any damage could be done, the defenders hurled into the ships enough blocks of stone prised from the city walls to sink them. Then the river Seine played a part. A sudden rise in its waters swept away a bridge, and the garrison in the tower protecting the approaches was cut off; the isolated men fought like lions and were only overcome when night fell. After a year of siege, Charles the Fat, who was encamped with a relief force on the heights of Montmartre, preferred to buy off the invaders. He had to pay 700 silver *livres* and allow them to go plundering up the Seine as far as Burgundy. Then, finding nothing left that was worth the taking the Norsemen decided to return and see what was happening in England.

Alfred's successors lacked his qualities, and through neglecting the fleet were obliged to pay Danish raiders large money bribes to be left in peace. Delighted with this, the raiders descended time and again on the English coast; until Ethelred the Unready, seeking to avoid payment of yet another instalment of Danegeld, foolishly authorized the St. Brice's Day massacre (November 13th, 1003) of every Dane in the kingdom. This brought an invasion force scurrying across the seas to avenge the outrage, and eventually led to the Danish conquest of England by Canute—resulting in constant turmoil that William of Normandy was soon to turn to his own advantage.

In order to put an end to the ravages of the Northmen, Charles the Simple, King of the Franks, accepted what had become a fact and by the Treaty of St. Clair-sur-Epte, in 912, ceded to Rollo, the chief of the Northmen, the tract of land between the Channel coast and the Seine above Rouen—the province that the Romans had called Lugdunensis Secunda, and to which its new owners (while gradually extending the frontiers south-west, almost to the Loire) gave the name of Normandy. For the next century and a half the Normans wisely continued settling in their fertile territory, though still a sea-faring race and having as great an interest as ever in events across the Channel.

Thus it was that on the death of the childless Edward the Confessor, the seventh Duke of Normandy (a bastard son of Robert the Devil by a tanner's daughter, Arlette, who gave birth to him in the castle at Falaise) laid claim to the throne of England; and decided to invade the country on hearing that Harold, whose regal pretensions were no stronger than his own, had hurriedly had himself proclaimed King.

The invasion of 1066, with its political and religious aspects, was the best organized and most successful amphibious operation of all time, until quite recent years. . . . Yet, amazingly, it met with no opposition at sea, although Harold had at his disposal enough ships and seamen to prevent the landing. This neglect on Harold's part was the basic cause of his ultimate defeat.

"There is no reason to doubt that Harold had mustered a considerable fleet. The Anglo-Saxon Chronicle states quite clearly that by the spring of 1066 the largest assembly of ships and men ever seen in England was gathered at Sandwich, to repulse the threatened invasion of William the Conqueror."[1] But this fleet was no longer guarding the approaches to the south coast when, at Michaelmas, the Norman ships hove in sight and made a landing at Pevensey. We shall come to the reason in a moment. First, a word must be said about William's preparations, which were in every way remarkable.

[1] Luard Clowes, *History of the Royal Navy*, Vol. I, p. 72.

His decision made, the Norman Duke's first move was to obtain the support of the highest spiritual power, the Pope. The approval of Rome to "bring England within the discipline of the Holy See again", and a Bull excommunicating Harold, favoured William's preparations —even on the military side—to an extent difficult to realize in present times. Next, he formed an alliance with Tostig, Harold's rebellious brother who had recently been governing Northumbria—and who was also a marriage-relation of William. Tostig was sent to Norway to enlist the aid of the northerners.

Meanwhile, William assured himself of neighbouring neutrality, as well as active help from grasping overlords, through the influence of his father-in-law, Count Baldwin of Flanders, who had been nominated Regent of France in 1060, during the minority of Philippe I. There was but one reverse in all this diplomatic and military activity—the hostile attitude of Conan, Duke of Brittany. But his death came opportunely— so much so, in fact, that it was said he had been helped on his way— and his successor, Hoel, preferred to avoid a similar fate and to furnish his powerful neighbour with a body of volunteers, commanded by his son.

It was the Norman barons who showed some reluctance to further their Duke's designs, and he had to persuade them with promises of money and the titles to English lands when conquered. He aroused their greed so much that "some came forward with the offer of ships, others with men-at-arms, and many promised to march in person under the ducal banner; clerks gave their money, merchants their cloth, and peasants their foodstuffs". Some sold their household possessions or mortgaged their land in order to furnish ships or pay for soldiers.

The energetic William borrowed money from all sides, against the promise of lands he had never seen. But confidence was high, and lenders came forward—obtaining rates of interest that broke all records! Small wonder that the spring and summer of that momentous year saw every haven and harbour along the Norman coast the scene of busy preparations.

Before long, the expedition found enthusiastic support from the Rhine to Aquitaine; the Counts of Anjou and of Poitou, of Penthièvre and of Burgundy, Teuton barons, all flocked to join William of Normandy— as did many greedy adventurers and loot-hungry soldiers of fortune. There was no age limit; the oldest member of the force was the Viscount of Coutances, Néel, in his eightieth year. Altogether an army of 65,000 gathered in a camp at St. Valéry-sur-Somme. The strength of the fleet that was to carry them has been variously estimated, but the figure given by the historian Augustin Thierry—four hundred large transports and a thousand small craft—would seem approximately correct.

All these had the lines of the Norseman's drakkar—long and lean like a serpent, with the head rearing up to form the prow and the tail curved to make the stern. The largest were two-masted, with a square sail, and could transport two or three hundred men. The small craft, raw-timbered, hurriedly constructed vessels, were not decked over and

Duke William's men start to build the invasion fleet (*from the Bayeux Tapestry*)

their motive power was the oar; their maximum load was about forty men and a few horses. They were in no sense warships; they were transports, only required to hold together long enough to give passage to the army. They needed good weather for the crossing, or would soon have foundered.

William had appointed the then wide mouth of the river Dives, between the Seine and the Orne, as a first rendezvous for his ships. The whole fleet set out on September 14th, and with the wind in the right quarter covered the distance of nearly a hundred miles to St. Valéry in a single night. The Duke was in Rouen, taking leave of his wife Matilda and arranging for his son Robert, aged 16, to be in control of the Duchy during his absence. He rode north to St. Valéry, and found everything in good order; the loading plans, which had been drawn up in great detail, were soon executed, and the army was ready to take ship and sail.

But the equinoctial gales were blowing, and continued to blow for another ten days, much to William's fury. If he did not soon succeed in crossing the Channel the whole enterprise would have to be abandoned until the following spring—which was what Harold thought, never believing that his rival could possibly be ready to invade before the summer ended. To add to William's troubles, the plague appeared in the camp. Men were dying from it every day; morale sank so low that William increased the rations and called in the aid of the supernatural.

The mouldering bones of Saint Valéry were hastily disinterred and paraded through the streets, with everyone on his knees praying for a change of wind. And on September 27th the sun rose on a gentle sea, with a breeze coming encouragingly from the south-west. William the Conqueror must have given a sigh of relief!

Tostig, in the meantime, having reached the Baltic with the few ships given him by William early in the spring, had succeeded in rousing the warlike spirit of Harald Hafager, King of Norway, one of the most celebrated sea-captains of the time and renowned for his expeditions which had taken him as far afield as Constantinople. He was only waiting for the ice to break to gather together a fleet of three hundred vessels and to attack the east coast of England.

Thus assured, Tostig took to sea again with sixty ships, looking in at the Frisians to augment his fighting strength with some of the island freebooters, and then filled in time by making a descent upon his late subjects on the Northumbrian coast. Harald had sailed for the Orkneys as soon as weather permitted, and then landed in Scotland; there he heard that Tostig had been repulsed and driven north. The two joined up, and their combined fleet sailed down the coast. They razed Scarborough, plundered the region of the Tyne, and advanced up the Humber and the Ouse. Two armies sent against them were defeated one after the other, and Tostig took York.

Throughout the summer Harold had been keeping watch on the Channel coast. But with winter approaching and no sign of the enemy from France, it seemed to him more important to race north and eliminate the invaders there; after that, he could return to his vigilance in the south. He reached York on September 25th, just after its capture by Tostig. Without losing a moment, he led his army to the attack and inflicted a heavy defeat on the invaders. Tostig and "the last of the Vikings" were slain. Olaf, the King of Norway's son, just managed to escape with the remnants of his forces and to get to sea with a mere twenty-three ships.

It had been a costly diversion! But William may well have been secretly relieved at the disaster to his turbulent allies, now that they had successfully played their role.

If Harold's fleet had not abandoned its watch while he was marching on York, his calculations might have proved successful. Perhaps he had taken the wish for reality in accepting reports brought to him from Normandy—by double-agents, possibly—that William had given up his plans because of the persistent, adverse winds. Or perhaps there had been no one, after Harold's departure for the north, capable of retaining the mariners—who had never, within living memory, been required to remain for so long in the King's service. "After the Feast of the Nativity of Our Lady (September 8th), their being no food left the crews refused to continue to serve; for the season of provisioning had begun, and no man could keep them there any longer."[1]

How the Norwegian diversion helped the Norman invasion

The way was clear for William, and the fine weather had returned. The whole of September 27th was spent embarking and putting to sea. William led the way in his own vessel, *Mora*, with the Papal banner fluttering at the masthead and the three leopards of Normandy embroidered on the sail. The concourse of vessels strung out behind him, and before long they were widely scattered on the waters. The *Mora* forged ahead during the night, and at daybreak the Duke and his companions found themselves alone and in sight of land. . . . They waited for other vessels to come up; and before the end of that day the whole

[1] *Anglo-Saxon Chronicle.*

force had got ashore unopposed near the village of Pevensey, whose inhabitants fled inland.

The rest is well known—with the news of the Bastard's landing Harold hurried south from York, and by forced marches reached Hastings by October 13th; only to meet his death and leave the Norman Conqueror free to assume the English crown.

III

THE BATTLE OF SOUTH FORELAND, WHICH SAVED ENGLAND'S INDEPENDENCE

Richard the Lion-Heart's fleet—Philippe Augustus, the "poor relation" in the Crusades—a Turkish ship's great fight against heavy odds—rupture between the French and English—the naval battle of Damme (1213)—Eustace the Monk, in control of the Straits of Dover, enables Louis of France to land and march on London—Hubert de Burgh's victory at South Foreland (August 24th, 1217).

IT was a peculiar enough position when the Duke of Normandy was King of England, yet held his possessions across the Channel as a vassal of the French King by the terms of the treaty of St. Clair. Yet how much more extraordinary was the position in 1154, when the English crown passed to Henry Plantagenet, who was a great-grandson of William the Conqueror through his mother; for in addition to Normandy he held the adjacent province of Anjou, inherited from his father, and Guyenne, Aquitaine, and Auvergne by his marriage to Eleanor, the divorced wife of Louis VII of France. These complications led to countless disputes, and it is hardly to be wondered that the Kings of France were very sensitive with regard to their powerful neighbour, whose French territories were more extensive than their own.

Henry II admittedly made homage to Louis VII for his French dominions, but was soon off to annex Brittany, which became an English dependency for a time.

Ships had little part to play in all that. France, in fact, had no real fleet. How could she have? She had only a few miles of Channel coast, north of the Somme; to the south, it was all held by the Anglo–Normans. The Biscay coast of the Languedoc did not become French until 1229, and Provence was in the hands of the Emperor. It was St. Louis, by his purchase of Aigues–Mortes in the mid-thirteenth century, to embark his crusaders, who first gave the French an outlet to the Mediterranean.

The English had therefore nothing to fear from French seamen. But the Flemish, under the leadership of the Counts of Boulogne and Flanders, had a fleet of six hundred vessels ready to sail in 1167. This was a far stronger force than England could oppose at sea, but she was saved by her soldiers. A concentration of troops in Kent was enough to discourage the would-be invaders. However, England had learnt her lesson, and resolved never to be caught in such a situation again. Twenty-five years later, Richard the Lion-Heart set off for the Crusades at the head of a splendid fleet.

The French Norsemen had become civilized; those in Scandinavia had had their day. They still occasionally raided the Orkneys and the coast of Scotland, and in 1075 King Haakon of Norway landed in Northumbria, but soon withdrew. The ageing Kings, Henry II and Louis VII, after several skirmishes between their forces, swore an ever-lasting peace; and there was even a question of their going on a crusade to the Holy Land together. But death intervened.

English ships made their appearance in the Mediterranean, as privateers as much as traders, and were soon at grips with the Barbary pirates, who were usually classed together as Saracens, whether Turkish, Syrian, or North African; in fact, they were all equally ferocious and dangerous.

Although no great sea battles took place during the Third Crusade, led by Philippe Augustus and Richard the Lion-Heart, there were several stirring naval episodes. In April, 1190, Richard mustered at Dartmouth the greatest fleet ever seen in an English port. Even in those days it could be called an Imperial Fleet, for Norman, Breton, Poitevin, and Aquitaine ships together outnumbered the English. This armada had a rough passage to the Mediterranean; when it reached Marseilles, on August 22nd, 1190, decimated by storms, Richard —who had made the journey overland with Philippe Augustus—had grown tired of waiting. He had hired ships and sailed for Genoa; from there he went south to Messina, where his flotilla caught up with him a month later.

Philippe Augustus, having no ships of his own in the Mediterranean —for the reason mentioned above—had been obliged to call on the services of the Genoese. A week before Richard, he reached Messina pale and ill, having been seasick all the way from Genoa. The Sicilians were disappointed by his poor showing, and all the more readily accorded an enthusiastic welcome when Richard's fleet arrived, the galleys in battle order and flying their gleaming banners and standards, with trumpets sounding.

The summer was almost at an end, the campaigning season was over for the year, so all these newcomers took up their winter quarters in Sicily. With the coming of spring the French King set sail with his hired ships, while Richard made a majestic departure with his impressive flotilla. The ships sailed in a curious triangular formation: in the van went three vessels having the ladies of the court aboard, among them the King's fiancée, Berangaria; there were thirteen ships in the second line, twenty in the third, and the seventh had as many as sixty. Finally fifty galleys, including the King's, brought up the rear.

However, this splendid formation was soon broken up by bad weather, and when the fleet reached Crete on April 17th, 1191,

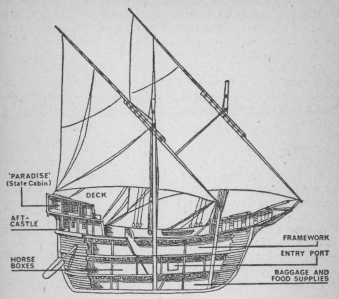

'PARADISE' (State Cabin)

DECK

AFT-CASTLE

FRAMEWORK

ENTRY PORT

HORSE BOXES

BAGGAGE AND FOOD SUPPLIES

Cross-section of a transport-ship with access for horses

twenty-five craft were missing; some of them were never heard of again. All the same, Richard made an impressive show in these Eastern waters; and, believing that the King of Cyprus had insulted him, launched a lightning campaign against the island. He soon captured it, and there married Berangaria before continuing towards the Holy Land. On June 1st the Crusaders of the two nations joined up again outside Acre, which was being besieged by the French. The English flotilla prepared to support its allies from the sea.

A few days later, Richard's ships were cruising off Beirut when they sighted a magnificent vessel, the largest and strongest that the English seamen had ever seen. This fine Turkish three-master, her vividly coloured paintwork glittering in the sun, was carrying seven or eight hundred reinforcements to the Muslims besieged in Acre; she was defended by all known means, including a somewhat unexpected missile to meet with at sea—"two hundred poisonous snakes collected by the Turks to destroy the Christians".[1]

Richard sent a galley to investigate; it returned with news that the ship claimed to be French, yet no one on board could speak that language, neither could they show a French flag or one of any Christian nation. It was highly suspicious. A galley sent in pursuit of the vessel was greeted with a shower of arrows and Greek-fire. This was proof enough, and Richard gave the order to attack.

Some English historians have given much attention to the fight that followed, not because it was any remarkable feat on the part of the English ships—whose great superiority in numbers was bound to bring victory—but because it was the first time since William the Conqueror that the King himself had led a fighting fleet; and also because of the outstanding defence put up by the Turk, which repulsed a score of attacks, so that Richard had to threaten his men with hanging or torture if the enemy were allowed to escape.

Time and again the English boarded the enemy, only to be thrown back by wave after wave of defenders who seemed to issue from the bowels of the ship in a constant stream. It was finally decided to ram this impregnable fortress. Galleys swept forward and drove their beaked prows into her sides; badly holed, this tough enemy at last went down. There were fewer than forty survivors; so furious were the victors, that only with difficulty did their leaders manage to save the lives of the rescued men, from whom they wanted to learn about the Turkish weapons.

The name of this valiant lone fighter has not come down in history, yet it is surely worthy of a place beside others who defied great odds, such as the French *Belle Cordelière* (in 1513), Grenville's *Revenge* (1591), the American *Cumberland* (1862), and the German *Bismarck* (1941).[2]

Three days later Acre fell to the Crusaders. The credit should go to the French who had maintained the siege for months, but all the glory went to the English whose arrival had turned the scales. Philippe Augustus, tired of always being in the position of poor relation, decided to return home and gave his bad state of health as an excuse. As a final humiliation he had to borrow two galleys from Richard to sail for France. During the voyage his bitterness increased. The English King had inherited far too much of France, he decided. There could be no end until it was wrested back. The misadventures of Richard the

---

[1] During the Punic Wars Carthaginian sailors were said to have made missiles of jars filled with vipers and scorpions.

[2] The accounts of some of these fights will be found on later pages.

Lion-Heart, held prisoner in Austria for seventeen months in the course of a Homeric journey home, gave Philippe Augustus time to prepare his attack on Normandy. It was no skirmish this time, but the first major Anglo-French conflict. Sometimes called the First Hundred Years' War, it really spread over half a century, and brought a revival of the bitter fighting in the narrow seas between England and Flanders.

Richard the Lion-Heart died in 1199. His brother, John Lackland, soon became known for the violence of his temper and his military reverses. By 1204 he had already lost all the Angevin territories to Philippe Augustus, and the Channel Islands represented all of the Duchy of Normandy still in English hands. He did away with his nephew Arthur, whose claim to the English throne was greater than his own. But to his credit, from the English point of view, he never neglected the fleet; in his direst straits, he still had the loyalty of the Channel seaports and their seamen. To them, England owed her independence at the time of the serious crisis which marked the end of John's reign. In short, John Lackland was beaten everywhere except at sea.

His first victory was at Damme in 1213. Damme is today a village some miles inland, near the Belgian–Dutch frontier. But until the fifteenth century, before the silting up of the Zwijn estuary, it was the port of Bruges. Its wide roadstead was the sea-lung of Flanders; through it flowed all the wealth of overseas trade. And on two occasions during the late Middle Ages it was the scene of a memorable victory by English seamen.

Philippe Augustus had assembled a large fleet in the Seine estuary, and an equally large army at Rouen, as preliminaries to a descent on England. It was the first time that a French king had undertaken a naval expedition—though it could hardly be called a fleet of warships. Philippe had merely mustered everything afloat between the Seine estuary and Calais, in order to transport his troops across the Channel. Nevertheless, he had a total of 1,700 craft. Just as this collection was about to put to sea, plans had to be changed because of the defection of the Count of Flanders. Philippe Augustus had been reckoning on his support, and now found it necessary to invade his lands instead. Consequently, the fleet received orders to proceed to Damme, and there to await the termination of military operations. Capacious as the haven was, some of the vast assembly of ships had to ride at anchor outside the harbour, while others were beached along the coast. Their crews, with time on their hands, went pillaging the country inland instead of caring for the safety of their vessels.

Meanwhile, John Lackland had put William Longsword, Earl of Salisbury, in command of five hundred sail. This fleet, crammed with English and Flemish knights and a strong body of archers and men-at-arms, streamed out of Dover Roads and was off Damme on May 31st, 1213. Salisbury ascertained that the enemy vessels had been left with little defence; the assault went in with a rush and soon overcame all resistance. Three hundred ships laden with food and arms were taken as prize, and a hundred set on fire—all with hardly a blow struck.

The French counter-attack did not come from the sea, but from the French troops preceded by the Count of Brittany's cavalry, that galloped up to drive off the English. Salisbury and his men would have been only too pleased to continue wreaking havoc, but they were driven off and forced back to their boats. Gaining the fleet, they stood off to see whether the rest of the French ships would sally forth.

The fight proved that the infant French Navy had much to learn, if only to guard its ships when at anchor. Unfortunately, Philippe Augustus became discouraged. "The French know little about the ways of the sea," he declared. And in order to prevent the same fate befalling the rest of his fleet, he set fire to it himself!

It was certainly a bad beginning; but the following year the victory of the French over the Emperor Otto and his allies, at Bouvines, deprived John of all support on the Continent. Nevertheless, the French felt the consequences of their naval defeat later. The English mastery of the Channel was sometimes challenged, but this was entirely due to a notorious adventurer who entered the French King's service in 1212, after having been in the pay of many countries—including England.

Eustace the Monk was born in a small town of Picardy, which made him a vassal of the Count of Boulogne. As the younger son of a noble family he was destined for the Church, and entered the Benedictine abbey of Samer, some ten miles from Boulogne. From there he was sent to Toledo, presumably for further instruction in the liturgy and canon law; but in fact he studied black magic, or negromancie, as it was then called. His return to Samer set the abbey in an uproar.

He did not stay long. Soon after his return he fought a duel to avenge the murder of his father, unfrocked himself, and took service with the Count of Boulogne. Having fallen into disgrace with the Count, he crossed the Channel to offer his sword to King John, and thus began his naval career. John welcomed him, and gave him thirty galleys with which to harry the Channel Islands.

The islands were devastated after fierce fighting in which Eustace, armed with a mighty axe, fought like a lion. Then he took his force round the Cherbourg peninsula to ravage the coast of Normandy.

King John, apparently delighted with the results of this expedition, showered favours on him and furnished him with the means to continue his piratical activities in the Channel. Then Renaud, Count of Boulogne, appeared at the English court, and Eustace the Monk decided that the moment had come to return to France and to offer his services to Philippe Augustus.

The French King was not too well endowed with experienced sea-captains. Moreover, he was at cross-purposes with Renaud of Boulogne. There is nothing like a common hatred to cement an alliance. Eustace was well received by Philippe, and was soon off again to harry the Channel Islands, but this time on behalf of the French. The Battle of Damme took place about then, but Eustace the Monk does not seem to have been present.

The episode which chiefly brought his name into prominence is one of the strangest in the history of France and England. After the Battle of Bouvines, King John's situation had sharply deteriorated both at home and abroad. Discontent was growing in England. The rebellious barons plotted to depose the King and sent a deputation to Prince Louis, the heir to the French throne, to offer him the English crown—provided he arrived with sufficient force to overthrow the tyrant. Philippe Augustus was lukewarm about it, for he feared the wrath of the Pope, whose support King John had cunningly gained by promising to go on a Crusade to the Holy Land. But Philippe's daughter-in-law, the pious Blanche of Castille, was eager to see her husband on the throne of England while waiting for that of France. It is said that "Woman's will is God's will"—and her's almost was.

The only sea-captain in France likely to make a success of the undertaking was Eustace the Monk—the pirate and turncoat, whose association with the mother of St. Louis is startling, to say the least. Eustace lost no time. By May, 1216, he had mustered a fleet of some six hundred sail at Calais; and although running into one of the Channel's sudden storms, which caused the loss of many of his vessels, Eustace succeeded in landing Prince Louis and his force on the Kentish coast. "Not a single captain of a loyal ship was there to intercept and seize Louis, and send his head to the King." [1]

The English seamen were lacking not so much in loyalty as in the means to act. Several of the Cinque Ports had remained faithful to the King. For months Eustace the Monk played the pirate in the Channel. His reputation for ferocity was such that Philippe Augustus could not even guarantee the safe passage of the Papal Legate to England. "We would gladly give you one for our kingdom, but if perchance you fall

[1] Luard Clowes, *History of the Royal Navy*, Vol. I, p. 186.

into the hands of Eustace the Monk or any others of Louis's men who infest the seas, and some misadventure befalls you, do not put the blame on us."

The turning-point came with John's death in the October of 1216. The snake was dead, the poison died with him! All the accumulated hatred was buried with him, and English unity was once again welded together in support of the nine-year-old Henry III, proclaimed king at Gloucester by a council of barons led by the venerable William Marshal, Earl of Pembroke. Their first task was to rid the land of Louis, who had had himself proclaimed king in London. His position was becoming untenable. Dover had resisted him, and its seamen were able to harass his sea communications. In May, 1217, he sustained a crushing defeat at Lincoln. He was urgently in need of reinforcements, and so it was essential that Eustace should retain command of the Channel. He did his best, notably by constructing on a large galley an after-castle on which he intended to mount a powerful catapult to bombard enemy vessels. Unfortunately for him, the seamen of the Cinque Ports got wind of these preparations and sallied across to make a surprise attack and completely destroy the floating fortress. A few weeks later Prince Louis's venture was brought to an end by the naval battle of South Foreland.

By August, 1217, Eustace had assembled a fleet at Calais—of three hundred vessels, according to some accounts, of one hundred, say others —and was ready to transport a large body of reinforcements for Prince Louis. It was a move that Pembroke had anticipated. But morale was low among the seamen; Pembroke rallied them by exploiting their increasing hatred of the pirate monk, especially since his sack of Folkestone in 1215, in revenge for being foiled in an attack on Jersey. "Traitor, arch-pirate, felon", were the mildest names bestowed on him. "A worse scourge there can never be." "His career of betrayals," Clowes writes, "had a far greater and more decisive effect than is generally supposed. The hatred which the English had conceived for him flames out in all the accounts of the great battle of South Foreland."

England was short of seamen just then. Pembroke marched such men-at-arms as he could collect down to Sandwich, to supplement the crews. These men were rather doubtful about their prospects. "We are neither sea-fighters nor pirates nor fishermen," they said. "You are leading us to our death!" Moreover, there were few ships ready for sea —in the event, the English Fleet numbered only about a third of the French.

It was on a fine, clear day—August 24th, 1217 (St. Bartholomew's

Day)—that the French Fleet was sighted in the Straits, sailing on a course which gave it the full advantage of a strong south-easterly wind. The alarm was given in Dover, where the undefeated governor, Hubert de Burgh, lost no time in going into action.

The sight of the meagre force he had collected—sixteen large vessels and a score of smaller ones—roused the French to ribald laughter. This draggle would soon be feeding the fishes! The jeering increased when Hubert de Burgh appeared to be trying to avoid contact, standing out to sea and tacking on a course as though bent on counter-raiding Calais, which the French knew to be strongly garrisoned.

"String them up!" shouted the French sailors. And Eustace added, "They'll get a warm reception, the thieving knaves!"

Even Eustace had not grasped the fact that his adversary was carrying out an entirely new manoeuvre—gaining the weather-gauge. This encounter was to lay the foundation of a doctrine of sea warfare upon which, throughout the days of sail, all victories were to be based.

The time of long-range fighting had not yet arrived—there were no cannon. Sea warfare was still regarded as a transposition of land fighting to the closed arena of two ships grappled to each other. Opposing fleets had sought only to get to close quarters as soon as possible, as best they could, often by use of oars. But on this occasion, by gaining the weather-gauge, Hubert de Burgh seized the initiative. He could choose his moment to attack, while the French could only sail before the wind.

Having gained the advantage of position, Hubert de Burgh eased his helm and swept down large before the wind on to the French ships in the rear. Those in the van, carried forward by the wind, were unable to help them. The numerical advantage was lost to the French; chances were now equal. More than equal for the English, in fact, as Eustace's ships were riding low and sluggish in the water, being heavily laden with the reinforcements and supplies for Prince Louis. Whereas the English "cogs" or tubs were riding high and dominated the enemy with their "castles", on which—another innovation—Hubert de Burgh had placed his bowmen; many of them were men of Philip d'Aubigny, the Governor of Jersey and an arch-enemy of Eustace since his raids on that island. More men were up in the rigging, ready with sacks of unslaked quicklime to toss by handfuls into the eyes of their enemies.

Four or five of the English fell upon the ship in which Eustace was flying his standard. The quicklime did its work, being whipped downwind and blinding the French sailors. The English quickly grappled and boarded the enemy, slashing the stays and bringing down masts and sails, which enveloped the Frenchmen and brought the ship to a standstill. The boarding parties cut the enemy to pieces and the decks ran with blood. A contemporary chronicler wrote that so much blood flowed that when the booty was being shared out an English soldier tried to snatch what he thought was a fine piece of scarlet bolting—cloth in which he already fancied himself—only to find that he had a huge clot of blood at the end of his grappling-iron.

Eustace had fought bravely at first. But when he saw that all was lost, he went and hid. He was dragged from the bilge of his ship disguised in borrowed clothing, and offered ten thousand silver marks if his life were spared. All in vain. There was competition among the English as to who should execute him. The privilege is said to have gone to a bastard son of King John, who gave Eustace only the choice of having his head lopped off on the bulwark or on a block. The body was thrown into the sea, but the head was subsequently stuck on a pike and exhibited in all the Kentish towns.

The early loss of the French commander hastened the defeat which followed. Some of the ships were boarded and taken in the same way as Eustace's. Others were holed by the favourite English tactics of running down and ramming, and quickly sank. The French were either butchered or drowned. Whole crews jumped overboard rather than await certain death by the sword. A mere fifteen French ships limped back to Calais, while those which had not been sunk were triumphantly towed into Dover.

It was the end of Prince Louis's reign in London. Threatened on all sides, cut off from reinforcements, he was only too glad to negotiate an honourable withdrawal. By winning the Battle of South Foreland, the English seamen had saved their country from a dire threat to her independence.

IV

THE BATTLE OF SLUYS, WHICH PAVED THE WAY FOR THE HUNDRED YEARS' WAR

Philippe the Fair's navy neglected by his successors—Edward III's claims to the French crown—efforts of the new French admiral, Hue Quiéret—raids-on the English coast—the "Grand Army of the sea" concentrates in the Scheldt— Edward III arrives on the Flemish coast—a naval reconnaissance made by cavalry—the battle on June 24th, 1340—both French admirals slain—a scene of carnage—the crushing defeat of the Grand Army, and its consequences.

HENCEFORTH, the history of England and France was to take two separate courses, and the two kingdoms—as always with neighbouring powers growing in strength—were to exchange many hard blows before learning to live in peace together. Not that they were permanently at war during the late Middle Ages; far from it. They even had the sense not to become too disturbed over the inevitable friction between their merchant shipping that occurred in spite of treaties. The shipmen of the two countries carried on their own private conflicts, and raided each other's shores with unbridled ferocity. Fishermen fought for the best fishing-grounds, the many pirates respected no one, and honest merchantmen put to sea ready to fight to the death.

Little improvement had so far been made in ship design. Most vessels were still two-masted craft of less than two hundred tons burden, not much longer from stem to stern than they were in the beam, and so were difficult to work. For purposes of war, the chief innovation was the fighting-top, or "tower", a circular platform with a waist-high screen, on which armorial banners were hung, that was fixed to the masthead. This housed the bowmen and throwers of quicklime and other fighting-men. The sea-fighters of the time were certainly not lacking in ingenuity. When an enemy ship was grappled, her deck was sprayed with soft soap or tallow to make it slippery for the defenders. Arrows with large iron shafts were shot into her sails; the billmen slashed at the stays to bring down the rigging and envelop the crew; while specialists dived overboard to try and bore holes in the enemy's hull—the forerunner of modern underwater attacks. Ramming—so greatly favoured by Mediterranean galleys—was not attempted nearly so much in these northern waters, for the lumbering sailing vessels rarely had the speed to do much harm.

The French King, Philippe IV (Philippe the Fair), showed an unusual interest in the sea, for a monarch of his time. At the end of the thirteenth century he obtained the services of several squadrons of Mediterranean galleys, which were brought round to the Channel by sea-captains from Monaco and Genoa. The King had other galleys

The ancestor of naval guns

built for him at Rouen and Harfleur, under the supervision of Genoese ship-builders in his pay. This was the beginning of the French naval yards; the royal fleet came into being, and henceforth its warships had their own special crews. The English ships were at a disadvantage against these galleys in calm weather, when the latter were the speedier and the more manageable; but in rough weather the sturdy English craft prevailed, and their high fore- and aft-castles facilitated boarding and entering the enemy.

The English King had no real standing naval force; and, like the French King, he had to call on merchant ships to transport knights and men-at-arms when he went to war. But there were far more English trading vessels than French, and therefore a greater number of experienced seamen. Moreover, the English monarch was able to call upon the Cinque Ports—with their additional "members" they were then many more than five—which, in return for certain privileges, were under obligation to furnish ships and men for the King's service.

Philippe the Fair's three sons all died without male issue, and in

Philippe VI

1328 his nephew, Philippe of Valois, came to the throne as Philippe VI. A year earlier, Edward III had succeeded to the English crown. He was a grandson of Philippe the Fair through his mother, Isabella, and claimed that he had a better title than Philippe of Valois to the French crown. It was, in a sense, the story of Prince Louis again, but in opposite manner. Edward's pretensions were naturally refuted by the French King, but as he persisted in them—the quarrel was envenomed by French interference with the Anglo–Flemish wool trade—war between the two became inevitable.

For the past fifteen years the embryo French navy had been greatly neglected; crews were no longer trained, and ships were rotting in the yards. Philippe VI and his ministers made the belated discovery that ships were needed in order to carry the war to England. There was not even an admiral,[1] though one was soon appointed—Hue Quiéret, Seneschal of Beaucaire, a good administrator but having little knowledge of the sea. He was ordered to make the ships seaworthy and to assemble a fleet of transports for "the Grand Army of the Sea".

The first ships ready for sea tried their hand by attacking English and Flemish merchant shipping. Bérenger Blanc raided vessels in the Thames estuary; while Nicolas Béhuchet, a tax-collector turned King's officer, a brisk and determined fighter, landed a force at Portsmouth on March 24th, 1338,[2] sacked the town and left it in ashes except for the parish church and the hospital. On his return across the Channel, he raided Guernsey.

Six months later, Quiéret himself carried off a great prize. While cruising with a squadron off the mouth of the Scheldt, he saw five fine English ships at anchor under Walcheren Island. Quiéret had the stronger force, and seized the opportunity. After a desperate fight, the English were all killed, and Quiéret towed the five "great ships" back to France. They were a very useful addition to the French Fleet, which had no ships of their size. Four cannon were mounted on each ship—something that had never been done before—and the five were renamed. The *Great Christopher*, which had been specially built for Edward III, became the *Christophe-de-la-Tour*. However, they were not destined to remain for long in French hands.

On October 6th, 1338, Southampton suffered as Portsmouth had earlier in the year. The English seamen took their revenge the following spring, raiding and setting fire to Le Tréport, destroying thirty vessels in Boulogne harbour and stringing up their captains, and leaving the lower town ablaze. All this dreadful toll on both sides increased the enmity, which hardened even more on the English side after the atrocities committed by Charles Grimaldi, seigneur of Monaco and in the pay of Philippe VI, when raiding the Kent coast with his galleys; on his triumphant return to Calais he paraded some captured English fishermen who had been hideously mutilated.

By the spring of 1340 Philippe VI had completed his preparations

---

[1] The term "Admiral" had a purely administrative connotation in those days. The English opposite number was "Captain and Admiral of the Fleet of the Cinque Ports . . .". (*Tr.*)

[2] In his *History of the Royal Navy*, Clowes inclines to the view that the raid on Portsmouth took place in 1337. The French naval historian, La Roncière, basing his argument on a letter from Edward III to the barons of the Isle of Wight dated April 15th, 1338, prefers March 23rd of that year.

for the great expedition against England. Nearly two hundred ships were ready in his Channel ports to carry "the Grand Army of the Sea" across the waters. The crews had been recruited from local fishermen; the archers and men-at-arms came chiefly from Picardy and Upper Normandy. There was a lack of good leaders, though. The Norman barons had little belief in the success of the venture, and their enthusiasm was lukewarm. Less than one hundred and fifty knights joined the expedition, bringing four hundred crossbowmen with them. The merchant ships, barges and fishing-smacks among the fleet had "twenty thousand wretched fishermen and bargemen" on board, most of whom had never handled a military weapon.

The only experienced seamen were the crews of the King's galleys, which were commanded by Admiral Hélie. There were also four Genoese galleys led by a wily and accomplished sea-captain, Barbavera, whose good advice at a later stage could have been of help; but the leaders of the expedition were in disagreement among themselves, and would not listen to the Genoese.

The force of two hundred and two vessels and more than twenty thousand men sailed from Boulogne and Calais and reached the mouth of the Zwijn on June 8th, 1340. Quiéret had received orders to prevent the English entering the Scheldt estuary to make a landing.

The Zwijn today is no more than a stream marking the frontier between Belgium and Holland; and the town of Sluys is, like Damme, several miles inland. But in medieval times Sluys was a fortified port guarding the wide estuary of the Zwijn and the Scheldt. Since then, the Dutch have built their dykes and gained many squares miles of land from the sea.

No sooner had the French Fleet anchored in the estuary than the crews went ashore marauding and pillaging, as occurred much too often in those times. The Flemish in these parts were already badly disposed towards the French; this further treatment was to have dire effect on the survivors of the forthcoming battle.

Quiéret drew up his ships in three divisions, one behind the other and with the ships facing either direction. The vessels were lashed together with heavy chains, while barricades of spars and planking were erected inboard, and small boats filled with stones made barriers across the forecastles to give shelter to bowmen and soldiers. In short, Quiéret had transformed his naval force into a floating fort.

The captured "great ships" were in advance on the left of the front line, to enable them to make good use of their cannon. On the extreme left, nearest to attack from the sea, was the *Great Christopher*, commanded by a Flemish sea-captain and defended by Genoese crossbowmen. Then came the *Edward*, the *Catherine*, and the *Rose*; with the *St. George*, in which Quiéret and Béhuchet were flying their banners, a little to the rear. The front division was formed of ships and crews from Flanders and the Seine estuary, the second division came from Boulogne and Dieppe, and the rear was held by Normans. Barbavera, who had again urged the folly of waiting on the defensive, was cruising off the estuary with his galleys, watching for the enemy.

Edward III had been warned by the Archbishop of Canterbury that the French were concentrating their forces, but in spite of confirmation by his sea-captains, John Crabbe and Robert Morley, was still only half convinced. "You're saying all that to stop me crossing to France," he cried. "But cross I shall, and those who are needlessly afraid can remain at home!" His captains protested that they would never desert their King in danger; and this so impressed Edward that he gathered a stronger force than he had intended. Two hundred ships of all sizes were eventually mustered at the mouth of the river Orwell, near Harwich. A squadron of fifty sail from farther north was ordered to make rendezvous off the Flemish coast. The Royal standard, impudently bearing the lilies of France in support of Edward's claim to be "King of England and of France", was flown in the great ship *Thomas*, which had aboard the leading names of English chivalry. A host of knights and their squires were in the other ships, so that the fleet made a brave and gay display with all the many-coloured banners and pennants fluttering in the breeze. Some of the knights had managed to get their horses into the holds of the larger vessels. One highly gilded and painted ship was carrying the ladies of the Court, who were to accompany the army.

This splendid company got under way at one in the morning of June 22nd. The weather was set fair, with a rising breeze from the north-east—perfect conditions for a swift passage to Flanders. Tacking to clear the coast, the fleet then made good speed with the wind abeam, the *Thomas* in the van and the great ships towing the smaller, through seas that were choppy enough to upset the soldiers.

At noon the next day the fleet made its landfall—the dunes of Blankenberghe, cried the lookout in the *Thomas*. The King decided to anchor there for the night. The smaller ships were hauled up the beach, and the soldiers bivouacked ashore to recover from the crossing. The local fishermen soon came hurrying to say that the French were concentrated in the Scheldt estuary a few miles to the east. Instead of sending a galley to investigate it was deemed more expedient to use some of the horses, as they had suffered badly from seasickness and would be only too glad to stretch their legs. So a few knights and a mounted escort were soon cantering across the dunes towards the Scheldt. Night was falling when they came within sight of Sluys and the French Fleet, but they were able to note its disposition and strength, and hurried back to report.

On receiving this intelligence, Edward III determined to attack the following morning, June 24th, the Feast of St. John.

The lookout in Barbavera's galley had seen the forest of masts and sails to the west, and the Genoese returned with all speed to the *St. George*. "Up anchor and set sail quickly," he urged Quiéret. "You're in a cul-de-sac here. At daybreak tomorrow the English will bear down on you; they'll be borne in by the wind, your bowmen will have the sun in their eyes, and you'll be trapped."

But Quiéret would have none of it. "Shame on any who depart from here!" he cried. Barbavera saw it was useless to insist, but resolved not to be trapped himself. And at the height of the battle next day, when matters were going badly with the French, he cut his cables and managed to get clear with his four galleys.

At five that morning, June 24th, the tide was just on the turn, and the English ships drew off on the ebb and proceeded to manoeuvre for position. The sun was well up by the time the whole fleet was in battle order, a few miles off the estuary and facing the immobile French formation. Edward was waiting for the tide to turn again. . . . At eleven o'clock a signal was flown from the *Thomas*; trumpets on all the ships summoned archers and men-at-arms to their stations. And then, with sails spread, the English were borne in to the attack by the current and a strong following wind.

Edward was in the van, with his largest ships and best captains. This spearhead of the assault steered straight for the extreme left of the enemy line, the most exposed; and the sight of the *Great Christopher* and the *St. George* in French hands roused the wrath of the English. As they drew within bowshot, the English archers sent their first flights of arrows whizzing over the enemy barricades, while the crews stood ready with their grapples and the men-at-arms prepared to board and enter the anchored vessels. Just then, like sudden thunderclaps, came the discharge of the French cannon. At that distance, every shot was effective. Before the English could get to grips, a Hull galley was smashed, and the ship carrying the ladies of the Court was sunk. The *Thomas*, too, was hit several times before grappling the enemy.

Two ships assailed the *Great Christopher*; and, pressing close behind, the other ships of the English van swung in bow to bow, threw out their grapples and fought furiously to gain an entry. With sword and pike, and a deluge of missiles from the fighting-tops, the French fought to thrust back the invaders; while their divers went overside to try and hole the English ships. Back and forth swayed the tussle, each fighter seeking the honour of being the first to gain an enemy deck. Edward was in the forefront of the fray, wielding his gleaming sword; Béhuchet sought him out, and succeeded in wounding him in the thigh.

But, as Barbavera had foreseen, the immobility imposed by Quiéret's plan prevented the ships in the second and third lines from aiding the first, on which the English attack was concentrated. Ship after ship was cleared from the left inward. The English archers were discharging their arrows at thrice the speed of the Genoese crossbowmen, and the

Ship in a storm (*from a Flemish engraving*)

French losses were visibly mounting. Fighting with desperate courage, the French were forced slowly back along the line. Quarter was neither asked nor given; each captured ship was cleared of its crew, dead and wounded alike being tossed overboard.

After several hours of fierce fighting, the four great ships were again in English hands. Quiéret, badly wounded, was captured and beheaded; and Béhuchet, attacked by knights enraged at his insult to their king, was also taken. A few minutes later his body was swinging from the yard-arm of the *Thomas*, as a reprisal—wrote the chroniclers— "for the horrible ravages beyond all law of man that he had committed in England". This summary justice had a disastrous effect on the French; they began to give way when they saw that their leaders' banners were no longer flying from the *St. George*, and that Béhuchet had been hanged by the enemy.

Until then, the men in the second line of ships had stoutly resisted the advance of the English, although their ranks were thinned by the deadly flights of arrows. A giant Norman, Pierre d'Estelang, standing in the bows of his ship, wielded his sword to such effect that he was said to have slain or wounded more than a hundred of the enemy before being brought down himself. He was left for dead, but in fact survived the fight.

The sun was slipping below the horizon. Dead in their thousands littered the decks. Groups of fighters, linked together in fierce hand-to-hand combat, had gone overside together. The waters were running red with blood; and the flames from burning vessels stood out more clearly as night began to fall.

The local fishermen, seeing the flames, came hurrying for the pickings, taking the hard-pressed French from behind. Panic overcame the remnants of "the Grand Army of the Sea". But in trying to flee from the scene of carnage, hundreds of men were drowned while struggling to reach the river banks in the gathering darkness.

Those aboard the royal galleys commanded by Admiral Hélie were more fortunate—more experienced in warfare, too—and succeeded in cutting their moorings and, aided by the ebbing tide, reached the open sea. These vessels, with a few Dieppe barges and large ships, were the only ones to escape from the disaster. Among them was the *St. James* of Dieppe, which attacked and captured a great Sandwich ship; when about to take its prize in tow, it was in turn attacked by a number of English vessels. The *St. James* fought them off throughout the night, so valiantly that when finally captured at daybreak the victors found more than four hundred dead on board.

For days after the battle of Sluys, wounded survivors were trickling back through Flanders "in rags, and much distressed in body", with arms in slings and heads bandaged. At the French Court there was great consternation. Nobody dared tell the King of the disaster, and eventually it was the court jester who blurted out the news.

Edward III now held command of the Channel, and could carry the conflict to French soil at any point he cared to choose. Six years later his choice fell on the Cherbourg peninsula. At the head of a vast fleet estimated at more than a thousand sail, Edward landed at St. Vaast-la-Hougue on July 12th, 1346, burnt the few French vessels in the harbour, razed Barfleur and Cherbourg, and started on the march eastwards along the Normandy coast that was to lead to the great victory at Crécy a month later, and then to the siege of Calais.

The Hundred Years' War had begun.

V

THE BATTLE OF LEPANTO, WHICH SWEPT THE TURKS FROM THE MEDITERRANEAN

The supremacy of the Venetian Fleet—the sack of Constantinople, April 22nd, 1204—Bajazet and Mahomet II—the Turks capture Constantinople—terror in the Mediterranean—Pius V and the Holy League—the Christian fleets concentrate at Messina—Don John of Austria destroys Ali Pasha's fleet at Lepanto on October 7th, 1571—the greatest galley fight of all time.

WHILE English and French ships were assailing each other in the Channel—a sea rivalry that was to last six centuries [1]—there was comparative peace in the Mediterranean. By the end of the twelfth century the ships of the Republic of Venice were supreme. In the ninth century, led by the Doge, Pietro Tribuno, they had saved Italy from the Huns; later, they had withstood the Saracens and the Normans of Sicily, finding renewed strength after each setback. Venetian ships played a considerable part in the Crusades, both in providing transport and in battle. Commanded by the nonagenarian Doge, Arrigo Dandolo, they were mainly responsible for the capture of Constantinople on July 17th, 1203, and were chiefly involved in the terrible battle of April 22nd, 1204, which astounded the world by "the spectacle of a Christian city taken and sacked by Christians who surely should only fight against the infidels whom they had sworn to destroy".[2]

The Venetians had learned early how to build large craft capable of carrying two hundred soldiers in addition to the rowers and seamen. An idea of the size of the great Venetian transports is obtained from the fact that, during the Second Crusade, fifteen of these vessels alone were able to carry ten thousand men and four thousand horses. The Venetian war-galleys, smaller than the transports, were the best of the time. The Republic was so proud of them that each captain had to swear to engage the enemy unless outnumbered by more than twenty-five to one. All the Venetian galleys had a strong iron beak protruding from the prow, and the largest ships carried a huge, weighted beam slung from the mainmast, for smashing the deck of an enemy. Cannon were mounted fore and aft, so that whether attacking or retreating a fleet of war-galleys endeavoured to keep line abreast. The "bow-

[1] From 1217 (South Foreland) to 1815.
[2] *Histoire de la République de Venise*, by Count Daru, Paris, 1819.

47

chaser" was a 36-pounder, and made many bloody gaps along the rowing-benches when it swept an enemy galley from stem to stern.

Venice kept to galleys long after the other Mediterranean sea-powers because the treacherous winds in the Adriatic were a handicap to sail. Even so, the Republic retained its supremacy in the Mediterranean at a time when the big round sailing-vessels, the "tubs", were beginning to make their appearance. The Battle of Lepanto, in the second half of the sixteenth century, was fought predominantly by oared galleys.

By the end of the fifteenth century, the expansion of the Ottoman Empire constituted a growing threat to the Mediterranean countries. Its pirate ships made sea trade almost impossible, and on land the Sultan's armies had penetrated into the Balkans. In 1394, Sigismund, King of Hungary, had appealed to France for help against the hordes of Bajazet, the Turkish Sultan. This new crusade was led by the Count of Nevers, with Admiral Jean de Vienne and Marshal Boucicaut. But it met with disaster. The Christian Army was cut to pieces at Nicopolis, on September 28th, 1396; Jean de Vienne, leading the attack, was killed along with two thousand knights, and Boucicaut was made prisoner. However, Bajazet failed to take Constantinople. It was not until 1453 that the city fell, after a long and celebrated siege by Mahomet II. The Turkish Fleet played a surprising part in the final capture, for Mahomet had not hesitated to dig a canal along which his vessels were towed into position to attack the city.

Henceforth, the Turks were able to extend their power by land and sea. Early in the sixteenth century Suliman the Magnificent was terrorizing central Europe. His sea-captains had conquered the Aegean archipelago, and were thrusting towards North Africa; aided by the corsairs of the Barbary coast, they attacked the seaborne traffic, capturing merchantmen and slaughtering their passengers and crews, except those judged useful as galley-slaves.

Stories of the atrocities committed in captured towns by the ferocious and fanatical janissaries (the shock troops of the Sultan), and the threat of slavery in the galleys hanging over anyone who ventured to sea, increased the Mediterranean peoples' fear of the Muslims. The Venetian Republic, although the leading naval power at the time, had thought it prudent to swallow its pride and pay the Sultan for safe-conducts in order to protect its profitable Levant trade. As for the French—who were hardly a Mediterranean power—they had treated with the Turks. Such was the situation when Pope Pius V made his appeal to Christian Europe to join in waging war against the hated Turks, and formed the Holy League for the purpose.

Philip II of Spain needed no urging; Naples and Genoa could do no less than follow his lead. France and Protestant England were not concerned with the situation. Venice remained undecided.

It was the Turks themselves who decided the Venetians to join the League. In 1489 the Republic had bought Cyprus from the heiress of the Lusignans; but in 1570 the ambassador of Selim II[1] claimed that the island was part of the Ottoman Empire. Venice rejected the claim, and war broke out. Mustapha Pasha, at the head of a large fleet, invaded Cyprus and laid siege to Famagusta, the capital, which was defended by the Venetian general, Bragadino. After a long and heroic resistance, the defenders capitulated in June, 1571; and Mustapha, in spite of having promised to spare their lives, had them all put to the sword. Bragadino himself was flayed alive.

The news of this fresh horror swept away any doubts that Venice might still have had, and the Christian fleets began to concentrate for battle.

Pius V had given the command to Don John of Austria, a natural son of Charles-Quint; he was a handsome young man of twenty-five, a bold leader on land and sea who already held the rank of Admiral of Spain. The Papal ships were commanded by Prince Antonio Colonna, the Genoese by Admiral Giovanni Andrea Doria, and those of the Knights of Malta by the Grand Master, Giustiniani. The Venetian Fleet, commanded by Sebastiano Veniero, was partly based on Crete and partly on Corfu. These dispositions had been taken to prevent the war-galleys of El Louck Ali, Governor of Alexandria and an ally of the Sultan, from entering the Adriatic. When Veniero sailed with both his squadrons to join the other Christian fleets at Messina—the rendezvous appointed by Don John—the way was left clear for El Louck Ali to attack Venice. However, he let the opportunity slip, preferring to spread desolation and terror along the Greek coast, although he was aware of the Holy League's preparations.

One of his best sea-captains, an Arab named Kara Khodja, had been sent with two of the swiftest galleys to keep watch on the Straits of Messina. Kara Khodja was most skilful in handling galleys. Better than anyone, he could make use of the slightest breath of wind to rest his rowers, who were the best-trained of all in the Muslim Fleet. He hoisted black sails at night, in order to move unseen, replacing them with white at dawn. By means of this stratagem he was able to venture up to the entrance to Messina harbour—and returned with all speed to El Louck Ali, to inform him that the Christian fleets were all assembled. Ali decided to join the rest of the Turkish Fleet which, under the

[1] The son of Suliman, who had died in 1566 at the age of seventy-two. (*Tr.*)

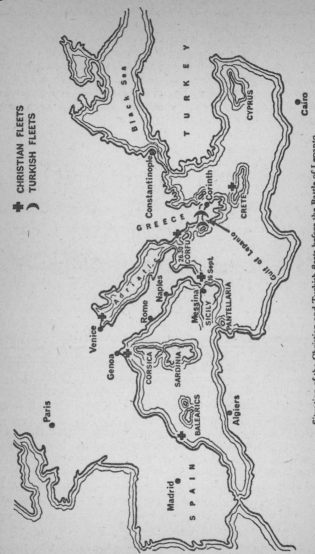

CHRISTIAN FLEETS
TURKISH FLEETS

Situation of the Christian and Turkish fleets before the Battle of Lepanto

command of Ali Pasha, was at anchor in the Gulf of Lepanto (also called the Gulf of Corinth).

There were, in fact, three hundred ships gathered in Messina harbour, following the arrival of the Spanish Fleet on August 25th, 1571. Don John had led it in, flying his flag in the *Reale*, a magnificent galley with sixty rowers which had been built three years earlier for the Viceroy of Catalonia. The foremost artists of Barcelona had painted the after-castle; the hull was brightly decorated, and its long beak had a carved lion's head at the tip.

The Spanish flagship *Reale*

Don John formed the whole Christian Fleet into five squadrons, each with ships of the different nationalities. When the galley fleet left harbour, there were seven fast galleys in the van, commanded by Juan de Cardona and flying a green pennant. The main body, with the *Reale* in the centre, had the galleys of Antonio Colonna on its right wing and those of Veniero on its left. The extreme right was held by the galleys of the Knights of Malta, flying a green pennant, and the extreme left by those commanded by Agostino Barbarigo, which were flying a yellow pennant. The vessels in the rear were commanded by the Marquis of Santa Cruz.

Most of the sailing-ships—about a hundred—were to follow, so not to delay the galley fleet should the winds be unfavourable. However, six great Venetian galleasses had been included in the galley fleet, as they could if necessary proceed with oars.[1] The idea was, when it came to a fight, that the galleasses should attack first, two abreast, and pound

---

[1] Galleasses usually cruised under sail, but used oars in battle. The galleass was an attempt to combine the speed of the galley with the fire-power and sea-keeping qualities of the galleon; it was a formidable ship. (*Tr.*)

the enemy with their heavy guns—softening him up, as it were, before the galleys dashed in to ram and board.

But first the fleet had to wait for fine weather, and it was not until September 16th that the *Reale* led the way out of the Straits of Messina. The standard of the Holy League was fluttering from her masthead, while on shore the Papal envoy gave the blessing of Pius V to the whole enterprise.

Messina, opposite the toe of Italy, is in the centre of the Mediterranean. Lepanto, in the Gulf of Corinth, where the Turkish Fleet was at anchor, is only about two hundred miles distant—less than a day's run for an ordinary ship today. The *Reale* and the Christian Fleet, however, took ten days.

This was due in the first place to a return of bad weather and the galleys having to struggle against head-winds, and then to the vessels having difficulty in keeping formation. Don John had changed his order to three columns in line astern; if the enemy were sighted the galleys would be signalled to come round to line abreast. The seven galleys in the van were to advance towards the Turks to give the fleet time to carry out the manoeuvre. During the day, the seven kept some twenty miles ahead, but dropped back to eight when darkness fell.

After ten terribly hard days for the rowers, Corfu was reached. The island had been devastated by El Louck Ali, and the people had just had news of the massacre at Famagusta. All this only served to strengthen the resolve of such a staunch leader as Don John. Four swift galleys under the command of Gil d'Andrada were sent off on reconnaissance. Meanwhile, the fleet moved cautiously down the coast and anchored at Gominessa, thirty miles south-east of Corfu. Andrada rejoined it there, after an absence of four days. His report was optimistic. According to him, the enemy had only two hundred craft at the most, and their crews had been decimated by the plague. Don John therefore decided to seek battle at once.

On the Turkish side, the commander-in-chief, Ali Pasha, had sent Kara Khodja on a similar mission. He managed to count the number of galleys while the Christian Fleet was still lying off Corfu. But the darkness which enabled him to perform this bold exploit also prevented him from seeing the whole fleet; so he, too, brought back an optimistic report. Ali Pasha decided to bring the enemy to battle believing he had numerical superiority. Thus it was that both fleets weighed anchor the same day and made for the mouth of the Gulf of Corinth. The Christians, however, had still to contend with bad weather, and spent four days at anchor in the bay of Phiscardo, under the lee of the island of Cephalonia. On October 6th the weather improved. That night, Don John moored off the mainland at Cursolari, barely twenty miles from the Muslim fleet at the entrance to the Gulf. Hardly had his vessels got under way again at dawn than the leading galleys sighted the Turkish sails. Don John had a Roman pilot put ashore, and he climbed a small headland to count them. He brought back the news that there were more than two hundred and fifty enemy vessels. Don John had only two hundred and two, not counting the sailing-ships. It was going to be a closer thing than he had thought. But the six great galleasses would give a good account of themselves, and in any case it was too late to draw back. Slowly the fleet moved into action.

The Turks had taken up their position across the entrance to the Gulf, with Ali Pasha in the centre, Mohammed Siroco commanding the right wing and El Louck the left.

The Christian Fleet passed through the narrow strait between the islet of Oxia and Cape Skropha, on the north of the mouth of the Gulf, and formed into battle order. The six galleasses were in the van, then one hundred and fifty galleys in line abreast, with the remainder in reserve under Santa Cruz. Don John had given orders for the left wing to reach as far inshore as possible, to prevent the Turks outflanking them. All this took time. Meanwhile, Don John was passing in front of the fleet in a galley, standing at the prow and holding high a crucifix, and being acclaimed by all the crews. When he was again aboard the *Reale*, a gun was fired as a signal to attack, although the fleet was not yet in position. At the same time, the purple-and-gold standard which had been specially embroidered for the battle was broken from the mainmast. It portrayed Christ crucified, with St. Peter and St. Paul on either side, and was fluttering bravely in the freshening south-east wind.

Ali Pasha was flying a white standard on which verses from the Koran were inscribed in gold letters. With the wind astern, his whole fleet in line abreast was bearing down upon the Christians, who were still manoeuvring into position. It was a critical moment, for they seemed likely to be separated indiscriminately and so have their fighting strength greatly weakened; but fortunately for them, the wind suddenly dropped just then. The Turkish crews at once began clewing and furling their sails, with a common accord and a rapidity which their enemies could not help admiring.

Oars alone now became the motive power for the battle. This slower approach of the Turkish galleys gave the Christians time to take up their battle stations. Nosing ahead of their line went the Venetian galleasses; the gunners were standing by their pieces, the musketeers

The Battle of Lepanto

were in the rigging, all ready to open fire. It was midday when the two galleasses in the centre and the two on the left belched forth with all their cannon, causing great confusion among the oncoming galleys. The shot ripped among the long sweeps, inflicting many casualties on the rowing-benches. The Turkish thrust lost impetus. The cannonade continued, the range closing all the time, but the Turks came on in close formation in spite of the hail of gunshot, and began to grapple and board their enemies.

Barbarigo, on the left wing, sustained the first attack from Mohammed Siroco, Pasha of Egypt, in a great Alexandrian galley; while some Turkish galleys managed to slip inshore, as Don John had feared, and take Barbarigo in the rear. The janissaries fought like demons, boarding Barbarigo's galley and clearing the deck as far as the mainmast. Barbarigo was wounded, and the situation was becoming desperate; then his other galleys counter-attacked, and the Turks in their turn were swept from the deck and into the sea. The fight was carried to the enemy galley, and after fierce hand-to-hand struggles in which Mohammed Siroco was killed, the galley fell into Christian hands.

This success seemed to make victory certain on the Christians' left wing. The Turks there began to lose confidence, and some beached their galleys or started to withdraw up the gulf. The rest continued the fight, and the slaughter was horrible. With pike and crossbow the veteran Italian and Spanish fighters met the onslaughts of the ferocious janissaries, whose bowmen were skilful but handicapped by their bows becoming loose after discharging a score of arrows. The confused fighting, in which many were killed or swept overboard, ended with the Christians capturing the enemy galleys. The Christian slaves at the oars were at once freed, and the Muslim prisoners chained to the benches in their place.

But matters were not going so well for the Christians in the centre and on the right. Ali Pasha had headed straight for Don John's flag-ship in the centre, holding his fire until the last moment. At almost point-blank range, his cannon fired first. The mainmast of the *Reale* was struck by a ricocheting ball; a whole bench of rowers was mown down, and bits of wood and human limbs were tossed into the air. The *Reale* was returning the fire as the two great galleys crashed into each other, splintering their long beaks.

Banner, standard, and pennant of a galley

Similar scenes were taking place on all sides. Amidst the din of firing, with drums beating and trumpets sounding, boarding parties hurled themselves on to enemy decks. The Christians chained to the rowing-benches of the Turkish galleys did what they could to help their deliverers. No quarter was given. Muskets were fired at point-blank range, and sword or dagger gave the mortal thrust.

The Spaniards had twice boarded Ali's galley, and had twice been thrown back. Then the janissaries obtained a foothold on the *Reale*, and began to gain ground. Don John had to draw his sword and lead a counter-attack. Nevertheless, the Spaniards were beginning to give way, and the splendid galley was in danger of falling to the enemy. Just then, Colonna came to the rescue, boarding Ali Pasha's galley by the stern. Caught between two enemy forces, the janissaries were soon overwhelmed.

No quarter was being given on these galleys either. Ali killed himself just as he was about to be taken. A Christian soldier took the head to Don John, who told him to throw it into the sea.

Total victory seemed assured. But Doria's squadron on the right wing had not yet engaged that of El Louck Ali on the Turkish left; both were manoeuvring to outflank the other to the south. Suddenly the Muslim galleys swung round and dashed towards the fighting in the centre before Doria realized what was happening. Ten galleys drove in a bunch against the Knights of Malta, the most hated of the Sultan's enemies.[1] Under this ferocious and unexpected attack, many of the knights were slain or wounded and their banner fell into El Louck's hands. Just in time, Santa Cruz came up with the reserves; Don John, having overcome his immediate enemy, threw his galleys into the fray; and Doria, coming to his senses, thrust towards the thick of the battle. El Louck saw that his attempt had failed, and thought only of escaping while there was time. Fighting his way clear, and helped by a following wind, he made off through the Straits of Ithaca with what remained of his squadron.

That was the end of the battle. There had been terrible slaughter. The number of Turkish dead was estimated at thirty thousand. Dozens of their captured galleys were towed away by the victors; the remainder had either been beached or had fled with El Louck Ali.

It was said that Pope Pius V was at work with his secretaries in his study on the day of the battle, when he suddenly stopped the proceedings and became deep in prayer. And it was at that moment, the

---

[1] Six years earlier, in 1565, the Knights had resisted all the might of Suliman, at the great siege of Malta. (*Tr.*)

story goes, that Santa Cruz and Don John were counter-attacking and making certain of victory for the cause of the Holy League.

That evening the blood-reddened sea was whipped up by a south-east wind which soon developed into a gale. Don John hastily led his

An English ship-of-war in 1558 (*from a tapestry in the old House of Lords*)

fleet to shelter in the Bay of Petala, first sending off two fast galleys to Messina with the news of the Christian fleet's resounding victory.

And twelve thousand Christians who had been condemned for life to the rowing-benches of Ali Pasha's galleys, and for whom the battle had held more horror than for the fighters, that night tasted the joys of a freedom they had thought lost for ever.

VI

THE INVINCIBLE ARMADA LIMPS HOME
IN DESPAIR

Philip II's preparations—death of the Marquis of Santa Cruz—the Duke of Medina Sidonia is surprised at becoming an admiral—the Felicissima Armada sets sail—Howard makes his dispositions—the Armada enters the Channel—the fighting on July 21st, 23rd, and 25th, 1588—arrival in Calais roads—the Spaniards' morale shows signs of cracking after the losses at Gravelines—the flight north—a worse enemy than the English—the long road home—cemetery of wrecks on the Irish coast—hunger, thirst, and storm—a disaster for the Spanish navy.

SEVENTEEN years after Lepanto, Philip II of Spain undertook what he considered to be another crusade when he sent his Great Armada against England, hoping to invade and conquer that heretic country and bring it within the Roman Catholic faith again. Needless to say, the Spanish monarch once more had the official backing of the Holy See. In 1570 Pope Pius V had excommunicated Queen Elizabeth, announced that her subjects were released from their oaths of loyalty, and called on the Catholic monarchs to undertake a holy war. Spain believed that she was particularly fitted for the task of punishing the insolent English heretics, having destroyed so many Muslim infidels at Lepanto. There was also the fact that Spain had suffered greatly from the attacks of English seamen—notably one, Francis Drake—on her ports and shipping.

Philip of Spain had an excellent base in the Spanish Netherlands for assembling an invasion army, and the governor and commander of the Spanish forces there, the Duke of Parma, was an experienced general and not without some knowledge of the sea. But there remained the problem, as always, of getting an invasion army safely across the Straits of Dover. However, at that time the Spanish naval resources seemed strong enough to be able to neutralize the English opposition—at least, on paper. The Spanish naval commander-in-chief, Alvarez de Bassano, Marquis of Santa Cruz—one of the victors at Lepanto, and who had more recently defeated the Portuguese in the Azores—was greatly in favour of the enterprise against England. He set about preparing the plans for the invasion, on a scale never before executed. They envisaged the use of 556 vessels and 94,282 men in an amphibious operation directed at the mouth of the Thames, with London as its objective.

Unfortunately for Spain, Santa Cruz died in February, 1588, while his plans were still being completed. Philip was then misguided enough to confer command of the Felicissima Armada—as it had been somewhat prematurely named—on Don Alonzo Perez de Guzman, Duke of Medina Sidonia. Although a Grandee of Spain, the head of an illustrious House, and Captain-General of the Coast of Andalusia, he knew nothing of the sea or of war—as he himself protested to his king— and his sole experience of travel by ship had taught him only that he was prone to seasickness.

Philip II dismissed his honest protests, and as a loyal subject Medina Sidonia could but obey. In March, 1588, he took over his command, hoisting his flag in the *San Martin*, a vessel of 1,000 tons and 48 guns, manned by 117 sailors and 300 soldiers. He had some hundred and thirty sail all told, carrying crews and soldiers totalling 29,552.[1] There was the armada of Portugal, under the orders of Medina Sidonia himself; there were the Biscayan galleons under Juan Martinez de Recalde, the Castilians under Diego Flores de Valdes, the Andalusians under Pedro de Valdes, the Guipuzcoans under Miguel de Oquendo, and the Levanters under Martin de Bertendona; there were also four galleasses of Naples under Hugo de Moncada. In addition, Juan Gomez de Medina commanded an unwieldy squadron of *urcas*—supply ships; and Antonio Hurtado de Mendoza commanded the light, fast ships, *pataches* and chebeks, for scouting and dispatch carrying. Finally, there were the galleys of Portugal under Diego Medrano.

To oppose this great fleet, Elizabeth had only thirty-four ships in commission, under command of the Lord Admiral, Howard of Effingham, whose flagship was the *Ark Royal*. But the Queen's ships were supplemented by a force of armed merchantmen almost equal in number, fitted out by the City of London or by the Queen's Commissioners and commanded by Francis Drake in the *Revenge*. Lord Seymour had a squadron supplied by the Cinque Ports and others, and was patrolling off the Flemish coast; and many volunteers put out to join the fleet as the enemy ploughed steadily up-Channel. All in all, 197 ships met the Armada, smaller in size than the Spanish on the whole—their total man-power was only 15,551—but superior in many other ways. The English ships were more manageable, their guns had a longer range, and their gunners were more rapid and accurate. The Spaniards had filled their galleons with infantry, then the best in the

[1] Including 2,000 convicts as rowers in the galleys and galleasses.

world, for they still thought of sea warfare as principally a matter of boarding and entering, as Lepanto had shown. So the gun-ports of their fighting ships had remained narrow, and this handicapped their fire. However, if ever they did manage to close and grapple, the Spaniards were redoubtable foes.

Medina Sidonia's instructions, though, were to avoid a fight as far as possible, not to be diverted by any English offensive but to sail for the Thames estuary and his rendezvous with Parma, to cover the passage of the latter's troops. He, in the meantime, was expected to have gathered or built the flat-bottomed barges needed to transport his infantry and cavalry. There were said to be twenty-five thousand soldiers encamped at Dunkirk, Gravelines, and Nieuport—including seven hundred English Catholics who had emigrated[1]—all waiting to embark so soon as the Armada hove in sight. . . . A similar situation to that of Napoleon, over two hundred years later, waiting at Boulogne camp for Villeneuve to appear with his squadron.

Queen Elizabeth, informed of all these threatening moves, had the more prominent Catholics arrested and saw to the defence of her shores. Seymour was blockading the coast of Flanders; Howard and Drake and Hawkins were with the fleet in Plymouth Sound, ready to defend the western approaches. But there were difficulties over supplies. Howard, who wanted to go and seek out the Spaniards in their own ports, was fretting at the adverse winds and fuming at the non-appearance of essential stores. "If this wind holds for another six days," he wrote urgently to Whitehall on May 28th, "we shall have them knocking at our door. . . . I have here the finest and bravest lot of soldiers, sailors, and captains ever seen in England. What a pity that they lack victuals when so eager to give their lives in the service of Her Majesty."

On the day Howard was writing those lines, Medina Sidonia was working his way out of Lisbon river. But hardly had he rounded Finisterre than a howling storm scattered his ships; many days passed before the last of them struggled into Corunna or other northern Spanish ports. Some had been driven as far as the Channel, and English merchantmen returning home reported that they had been fired on between Ushant and the Scillies. Soon, all London was persuaded that the Armada was approaching up-Channel.

In fact, it was regrouping at Corunna. News of this reached Howard; having at last received supplies, and with a fresh wind springing up from the north-east, his fleet of some ninety ships spread their sails for

[1] A century later, French Protestants were to be found fighting on the Allied side against the Catholic bloc.

a quick run to the Spanish coast. That was on June 23rd. But when in the middle of the Bay of Biscay the wind hauled round to the south, and there was nothing for it but to turn and run back again. They dropped anchor in Plymouth harbour on July 12th—the very day that the Armada's galleons were weighing theirs at Corunna.[1]

Difficult though it is to believe, Howard then received orders from Whitehall to demobilize half of his crews! Disregarding this command, the Lord Admiral kept his men together on half rations, eked out by additional supplies purchased out of his own pocket. Drake, meanwhile, had been rebuked by his Sovereign for having "wasted" powder and shot on mere target practice.

The enemy was approaching, nevertheless. . . . With a favourable wind in their sails, the Spanish Fleet had raised the Lizard on July 19th. The captain of the barque *Golden Hind*, one of the screen assigned to cruise in the mouth of the Channel, came bustling back with full sail to bring the news to Plymouth.

Howard at once began warping out of the Sound. The wind had shifted round to west-north-west, and so the Spaniards held the important advantage of the weather-gauge. They came steadily up-Channel in what was little less than military formation. Nosing ahead, like a cavalry advance guard, went the galleasses; next came the main body, led by Medina Sidonia, with the Biscayans of Recalde bringing up the rear. They were the first to be attacked, on July 21st, by a group of English ships that had worked around and passed astern of the Armada, with the object of getting the weather-gauge.

None of the three clashes as the Spaniards moved up-Channel, closely pursued by the English, was in any way conclusive—neither Drake's action off Plymouth on July 21st, Howard's off Portland Bill on the 23rd, nor the several fights off the Wight on the 25th. Howard wished to avoid a close fight at all costs, for the castles of the Spanish ships loomed so high above the English as to give them great advantage if it came to grappling and boarding, and also with their musket-fire. So the English prudently kept their distance, subjecting the enemy ships to long-range bombardment. But the first losses among the Spaniards were due to collisions. The *Santa Catalina* lost her bowsprit and foremast; while Pedro de Valdes's flagship, *Nuestra Senora del Rosario*, was so badly crippled that she had to be abandoned, and was later snapped up by Drake as a prize.

The chief disaster of the day was when the *San Salvador*, the treasury

[1] All the dates in this account are Old Style—that is, according to the Julian calendar, and ten days behind the Gregorian proclaimed by Pope Gregory XIII in 1582. Most of the European countries were using the latter by 1588; but England, of course, was not—and did not accept it officially until 1752.

ship, was seen to be ablaze; her poop and two decks of her stern-castle had disappeared. Two of the barrels of gunpowder stored aft had accidently blown up. Her crew was promptly taken off, together with the King's money. . . . She went down soon afterwards.

Nevertheless, the might of the Armada was little diminished, and a favourable wind was sweeping it up-Channel still. But the capture of Pedro de Valdes and his ship, and the loss of the *San Salvador*, had depressed the Spaniards; while the English had the satisfaction of knowing that in fire-power and seamanship they were superior to the enemy.

At dawn on the 23rd the Armada had Portland Bill almost abeam, and the wind had hauled round to the north-east. Howard was to leeward, leading his line towards the land in an effort to work round the Spaniards' left wing and so recover the wind. It was a chance for Medina Sidonia to intercept and get to grips with the English ships. But they held off the Spanish by pouring in a series of broadsides. Both English and Spanish blazed away without doing each other much harm, but expended most of their powder and shot. By evening the wind was again fair from the west, which favoured the English strategically but enabled the Armada to plough steadily on again to its rendezvous with Parma.

The third action, off the Wight on the 25th, began with Hawkins and his squadron trying to capture a Spanish straggler, the *Santa Ana*. Some of the Armada went to her aid, and for a while the two groups banged away at each other. But there was hardly any wind, so little manoeuvring was possible, and the action was as indecisive as the previous two. Howard was biding his time, hoping to obtain fresh supplies of ammunition at Dover. While Medina Sidonia, as the Armada drew ever nearer to the Flemish coast, plumed himself on his chief task having been virtually accomplished. On July 27th the Invincible Armada anchored in Calais roads. Only three of the fighting ships were missing—the two lost in the first engagement, and the *Santa Ana*. The last had not been captured, but was swept on to the French coast near Le Havre and became a total wreck. Still, three out of one hundred and twenty was no great loss, and Medina Sidonia had every reason to congratulate himself.

Yet history has shown that it is no easy feat in wartime to take a fleet up the Channel against the winds and the currents, and with British warships out in force. In the century after the Armada the French admiral Tourville was becalmed and—as will be seen—robbed of complete victory over an Anglo-Dutch fleet. No one did any better during the era of sail, and not until the Second World War was the

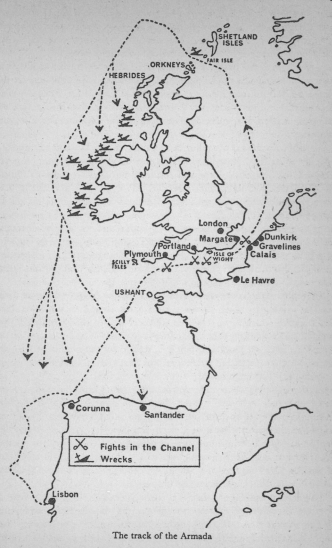

SHETLAND ISLES

FAIR ISLE

ORKNEYS

HEBRIDES

London

Margate

Portland

Plymouth

Dunkirk

Gravelines

Calais

ISLE OF WIGHT

SCILLY ISLES

Le Havre

USHANT

Corunna

Santander

✕ Fights in the Channel

🦅 Wrecks

Lisbon

The track of the Armada

feat accomplished, when the *Scharnhorst* and *Gneisenau* slipped out of Brest and escaped with their escort into the North Sea under the nose of the Royal Navy. And what recriminations that brought forth!

Yet now that the Armada had carried out the most difficult part of its task, Medina Sidonia was uneasy. He and his Staff were aware of their risky position. King Philip would have done well to have ordered Medina Sidonia to attack the English at the beginning, for they were still there on his heels. But they were no more dangerous than ten days previously, when the Armada had entered the Channel—less so, in fact, since they had expended all their powder and shot. But Medina Sidonia did not know that, and in any case he had little left himself.

Meanwhile, the Armada lay in an exposed and dangerous anchorage. Why was it there at all, when its Admiral had been ordered to make for the Thames estuary? The chief reason was that he had not heard from Parma. Four days previously, Medina Sidonia had sent off a pinnace with a messenger to tell Parma to make ready to meet the Armada off Dunkirk. The messenger had not returned. Medina Sidonia had anxiously continued his progress as far as Calais; whereas, helped by wind and current, he could have easily reached the Downs off Margate. But he feared that once he had passed the Straits he would be unable to make his junction with Parma. So he had anchored in Calais roads and sent off more messengers to the reticent general, and tried to obtain supplies of round and shot. Parma was then at his headquarters in Bruges. He was helpless to aid the Admiral. His barges were leaking; they had no stores aboard; the seamen were deserting, and the coast was being patrolled by Seymour. At best, it would be a fortnight before Parma was ready. But were the English just going to watch and wait?

Howard, carried forward by the same wind and tide, had also dropped anchor, and the English ships were standing off "just a long culverin-shot" from the Spanish. Seymour's squadron, summoned from its blockading station, joined Howard and brought the strength of the fleet to one hundred and forty. Eight were sacrificed to make fireships. During the night of July 28th, when the tide had turned and was setting strongly towards the anchorage, the Spaniards saw the eight black shapes belching flames and bearing down on them.

The Dons gave way to panic. They cut their cables and made for the open sea, scattering here and there in great confusion. The first victim of the sudden flight was Moncada's *San Lorenzo*, the *capitana* of the galleasses. She had fouled her rudder on a neighbour's cable, and was drifting inshore. At daybreak the English saw she was aground near the entrance to Calais harbour; Howard ordered off some ships' boats to board and capture her. There was a furious fight on the beach, in which Moncada was killed.

At daybreak Medina Sidonia discovered that his fleet was dispersed and that many ships were dangerously close to the Dunkirk banks; and that the enemy were coming in to close the range, carried forward by the wind and current. The battle took place off Gravelines, with the English concentrating their fire on the isolated Spanish ships, the rest of the Armada to leeward being unable to help them.

There are conflicting reports as to the number of Spanish ships lost in that fateful action. But although it may not have been more than four or five most of the other ships were certainly badly mauled and all had heavy casualties; morale was very low. Medina Sidonia's pilots had warned him that, with the wind in such a quarter and increasing all the time, his whole fleet was in dire peril of being driven on the Zeeland shoals. . . . But, even as they braced themselves for the shock of stranding, the wind backed—backed right round to the south-west. The battered Armada made sail to the north-east, into the North Sea.

There was no question now of a rendezvous with Parma and a landing on the English coast! Most of the ships were completely out of ammunition; fortunately for Medina Sidonia, the English were in no better case. Howard felt sure that the fighting off Gravelines had badly affected the enemy's morale. There was no question now of staving off a threat of invasion, only of the number of enemy ships that could still be destroyed. But the much-needed supplies of powder and shot had not been received, Howard was without the means of bringing the Spaniards to action, and could only tag along behind. The two fleets sailed northward, until at about the height of New-castle the English turned away; on August 8th they came scudding into Margate roads and dropped anchor. But the misfortunes of the Spanish had only begun.

After Gravelines, the Invincible Armada was no longer a fighting force. The Spaniards were badly demoralized and in a worse state than if they had lost half their fleet. In point of fact they had not lost even a twelfth of it, and yet they were now thinking only of their safety. But where did safety lie? There could be no question of putting about and returning to the Channel; the Armada was more than likely to meet with head-winds, and certain to be attacked by the English—without having a single cannon-ball to fire in reply. The suggestion to lay up for the winter in some port of the German Bight or in a Norwegian fjord was soon dismissed. Finally, the Spanish admiral resigned himself to attempt the long road home round Scotland and Ireland, in spite of the distance, the threat of starvation, and the small amount of drinking water remaining. The leaking, splintered ships were patched up as well as possible, and then they headed north running easily before the wind. By August 20th they had cleared the Shetlands and were meeting the Atlantic billows. Now a much more deadly enemy than Howard and company was awaiting the crippled Armada.

All seemed to go well at first. The wind hauled round to the north-east, helping the ships on their homeward course. Medina Sidonia believed himself saved, and sent off a fast pinnace to report to the King. "God," he said, "has seen fit to direct the course of events other than we would have wished." It was then that the *Gran Grifon*, the *capitana* of the hulks, struck a rock off Fair Isle; her captain, Juan Gomez de Medina, and his crew scrambled ashore, and had to spend the winter on that bare island. This was only the beginning of the troubles. For the next two weeks the Armada met with nothing but storms from the worst possible quarter, the south-west, and with baffling head-winds. Nineteen ships were cast away on the rocks of the Hebrides or strewn along the unwelcoming shores of Ireland—one for every three or four sea-leagues. Probably the most tragic shipwreck of them all was the galleass *Girona*, which had picked up some casta-ways, Admiral de Leyva among them, who had twice been ship-wrecked; she was driven ashore near the Giant's Causeway with the loss of all hands. Barely a thousand of the six or seven thousand casta-ways escaped with their lives—and they were so badly treated by the population as to wonder whether a quick death would not have been preferable.

In addition to the 19 ships whose fate is known, 35 others were never heard of again; so that the total losses amounted to 63 out of the 127 which had set out from Lisbon. The survivors were in a pitiable condition when they straggled into Spanish ports. Many had no food or water left. The *San Juan*, Recalde's galleon, had managed to anchor off the coast of Ireland and the crew had made an armed raid to take on fresh water and some supplies. Nevertheless, before making a home port, two or three men a day were dying of hunger and thirst. Alto-gether, two hundred died on that ship!

It was not until the end of September that the last ships of the ill-fated Armada limped into the northern ports of Spain. Philip II did not seem greatly affected by the disaster. "I sent my ships to fight against the English, and not against the winds and the waves. Praise be to God!" was his calm comment. But the brutal facts were there. Spanish sea-power had suffered a blow from which it never recovered; and as a consequence the vast Spanish Empire—over which, Charles-Quint had affirmed, the sun never set—was gradually lost.

VII

DE RUYTER, THE MAN WORTH AN ARMY

Anglo-Dutch rivalry—the Navigation Act of 1651 sparks off hostilities—the opening clashes—De Witt's dissatisfaction with the Dutch captains—Tromp's Broom—Dutch victory off Dungeness (December 10th, 1652)—Battles of North Foreland and Scheveningen (1653)—death of Tromp—Second Dutch War—the bloody battle of Lowestoft (June 13th, 1665)—Ruyter's great days—the "Four Days" Battle (June 11–14th, 1666)—the gallant Admiral Harman—the Dutch sail up the Thames (1667)—Third Dutch War—the first Franco-British Alliance—Battle of Sole Bay (June 7th, 1672)—the Schoonveldt and Texel fights (1673)—the end of an unhappy alliance— Duquesne against Ruyter in the Mediterranean—French victory at Augusta, and the death of Ruyter.

WITH Spain no longer a great sea-power, and France still without a fighting navy, England's supremacy at sea seemed unlikely to be challenged. In the event, it was a quite small nation that rose to oppose the English in their own waters.

The United Provinces of Holland had finally shaken off the Spanish yoke, and the country's independence was recognized by the Treaty of Westphalia in 1648. Its long coastline and its intricate waterways running into the wide estuaries of the Scheldt and the Meuse, made it a natural breeding-ground for sailors. Half a million of the two and a half million Dutch earned their living by fishing or in the mercantile marine. "Amsterdam," the saying goes, "is built on herring-bones." These sea-rovers had virtually the monopoly of the carrying trade of Western Europe. By 1650 there were 140 Dutch merchantmen on the East Indian run, 1,600 Dutch coasters in the Baltic, and nine-tenths of the English sea trade was being carried in Dutch ships. It was a state of affairs that could not be allowed to continue—and four years after the Treaty of Westphalia the Dutch were at war with the Commonwealth.

It was of course a naval war, in which the English had the advantage in the number and size of their warships, which also carried the heavier guns and were the better rigged. On the other hand, with their shallower keels the Dutch were able to manoeuvre more freely among the sandbanks and shoals between the Zeeland coast and the Straits of Dover—the natural battleground of the English and Dutch.

Although the Dutch had many captains who were good seamen, few of them had much experience in warfare. Indeed, such were the short-comings of some in the face of the enemy that the States General sent "political commissaries" to sail with them, having authority to take immediate action against "those who failed in their duty". Discipline, too, was slack, and attempts were made to stamp out the frequent mutinies by imposing harsh punishments.

On the English side, the Civil War had caused deficiencies in the navy, and good officers were at a premium. Their places were filled by army officers, who made up for their lack of naval knowledge by introducing greater discipline. The first naval commander to engage the Dutch, Robert Blake, had been a colonel in the Parliamentary army, and was appointed "General-at-Sea" in 1649. George Monck, who was created Duke of Albemarle after his naval victories in the Second Dutch War, had also had a military career. Such practices were by no means unusual in those days. The captain left the navigation of the ship to the pilot, and only took over effective command when battle was joined. The French admiral, Jean d'Estrées, and the Dutch, Van Ghent, were soldiers before serving at sea; and many of the officers needed for Louis XIV's navy were recruited from the army by Colbert, the Minister responsible for the revival of the French marine.

There were, however, some professional naval officers. Sir George Ayscue, Blake's second-in-command, had served at sea all his life. The Dutch admiral, Marten Harpertszoon Tromp, born in 1597, had sailed the seas almost since his infancy, and so had his son Cornelius, who was a worthy successor to his father. There was also Michiel Adrianszoon de Ruyter, ten years younger than Marten Tromp and the most distinguished of all Dutch naval commanders, who was mortally wounded during a battle in the Mediterranean in 1676, after having spent sixty years at sea and fought in forty battles.

The main cause of the First Dutch War was the notorious Navigation Act passed by Cromwell in September, 1651, which banned all foreign merchant ships from bringing cargoes into English ports, except those carrying cargo from their own country. The Dutch merchantmen faced ruin. The United Provinces sent a deputation to protest, but Parliament refused to repeal the Act. The Dutch therefore decided to build up their fleet, and on May 10th, 1652,[1] ordered their sea-captains to oppose, by force if necessary, any attempt to search Dutch ships. War seemed inevitable, and it was triggered off twelve days later. Three English frigates commanded by Captain Young were cruising

[1] Date according to the Gregorian calendar, which is now used throughout this book.

off Start Point when they encountered a Dutch convoy escorted by three men-of-war; the Dutch commander refused to render the traditional salute of the flag, and the English opened fire.

A few days later, Marten Tromp with a squadron of forty warships was forced by bad weather to seek shelter in Dover roads. War had not yet been declared, and the Dutch admiral had not neglected to inform the Dover authorities of his peaceful intentions. However, in spite of a shot being fired across his bows, he refused to salute the flag of Dover castle; and as soon as the weather calmed, at two in the afternoon of May 29th, he bore away into the open Channel still without having conformed to the request.

Blake was at Rye with a dozen ships, and Bourne was lying in the Downs with nine others. Both set sail as soon as Tromp had been signalled, and converged upon him from east and west, two hours after he had left Dover. Blake loosed off three shots to make the Dutch admiral haul down his flag. Tromp naturally would not do so, and this time battle was joined. The fighting raged furiously from six in the evening until nightfall; two Dutch ships were captured, though Tromp recovered one of them soon afterwards. Ten English ships, however, were badly mauled, and Blake's flagship, the *James*, had its hull peppered with more than seventy shots.

Only a formal declaration of war was lacking, and this was made by the Commonwealth on July 17th; though neither side had waited until then to begin offensive operations. Leaving Ayscue to keep watch in the Straits, Blake had sailed north on July 1st to seek out the Dutch herring fleet of six hundred craft which was fishing off the Shetlands. By the 22nd he had forced a hundred to discard their catch or had taken the vessels as prizes. In the meanwhile, Ayscue had intercepted a Dutch convoy between Cape Blanc and Cape Gris-Nez, captured seven ships and driven the others ashore. He then anchored in the shelter of the Downs. Tromp, who was on the lookout for him, arrived off the Goodwins on July 21st, but adverse winds from the south-east prevented him attacking. "In order not to lose time or the benefit of the wind", the Dutchman decided instead to go after Blake in the hope of protecting the fishing fleet and also a convoy of East Indiamen returning by way of the north of Scotland to avoid the risky passage up the Channel. By August 3rd Tromp was off the Orkneys; but instead of meeting with Blake and his squadron, Tromp ran into a strong gale that blew for three days, battering the Dutch flotilla so much that it had to turn for home. This lack of success infuriated the Dutch, and Tromp had to resign his command.

De Ruyter had fared better in the Channel. Sailing out of the Scheldt with twenty-three ships and sweeping down Channel, on August 26th he met with Ayscue's squadron that had just put out from Plymouth. Action was joined, and a stubborn fight ensued which lasted from one in the afternoon until dusk. Little is known of the result, except that both sides claimed a victory! The Dutch had some reason to be pleased, judging by the lukewarm reception that news of the fight received in London.

Admiral Ruyter (*from a Dutch engraving*)

At the end of September, after another indecisive engagement, Ayscue was dismissed his command but granted an honourable pension by the Council of State.

Blake had not been idle after his return from Scottish waters. In September he attacked and seized some French ships—although England and France were not at war—carrying fifteen hundred reinforcements to Dunkirk, which was under siege by the Spanish. "It mattered little to the English who held Dunkirk," Clowes comments on this incident. "But in view of the state of affairs in the Mediterranean it was essential to be on good terms with the Spanish, and it was too bad if this was at France's expense." As a result, Dunkirk was captured. Happy at having dealt this unexpected blow—which had been against a force much inferior in numbers to his own—Blake continued to keep watch and ward in the Straits. On October 8th he encounted Admiral De Witt's squadron near the Kentish Knock, a sandbank a few miles off the North Foreland. Action was joined at three in the afternoon. Blake gained the weather-gauge, and this time the Dutch got by far the worse of the gun-duel into which the action developed. Some of their ships even ran foul of one another in their panic. The rest fled, and the following day De Witt called his captains together to ask them to give better service to their country. Yet, on October 10th, when there came an opportunity to give battle again, half of them refused to fight "against an enemy so superior in strength". "I have never seen such cowardly captains," wrote the disheartened De Witt, after returning to the Scheldt with his battered squadron.

For the Dutch captains it should be said that, although the English were only slightly superior numerically, their ships had by far the greater weight of metal. No Dutch ship could match the *Resolution* or the *Sovereign*, and few could equal the *Fairfax*, the *James*, the *Andrew*, and other second-raters of Blake's squadron. As for De Witt, he was so unpopular that when, at the beginning of the action, he had wanted to shift his flag to the *Brederode* (Tromp's old flagship), the officers and crew had refused to allow him on board.

The outlook seemed bright for England. But because of financial difficulties, and thinking that with the approach of winter there would be no further threat from the Dutch Fleet, the Council of State rashly ordered a number of the larger ships to be laid up for the winter.

The States General, however, stung into action by De Witt's defeat, and not wishing its merchant ships to be denied passage to the Atlantic via the Straits of Dover, recalled Tromp and placed the best of their sea-captains under his command—Evertzen, Floriszoon, Ruyter. . . . The disgruntled De Witt pleaded ill-health and went into retirement. The need to refit and the low morale of the crews delayed sailing, but eventually Tromp was able to make towards the Straits with a vast concourse of vessels—about a hundred warships escorting five hundred merchantmen whose destinations were French Channel ports, the Mediterranean, the West African coast, or the East Indies.

The English were quite unprepared for the appearance of this armada. Troops were hurriedly sent to guard the Kentish coast, while Blake hastily mustered what ships he could, sailing out to intercept the Dutch with 42 men-of-war, frigates, and armed merchantmen, and a dozen smaller vessels—giving him a total of 1,400 guns and 5,800 men. Whereas Tromp, after leaving several of his ships to protect the convoy, still had 81 vessels—2,200 guns and 8,000 men.

The encounter took place on December 10th off Dungeness, which then as now was passed by more shipping than any other point of the globe. The Dutch had the advantage of numbers, but the English were favoured by the wind, which by shifting round and veering between north-east and north-west prevented part of the Dutch fleet from taking part in the action. The Dutch van, led by De Ruyter and sailing close to the wind, opened fire first, at about noon. An hour later, action was fully joined. Blake's *Triumph* was particularly sought out, and fought valiantly until nightfall, ably supported by the *Victory* and the *Vanguard*. Two other English hotly engaged were the *Garland*, a third-rater, and the *Bonaventure*, an armed merchantman. Tromp's flagship, the *Brederode*, was attacked on both quarters but managed to disengage, and towards the end of the day captured the *Bonaventure*, in which the captain and greater part of the crew had been killed. The *Garland*, too, was eventually captured after sustaining many casualties; and three other English ships were sunk. The only Dutch vessel lost was the victim of an explosion on board.

Blake was obliged to take refuge in the Downs with his battered fleet. Tromp, patching up the damage to his ships there and then, vainly tried to follow up his victory. Adverse winds prevented him, but he had the satisfaction of seeing his convoy proceed without further molestation.

The Battle of Dungeness was the first really great victory of the Dutch. Soon afterwards the legend came into being that Tromp had tied a broom to his masthead, signifying that he had swept the English from the sea.[1] Blake, mortified by his defeat, tendered his resignation, but it was refused. This was no time for the country to lose the services of such a man. The Administration had learnt its lesson, and appropriate steps were taken to ensure that the insolent Dutchman would have his broom rammed down his throat if he showed himself in the Channel again.

So it was that when Tromp next appeared, the following February, escorting a homeward bound convoy of two hundred sail, he found himself waylaid off Portland by seventy warships under the combined command of Blake and Monck. The two fleets were about numerically equal. Tromp had the wind astern; the English were to leeward. Leaving his convoy to sail on, the Dutch admiral pressed forward to attack.

The battle raged for three days and heavy toll was taken on both sides. Some ships were captured and recaptured several times. Blake and Bourne were both badly wounded, and the captains of the *Vanguard* and the *Triumph* were killed. The total Dutch losses amounted to four warships and thirty merchantmen, but most of the convoy managed to escape. The battle had drifted eastward all the time, and ended on March 3rd; Monck, who had anchored in the shelter of Cape Gris-Nez prepared to cut the enemy's retreat, saw at daybreak that there was not a sail in sight. On the English side, only the *Samson* was missing; but

[1] Clowes gives the explanation that a broom was usually tied to the masthead when a vessel was for sale; and Tromp, anchored off St. Martin-de-Ré after his success in the Channel, was merely auctioning some of his prizes.

three other ships had been so damaged as to be almost useless, and another had been accidentally set alight. Most of the other ships were in need of a lengthy refit.

In the weeks that followed, the Dutch kept harrying English shipping in the Channel, and even bombarded Dover. The decisive battle came on June 11th, off the North Foreland, when Monck with 110 ships encountered Tromp with 90. It ended in an English victory. After a four-hour gun-duel, the Dutch had lost 10 ships, and 1,350 men—including 6 captains—had been taken prisoner. Tromp had to fire on his own vessels in a vain effort to prevent them from retiring. He was finally forced to draw off, and took refuge within the Weilings sandbanks at the entrance to the Scheldt, where the English dare not follow him for fear of losing their ships of deeper draught. De Witt told everybody at the Hague that the English ruled the sea, and Ruyter vowed that he would quit the service if nothing was done to improve the fleet.

Nevertheless, Marten Tromp did not despair. Although peace talks had begun, he sallied out of the Meuse on August 3rd, 1653, at the head of eighty warships. As soon as news reached Monck, he weighed anchor but was unable to prevent De Witt joining Tromp with an additional squadron. On the 9th, the two fleets were within half a mile of each other, but the north-west wind freshened so much that it was impossible for them to engage. The wind dropped on the 10th; and at seven in the morning, battle was joined off Scheveningen. It was to be the last battle of the war, and Tromp's last, too.

Tromp, as usual, was in the thick of the fighting. His *Brederode* took on a whole squadron almost single-handed, belching fire so rapidly that his ship became shrouded in smoke. When it cleared, a flag calling his rear-admirals aboard for a council was seen to be hanging out. Those who managed to answer the summons were dismayed to learn of the death of their leader; he was lying on deck, having been shot through the heart by musket-fire from one of the vessels of the Blue squadron.

Tromp was the only admiral who was universally admired in Holland, whose orders were never questioned; he was popular with his seamen, and was the bravest and cleverest of all the enemies of the English at sea. To give the news of his death there and then would have meant risking his ships abandoning the action. Tromp's flag was left flying, and Evertzen took command and resolutely continued the fight. Taking advantage of the wind, the Dutch sent down their fireships among the enemy squadrons. The *Triumph*, flagship of the Admiral of the Red, was set alight and only just saved from destruction; while Rear-Admiral Graves of the White was burnt to death on the *Andrew* with a great many of his crew. The *Oak* went down with all hands; the burning *Worcestor* fouled the *Garland* and set her alight too, and both were lost.

Then the wind changed. And the English, in spite of their heavy losses, were able to assert their superiority. The *Brederode* narrowly escaped capture. The Dutch lost ten ships, and when darkness began to fall Evertzen made the signal to withdraw.

After this defeat and the loss of their great leader, the Dutch dared not venture out against the English for a time; and peace was signed first, on April 15th, 1654.

Ten years later, war broke out again between England and Holland. It was partly the fault of the Dutch, who had not ceased harrying English shipping in distant waters. But it was also due to the desires of the newly restored Charles II to have a strong new fleet capable of bringing to heel all the other maritime powers of Europe; to say nothing of his brother, the Duke of York, who nurtured a strong personal animosity against the Dutch Protestants. Without waiting for a formal declaration of war, he—as Lord High Admiral—had sent Sir Robert Holmes with a squadron to attack the Dutch trading-posts on the Guinea Coast. Holmes then crossed the Atlantic to deal similarly with their establishments in North America, where New Amsterdam was recaptured and renamed New York, in 1664. Ruyter was sent to retrieve the situation, which he succeeded in doing on the West African coast; but his expedition against Barbados was less successful. Meanwhile, in European waters, the Duke of York had seized about a hundred Dutch merchantmen. By then, matters were considered to have reached a point whereby a state of war officially existed between England and the Low Countries.

The Dutch Fleet had been built up again by De Witt, in spite of his retirement. In the absence of Ruyter, who was Tromp's obvious successor, the command was given to Jacob van Wassenaer, Lord of Obdam, with Kortenaer, Evertzen, and Tromp's son, Cornelius, as his squadron commanders. The Duke of York had under him Prince Rupert, Montagu (the Earl of Sandwich), Penn, Lawson, and Ayscue. The first encounter between the two fleets took place off Lowestoft on June 13th, 1665.

Obdam had put to sea on May 23rd with a considerable armament: 103 warships mounting 4,869 guns and carrying 21,556 men. On the 30th he had snapped up a valuable convoy outward bound from Hamburg, escorted by a single 34-gun ship. There was great outcry in England when this became known, and the Duke of York had hurriedly led out the fleet.

Prince Rupert was in the van, with the Duke in the centre, and Sandwich in the rear. With the wind in the south-west, the English had the advantage; Obdam made desperate efforts to gain the weather-gauge, but only succeeded in getting into confusion and letting the English in among him. During the resulting vast mêlée, the two commanders-in-chief found themselves ranged alongside, Obdam in the 76-gun *Eendracht*, the Duke in the 80-gun *Royal Charles*, and the Dutchman almost succeeded in closing and boarding his enemy. The Duke himself was slightly wounded and was spattered with the blood and brains of those killed at his side by a cannon-ball. Indeed, matters might have gone far worse with him; but the *Eendracht* suddenly blew up, and Obdam perished with practically all his ship's company—there were only five survivors.

The confusion following on the death of the Dutch commander-in-chief became even greater when Kortenaer and Stellingwerf were killed soon afterwards. Cornelius Tromp, believing he was the senior surviving flag-officer, took over command of all the ships in his vicinity. While Evertzen, the second-in-command of the fleet, was directing the action in another area. Signalling was so poor that forty-eight hours later Tromp still did not know what had happened to Evertzen, and mentioned his anxiety in his report to the States General.

The Dutch seamen, nevertheless, fought magnificently. The 76-gun *Oranje* captured the 52-gun *Montague*, which was retaken by the *Royal James* after a furious fight in which the latter's captain was killed and the *Oranje* herself went down in flames. The 56-gun *Staden Landen* seized the 46-gun *Charity*, which had already been badly battered by three other Dutch ships. Admiral Lawson was among the dead.

However, by seven in the evening the Dutch had had enough, and Evertzen gave the signal to break off the action. In the confusion, three Dutch ships belonging to three different divisions ran foul of one another, set each other on fire and went down in flames; while four others met the same fate when the English launched their fireships. Fourteen Dutch vessels were captured. It was only the courage of Cornelius Tromp in covering the withdrawal that prevented the Duke of York from inflicting a crushing defeat.

The Duke was acclaimed on his return. But public opinion was against the King's brother and Heir Presumptive running such risks in future.[1] Lord Sandwich was appointed in his place, but lack of success soon led to dismissal. De Ruyter, returning from the West Indies, managed to slip safely home, although Sandwich was waiting to intercept him in the southern waters of the North Sea and had sent Vice-

[1] Charles II had married the Infanta of Portugal, a rich but unattractive heiress.

Admiral Sir Thomas Tyddemann up to Bergen with a squadron for for the same purpose. De Ruyter received a great welcome and was promoted to high command of the Dutch navy. He took charge of all operations, and was soon giving the English some hard knocks.

On January 16th, 1666, France entered the war on the side of the Dutch; though Louis XIV showed little eagerness to intervene at sea. His Mediterranean squadron of thirty-six vessels, commanded by the Duc de Beaufort, was brought round to Brest but never ventured beyond the western approaches of the Channel. However, the news of its presence caused the English to commit a grave strategic error. On Charles II's orders, Prince Rupert was sent down-Channel with a third of the total naval forces, while Monck remained with fifty-six warships to meet the eighty Dutch under Ruyter.

Such were the conditions in which the famous "Four Days' Battle" began on June 11th, 1666. "Each side claimed the victory; but it undoubtedly went to the Dutch, although there was equal valour on both sides."[1]

On the very day that a strong east wind was carrying Rupert down-Channel, Ruyter was making use of that wind to clear Dutch waters. By the morning of June 11th he was between Dunkirk and the Downs, when the wind shifted round to the south-west. He anchored there and then, with his van under Evertzen standing out to the north-west, himself in the centre, and his rearguard under Cornelius Tromp to the south-east. By nine o'clock visibility was good, and Monck was seen to be at anchor to windward. The English were much the smaller force; but Monck, signalling to engage forthwith, bore down on his foe with great determination. He seized the initiative by advancing on the Dutch van in line ahead, but this meant making an angle of forty-five degrees with the line of the anchored Dutch, so that a third of his ships were still out of range when action was joined. Cornelius Tromp had at once weighed anchor and, casting on the starboard tack, stood off to the French shore. Ruyter and Evertzen were still too far to leeward to be able to help Tromp at this stage. However, the ebb and flow of the fight brought the English into dangerous shoal water, and they were forced to put about. This gave the Dutch centre and rear, which had not so far engaged, the opportunity to fall on the weakened English rear—which Monck's manoeuvre had brought to the head of the line. Ruyter took full advantage of the situation, cutting out several English ships and dealing with them individually.

The first was the *Swiftsure*, wearing the flag of Vice-Admiral Sir William Berkeley, whose brother Charles had been killed the previous

[1] J. Barrow, *History of England*, Vol. X, p. 41.

year at the side of the Duke of York during the Battle of Lowestoft. Beset on all sides, Berkeley put up a magnificent defence, refusing to strike his flag; the end came only when he was hit and killed by a bullet.[1]

Meanwhile, a 60-gun auxiliary and the 44-gun *Loyal George* had been captured by Ruyter. Sir John Harman narrowly escaped a similar fate to Berkeley's when his ship *Henry* had her masts and rigging shot away and was on fire. A Dutch fireship had struck her on the starboard quarter. Thomas Lamming, the first lieutenant, leapt through the flames and cut it loose. Hardly was this danger overcome than a second fireship caught her on the port quarter; the blaze spread with such rapidity that about fifty men jumped overboard, and Harman had to draw his sword and threaten to kill any who tried to follow. His example rallied the crew, and the fire was brought under control. A third fireship was then seen bearing down, but Harman sank it with his guns. Evertzen then ranged alongside and called on him to surrender. "I haven't come to that yet," retorted Harman, who had had his leg broken when a mast fell on him. And his next broadside stretched the valiant Dutch admiral dead.

The battered *Henry* managed to limp into Harwich; and Harman, in spite of his broken leg, got her patched up and put to sea again, but was too late to strike another blow at the Dutch.

In addition to Evertzen, the Dutch had lost a flag-officer, Stachouwer. Cornelius Tromp had been obliged to shift his flag to another ship, and Ruyter's looked about to sink at any moment. On both sides, two or three vessels had blown up or sunk.

Only the coming of darkness brought an end to the fighting. Monck withdrew westward, on the port tack, without interference from the Dutch. The two fleets used this respite to patch up their ships as well as possible, and at daybreak Monck returned to the attack with forty-four vessels against eighty Dutch. Ruyter had the wind of him at first, but by skilful manoeuvring Monck succeeded in gaining the weather-gauge. The Dutch squadrons were in some confusion, many of them masking the fire of others.

It was then that Cornelius Tromp made the mistake of trying to work round the English; by so doing, he exposed his ships to a raking fire, one after the other, and also became separated from Ruyter—who was having difficulty enough in co-ordinating his fleet. Two of his Vice-Admirals had sheered off because things were becoming too hot for

---

[1] The Dutch later wrote expressing their admiration of his great valour, and asking whether they should return Berkeley's body to England or bury it with honours in Holland.

them. Tromp was beset on all sides, and was soon in such a critical situation that Ruyter had to plunge into the mêlée before his ships were properly deployed. It was a fine opportunity for the English to work havoc among the mass of ships that were herded together like a flock of sheep, too numerous in fact for effective overall command. But Monck had insufficient strength to take advantage of it. He was unable to prevent the Dutch from reforming, and when night fell he drew off towards the north-west.

That day's fighting had been almost as costly as the first, with three ships lost on each side. Another Dutch admiral had been killed— Abraham van der Hulst, who was serving under Tromp.

On the third day the wind was coming from the east. Monck, with only twenty-eight ships still fit for battle, continued his slow withdrawal to the west; the tough old sea-fighter was waiting for Rupert to join him before engaging the enemy again.

There was little Ruyter could do to thwart Monck's intentions, but he added to his score by seizing the 90-gun *Royal Prince*, Sir George Ayscue's flagship, which had the misfortune to go aground on the Galloper Shoal. Surrounded by the enemy and with a hundred and fifty of his crew killed, Ayscue had to surrender to Tromp. The latter would have been delighted to take the prize back to port, but Ruyter would not allow this and gave orders to burn her.

For a third force had just appeared on the scene. While the dramatic events were occurring on the *Royal Prince*, a score of sail was sighted to the west. For a moment, the Dutch joyfully thought it must be Beaufort's squadron. Caught between two fires, the English would now be completely destroyed! But it was Prince Rupert, and his arrival caused Ruyter to be more prudent. He now had about sixty of the enemy to face, half of them undamaged ships, whereas his remaining seventy-eight— lighter craft, on the whole—were already battle-scarred.

On June 14th, the fourth day of the battle, the wind freshened and verred to the south-west again. The enemy fleets pounded each other for a couple of hours, sailing on the port tack and in two parallel lines. Monck succeeded in breaking the Dutch line to leeward, but with the wind strengthening the fighting became confused. Indeed, the wind was almost of gale force, and Ruyter withdrew, rightly satisfied with the results of the four days' fighting. His own losses amounted to six or seven ships, but he had sunk or captured a score; five thousand English had been killed, against two thousand Dutch.

The English Fleet was far from being destroyed, and it still remained a threat to Dutch shipping. Nevertheless, Europe was unanimous in congratulating the Dutch admiral on his men's fine performance in battle. "The Lord Ruyter," wrote Louis XIV, "did such deeds with heart and mind as surpasses all human endeavour."

For the campaign of 1667, Ruyter was planning to sail up the Thames and the Medway to destroy shipping and naval stores and blow up the arsenals. Every detail of the operation had been carefully studied. The Dutch had obtained precise information as to where English warships were lying, and had enlisted the help of renegade river-pilots. Ruyter gave command of the van to Rear-Admiral van Ghent, who had previously been an army colonel and so was equally at home on land and sea. An ideal leader for a combined operation! A renegade Cromwellian soldier, Colonel Dolman, was to lead the landing party.

Ruyter sailed from the Helder on June 6th, then remained several days in the Scheldt estuary while his fleet assembled and his military forces embarked. He finally put to sea on the 14th with 51 ships-of-the-line, 3 frigates, 14 fireships and a number of small craft. By the evening of the 15th he was within twenty miles of the Thames estuary when a south-westerly gale sprang up. However, the bad weather did not persist, and in the evening of the 17th the Dutch were anchoring at the Nore, near the entrance to King's Channel. The next day, Londoners were horrified to learn that a Dutch fleet was proceeding up the Thames. "Trading ceased, banks suspended payments, people left their work and gathered in the streets; many of the inhabitants fled, taking their valuables with them."

Van Ghent had at first been held up by adverse winds; but towards evening on the 19th, aided by a breeze from the south-east, he reached Gravesend. The wind having then dropped, he was unable to seize the ships he could see in the distance, farther upstream. In any case, his main objective was the naval installations at Chatham, on the Medway. On the 20th he sailed back down the Thames, joined up with reinforcements sent by Ruyter and raided Sheerness.

Instead of forcing their way at once up the Medway, which had only a chain across it by way of a boom, the Dutch missed the high tide on the 21st. Monck took advantage of this to bar the river by anchoring four fireships and another half a dozen craft behind them. But it was of no avail. The Dutch broke through next day, burnt half a dozen ships, and then withdrew bearing away with them the *Royal Charles* although "the state of the wind and the tide were such that even the best of the Chatham pilots would not have liked to undertake it".

It was a fine exploit, and Ruyter did not want to risk a set-back which would have reduced its effect. However, by order of the States General he stayed at the Nore, making two more raids into the Thames. He

then sailed down the Channel, intending to mete out the same treatment to Plymouth as he had to Chatham. But envoys reached him with
the news that peace had been signed. The Treaty of Breda had put an
end to hostilities between England, France, and the United Provinces
on July 21st, 1667.

There was peace for five years; then, on April 7th, 1672, England
and France declared war on Holland.

This time France had led the way, dragging England after her;
for Charles II was dependent upon the subsidies of his cousin, Louis
XIV. The situation of the Dutch seemed hopeless, now that the strongest
military nation and the strongest naval power were arrayed against
them. And it probably would have been hopeless but for Ruyter.

In spite of his sixty-five years Ruyter was still a staunch fighter, a
skilful seaman, full of sound commonsense, brave without being fool-
hardy, and a man who would take no unnecessary risks—as he had
shown during the "Four Days' Battle" and his forays up the Thames.
On the outbreak of war the States General had again given him command of the fleet. Ruyter was convinced that his country's best chance
of victory was at sea, and by April 23rd he had already made his way
out of the Meuse with the first ships ready for sea, and was waiting at
the Texel for the rest of the fleet to join him. He finally sailed on May
12th, having been informed that the French Fleet was proceeding up-
Channel to join the English. Ruyter's first idea was to attack the latter
at their anchorage in the Downs before the French reached them. But
it was already too late. A Danish merchantman hailed in the Straits
gave news of having counted eighty-three warships and thirty fireships
lying off the Isle of Wight on May 14th. . . . The two fleets had made
their junction.

Ruyter considered the possibility of seeking an encounter in the
Channel, but a council of war held on the *Zeven Provincien* was not in
favour of it. A foray into the Thames as in 1667 was proposed, "to see if
there was an opportunity of insulting the enemy". Again it was Van
Ghent who, with thirteen ships, pursued eight English vessels entering the estuary with the tide on May 24th; but the eight were the
better sailing-ships and eluded him, taking shelter under the guns of
Sheerness.

In the end Ruyter waited for the Allied fleet on the route it would
have to take to reach the Thames. He sighted it on May 29th, but fog
and then stormy weather prevented action being joined. Finally, on
June 6th, after a week of tacking to and fro in the North Sea, Ruyter's
scouting vessels reported that the combined fleet was moored in Sole

Bay, north of the Thames estuary. A light north-easterly was blowing. giving the Dutch the advantage for an attack.

The Dutch Fleet consisted of 78 ships mounting a total of 4,188 guns, 24 corvettes and scouting vessels, and 36 fireships; the man-power amounted to 19,930. Its three squadrons of almost equal strength were commanded by Bankert, Ruyter, and Van Ghent. Opposing them were 84 warships with 4,954 guns, 17 frigates, 23 fireships, 30 supply ships, and 2 hospital ships, with a total of 30,500 men. Of this force, 30 of the warships were French, 6 of the frigates, 8 fireships, and 6 supply ships, all these mounting 1,664 guns and carrying 10,140 men. They consisted of the Brest squadron, commanded by Duquesne, and the Rochefort squadron under D'Estrées, who was the French commander-in-chief.

Abraham Duquesne is a great name in French naval history. He was born at Dieppe in 1610, became a naval captain before he was twenty-six and a Rear-Admiral at thirty-six. He was a fine seaman but at the same time a "crotchety and pernickety" leader, touchy about the privileges of his rank, and a nightmare to the administration; he was always demanding the best of everything, the best rope and tackle and so on, but he was a true perfectionist. One of his contemporaries wrote of him: "There can be no one in France, or even in Europe, who applies himself more soundly and competently to his task." The navy suppliers who wearied Colbert with their complaints about him were roundly ticked off: "Even if he has some faults, it's their job to put up with them and to see that he's satisfied."

Unfortunately, Duquesne and his commander-in-chief, D'Estrées, were on bad terms. Jean D'Estrées was a difficult man to get on with, too. He had served in the army until he was forty-six, in which time he had made himself so unbearable that the Minister of War, Louvois, gladly transferred him when Colbert asked for officers for the fleet that was being formed. On November 12th, 1669, he had been made Vice-Admiral after only twenty months' service at sea. While his courage was not in doubt, the same could not be said of his knowledge of naval tactics, although he himself was "so convinced of his capabili-ties that he never took any advice from those who were most competent to give it".[1] He had already had Duquesne under his command, in 1670, during a campaign along the West African coast, in the course of which a whole series of trifling incidents were magnified into real dis-putes—a distressing state of affairs, and one that boded no good for the coming campaign.

The two squadrons had sailed together from Brest on May 10th,

[1] La Roncière, *Histoire de la Marine Française*, Vol. V, p. 551.

and anchored off Spithead on the 13th. Charles II went down to review them, and inspected the flagships—*St. Philippe* (D'Estrées), *Terrible* (Duquesne), and *Superbe* (des Rabesnières Treillebois)—complimenting the French admirals on "the ship-shape order of their vessels". On May 17th the English Fleet commanded by the Duke of York—who had taken over again on the death of Monck early in 1670—arrived and anchored off St. Helen's Head. Most of the ships had come round from the Thames, and only missed the Dutch by a day or two. There had been great difficulty in scraping the crews together, and the London press-gangs had "raked in even coachmen, servants, and loose and un-known persons!"

The combined fleet was deployed in three squadrons: D'Estrées commanded the White squadron, with Duquesne's division in the van; the Red squadron under the Duke of York was in the centre; and Montagu, Earl of Sandwich, commanded the Blue. On May 25th the fleet passed through the Straits of Dover, but the watchful activity of the Dutch prevented it from waiting for an expeditionary force which was being assembled with the object of making a landing at the mouth of the Scheldt or the Meuse.

At nine on the morning of May 29th a French scout, the *Eole*, reported that the Dutch were about five leagues to leeward—the wind was blowing up from the south-west—and in line of battle on the starboard tack, some eight leagues off the Zeeland shoals. By three in the afternoon the enemy fleets were within a league of each other, to the north-west of Ostend, and the Duke of York gave orders to drift with the current. But the Dutch did the same; the distance between the two fleets was not diminishing, and the Allies was being drawn towards the shallows. At seven o'clock Duquesne, in the van, finding only eleven fathoms of water under him, fired several shots as a warning of "Danger ahead". The Allied Fleet put about, and so became separated from the Dutch by sandbanks on which its ships would certainly have foundered because of their deeper draught.

The following day, mist and a gusty wind prevented any contact. Ruyter was still in sight on the 31st, about two leagues to leeward, off Ostend; but the Duke refused to be enticed so near the enemy coast, and decided to put in to Sole Bay to water. The fleet dropped anchor there on June 2nd.

The Lord High Admiral was so convinced of his safety that on June 6th he recalled the two English frigates from patrol. The *Eole*, however, asked for and obtained permission to remain at sea. During the day the wind hauled round to the north-east, putting the fleet on a lee shore, and Sandwich went on board the flagship to urge the Duke to weigh anchor at once. But he was accused of being fainthearted, and left the *Royal Prince* after a violent dispute with the Duke.

At half past two that night the *Eole* came running for the anchorage, firing her guns to warn the fleet that she had sighted the enemy. At daybreak the Dutch came sailing in to the attack, their three squadrons in line abreast. Among the Allies there was a hasty scramble to put to sea; much gear and thousands of men were left behind. D'Estrées's squadron cast on the port tack to clear the coast, while the Duke and Sandwich took the starboard tack, steering east. There was a good deal of confusion among the fleet, the Red squadron being to leeward of the Blue, with the French well away to the south. The falling wind and the inshore current added to the difficulties. There were, in fact, two separate battles that day—Sandwich's squadron against Van Ghent's, to the north, and the French against Bankert's to the south. But the latter, with only twenty-six ships against thirty, was anxious to avoid being boarded; and as he had the weather-gauge, he kept his distance while still remaining just within gun-range (at that period, it was about five hundred yards). There was a particularly warm engagement in the rear, in which the *Superbe* lost her admiral and twenty-three of her guns blew up. In the centre, the captains of the *Tonnant* and the *Excellent* were wounded. The *St. Philippe* was holed on the water-line, and then the Dutch sent half a dozen fireships down on her, but they were either avoided or sunk. The *Emerillon*, battling into the wind, was sunk before reaching her objective.

Duquesne, with the van to leeward, had virtually been out of the fight all this time. He had reached the position assigned to him by D'Estrées, but Bankert had then drawn off on the other tack; it was not until five in the afternoon that a few ships of Duquesne's division were able to engage the enemy. On the whole, D'Estrées's and Bankert's squadrons did little more than bang away at each other. Only one Dutch ship, the *Oranje*, suffered any real damage.

It was a very different matter to the north, where the battle raged furiously. At first things went badly for the English, who had been taken by surprise. The Dutch concentrated their fire on the Blue squadron and the leading vessels of the Red. The *Royal James* was closely engaged by the *Groot Hollandia* accompanied by half a dozen fireships; the latter were destroyed one after the other by the *Henry*, which had gone to the help of the flagship, but the *Henry* received such a battering—her captain, Francis Digby, was killed—that she had to withdraw. The *Edgar* only just managed to avoid a couple of fireships.

Sandwich tried to restore matters by grappling and boarding the *Groot Hollandia*, and his boarding-parties soon cleared her deck. But their numbers were insufficient to follow up the attack, and shortly afterwards the *Royal James* had to anchor in order to cut herself clear of the Dutch ship, which was more of a dangerous encumbrance than a conquest. But, thus isolated from the rest of the squadron, the *Royal James* was attacked by Rear-Admiral Sweers in the *Olyfan* and then set ablaze by a fireship—burning so furiously that she had to be abandoned. The Earl of Sandwich was forced to leap into the sea and was drowned. Van Ghent, the opposing admiral, was killed at about the same time.

The Red squadron was just as fiercely engaged. The *Royal Charles* had been badly damaged. The *Royal Prince*, attacked by the *Zeven Provincien* and the *Ridderschap van Holland*, and with two fireships sent against her, lost her main-topmast and had two hundred men killed or wounded. The Duke of York had to shift his flag to the *St. Michael*.

The *Royal Catherine*, astern of the *Prince*, was in a still worse plight; badly battered and set ablaze by a fireship, she was obliged to strike her flag. Two Dutch ships approached to take her in tow. While the prize-crews were looting her, the bo'sun, Small, rallied some of the men and they attacked the Dutch. Some French pinnaces in the vicinity went to their assistance, and the *Royal Catherine* was recovered. But she had been so badly mauled that the only thing to do was to tow her back to the anchorage in the bay.

The situation was not very promising when the Duke of York took command again in the *St. Michael*. Ahead of him were the Lowestoft shoals, on which his ships risked running aground. To leeward, working inshore, was Ruyter's squadron; out at sea was Van Ghent's squadron, which had only to let the wind carry it for the English to be caught between two fires. But Sweers—who should have been in command—was unaware that Van Ghent had been killed, and the squadron was in a state of confusion. The *Olyfan*, moreover, had suffered much damage in the fight with the *Royal James* and was isolated from her squadron. Schram, next in seniority to Sweers, made no attempt to take control (he was later court-martialled). The Duke took advantage of this to reform his squadron; the *Phoenix*, the *Resolution*, and the *Cambridge* moved into line ahead of the *St. Michael*. One Dutch ship had her main-mast shot away, another was sunk, and soon it was Ruyter who found himself in difficulties. The gallant Harman, who had shown such remarkable courage during the "Four Days' Battle", attacked him from leeward, while Admiral Kempthorne with six ships bore down on him from the other quarter. Fireships were sent down on the Dutch from all directions. . . . But Aert van Nes came to Ruyter's rescue with five or six ships, crowding on sail to pass ahead of the Duke—pouring a broadside into the disabled *Henry* on the way—and then led Sweer's squadron resolutely against the enemy. The *Victory* was disabled and had to drop out of line; the *St. Michael* was so badly mauled that the Duke of York was soon obliged to shift his flag again. He had a short respite, however, because Van Nes went to the help of Ruyter, who was being closely assailed by the Blue squadron—which Kempthorne was commanding, now that Sandwich was dead. At this point the isolated *Stavoren* was disabled and captured by the *Cambridge*.

Ruyter's flagship

It was now past six o'clock. The Duke put off in a pinnace from the disabled *St. Michael*, and hoisted his flag beside Spragg's in the *London*. The transfer took three-quarters of an hour, due to a freshening wind and a rising sea. Night was coming up, and Ruyter drew off to the south to join up with Bankert, who was several leagues to leeward. The Duke tried to counter this by bringing his squadron round to windward, but the battle was in fact over. It had cost the Allies the *Royal James* and a few fireships, and eight English vessels and the French *Superbe* were in sorry state. Sixteen hundred men—among them two admirals and seven captains—had been killed or drowned. One Dutch ship had been sunk and another captured, seven were badly damaged; another blew up later that night. Van Ghent had been killed, Bankert wounded. . . . Ruyter declared afterwards that he had never seen a battle so terrible. Yet it was his thirty-third!

The action was finally broken off on June 9th; both fleets were almost out of ammunition. Ruyter anchored off Walcheren, while the Allied Fleet repaired to the Thames "in great distress".

Controversy soon broke out as to who had won at Sole Bay, just as it did centuries later after the Battle of Jutland. At first the English had nothing but praise for their allies. "The French squadron fought with extreme courage," Admiral Kempthorne wrote to a friend on the night of the battle. The Dutch were of the same opinion. "No one could speak more highly of a nation than did Ruyter and his officers concerning the French squadron," Colbert was able to write to his brother, De Croissy, the French Ambassador to the Court of St. James. The first discordant notes in this harmony were sounded—not surprisingly—among the French themselves. Such were the pitiful consequences of the animosity between D'Estrées and Duquesne. If only this dirty linen had not been washed in public!—but echoes of the dispute soon reached London, where mischief-makers were quick to affirm that the French had looked on while the English fought, and had merely "skirmished with a few Zeeland vessels which had been left to keep them quiet", and that the damage done to the English fleet was due to their inactivity.

The quarrel between the two French admirals continued until January, 1673, when Duquesne, at his own request and against Colbert's advice, appeared at Court to state his case. But D'Estrées had much the greater influence in high circles, and the unfortunate Duquesne was relieved of his command.

Perhaps it was some consolation for him to learn that there was also dissension in the enemy camp. In Holland, crowds had to be stopped from pillaging Ruyter's house because they supposed him to be in the pay of the French; and two of his admirals were brought before a court-martial to clear themselves.

No one, in fact, seemed satisfied with the outcome of the battle. But considering that the English were unable, because of their losses, to land a force on Dutch soil and take advantage of the disorders there, as they had intended, the Battle of Sole Bay would appear to have been a victory for the Dutch. Especially as England signed a separate peace treaty with the Dutch—due in part to distrust of the French—on February 9th, 1674.

However, in 1673 the English and French were still allied against the Dutch. Prince Rupert was in command of the Allied Fleet (the Duke of York had been removed by the provisions of the Test Act), with D'Estrées again leading the French squadron. In the place of Duquesne was the Marquis de Martel, an experienced sea-captain and an old campaigner, but who had an even stronger dislike for

D'Estrées—so strong, in fact, that it eventually landed him in the Bastille.

So the combinéd force was no more united than it had been the previous year. Rupert got on no better with Spragg, his second-in-command, than D'Estrées did with Martel; furthermore, Rupert made no attempt to conceal his dislike of the French and his doubts as to their loyalty. Ruyter, on the other hand, had the sure support of Cornelius Tromp—who had returned to the service after a long absence —and of Bankert, two keen and able sea-captains.

Charles II and Louis XIV were still hoping to carry out the previous year's plan of landing troops on the Dutch coast. But this time, Rupert had instructions first to seek out and destroy the Dutch Fleet. Ruyter, for his part, was planning new forays into the Thames, hoping to bottle up most of the English fleet. But Rupert was warned in time by French agents, and on May 6th hastily left Sheerness with 45 ships to anchor off Dungeness. When the Dutch admiral sallied forth on the 12th with 36 warships, 12 frigates, 16 fireships, and 8 block-ships, he found the English prepared for him. He also learnt that the French had just sailed from Brest and were coming up the Channel, so he gave up his attempt and returned to shelter in the Schoonveldt roads, behind the sandbanks stretching from Walcheren to the mouth of the Scheldt.

When D'Estrées joined Rupert the strength of the fleet was brought up to 84 warships, 10 frigates and 42 fireships.[1] Unlike the Duke of York, the Allied commander this time was quite determined to seek out the enemy, even in his own waters. Rupert set sail from Rye on May 30th, and two days later sighted the Dutch fleet lying off the Scheldt, between the Roen and the Stone banks.

For the next six days storms prevented action from being joined. The two fleets rode at anchor, and the English took the opportunity to study the tides, currents, and depths of this part of the Dutch coast. Such new, practical knowledge was extremely useful to have; but it was discouraging to realize how dangerous that coast could be. Ruyter and his captains, of course, knew it like the palms of their hands, and they wished for nothing better than to entice the enemy into those waters, reckoning that their best allies would be the inshore currents, the westerly winds, and the shoals.

The storms died down on June 7th—the anniversary of the Battle of Sole Bay—and the wind was coming from the north-west. When the tide turned, Rupert hoisted the signal to weigh. He was commanding the left wing, opposed to Tromp; D'Estrées had the centre, facing

[1] Martel, with three ships, only reached Brest in time for the latter part of the campaign.

Ruyter. The Dutch tactics proved successful. The greater numbers of the Allies gained them no advantage, as the captains were so afraid of foundering on the shoals; while the Dutch were in their element. By evening, Ruyter had reformed his line a league and a half farther out than at the beginning of the action, in spite of an off-sea wind which should have favoured his enemies.

Rupert had been foiled in his design, but it was an indeterminate encounter with few losses on either side. Two English ships had to return to the Thames for repairs. A Dutch vessel, which had gone aground at the mouth of the Scheldt, sank the next day. The French had wasted eight fireships and the Dutch four.

The storm rose again the next day and held for a week, preventing further fighting. Rupert remained in the area, but his difficulties increased with every day that passed. Food was running short, and the wounded could neither have proper attention nor be sent home. Ruyter, meanwhile, was joined by other ships which brought up his strength almost to that of the Allies. On June 14th the wind shifted round to the north-east. Rupert decided that the time had come to withdraw, but Ruyter was preparing to attack, and out beyond the shoal waters this time.

That day's action was extremely confused. Rupert was taken by surprise when the Dutch bore down, and ordered his ships to cut their cables; while D'Estrées seemed in less of a hurry and weighed anchor, apparently not understanding the intention of his commander-in-chief, who had made no signal. Spragg's division, too, remained inactive, waiting for its commander to return from Rupert's flagship with orders.

The result was "a great skirmish", with a great deal of gunfire, after which Ruyter discreetly drew off during the night, not wishing to be too far from the coast; while the Allies were well content to run for shelter in the Medway and the Thames, not making the Duke of York's mistake of anchoring in an exposed bay.

For all his faults D'Estrées was not without a certain amount of common sense, and he drew the right conclusion when he wrote to Colbert that Ruyter had "gained time and made us lose some in doing repairs and replenishing our powder and shot".

Two months later, on August 21st, 1673, the two sides were facing each other again, off the Texel. The encounter was just as indecisive as the two Schoonveldt battles, and at the end the Allied commanders were more at variance than ever. Rupert attacked the Dutch but apparently received little support from Spragg—who nevertheless lost his life—or from the French; only Martel's division showed any spirit, at the beginning of the action, while D'Estrées maintained an extra-ordinarily passive role throughout.

The Sole Bay controversy broke out again, fanned by a pamphlet which Martel secretly circulated and which was nothing less than a downright accusation against his commander. In England it was being said that the King of France had certainly ordered his captains to stand off and let the English and Dutch destroy each other. A strong movement to bring the war to an end had already formed in England when the French squadron sailed for home from the Thames, on September 28th, 1673.

Thus ended the first attempt at Anglo–French naval co-operation. It had not even lasted two years. Another one hundred and fifty were to pass before the two navies again fought side by side.

The French were now left to fight the Dutch alone, and the Spanish too, for the latter declared war on October 15th, 1673. On land, the French victories at Maastricht and on the Rhine were of little effect; behind their flood defences, and well supplied by convoys from their colonies, the Low Countries seemed as impregnable as an island. At sea, the French naval forces were barely up to the Dutch strength and were divided between the Mediterranean and the Atlantic. Colbert summed up the matter when writing, on May 17th, 1674, that "His Majesty, abandoned by England and obliged to maintain such great armies, cannot have the same strength at sea, and as it has been thought sufficient to keep 40 vessels in the Atlantic and 30 in the Mediterranean, with 24 galleys, the Dutch will have the supremacy in all waters".

In fact, no resistance was made to the Dutch in the Channel or in the Atlantic, and Ruyter sailed across to attack the French trading-posts and garrisons in the West Indies. But the garrison on Martinique repulsed him.

D'Estrées had remained in command of the Atlantic squadron; the Mediterranean command was given to the general of the galleys, Victor de Rochechouart, Duc de Vivonne and brother of Madame de Montespan. He was a brave soldier, but needed the support of a good and experienced naval commander—and Duquesne, then sixty-four years old, was brought back to active service. Their first task was to give support to a revolt against the Spanish that had broken out in Messina. This was a minor campaign, but enabled the navy that Colbert had so patiently built up over the years to gain its first victories. On February 11th, 1675, Vivonne's squadron, with Duquesne in the van, put to flight a numerically superior Spanish squadron under Don Melchior de la Cueva, and captured a 43-gun ship. On August 17th the Sicilian port of Augusta fell to Duquesne and Tourville. The Spanish called on the Dutch for help, and at the end of December Ruyter made his appearance in the Mediterranean.

The first encounter between French and Dutch, off Alicuri on January 8th, 1676, was indecisive; chiefly because Ruyter had thought it prudent not to risk a full-scale battle in case failure in sight of the Sicilians might "cause their small remaining amount of loyalty to vanish entirely". But Duquesne's prestige rose—he had "made Ruyter give way".

The following April a combined Spanish and Dutch Fleet tried to recapture Augusta. It was met by a French fleet commanded by Duquesne; Vivonne was away on a political mission. Duquesne had 30 ships with 1,722 guns and 10,300 men. The enemy fleet, under Ruyter, was of similar strength. Action was joined at about four in the afternoon of April 22nd, off Syracuse, and the battle raged furiously until long after dark. On the French side alone, 30,000 cannon-balls were fired. D'Alméras, commanding the French van, engaged in a struggle to the death with Ruyter, for both men lost their lives. D'Alméras was killed outright, and Ruyter was fatally wounded. The Dutch Admiral's biographer, Brandt, described the circumstances:

"He was on the poop-deck, giving orders and encouraging his men, when he was struck by a cannon-ball that carried away most of his left foot and broke his right leg in two places . . . the force of the blow made him fall to the deck below, a distance of about seven feet, giving him a deep cut on the head."

It was ten at night, under a bright moon, before the action was broken off. The Hispano–Dutch Fleet sought refuge in Syracuse harbour; Duquesne, being almost out of ammunition, made no attempt to cut off its retreat. The French might have gained an even more decisive victory if they had been able to get the wind of the enemy or had shown more discipline, and if D'Alméras's death had not thrown the van into some confusion. It would have been better for the Dutch to have lost half their ships rather than Michiel de Ruyter, "the man worth an army". The Admiral's wounds were serious, but his life was not thought to be in danger. He developed a high fever, however, and died at nine in the evening of April 29th, at the age of sixty-nine.

The consequences of his death soon made themselves felt. Six weeks later, on June 2nd, 1676, the French Fleet at full strength surprised the Dutch and Spanish at anchor at Palermo. It was more a massacre than a battle: the Dutch lost 250 men, including 2 admirals, and the Spanish lost 1,800, including 3 admirals, and 10 vessels were sunk or set alight. Only lack of powder and shot prevented the French from doing more damage. Their losses were less than 200 dead and wounded.

Success in the Mediterranean, however, was not enough for the French to win the war; and their navy was not yet strong enough to cut Dutch communications in the Atlantic and the North Sea. The Dutch could hold out indefinitely. But Louis XIV was weary of the war, and peace was signed at Nimeguen on May 16th, 1678.

VIII

FROM BEACHY HEAD TO BARFLEUR POINT

*Anglo-French rivalry at sea—the Battle of Beachy Head (July 10th, 1690)—
Admiral Tourville's difficulties with his superiors—his courageous fight off
Barfleur against the combined Anglo-Dutch Fleet (May 27th, 1692)—its
tragic conclusion at La Hougue, due to one Minister having wanted to spite
another!—Tourville takes heavy toll of the Smyrna convoy—Jean Bart re-
captures a wheat convoy from the Dutch.*

CHARLES II was succeeded by his brother James, but the reign was
short. Parliament and public opinion were hostile to his professed
Roman Catholicism, and after three years the crown was offered to
the Protestant William of Orange, the husband of James's daughter,
Mary, by his first wife. James II fled to France, where his cause was
supported by Louis XIV. The French King's recognition of James as
the rightful British sovereign was tantamount to a declaration of war.

King William soon brought about a Grand Alliance: England and
the United Provinces, naturally; the Emperor of Germany, because the
French were thrusting into the Rhineland; and Savoy and Spain, because they did not want to be left out. . . . In short, France found the
whole of Europe arrayed against her. However, Louis XIV's Minister
for War, Louvois, had created a fine army; and over the years,
Richelieu, Colbert and his son, Seignelay, had built up a navy which
was at its best at a time when the Dutch, worn out by so many wars,
were neglecting their navy, and when the English Fleet was dispersed
in distant waters. It was a propitious moment for the French. They
could easily have gained the mastery of the narrow seas; but instead of
seizing the opportunity, Louis XIV wasted time and ships supporting
the attempts of James to reconquer his kingdom.

The ex-King landed in Ireland in March, 1689. The French were
bringing him three thousand reinforcements, and preparing to put
them ashore in Bantry Bay, on May 9th, 1689, when Admiral Herbert,
Viscount Torrington, hove in sight with twenty-seven ships, of which
nineteen were ships-of-the-line. The French squadron covering the
landing greeted them with such an intense fire that, according to one
French writer, "the English at once closed their gun-ports for fear of
having their gunners filched". The *Ardent*, flying the flag of the French
admiral, Château-Renault, engaged Torrington for four hours,

driving him out to sea and inflicting grievous damage. The English withdrew with two ships disabled and casualties in men that were double those suffered by the French.

But the real contest came the following year, in July, when the largest French fleet ever seen sailed up the Channel. Commanded by Vice-Admiral Tourville, it numbered 75 ships-of-the-line, 6 frigates, and 20 fireships.

Anne Hilarion de Costentin Tourville was then forty-eight. He had entered the navy at an early age, under the aegis of the Knights of Malta—whose Order was a real nursery of seamen in the seventeenth century. At fourteen he had been a pretty-looking lad, with fair hair

and blue eyes, who was thought better suited for conquering the hearts of the ladies at Court than for capturing the ships of the King of England. It was said that his first captain looked disgusted when he joined the ship, and that the lower deck at once named him a milksop. But a few weeks later, when the ship went into action, the "milksop" showed what he was made of and there were no more sneers about him. He was a captain of the King's ships at twenty-seven, and in command of a squadron when thirty-three, having fought under D'Estrées at the Battle of Sole Bay, under Duquesne at Augusta and Palermo, and having taken part in the fighting before Algiers and Tripoli.

Prow of a ship-of-the line (*from the Colbert Atlas*)

The large fleet placed under his command in 1690 was due to a memorandum submitted to the King by Jean Bart, in which that intrepid corsair proposed to force the Thames as Ruyter had in 1667. Jean Bart had been present at that occasion as a sailor in the Dutch flagship. Such a direct attack at the heart of the enemy nation would give better results than engaging in secondary operations—and it was now or never, for the Brest fleet had been joined by the Toulon fleet, under Château-Renault, and fifteen galleys were on their way from the Mediterranean too, having just put in at Rochefort.[1] With such a force, there was every hope of wresting control of the Channel from the Anglo-Dutch fleet—an essential preliminary to an invasion of England.

[1] The idea of including galleys came from Seignelay, who had succeeded his father, Colbert, as Navy Minister in 1676. Galleys had not been seen in the Channel since the time of Philippe the Fair. It was an excellent idea, but unfortunately the galleys had still not arrived on the scene when Tourville, becalmed, could have made good use of them.

What a splendid display of naval power was given to the people of Brest when Tourville put to sea on June 22nd, 1690! Taking the van was the White-and-Blue squadron of twenty-four ships commanded by Victor-Marie D'Estrées, the son of the Admiral D'Estrées who had fought with the English against Ruyter. Then came Tourville in the *Soleil Royal*, a superb 98-gun ship-of-the-line, leading the main body of twenty-six vessels, the mightiest and finest of the whole fleet. The Blue squadron held the rear—twenty-five ships commanded by Château-Renault in the *Dauphin Royal*. The fleet contained ships bearing the most historic French names, captained by the country's finest seamen: Panetié in the *Terrible*, Gabaret in the *Intrépide*, Amfreville in the *Magnifique*. . . . Jean Bart, in the *Alcyon*, was with the van, with the responsibility of relaying signals. The fiery Chevalier de Forbin, in the *Fidèle*, had a similar role in the main body. Finally, there were five fireships, whose names were well chosen for their job, meaning the *Imprudent*, the *Impertinent*, *Nuisance*, *Firebrand*, and *Scatter-brain*.

The hulls of the men-of-war had been brightly painted, contrasting with the wide white bands that marked the lines of gun-ports. The gilded carvings on the huge after-castles were glittering in the sunshine; though some of the ships, like the *Soleil Royal*, had their decorative work discreetly coated with pearl-grey paint. Their masts and rigging

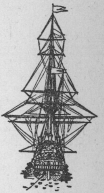

Poop of a ship-of-the-line (*from the Colbert Atlas*)

pointed high in the sky, and their great spreading sails were decorated with allegorical figures and emblems of all kinds.

Tourville was hoping to be off the Isle of Wight in less than forty-eight hours; but when the last of his ships had cleared Brest roads the wind dropped, and the fleet stayed becalmed for the next three days. An intercepted letter had caused Tourville to expect to come upon an Anglo-Dutch fleet of fifty-eight ships at anchor off St. Helen's Head. But when he finally made the Isle of Wight on July 5th he found the anchorage empty. Jean Bart responded to his call for a volunteer to reconnoitre the coast. When darkness fell, Jean Bart put off in a long-boat, taking some fishing-nets with him, and discovered the enemy fleet anchored off Beachy Head, not far from Pevensey (which the French called "Béveziers"; this was the name they gave to the battle that followed).

Jean Bart calmly explored the anchorage, replying "Fisherman"

whenever he was hailed by a lookout. On the 8th he was back to report to his commander-in-chief that there were eighty-four ships at anchor; actually, there were only sixty.

Tourville, in any case, was eager to get at the enemy. But in those days sailors could not always do as they wished. There was little wind, and that little was adverse. All the French ships could do was to drift with the current, dropping anchor on the ebb tide. Whereas the English, having such of the weather-gauge as there was, could take the initiative whenever they pleased.

Admiral Arthur Herbert, Viscount Torrington, had been greatly surprised to learn of the presence of the French Fleet, for he had not a single ship scouting to the west of St. Helen's Head. But he was determined to engage the enemy at once, and the Dutch admirals serving under him had some difficulty in persuading him to await the arrival of reinforcements. However, soon after day-break on July 10th his flagship, the *Royal Sovereign*, was signalling to the fleet to weigh anchor.

Tourville was ready for him. The divisions of his three squadrons were hove-to in battle order, though D'Estrées had been obliged to cede the place of honour in the van to Château-Renault's squadron, which was more favoured by the wind.

Torrington had the advantage of wind and current, and his fleet came bearing down on the French, with his van—a Dutch squadron commanded by Evertzen—imprudently forging far ahead and driving into the heart of the French van. A furious gun-fight developed between the Dutch and the French ships. The *Dauphin Royal* received particular attention, the Dutch having recognized her as Château-Renault's flagship. Two great men-of-war attacked her; cannon-shot hurtled in both directions, tearing holes in sails, splinter-ing masts, and bringing down rigging. The cries of the wounded and the dying could be heard between the thunderous discharges of the guns. The decks ran with blood, and down below the surgeons had rolled up their sleeves and were at work on the first of the wounded.

Just astern of the *Dauphin Royal*, the *Ardent* was in such bad shape that Château-Renault gave her captain permission to take her out of the line; and he let her drift before the wind, getting away from the scene of action in order to patch up the damage.

By then, the critical moment for the French had passed; the rest of their van had succeeded in wearing round the Dutch line so that it came under cross-fire—not only from Château-Renault's ships but from the following main body under Tourville—while the main Allied force was still out of range. With the exception of a few Dutch that managed to escape through the gap left by the *Ardent*, all Evertzen's ships were badly mauled. The French poured in a crippling fire from all sides; rigging was shot away, decks and superstructure were repeatedly holed. The Dutch fought back with desperate courage. . . . The *Vriesland*, attacked on both quarters and with two hundred and thirty men killed or wounded, refused to strike her colours while she had still a gun or two to fire. When she finally surrendered, the officer in charge of the prize-crew reported that "there was not a foot of space above the water-line that had not been hit, and the deck was strewn with dead and dying".

The English eventually arrived on the scene and were greeted in a befitting manner by the French. Admiral Ashby in the *Sandwich* was so hotly received by the guns of the *Soleil Royal* that he promptly sheered off. Other vessels of his command, however, caused much damage to the French *Tonnant*, which was disabled for a time. But four English ships, their masts gone by the board, had to abandon the action.

One may wonder what Torrington was doing in the meantime. Apparently having little desire to measure himself against the first-raters in the French centre, he had taken advantage of the "doubling" of the Dutch line to fall on the weaker ships of the French rear. So that instead of seeking out the *Soleil Royal*, Torrington's flagship turned her guns on the *Content*, the *Entreprenant*, and the *Apollon*, mere 50- or 60-gun ships against whom an easier victory was expected. But these smaller vessels fought with such great courage that the *Fougueux* with her 58 guns forced the English flagship to break off the action, in spite of her superior armament. Never before had French gunners served their pieces so quickly nor been so deadly in their aim. Two of the French ships, however, were obliged to fall out of line. The *Terrible* had part of her stern blown away. The Admiral of the Blue, Sir Ralph Delaval, attacked Gabaret's division and had two ships dismasted for his pains; while the 48-gun *Vaillant* had the better of one of his 90-gun three-deckers.

All was going well for the French; a magnificent victory seemed within their grasp. With the approach of darkness the wind veered round gradually to the north-west, then to the west—giving the weather-gauge to Tourville. And he still held the Dutch squadrons within his grip; not one of their ships, he was hoping, would ever see Holland again. If only the wind would hold, he could deal a mortal blow to the English. They were already showing signs of being disheartened; in a final effort, they sent a fireship down towards the French, but it was shot to pieces by gunners of Gabaret's division before reaching its destination, making a wonderful firework-display.

Torrington then signalled to withdraw, and ordered out his boats to tow the crippled ships away. Unfortunately for Tourville, the wind had not held, and the tide was on the turn too. Torrington ingeniously ordered his vessels to drop anchor; and Tourville saw too late that the ebb was carrying him westward, away from the enemy fleet, which was thereby saved from disaster.

"The enemy has fled," Tourville wrote in the dispatch he sent off by a corvette, "having ordered out his pinnaces to tow his ships away, leaving ten disabled vessels which we would take if there were a breath of wind. We have captured one ship, dismasted eleven, sunk two, and three fireships, and sunk a fourth fireship that was bearing down on us." If only Noailles had been there with his fifteen galleys! Alas, they had only just rounded Finisterre.

Night had now fallen, but the scene of the action was lit up by burning ships. One, Van de Putte's flagship, was still ablaze at daybreak; another, the *Noord Quartier*, sank during the night.

The French did not intend leaving matters there. For the next two days and nights, Villette and his division harried the hapless Dutch who had been unable to follow Torrington to the shelter of Thames-mouth. Keeping close on their heels, watching—in vain—for the slightest breeze that would enable him to finish off the badly maimed Dutch, Villette succeeded nevertheless in sinking the *Wapen van Utrecht* and in forcing two other vessels and a fireship to go aground; their crews then sank them to prevent their falling into the hands of the French. The *Tholen*, too, was dealt a mortal blow; and a 70-gun warship was beached and burnt by her crew. When the shattered Dutch squadron arrived within sight of Dover, seventeen of its ships were missing. Tourville had not lost a single one.

The Dutch had paid heavily, far more than the English, and there was great indignation in Holland. While in England, where a landing by the French was feared at any moment, the Trained Bands were mustered—and the defeated Admiral was sent to the Tower.[1]

A few weeks after the Battle of Beachy Head, Tourville was obliged by bad weather and sickness among his crews to lay up the Fleet for the winter. Six thousand seamen, ill with scurvy or other diseases, were landed at Brest, after two thousand eight hundred had already been put ashore at Normandy ports—in all, a good third of Tourville's

---

[1] Torrington was kept in the Tower for several months, until brought before a court-martial at Sheerness on November 10th, 1690. He was acquitted by his brother-officers. But King William could never believe that he had not deliberately sacrificed the Dutch ships, and dismissed him from his country's service.

total man-power.[1] They were victims of the unhealthy conditions which prevailed in the ships of all countries at that period, and which took a far heavier toll than the fire of the enemy.

Long periods at sea were shown to be so gruelling that Tourville proposed leaving the burden to the enemy the following year. "Let our enemies wear themselves out at sea," he said, "and then we will sail out and attack them off Ushant when they're tired from their long patrol and want to return to port."

Seignelay had died in November, 1690, and his successor at the War Ministry, Pontchartrain, failed to see the wisdom of Tourville's advice. Instead, he lent an ear to those who thought it better to seek out the enemy in the Channel and "maintain our sense of superiority". Pontchartrain was hoping, too, that Tourville would succeed in capturing the huge Smyrna convoy, whose riches would help to reduce the deficit that the war had made in the Royal budget.

So Tourville was back at sea in the summer of 1691, cruising between Ushant and the Scillies with sixty-nine ships for seven weeks on end, without once setting eyes on the English Fleet. He missed the rich Smyrna convoy but fell upon one from Jamaica, capturing two of the escort ships and a few merchantmen.

The French saw no outcome to the war unless an invading force could be landed in England. James was still hopeful of success, with the backing of the French King, especially as William's hold on the throne was still not secure. It was rumoured that he could not count on the Navy. Many of its officers had served under James when he was Duke of York and Lord High Admiral—the present commander-in-chief for one, Admiral Russell, who had succeeded Torrington—and some were believed to be waiting for a favourable opportunity to change their allegiance; Carter, Admiral of the Blue, was one of those named openly. In any case, whatever was being said at Versailles and in London, Queen Mary thought it advisable (William was in the Netherlands) to summon Russell; and subsequently he and his senior officers signed an address of loyalty to the Queen.

Meanwhile, an invasion force, commanded by James and Marshal de Bellefonds, was encamped near St. Vaast-la-Hougue, on the east coast of the Cherbourg peninsula, and was relying on Tourville to ensure its safe passage to England. But Colbert's efforts to make France a maritime power were being woefully wasted under Pontchartrain's administration. Supplies and ammunition were slow in reaching the naval bases. There was a lack of sailors; and Tourville, peremptorily

[1] Tourville had sailed from Brest with 26,770 men, according to one source; 20,216, according to another.

ordered to put to sea, left Brest on May 12th, 1692, with only thirty-nine warships, leaving a score or more in harbour because no crews were available to man them. Twelve ships were on their way from Toulon under Victor-Marie D'Estrées, but they did not reach Brest until after Tourville had sailed, and were then held back by adverse winds. Ships were sent from Rochefort, too, but only five had joined Tourville by the time battle was about to begin. So that he had but forty-four ships, when more persistent effort could have given him double the number.

It might at least have been expected that he would be allowed some latitude in choosing the conditions in which to fight or in adopting the best measures for the success of the operation. But no . . .

". . . His Majesty definitely desires him to leave Brest on the said day, April 25th, even should he have information that the enemy is at sea with a force superior to that in readiness to sail with him. . . . Should he meet with enemy ships he is to chase them back to their ports, whatever number they may be . . ."

The royal instructions were, admittedly, directed primarily at putting the invasion force ashore successfully; everything was to be sacrificed to that end, after which a more prudent attitude was permitted, if not prescribed:

"If, having escorted the troopships to the landing area or the landing being in progress, the enemy attacks with a number of ships greater than he has under his command, His Majesty desires him to engage them and to persevere, so that even should he be at a disadvantage the enemy is unable to prevent the landing. But, when the landing has been completed and the troopships are on the return journey, should the enemy then attack him, His Majesty does not permit him to engage unless the enemy force is superior to his own by no more than ten vessels; *but His Majesty desires him to approach close enough to discover for himself, when that should oblige him to fight.*" [1]

That final phrase (my italics) was superfluous for a man like Tourville. It touched him to the quick. So now his courage was doubted! There was no need to wonder who had added that spiteful insinuation to his Instructions. It smelt of Pontchartrain from a mile off. In all the navy, there was no officer more vigilant than Tourville for the honour of his national flag. He had in the past attacked a whole division of the Spanish Navy because it refused to salute the French flag, and had inflicted a hundred and ninety casualties—at a time when the two

---

[1] Instructions of March 26th, 1692—Archives Nationales, Paris (K. 1360, No. 13). The full text was published in *La Bataille de La Hougue*, by Georges Toudouze, Paris, 1899.

nations were at peace. There were sixty-nine casualties among his own men; but the Spaniards had given him the salute—a nine-gun salute, which he had returned shot for shot.

As though it was not enough to tell him not to be afraid to seek out the enemy himself, Pontchartrain also wrote to Tourville on May 20th: "It is not your place to query the King's orders, but to carry them out and sail up the Channel; write and tell me if you intend doing so, if not the King will replace you with someone more obedient and less circumspect than you."

Sail up the Channel. . . . Tourville had been beating up against the wind for the past three days. As for going in to fight, he was soon to give further proof of that—even with the enemy two to one against him!

For the English and Dutch, contrary to what was hoped at Versailles, had joined up before Tourville had even put to sea. Admiral Russell had 63 ships-of-the-line, and 36 Dutch under Admiral Van Almonde had reached him on May 9th. So there were 99 warships against Tourville's 44; 38 frigates and fireships against his 13; 6,756 guns against his 3,240; 53,463 men against 20,900.[1]

On May 27th the wind shifted round to the south-west, and the French squadron was able to make good progress up the Channel, keeping inshore and dropping anchor on the ebb tide to prevent being carried out to sea again. Tourville had two frigates scouting beyond the Cherbourg peninsula—the Chevalier de Forbin's *Perle* and Roche Allard's *Henry*. Russell had weighed anchor as soon as the wind had got up, and his scouts—the corvettes *Chester* and *Charles Galley*—were well out into the Channel. Both French and English scouts sighted the opposing forces at daybreak on May 29th, and went scudding back to their respective flagships, signalling by flag and gunfire the position and numbers of the enemy formation. Roche Allard's report must have given Tourville plenty to think about: an absolute forest of masts and white sails had suddenly appeared about seven leagues to the north-east of Barfleur Point, "all aglow with sunrise". If Tourville was still hoping to come upon the English before the Dutch had joined them, he now knew the worst. The combined enemy fleet was there, deploying on a line approximately north–south, with the wind abeam. In the van was the White squadron consisting of Van Almonde's thirty-six ships; in the centre was the Red squadron under Russell, with Sir Ralph Delaval as his Vice- and Sir Cloudisley Shovel as Rear-Admiral, having thirty-one ships in three divisions; while the Admiral of the Blue, Ashby, kept the rear with thirty-two ships, his Vice-Admiral

---

[1] These are the figures given in Clowes's *History of the Royal Navy*, Vol. II, p. 340; Toudouze, *op. cit.*, gives 7,154 guns against 3,114.

being Sir George Rooke. How was it possible that Tourville could have been sent on such a hopeless venture? It is difficult to believe that nothing was known at Versailles or at La Hougue of this enemy concentration, which had been effected nearly three weeks previously. In any case, not until the last moment were some barges, or corvettes, sent out to find Tourville, with orders for him to put about and wait for reinforcements. Only one of them reached the *Soleil Royal*—when the guns were already firing.

And perhaps it was better so, after all, for this was to be Tourville's finest hour—the most magnificent, the most thrilling of all the battles fought by the French Navy until present times. "The strongest proof of military spirit and valour ever given by any navy," is the comment of one foremost naval historian, Admiral A. T. Mahan.

The two fleets drew near each other very slowly. There was only a faint wind, but it was from the south-west, and so Tourville had the weather-gauge. If he refused to engage, Russell would never be able to get within gun-range nor manoeuvre to encircle him. But if he let the wind carry him forward, he was practically certain to meet with a crushing defeat—glorious, perhaps, but complete, with the death of thousands of his men and the loss of many ships!

Tourville must have weighed all that in his mind. But what mattered more with him was respect for the orders he had received; and, more particularly, there was the affront given through his person to the whole Fleet—and so the need for a magnificent, dramatic gesture which would show the King of France what could be expected of his sailors. Without seeking anyone's advice, without holding a council of war, Tourville "went into action like a madman, deliberately seeking out the English admiral and bringing his ship abreast of the other".

The French Fleet, like the Allied, was deployed in three squadrons of three divisions, line abreast. The Blue-and-White squadron was on the right wing, the White in the centre, and the Blue on the left—which was the north of the line. The only obvious difference between the two fleets was in the numbers. The French Blue-and-White, commanded by the Marquis d'Amfreville, with Nesmond and De Relingue under him, had only fourteen ships against thirty-six Dutch. Tourville, in the centre with the divisions of Villette-Mursay and Langeron, had only sixteen to Russell's thirty-one. While the left wing, commanded by Gabaret with the support of Panetié and Coetlogon, opposed fourteen to Ashby's thirty-two.

Nevertheless, at Tourville's signal to engage the enemy, one and the same order was given by the captains of all forty-four ships: "Make ready!" And the French Fleet, wind astern, advanced towards its fate. "The resolute manner in which his ships bore down was remarked by all," Clowes writes of the enemy—and the English, in a word, could not get over it. Had the French admiral gone out of his mind, to engage in such conditions—when nothing was easier than to avoid it ("and he would have had at least a dozen excellent reasons for doing so", Clowes comments). Or could it be . . .? Doubts began to form in the minds of some of the Dutch captains—those who had taken part in the Battle of Beachy Head two years ago remembered that Torrington had let them down. Might there not be some truth in the rumours recently circulating in south-coast ports, and Russell be about to betray King William and Holland and go over to the French and ex-King James?

Rest assured, good Dutchmen; no treachery is in store. Tourville is counting only on his own ships, in a fair fight. Moreover, the English captains are smarting under the doubts cast upon their loyalty. . . . Carter, the Admiral who had been most suspected, was to show how little truth it held—when, mortally wounded, he cried to his flag-captain, "Fight on as long as the ship floats!"

At the Battle of Beachy Head, it will be remembered, Torrington had allowed his van to become engaged before his main body was near enough to support it. Tourville did not fall into that error, and it was "all together", the whole fleet in line abreast, that he bore down on the enemy with his *Soleil Royal* directed at Russell's *Britannia*.

Unfortunately the wind dropped just then, and the two fleets remained becalmed for a while, "just within musket-shot of each other". To reach his station in the line, Rear-Admiral De Relingue's *Foudroyant* had to be towed by one of her pinnaces. Most of the ships, in fact, had ordered out their boats, and the duel between the small craft of both sides was to be as vigorous as between the great ships.

Neither Commander-in-Chief had yet given the signal to open fire, but a Dutch ship nervously let off a broadside at the *St. Louis*. And a second later both lines were belching fire from one end to the other. It was then ten in the morning. The thunderous roar of ten thousand guns was to be heard until evening all along the coast from Cherbourg to Le Havre.

Few sea battles have been more furiously fought than this. Tourville's state of mind was well known, and his admirals and captains were with him entirely. One and all gave their leader complete support, and fought "like a band of brothers".

When Relingue, for instance, signalled "a great gap" between the van and centre, through which the enemy might work round Tourville, it was at once filled by Amfreville and a few of his squadron who sustained the attack, vastly outnumbered though they were. Gaps there were bound to be, when forty-four ships fight ninety-nine; yet if the French closed up, it would be so much easier for the Allied fleet to encircle them. Russell had already tried, early on, when he had sent the Dutch to work round the southern end of the French line; but Perrinet, in the *Bourbon*, had nipped the attempt in the bud by "doubling" the last of the Dutch, aided by four other ships including the 92-gun *Monarque*, Nesmond's flagship, which crowded on sail to arrive within gun-range all the sooner. Believing that "they were going to perish in this carnival", the French fought with the courage of despair; while the English and Dutch grew more and more exasperated at having to fight so hard for what had seemed an easy victory.

In the heart of the mêlée, like a towering fortress, was the splendid *Soleil Royal* belching death from her 106 gun-ports as she fought three assailants at once. The *Britannia*, the *London*, and the *St. Andrew*, each of a hundred guns, were trying in vain to grapple and board her. None could get close enough, and twice the English had to break off. And all the time Tourville on the poop-deck was not only fighting his own ship but directing the action of the French fleet too.

At about one in the afternoon he ordered out his boats to tow him to windward. His rigging was badly torn, but nothing essential had been shot away. Just imagine those men straining at the oars to haul the great ship along, amid the cannon- and musket-fire from all sides! No sooner had the *Soleil Royal* been drawn out of line than Amfreville and five ships of his squadron, taking advantage of the wind having briefly got up again—from the north-north-west now—made all haste to replace Tourville against the English centre, "in the most devoted manner".[1]

On the French left wing, matters were not going so well for them; Panetié's division had been slower to get within range, because of the dying wind, and some of the ships of Ashby's squadron found themselves unopposed. With the wind in the north-west, the latter were able to interpose themselves between Panetié and Gabaret. Panetié's three ships would certainly have been lost, without benefiting the rest of the French fleet in any way, if Panetié had not wisely drawn off to the south-west. Come what may, by drawing Ashby away from the centre of the battle, Panetié was relieving his leader of that many adversaries. Ashby did follow him, and for the next four hours Panetié had the satisfaction of keeping the thirty ships of the Blue employed in chasing his three, when the former "had better to do elsewhere". Eventually Panetié's three almost made contact with Nesmond on the right wing, where he was barring the way to the Dutch.

All the same, during the afternoon Russell almost succeeded in com-

[1] Clowes, *op. cit.*, p. 351.

pleting the encirclement of the French, as can be seen from the sketch given here (which was made by someone present at the battle and was later discovered by Toudouze, who reproduced it in his book). Tourville's only hope was to continue trying to break the centre of the Eng-

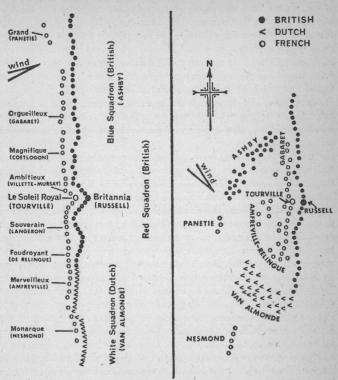

The Battle of Barfleur, May 29th, 1692. The French fleet attacks, wind astern

The situation at 4 p.m. The French are almost surrounded, but Tourville manages to break out

lish line, which he had been furiously assaulting ever since the beginning of the action. In any case, such seemed to be his intention, and the struggle in that cauldron became of dramatic intensity.

Eight or nine ships in company with the *Soleil Royal* performed wonders against greatly superior forces. There was Châteaumorant, the commander-in-chief's nephew, whose *Glorieux* was flying the Maltese cross from her mainmast; even the enemy remarked on the mettle of his ship's crew. There was Forbin, whose *Perle* lost a third of her complement in the fight; and Villette's *Ambitieux*, which got the better of Sir Ralph Delaval's *Royal Sovereign*; and many others which left their mark on the English . . . "their *Chester* drew off with her rigging and sails in tatters, and the *Eagle* had seventy killed, twice that number wounded, and her bowsprit and foremast were shattered".[1] Among the French the *Henry* and the *Fort* were both disabled, and had to be towed away by their boats.

When Coëtlogon, in the rear, saw that his commander-in-chief was in dire peril, he cried to his men: "We'll save this brave man or die with him!" And, ignoring the signal of his Rear-Admiral, Gabaret, his *Magnifique* and Bagneux's *Prince* sped to the help of Tourville. This left a gap in the French line, but the ships in the vicinity closed it as quickly as possible, their captains still fighting "like a band of brothers".

Visibility was already poor, and just as the confused fighting was at its height the mist came down so thickly that the guns stopped firing, for no one was able to distinguish friend from foe—and just at a critical moment for Tourville. Sir Cloudisley Shovel, the Rear-Admiral of the Red, had almost worked round the *Soleil Royal* and her supporting ships. This fortunate respite saved Tourville; and when the wind had got up again and cleared away the mist, the tide was on the turn. On the advice of Villette, Tourville signalled to the fleet to drop anchor. Their enemies began to be carried eastward; but Ashby soon took in the situation and his Blue squadron dropped anchor too, being now on Tourville's rear as a result of following after Panetié. The French were thus less concentrated and caught between two fires; and, moreover, were without Nesmond's five ships and Panetié's three, which remained too far off from the main action in spite of their efforts to draw near.

This quiet interval was soon over: the wind shifted round to the north-east, swept away the last wisps of mist, and the guns began firing again more furiously than ever. The English seemed determined to put an end to the battle and convinced that they could do so; indeed, there was a moment of panic on some of the French ships. But it passed, and the French gave as good as they got. The English were now to windward, and Russell took advantage to send down his fireships. The *Soleil Royal*—honour to whom honour is due—had five of them intended for her, but managed to avoid them all; the first by swinging the helm to port, the second at the cost of an anchor (the cable being hurriedly cut), and another was adroitly diverted by the ship's boats.

[1] La Roncière, *op. cit.*, Vol. VI, p. 114.

.. Villette, for his part, was threatened by three fireships, which he, too, managed to avoid.

Darkness was falling, and the French had held out; not one of their ships had been lost, none had received crippling damage. And now the enemy was drawing off to the east, the Red squadron first, then the Dutch, and finally Ashby's—which, being to the west of the French, unhappily sailed with the current through the gaps in their line, presenting Tourville and his courageous company with a great opportunity. It was not missed. Each English ship was raked with cannon- and musket-fire as she passed through the line; not a shot was wasted. The flagship, the *Royal William*, came under heavy fire from the *Soleil Royal*, the *Magnifique*, and the *St. Philippe*, which poured in broadside after broadside and left her disabled. The *Duke* received similar treatment, and her captain and Rear-Admiral Carter were both killed.

The night was thickening, and the moon rose on a silent sea; the battle had ended. For nearly fifteen hours, an Anglo-Dutch force of ninety-nine ships had endeavoured to destroy forty-four French, and were now withdrawing from the scene of action leaving the forty-four still afloat; damaged and exhausted they certainly were, but still navigable and capable of fighting, even the *Soleil Royal*, in which—to quote an English observer—"all the scuppers were running with blood".

"Tourville and his captains had made a most gallant defence and had, indeed, done wonders. . . . Had Barfleur had no morrow, the action would have been a French triumph. . . ." Such are the terms in which Clowes writes of the Battle of Barfleur Point—a battle which receives hardly any mention in French history. For it did have a morrow. Inevitably so, because in the seventeenth century—before Cherbourg and Le Havre existed as fortified ports—this stretch of the French coast provided practically no shelter to ships. There was no advantage to the French Fleet in being close to its own shores, when no haven was at hand where its ships could patch up their damage, land their wounded, and take in supplies.

The enemy, admittedly, was in like case; they had suffered much damage, too—the English especially, for the Dutch squadron had not been closely engaged. The *Zevent Provinciens*, the most badly mauled of the Dutch ships, had only nineteen killed and fourteen seriously wounded. But a good score of Russell's ships were disabled and holed, and had to be towed back to English ports. Nevertheless, there still remained quite enough to carry the fight to the enemy, and there was little sleep on either side that night. With oakum and melted pitch the broken seams and the jagged holes were stopped up, while carpenters repaired the rigging and masts, and chaplains and surgeons attended to the dying and the wounded. The French had 1,700 killed and wounded, but the Anglo-Dutch losses were estimated at 2,000 killed, including 2 Admirals, with 3,000 wounded.

A thick mist that persisted throughout the night aided the French in their withdrawal westward. Amfreville, Villette, and Panetié managed to group twenty-seven ships, and these were joined soon afterwards by Tourville with seven others; only nine under Nesmond's command were missing.[1]

It was not until eight on the morning of the 30th, as the mist was clearing, that the Dutch squadron caught sight of the French sailing before a light north-easterly wind, a good league ahead. Russell, when informed, gave orders to pursue them; but towards the end of the morning the wind shifted round to the south-west. By four in the afternoon neither fleet was making any headway against the ebb, and both anchored some distance off Cherbourg.

Unhappily for the French, Tourville could not bring himself to abandon the *Soleil Royal*, although that once-splendid ship was battered and leaking and had become a hindrance to the fleet. Her presence had enabled the Allied ships to gain on the French, and the distance between them had narrowed considerably. The tide turned at ten in the evening, and both fleets weighed anchor. Soon after midnight the *Britannia* lost her foremast, which had been damaged during the battle, and the other ships of her squadron hove to while the necessary repairs to her were carried out. Asby's squadron and the Dutch continued after the French. Panetié, commanding their van, succeeded in making the safe anchorage of St. Malo with twenty-two ships; while he had sailed south, between the Cherbourg peninsula and the Channel Islands, his pursuers had continued westward, past Alderney. The whole French Fleet might have been similarly saved, were it not for the slower progress of the *Soleil Royal* and the ships with her; they missed the tide and then lost their anchors. Tourville had to resign himself to shift his flag to the *Ambitieux*. But it was too late to save the *Soleil Royal*, which went aground near Cherbourg, together with the *Triomphant* and the *Admirable*, during the morning of May 31st. Tourville led the remaining ten ships, which had been unable to follow Panetié in time, to anchor off St. Vaast-la-Hougue; he hoped that there, with the protection of a few shore batteries and some assistance from Marshal de Bellefonds's force, his ships would be safe—and Barfleur would remain a French triumph.

---

[1] Nesmond had drawn off eastward with seven ships. He left the two most badly damaged at La Hougue, sent two others into Le Havre, and with the remaining three sailed on into the North Sea, round Scotland, and so returned safely to Brest.

Four years previously, in 1688, Louis XIV had ordered Vauban, the great military engineer, to begin work on the defences of Cherbourg. The citadel was well advanced when "Monsieur de Louvois, more to annoy Monsieur de Seignelay than for the good of the Service, obtained an order from the King for it to be demolished". It was Louvois, too, who had opposed the building of fortifications at St. Vaast in 1690. Tourville, lacking in foresight for once, had not insisted, considering it to be too distant a haven after a battle which seemed likely to take place between Ushant and the Lizard.

As a consequence of all that, Tourville's ships had to rely mainly on themselves to resist the assault that the English could be trusted to deliver.

Sir Ralph Delaval had already made one attempt to destroy the *Soleil Royal* and her two companions in distress, on May 31st, only a few hours after they had gone aground. But it had been unsuccessful; the guns of the *Soleil Royal* had kept Delavel's ships at a distance. He was back again the next day, with a change of method. Instead of sending in his ships, he ordered out all the boats to escort the fireships. The French gunners blew up one fireship, and another struck a reef, but two succeeded in reaching the stranded warships. Captain Thomas Heath of the *Blaze* got his grapples on the stern of the great three-decker while her guns were still firing. A few moments later, the *Soleil Royal* was a mass of flames, and blew up "with a frightful roar", tossing her crew into the air "like flies". The *Triomphant* fell a victim to the fireship *Wolf*, and the *Admirable* was set alight by some of the boats' crews. Louvois could rest happy! The valuable use that could have been made of the shore batteries was demonstrated by the six guns of a makeshift fort, which had greatly aided the *Soleil Royal* in holding off the first attack. Even a minor fortification would have obliged Delaval's ships to keep their distance, and events would have taken a different turn.

While this drama was being played out at Cherbourg, Russell was blockading La Hougue with most of his fleet and a similar attack was being prepared by Vice-Admiral Sir George Rooke.

When Tourville made St. Vaast with his ten ships on the evening of May 31st he moored them near the two left by Nesmond, in the shelter of a long, narrow sandbank called Le Crocq de Quinéville that extended out to sea from the little peninsula of La Hougue. Tourville was no longer free to make his own decisions. His Instructions placed him under the orders of the commanders of the invasion force—ex-King James, Marshal de Bellefonds, and the commissary, Bonrepaus. The last-named, probably having little desire to become embroiled in the

E

coming disaster, kept out of the way at this crucial time. It might have been possible for the ships to have tried to escape, after quickly taking on fresh supplies of ammunition from the dumps at Carentan and Valognes. But the whole of June 1st was lost in discussion and argument, and at the end the decision was taken to beach six of the ships behind La Hougue and the other six by the neighbouring islet of Tatihou, and to unload them of everything possible. As often happens with salvage operations carried out in such desperate circumstances—and in this case the officers were completely exhausted, having had no rest since the long, hard battle on May 29th—the unloading was done in great disorder, and at times was more like looting than salvage work. The army officers, who did not have the same excuse, remained inactive. Marshal de Bellefonds had promised one hundred and fifty boatloads of men to help defend the ships, but in the event he produced barely a dozen.

Early in the morning of June 2nd, the English fireships and boats came in on the tide and set fire to the six vessels by Tatihou islet, without any resistance being offered by the garrison on the islet—nor from James and Marshal de Bellefonds ashore at St. Vaast, where they "watched the dismaying sight as calmly as if they were at a firework display".

Disgusted by this complete lack of initiative, a few naval officers set about organizing some defence at St. Vaast before the enemy attacked the ships there. Tourville, Relingue, Villette, and some sailors halted the first attempt, at high tide the next morning. A few guns, hurriedly mounted on a barbette by the Chevalier de Gassiou, sank several of the boats and killed a number of the crews. But the English were in strength, and before long their fireships had set the remaining six vessels alight. The hard-won glory of the Battle of Barfleur vanished in the smoke of this dismal holocaust.

Still the military made no move! Not even to protect their own transports, to which the English next turned their attention. Some were burnt, and the remainder only escaped destruction because the English had to retire on the turn of the tide.

If the fifteen ships destroyed by fire had been lost during the battle off Barfleur the material loss would have been the same but not the effect on national morale—because, for one thing, the losses would not have occurred within sight of civilians. Fifteen ships the fewer, whatever was said, did not greatly affect the strength of the French Navy.[1]

---

[1] Tourville had put even more enemy ships out of action at the Battle of Beachy Head.

1 LE MAGNIFIQUE
2 LE St PHILIPPE
3 L' AMBITIEUX
4 LE FOUDROYANT
5 LE MERVEILLEUX
6 LE TERRIBLE
7 LE St LOUIS
8 LE TONNANT
9 LE BOURBON
10 LE GAILLARD
11 LE FORT

Position of the French ships at St. Vaast-la-Hougue, June 2nd, 1692

"More ships can be found, but not another Tourville", Louis XIV had exclaimed when enquiring after his Admiral, on receiving news of the battle. The King was right. Three days after the disaster at La Hougue, D'Estrées announced that he was ready to put to sea from Brest with sixty-four ships; and the following year found Tourville off Lagos with a fleet of ninety-three! No, what was far more serious was the moral defeat—felt not so much by the sailors themselves as by the Navy Minister, who began to show defeatist tendencies, and by the administration, in which the first cracks soon appeared. "We've neither the feelings nor the words of defeated men!" exclaimed the sailors. And D'Estrées demanded swift action: "I make much of the fact that we lost no ships in the fight (the Battle of Barfleur), for it is sufficient proof of our superiority over the English and the Dutch." Russell himself wrote to his adversary—it was not unusual, in those days—to compliment him "on the great valour he had shown by attacking in such a dauntless manner, and by fighting so valiantly although having an unequal force".

Clowes, in his *History of the Royal Navy*, follows the account of the business at La Hougue by that of "The Disaster to the Smyrna convoy". This was Tourville's reply to Admiral Rooke, whose fireships had destroyed the vessels beached at La Hougue. Rooke, escorting a huge convoy of four hundred merchantmen with twenty-three ships of war, was set upon by the combined squadrons of Tourville and D'Estrées off Lagos, on June 27th 1693. In the running fight that ensued the English lost ninety-two ships—they themselves admitted the figure—set alight or captured, without counting two of the escort. The following year, Jean Bart added lustre to his name in a brisk fight off the Texel; with only six second- and third-raters against eight powerful ships commanded by Admiral Hyddes de Vries, he wrested back from the Dutch a wheat convoy of a hundred ships recently captured from the French, and also took three of De Vries's escorting warships.

No, the French had not been swept from the seas by the losses at La Hougue; but that reverse indubitably had a grave effect upon French opinion and the national morale, and was a major cause of France eventually losing a war that had begun auspiciously for her.

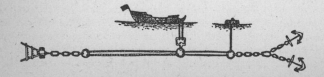

IX

BRITAIN'S COMMAND OF THE SEAS

How Sir George Rooke transformed the fiasco at Cadiz (August 22nd, 1702) into a resounding victory at Vigo Bay (October 22nd following)—capture of Gibraltar, August 4th, 1704—the Battle of Velez-Malaga, where the Count of Toulouse would have done better not to have listened to his advisers—how this lost opportunity gave the British command of the Mediterranean—French privateers' success in the Channel—the veteran Court de la Bruyère saves the Spanish squadron outside Toulon—the Seven Years' War—attempted landing by the British at St. Cast—Choiseul has big ideas—Monsieur de Conflans's day out—Admiral Hawke's successful swoop into Quiberon Bay (November 20th, 1759).

MOST of the battles here described so far—and many of those to follow —took place within sight of land and with one fleet at its moorings: Damme, Sluys, La Hougue, the Battle of the Nile, Copenhagen, Navarino. . . . But their place in the history of sea warfare is quite as important as that of the battles of movement during the era of sail, battles such as Beachy Head, Barfleur, "the Glorious First of June", Trafalgar. . . . It could be fairly said that, with the exception of Trafalgar, the greatest successes of the British navy were against ships at their moorings.

A further instance was the Battle of Vigo Bay, the famous action against the galleons of the "silver fleet" which gave England an early success in the War of the Spanish Succession.

That war had begun badly, though, with an attempt to capture Cadiz. Fifty English and twenty Dutch ships sailed from Spithead on June 29th, 1702, carrying ten thousand sailors and four thousand Dutch soldiers, under the command of Admiral Sir George Rooke. This fleet took more than a month to beat out of the Channel and cross the Bay of Biscay, and did not arrive off Cadiz until August 22nd. There were only two French ships and eight galleys to oppose the landing, which was effected without much difficulty, at Rotta, on the west of Cadiz Bay. The small town of Puerto Santa Maria was captured on September 1st—and the misfortunes of the invading force began, for the troops soon succumbed to the delights of this southern paradise, and drinking and looting destroyed all military discipline. Soldiers and sailors alike "behaved in the most disgraceful and abominable manner".[1]

[1] Clowes, *op. cit.*, Vol. II, p. 379.

The French and Spanish mounted a counter-attack from the sea, and their fire completely demoralized the invaders, who hurriedly re-embarked on September 15th. The next day Rooke sailed away from the scene of this shameful episode.

However, the shame was soon wiped away by a resounding victory. An indiscreet remark let drop by the French Consul at Lagos enabled the captain of one of the English ships to put his Admiral on the track of an enemy treasure fleet—the thirty Spanish galleons of the "silver fleet" which had been escorted from the West Indies by the French admiral, Château-Renault, with thirty warships. The galleons held the greatest wealth ever brought across the Atlantic. Château-Renault had been escorting them to Pasajes, but the port was being blockaded by the English. He had wanted to continue to La Rochelle or Brest, but the Spaniards were opposed to this; so finally he had taken his charges into the long and narrow Vigo bay, and moored them in the creek at the very end. Fifteen of his own ships were anchored in front of them, strung in a line from shore to shore; and as further protection a boom of masts, barrels, and chains was made across the narrowest part of the bay, anchored to the bed and protected by a 70-gun ship at either end. These narrows were, moreover, guarded by two small forts, one on each shore. Château-Renault confidently believed that the galleons were quite safe behind such protection. The unloading of them began, but with deplorable slowness.

The news of this great treasure revived the morale and spirits of the English. At a council of war held on Rooke's flagship, the *Somerset*, it was decided that such a prize could not be allowed to escape; and, giving up all idea of returning to the attack of Cadiz, the Anglo-Dutch Fleet sailed north to Vigo. It was off the entrance to the bay on October 22nd, and in the mist was mistaken for a supply convoy expected from Corunna.

Rooke placed his Vice-Admiral, Thomas Hobson, in charge of the attack, as it was impossible for the whole force to be deployed in the bay. The plan was for Hobson, in the *Torbay*, to go in with thirty vessels and fireships, while at the same time troops landed on both sides of the bay would advance and capture the two forts.

The whole operation went with a swing. The troops soon took the fort on the southern shore; and the field-works of the Corbeyron on the northern shore, which were commanded by Manuel de Velasco, the general of the galleons, fell not long afterwards. Meanwhile, the *Torbay* had been sailing up the bay until the wind dropped, and she came under fire from the *Espérance* and the *Bourbon*, the two French ships at either end of the boom. Then Lieutenant de l'Escalette succeeded in grappling his fireship, the *Favori*, to her. But the *Favori* had been improvised from a merchant-ship that still had her cargo of tobacco in the holds; and when she exploded the bales were thrown into the rigging of the *Torbay* and smothered the flames. Hobson's other ships

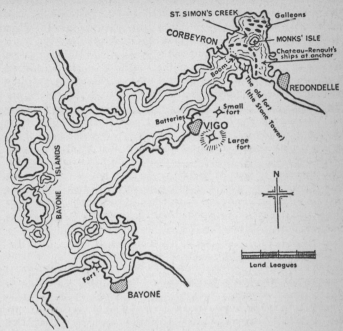

The Spanish galleons trapped in Vigo bay, September 22nd, 1702

had broken through the boom by now, and had overcome the two protecting vessels. The captain of the *Espérance* beached her, while the *Bourbon* was boarded by Dutch from the *Zeven Provincien*, in which Admiral Van der Goes was flying his flag.

The 90-gun *Association*, which had been giving supporting fire to the troops advancing along the northern shore of the bay, went to the assistance of the *Torbay*, which was in sorry plight. But soon afterwards Hobson shifted his flag to another ship of his division, the *Monmouth*.

Hardly half an hour had passed since the beginning of the operation and already Château-Renault found himself in a critical situation. There was an off-sea wind, preventing his ships from manoeuvring—

even if they had had the room. Only a few could bring their guns to bear on the boom. Château-Renault's flagship, the 76-gun *Fort*, soon emptied her powder magazines; and rather than let her fall into the hands of the enemy, Château-Renault ordered her to be set alight, and the rest of his warships too. The captain of the *Oriflamme*, De Fricambault, lost his life through having given Château-Renault the mistaken advice to seek shelter in Vigo Bay, "where with a little protection we should be safe from any attack". The blaze in his ship spread so rapidly that he was unable to get off in time. Three of the French ships went aground. Five, in addition to the *Bourbon*, were taken by the attackers. The whole operation had been carried out so briskly, and the ships had caught fire so quickly, that half the French crews were almost naked when they scrambled ashore.

The treasure galleons, deprived of their defenders, could do no better than set fire to themselves too. Nineteen of them were destroyed by the flames or sank. Great though the haul was, a considerable part of the treasure went to the bottom of the bay. Since then, many attempts have been made to recover the jewels, bars of silver, and precious stones from the rotting galleons that lie deep in the mud. Minor successes have from time to time roused the imagination and spurred the efforts of other treasure seekers. Companies have been formed to carry out salvage operations; in 1766, some crates of silver piastres were recovered; in 1825, silver plate; and in 1870, China porcelain. The Treasure of Vigo Bay is still talked about, and will no doubt continue to be for many years to come.

Early in 1704, Rooke set sail again for Spain, this time with the Archduke Charles of Austria on board his flagship, and with orders to land him at Lisbon. The Archduke was England's choice for the Spanish throne. Rooke and his squadron had to struggle against headwinds, and were once forced back to port before finally clearing the Channel; it was not until March that they entered the Tagus and put the Spanish Pretender ashore. Towards the end of May the squadron passed through the Straits of Gibraltar, on its way to give support to military operations along the coast of Catalonia and on the Italian Riviera.

At Brest the French were preparing to put to sea, too. The command of the fleet had been given to a young man of twenty-six, Alexandre de Bourbon, Count of Toulouse, one of the legitimized sons of Louis XIV and Madame de Montespan. He had received the title of "Admiral of France" at the age of four, but he had other and more substantial claims to his new command. Toulouse had always wanted to be a sailor, and he might well have become a great naval captain if circumstances had allowed him to continue his career at sea. Moreover, as his Chief-of-Staff and "mentor"—his "dry-nurse", said the English—he had an experienced navy commander in Victor-Marie D'Estrées.

Toulouse sailed from Brest on May 14th at the head of a squadron of 26 ships-of-the-line, 4 frigates, and 6 fireships, and made for the Straits of Gibraltar, having orders to give cover to a convoy of galleons bringing the indispensable sinews of war from the Spanish possessions in South America. With Rooke having already sailed eastward into the Mediterranean, and a gale blowing in from the Atlantic just at the right moment, the convoy had reached port safely when the Brest squadron dropped anchor in Cadiz Bay on May 25th.

Rooke seemed to be out of luck that year. Having missed the rich convoy, he then went and bombarded Barcelona—without doing much harm—and the French squadron slipped through into the Mediterranean while the Straits were unguarded. Rooke again missed the French on their way to Toulon, decided not to pursue the operation against the Italian coast, and sailed out of the Mediterranean on June 24th.

Then his luck changed. He was joined off Lagos by Admiral Shovel, who had sailed from England to try and overtake the Brest squadron and bring it to battle. Rooke thus found himself in command of a considerable force—some fifty English and Dutch warships, with a number of frigates and fireships, and several thousand soldiers in trooptransports, commanded by the Prince of Hesse. It was a marvellous opportunity to seize the rocky fortress of Gibraltar, which was guarded —so to speak—by Admiral Diego de Salinas with fifty-six soldiers and about a hundred militia, and by a small French vessel, the 10-gun *St. François*, which carried a crew of eighty.

This defending force of 240 men could do little against the 22 ships under Admiral Byng and the 1,800 soldiers commanded by the Prince of Hesse which were put ashore at Algeciras on July 31st. The defenders held out for three days, nevertheless, inflicting considerable casualties among the attackers. But on August 4th, 1704, Rooke took possession of Gibraltar "in the name of King Charles of Spain". As the Archduke never reigned over Spain—by the Treaty of Utrecht in 1713 the Powers recognized Philip V as King—the British remained at Gibraltar in their own right.[1]

Toulouse was at Barcelona with his squadron, which had been increased by units from Toulon, when the news of the capture of Gibraltar

[1] The same Treaty of Utrecht ceded Gibraltar unreservedly to the British. (*Tr.*)

reached him. The significance for Mediterranean naval strategy was obvious to any sailor. Toulouse's force was about equal to Rooke's in ships and armament. He weighed anchor, and sailed south. He put in to water at Velez-Malaga—about ten miles east from Malaga—and it was there that Rooke came up with him.

The battle that took place two days later, on August 24th, 1704, has been named Velez-Malaga by historians of both sides. It was the last general naval engagement of the War of the Spanish Succession, and the greatest of all until the Napoleonic Wars. In some respects it can be compared with the Battle of Jutland during the First World War, for the result of that, too, has given rise to much argument. Toulouse undoubtedly gained a tactical victory, as Rooke retired at the end of the day with losses twice those of the French. But by neglecting to follow up his advantage over a weakened enemy, and one whose magazines were almost empty, Toulouse lost the chance of a decisive victory; so that, as La Roncière wrote, "there were no laurels for the vanquished, so they reaped the fruits".

So it was at Jutland two centuries later, where the British losses in tonnage were double those of the Germans, and they had half as many casualties again as the enemy; yet for the rest of the war the German High Sea Fleet hardly ever ventured out again. Similarly, the damage that the French inflicted on Rooke's fleet did not prevent the British gaining command of the Mediterranean, through the capture of Gibraltar.

The French Fleet was hindered by the flat calm and the inshore current from getting out to sea, and eventually the ships had to be towed out by the twenty-four galleys accompanying them. This was

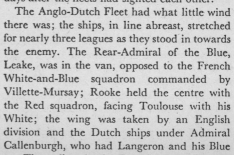

the reason for action not being joined until two days after the fleets had sighted each other.

The Anglo-Dutch Fleet had what little wind there was; the ships, in line abreast, stretched for nearly three leagues as they stood in towards the enemy. The Rear-Admiral of the Blue, Leake, was in the van, opposed to the French White-and-Blue squadron commanded by Villette-Mursay; Rooke held the centre with the Red squadron, facing Toulouse with his White; the wing was taken by an English division and the Dutch ships under Admiral Callenburgh, who had Langeron and his Blue squadron opposite them. The galleys in the French second line, to leeward, did not take part in the battle.

The squadrons of Leake and Villette-Mursay were soon hotly engaged. The leading French ship, the *Eclatant*, replied to a broadside from the *Yarmouth* with a devastating fire that sent her out of the line with "her sails torn to shreds"; while Leake's flagship, the *Prince*, had ninety men killed or wounded by the exchanges with Rear-Admiral D'Infreville's *St. Philippe*. Admiral Shovel, flying his flag in the *Barfleur*, was in the thick of it as usual. Villette-Mursay's flagship, the *Fier*, was "punishing a swarm of the enemy", and was gaining the head of the line to put about, when a bomb hit the poop-deck, shattered the stern, and set fire to her aft. "A hundred men were killed, and as many wounded or badly burnt. Marillac had his shoulder broken by a cannon-ball, d'Escoulan was wounded in a place that left him unfit for married life . . . a gentleman named Plaimbeau was blown into the sea by the bomb."[1] The *Fier* had to draw off, to bring the fire under control. The *Magnifique*, too, was badly damaged and had to be hauled out of the line by two of the galleys.

If Admiral Shovel had seized the opportunity thus presented by the gap left in the enemy line, his division could have encircled the leading French ships. But instead he bore down on the centre, where the fighting was fiercest. "It was the hottest day's fighting of my whole career," Sir George Rooke wrote in his report, in which he seemed surprised that Shovel and the other Rear-Admirals had shown small regard for their opponents' resistance. He added that the ships in the French centre had fought "most bravely and with all their heart. . . . We spent all night repairing our damage."[2]

Rooke's report also mentioned that a number of his ships, of all three squadrons, had to draw out of the line at one time or another during the battle. His own ship, the 90-gun *Royal Catherine*, got the worst of the exchanges with Toulouse's 104-gun *Foudroyant*, and fared no better against the next in line, the 86-gun *Vainqueur*—which, having fought off three English ships one after the other, left the next with her sails in tatters. The *Vainqueur* had a hundred killed or wounded, including her captain, Alphonse de Lorraine-Armagnac. At about two in the afternoon he received a terrible injury to his stomach. "That's nothing," he said, cramming his intestines back. "Every man to his station, and increase the firing!" He lingered on until midnight, never uttering a word of complaint and continuing to encourage his second-in-command.

Fighting equally furiously on the other quarter of the French flagship was Relingue's *Terrible*, sending broadside after broadside into the

---

[1] From Villette's report, quoted by La Roncière, *op. cit.*, Vol. VI, p. 354.
[2] Quoted by Clowes, *op. cit.*, Vol. II, p. 40.

Eagle and obliging her to draw off with sixty-four of her crew dead or wounded. Relingue lost a leg in this action.

At the rear, Callenburgh's flagship, the *Albemarle*, took a drubbing from the *Soleil Royal*; but his division had the better of the French, causing three of them to withdraw from the fray.

At seven in the evening, after nine hours of battle, Rooke signalled to withdraw. No ship had been captured on either side, but the Anglo-Dutch losses in men were not far short of 3,000, against only 1,700 French though the latter contained a high proportion of officers— "163 captains, officers, and worthy people". The Count of Toulouse was unaware at the time of the considerable casualties among the enemy crews, nor that their ammunition had been almost expended. The French still had more in their magazines than had been used during the battle. When Toulouse raised the question of continuing the fight next day, his flag-captain, the Marquis d'O—who had been his tutor—counselled prudence, and was supported by most of the Rear-Admirals and Captains. Only the suffering Relingue, and Pointis and D'Estrées, were in favour of pressing the enemy without delay.

The young Admiral of France let himself be persuaded by the majority. This was a great mistake. The Anglo-Dutch Fleet had not enough shot left for each gun to be fired more than ten times. Admiral Leake's flagship could have fired no more than three broadsides from the upper gun-deck, and none at all from the lower. Nevertheless, Rooke kept the French in view for forty-eight hours, then set sail for Gibraltar. According to more than one witness of the fleet's arrival there, the ships were in a sorry state.

"There was not a single vessel without some masts and yard-arms missing, or at least some damage to her superstructure. The largest had their poops covered with tarpaulin, so that nobody should see the bad state in which *Monsieur l'Amiral* had left them. They admitted they had been well beaten, and were generally agreed in telling us that the French were a brave lot and had shown their worth, and that *Monsieur l'Amiral* and his two supporting ships in particular had kept up a surprisingly rapid fire, with their gunners firing as fast as the musketeers. . . ."[1]

If only Toulouse had known. . . . From his camp before Gibraltar, the Marquis de Villedarias sent couriers in all directions to try and contact the Admiral. But it was too late. Lost opportunities in war do not occur again. In France, many a *Te Deum* was sung; and in England, Queen Anne bestowed titles and decorations on her sea-captains. In

[1] From the Travel-Diary of Sieur de Rozel *fils*, then a prisoner at Gibraltar; quoted by La Roncière, *op. cit.*, Vol. VI, p. 362.

short, both sides were satisfied! Rooke, who could have been decisively beaten, was able to have his ships repaired at leisure, at Gibraltar. The Rock remained in British hands, and "from then until the end of the war, France never again risked a fleet in full-scale battle".[1]

The Royal Navy's command of the seas can be said to date from this time, and was practically undisputed during the almost constant wars of the eighteenth century—at least, until the War of American Independence. But if the Count of Toulouse had taken D'Estrées's advice and followed up a battle that had already gone in his favour, then things might have been very different.

The war at sea continued, however. . . . Instead of pitched battles between squadrons in classical formation, stretching in long lines over the waters, there were clashes between lone privateers, raids on the enemy coast—and never a year without at least one major seaborne operation. In 1705 a British force was landed at Barcelona to march on Madrid in conjunction with its Portuguese allies, and Philip V was forced to evacuate the Spanish capital. In 1707 the naval base of Toulon was attacked by a British squadron of fifty-six ships. The French reckoned themselves victorious, as the enemy was beaten off. But it was more like a defeat for them, as their warships moored in the harbour escaped destruction by British guns only through being scuttled there and then. They never recovered from the treatment. However, the French were cheered by successes in the Channel that year, due to two daring corsairs, Forbin and Duguay-Trouin.

On May 11th, 1707, the Chevalier de Forbin sallied forth from Dunkirk at the head of 8 ships of 40 to 60 guns. Two days later he came upon a British convoy of 56 merchantmen about 18 miles west of Beachy Head; it was being escorted by 3 warships of 70 to 76 guns and a 40-gun frigate. The French attack was swift and sure. Three of their ships—the 54-gun *Blackwall* (a prize that had been allowed to keep her name), the 44-gun *Griffon* and the 56-gun *Dauphine*—closed and boarded the 70-gun *Hampton Court*. The French swarmed over her bulwarks and fell on their opponents, slashing out right and left, and captured her after a terrific fight in which the captain and many of the crew were killed. Meanwhile, Forbin's 60-gun *Mars* had ranged alongside the 70-gun *Grafton*, wasting no time in an exchange of gunfire either, and laid her aboard. But only a score of the French had reached her deck, in face of a hail of grape-shot, when the lashings holding the two ships together were sliced away by a chance shot. The *Mars* drifted astern with the current, and her boarders were left isolated on the enemy deck. Before long, only one was still standing, a Lieutenant

[1] Clowes, *op cit*, Vol II, p. 104

d'Olonne, several times wounded. But then the *Blackwall* and the *Fidèle* came to the rescue, their guns ready to rake the *Grafton*, and the latter was forced to strike her colours.

Two fine new ships were thus taken by Forbin. The 76-gun *Royal Oak* escaped, but only to go aground near Dungeness with eleven feet of water in her hold. Twenty-two of the merchantmen were captured, and twelve hundred prisoners taken. The French had two hundred and twenty killed and wounded. It had been a hotly fought action, so much so that the chaplain on the *Mars*, "a Parisian who had never previously been out of sight of the towers of Notre Dame, left the ship when we got back to Dunkirk and told me he wouldn't return to sea even if the King made him an Admiral".[1]

Four months later, Forbin had another success. He put out from Brest this time, in company with Duguay-Trouin, who had recently returned by way of the west coast of Ireland from a fruitful raid into Norwegian waters. Each had 6 ships under his command. Two days after leaving harbour, on October 21st, they were cruising 6 leagues or so off the Lizard when Forbin signalled to give chase—there was good hunting ahead! Some reinforcements were on their way to Lisbon in 130 transports escorted by 5 ships under Commodore Richard Edwards. These were the *Cumberland* and the *Devonshire*, both of 80 guns; the *Chester* and the *Ruby*, 2 smaller vessels; and the 76-gun *Royal Oak*, seaworthy again after her last encounter with Forbin.

The *Cumberland*, raked by the guns of Duguay-Trouin's *Lys*, grappled and boarded by the *Gloire*, peppered with grape-shot and having two hundred men out of action, did not even have to haul down her colours, for the bo'sun of the *Lys* had already cut them down when the fighting was at its height. The *Devonshire* was giving a good account of herself when she caught fire and blew up. The *Royal Oak* again escaped destruction, for she was being overhauled by the *Achille* when some of the latter's ammunition exploded, carrying away her top deck and forecastle and putting a hundred and twenty of her crew out of action. The remaining two British ships had already struck their colours.

Fifteen of the transports were added to these prizes. But Forbin, never satisfied, blamed Duguay-Trouin's headlong attack for the rest of the convoy having escaped. Nevertheless, the affair has gone down in British history as "the disaster of the Portugal convoy".

In spite of these losses in home waters, it is evident that throughout the wars of the eighteenth century Britain already "ruled the waves".

[1] *Mémoires du Comte de Forbin*, Amsterdam, 1730, Vol. II, p. 235.

Yet if the dash and drive of French sea-captains had received some support from their leaders and Ministers, who were more concerned with intrigue at Court, the Royal Navy would have met with stronger challenge. Some proof of this was provided by the Battle of Toulon in 1744, during the War of the Austrian Succession—known more familiarly as the War of Jenkins' Ear. This picturesque name sprang from the fact that a master-mariner, Robert Jenkins, was summoned to the Bar of the House of Commons and there produced a desiccated object, carefully wrapped in cotton wool, which he affirmed was the ear sliced from his head by a Spanish coastguard. War was declared— the ear was obviously only a pretext—and once again France and Spain were ranged against England.

Early in 1744, Admiral Mathews was blockading the naval base of Toulon. The twelve Spanish ships commanded by Don Jose Navarro, which were bottled up in the harbour, tried to break out with the support of the French Mediterranean squadron, then commanded by a bold and brave veteran of nearly eighty, Court de la Bruyère. In 1694 he had been Jean Bart's first officer in the *Maure* at the Battle of the Texel, and was given command of an improvised warship, a supply vessel named *Portefaix*, during the fighting; and with his new command he had contributed in a large measure to the defeat of the Dutch and the capture of the famous grain convoy. Fifty years had passed since then, but the old sailor was still game; he had not despaired on receiving orders to force the blockade and protect the sally of the Spanish ships.

The combined strength of the French and Spanish was twenty-eight ships—the same as the British, who were to windward. But the British failed to make the most of this advantage, largely because the Franco-Spanish van was not engaged. Mathew's centre attacked the enemy rear, his van attacked their centre, but his own rear—under Lestock— remained obstinately out of range, though observing Mathew's signals to the letter. Apparently Lestock was far from being on good terms with his commander-in-chief. And the upshot was, after an indecisive though furious battle in which each side suffered some eight hundred casualties, that Admiral Mathews broke off the action and withdrew to Gibraltar to repair his battered ships.[1] Court de la Bruyère was left in command of the approaches to Toulon; and so, with the naval base uncovered, he could count it a victory.

The conduct of this encounter had repercussions upon British naval

[1] The most seriously damaged were the *Marlborough* and the *Namur*. The Spanish *Poder*, her main and fore-mast gone, and with 200 killed or wounded, struck to the *Berwick*; but Court de la Bruyère succeeded in recovering the Spanish ship.

tactics. Admiral Mathews was relieved of his command,[1] although the entire fault appeared to have been Lestock's, for having ignored the sacrosanct "Fighting Instructions" of the Admiralty. This official fighting code had been slightly modified by Sir George Rooke in 1703, but the "Instructions" were still far too formalist and inflexible: the van had to oppose the enemy's van, the centre oppose his centre, and so on—as at the Battle of Barfleur, for instance. And who, now, would dare act contrary to this official code? Not until Nelson was its rigid doctrine swept aside.

If it was any consolation to Mathews, his opponent was little better treated in France. Some trumped-up charge was brought against Court de la Bruyère because, for political reasons, the Spaniards had to appear as the sole victors of the day's fighting. Although it was the French admiral who had saved them, Don Navarro was created "Duke of the Victory".

The Treaty of Aix-la-Chapelle in 1748 did no more than give both sides a chance to recuperate, and by 1756 hostilities had again broken out. This time, Britain had Prussia for an ally, and France had Poland and Russia—which meant that the war at sea was played out between Britain and France. Their respective naval forces amounted—on paper—to 121 and 45 ships. At least a dozen of the French ships were not in commission, due to lack of money. "No money, timber, work-men, or supplies . . ." reported Marshal de Conflans on the state of Brest arsenal, on November 7th, 1759, after he had been put in command of a fanciful plan for a raid on the English coast. But this distressing state of affairs could hardly be otherwise, for in the past six years the French Marine had had five different Ministers! The latest, Berryer, owed his position to the influence of the King's mistress, Madame de Pompadour, and was regarded with contempt by all the regular navy officers.

Britain, too, had her domestic troubles. William Pitt, who had come to power in 1757, was a resolute enemy of France, but there was much departmental inefficiency. Admiral John Byng, sent out to Minorca without proper support to dislodge the French—who had seized the island in 1756 and had already repulsed an attack by the Gibraltar squadron—failed to restore the situation and was recalled in disgrace.[2]

---

[1] Mathews, Lestock, and some of the captains were court-martialled. Mathews was placed on the Retired List, but Lestock was acquitted. "The verdict of the Court, by condemning the Admiral who had fought while acquitting the one who had not, bewildered and irritated public opinion . . ." (*Toulon*, by David Maunay, *Encyclopaedia Britannica*, 11th edn.).

[2] Byng was court-martialled at Portsmouth on January 27th, 1757, and condemned to be shot, under a law passed during the reign of George II which laid down the death

This French success in the Mediterranean had no effect, however, on the course of a war for the expansion of empire overseas, and in which the British Army on the Continent had the powerful support of Frederick the Great.

To force the French to maintain large garrisons on the Channel coast, and so prevent them being sent to reinforce the army in the field, the British carried out one or two diversionary raids as they had during the Dutch Wars. On September 4th, 1758, Admiral Howe landed a considerable force commanded by General Bligh on the beach at St. Cast. But little progress was made. The Governor of Brittany, the Duke d'Aiguillon, soon organized a stiff resistance; and on September 10th the enterprise ended in a disastrous withdrawal under heavy enemy fire. The French gunners, having used all their ammunition, fired anything that came to hand—including the chandeliers from the nearby church! The total British losses were four thousand dead and eight hundred prisoners.

Overseas it was a very different story. Marbeuf, with only half a dozen ships, was soon swept out of the Indian Ocean by the superior British force. In Canada, Boscawen's flotilla of 40 warships and 167 transports had little difficulty in recapturing Louisburg, which had been ceded to the French by the Treaty of Aix-la-Chapelle, thus leading to the successful investment of Quebec and the final expulsion of the French from Canada.

It was in these circumstances that Choiseul, who had been appointed Minister for Foreign Affairs in November, 1758, and Marshal de Belle-Isle, the Minister for War, conceived the idea of paying the British back in their own coin by effecting landings on their soil. Aiguillon, who had been so successful in repulsing the British at St. Cast, was given command of the operation. It was most ambitious; there were to be two simultaneous landings, one on the western coast of Scotland and the other at the mouth of the Thames.

But where were the ships for equipping such an expedition? The Toulon squadron was down to a dozen, and the score of ships at Brest was badly in need of overhaul and refit. In any case, before a naval force could be concentrated, the strangling blockade of the British had first to be broken: Boys was keeping watch off Dunkirk, Rodney was

penalty for "any person in the Fleet who, through fear, negligence, or indifference
.. failed to do his duty". The Court unanimously recommended him to mercy, but he was executed on board the *Monarch* on March 14th.

His tombstone has the following inscription: "To the perpetual disgrace of public Justice, the Honourable John Byng, Admiral of the Blue, fell a martyr to political persecution on March 14th of the year 1757, at a time when courage and loyalty were insufficient guarantees of the honour and the lives of naval officers."

off Le Havre, Hawke outside Brest, and Broderick and Boscawen were in the Mediterranean.

The Toulon squadron set sail, commanded by De la Clue, but did not get very far. No sooner had it passed the Straits of Gibraltar than Boscawen came up with it, on August 17th, 1759. Half of-the French ships managed to take refuge in Cadiz Bay; the remaining seven were attacked by fourteen British. The captain of the *Centaure* sacrificed his ship to cover the retreat of the others, but only two succeeded in escaping; two were captured, and the other two beached themselves.

In spite of this disaster, the expedition was not abandoned. The Duke d'Aiguillon had 17,000 men in camp in the Morbihan, southern Brittany, and was only waiting for the necessary transports; attempts were being made to send a few from almost every Channel and Atlantic port, but inevitably there were losses. At Brest, because of the dearth of sailors, Marshal de Conflans had to "borrow" three or four thousand soldiers from the invasion force to help get his twenty-one ships ready for sea. But no one's heart was in the affair . . . "there are not half a dozen navy officers who think the squadron can get out, and consequently all remain ashore and do nothing to help with necessary preparations".[1] There was a lot of useless talk and scoffing, and Conflans did not interfere. He had been a brilliant navy commander in his younger days—during the previous war he had captured two British ships—but age and honours were weighing him down, and the military complained of the "lethargy" of this sixty-nine-year-old Marshal of France.

Admiral Hawke was fifteen years younger,[2] and belonged to the school whose aim was to "totally destroy the enemy whenever and wherever he can be met". He had now been at sea since May—for some five months—and although the gales had forced him back to port several times, he had always returned to keep watch and ward off the coast of Brittany between Ushant and Quiberon Bay. His obstinacy was exhausting his men but making them into better sailors than the French crews, who were going to rust through long inactivity in port.

"I leave it to your experience and courage," Louis XV wrote to Marshal de Conflans on October 14th, 1759, "to take advantage of every favourable circumstance to attack the squadrons cruising between Ushant and Belle-Isle. . . . I also give you full liberty to go and escort the Morbihan transports when they are ready to sail. . . ."

---

[1] Letter dated October 18th, 1759, from Monsieur de Balleroy to the Duke d'Aiguillon, for whom he acted as liaison officer with the naval authorities at Brest.
[2] Hawke had been captain in the *Berwick* at the Battle of Toulon in 1744.

Conflans, after a few weeks of thought and preparation, replied on November 10th that "only favourable winds are now needed to sail down the coast to Morbihan". For the moment a south-westerly gale was sweeping Brest roads. It had driven Hawke back to Torbay, and the news of his arrival there caused some consternation at the Admiralty. But on the 14th the wind hauled round to the north, and Conflans seized the opportunity to slip out while his exit was still unguarded. By eleven in the morning the three divisions of the Brest squadron were standing out to sea. The van was under the command of Beaufrémont, in the *Tonnant*; the centre was commanded by Conflans himself, flying his flag in the *Soleil Royal*, and the rear by Du Verger in the *Formidable*. Twenty-one ships in all, in three equal divisions of seven. The only signs of the enemy during the next few days were two or three frigates on the horizon. The wind had dropped, and the squadron drifted gently out to sea for a time; then it got up again, but from the south-east, and so strongly that the ships had to heave to. But late at night on the 19th it began to blow from the west at last, and Conflans was able to make for the coast of Morbihan, expecting to be just north of the mouth of the Loire by the following morning—he was then twenty-three leagues south-east of Belle Isle. However, the wind increased during the night and backed north-west, and also brought a nasty surprise—at daybreak on the 20th, when Conflans was still twenty leagues off Belle Isle, some sails were sighted on the port bow. Conflans thought they could only be the few ships of Commodore Duff, who was known to have been blockading Quiberon for some time. "Pursue the enemy!"

Yes, indeed—Duff was keeping his distance. But other sails had appeared to the south-west; by mid-morning their identity had become obvious. Twenty-three ships of the line were crowding on sail to get within range of the French. It was Hawke, of course.

With Duff's seven, there were thirty ships against Conflans's twenty-one. And the weather was deteriorating, like the strategic situation of the French. What was Conflans to do? ". . . the circumstances of the moment, allied with the aim indicated in your letters, and seeing that the enemy force of thirty was superior to my own, all decided me to head for the coast of Morbihan".

Conflans was fifteen miles west of Belle Isle. A glance at the map shows that once he got beyond that island and the treacherous reefs to the east he would be in the relatively narrow waters of a bay in which navigation was dangerous—and where, he thought, the thirty ships of the enemy would not dare to follow him.

In that, he was mistaken. Hawke was not a man to be intimidated

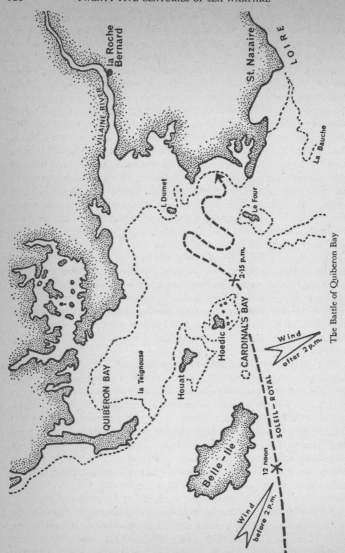

LOIRE

St. Nazaire

la Roche Bernard

VILAINE RIVER

La Bauche

I. Dumet

Le Four

2:15 p.m.

CARDINAL'S BAY

Wind
after 2 p.m.

The Battle of Quiberon Bay

QUIBERON BAY

la Teignouse

Houat

Hoedic

SOLEIL-ROYAL

Belle-Ile

12 noon

Wind
before 2 p.m.

by difficulties of navigation. He had met with plenty during the past six months of keeping watch and ward at the Channel approaches. And so, with the wind astern and a full spread of canvas, the British squadron came scudding after the French; and by two-thirty in the afternoon had begun to engage the rear division, which was in even greater disorder than the rest of its squadron, due to the increasing wind and mounting sea.

The *Magnifique* was the first to be attacked, and for an hour held off three enemy ships. Then a fourth worked round to leeward of her. The *Magnifique* ran out her guns to deal with the enemy on that quarter, but shipped so much water through the gun-ports that she had to close them hurriedly. The *Héros* came to her aid, and was attacked from all sides; her fore-topmast was brought down and then the mizzen-mast came crashing on to the enemy ship that had ranged alongside. The *Héros* became little more than a wreck, and struck her colours after two hours of desperate fighting; four of her consorts intervened, however, just as she was about to be taken as a prize, and she was left riding at anchor.

The *Formidable*, Du Verger's flagship, had shortened sail in an attempt to cover the retreat of the rear division, and soon found herself alone among the enemy. By five o'clock she had succumbed under the weight of numbers, and was finally captured by the *Resolution*. Then the *Superbe* capsized in the course of a furious engagement, through shipping a heavy sea when she ran out her guns to drive off an attacker that had worked round her—a disaster that the *Magnifique* had only just avoided.

Conflans, meanwhile, in the *Soleil Royal*, had been leading his line into Cardinals' Bay for a full hour, without apparently troubling himself about what was happening to his rear. The reasons he gave in his report later were not entirely satisfactory. However, at about half past three the *Soleil Royal* began casting on the port tack to "join several of our ships that were being driven together in some disorder by the heavy seas". The confused state of the French squadron can be gathered from that understatement. Another disaster occurred as the ships in the van imitated the *Soleil Royal*'s movement. A heavy sea swamped the *Thésée* as she came round into the wind, for the gun-ports of her lower deck had been left open, and she, too, capsized.

Nevertheless, by turning to face the enemy, Conflans stemmed the force of the attack. The *Soleil Royal* and other powerful ships—the *Tonnant*, *Orient*, and *Intrépide*—held off the British for a time. The winter daylight was already fading, and soon after five o'clock the action was broken off. The French had lost three ships. But what was far more serious for them, the squadron had been driven on to a lee shore and was trapped in the bay into which Conflans had led it. Only eight ships—the *Tonnant* and the *Magnifique* among them—eventually escaped and reached safety in Aix roads, off Rochefort. The *Soleil Royal* went aground near the mouth of the Loire, and Conflans gave orders on November 22nd for her to be burnt, fearing an attack like that against her glorious predecessor sixty years earlier. The *Héros* was burnt by the British; in any case, she was completely disabled and taking water. The *Juste* was beached, and seven others took shelter, together with the frigates, in the mouth of the Vilaine. They were to remain there for some time—two got back to Brest fourteen months later, in January, 1761, but the others were still there after two years.

The British had lost two ships, victims of the treacherous reefs in the bay. That was a risk Hawke had knowingly accepted, and one fully justified by results.

There was no longer any fear of a French invasion of Britain; and command of the seas enabled the British to build up a Colonial Empire at the expense of the French. For a time, after Beachy Head, it had seemed that Tourville might have gained the mastery; but now the English indeed ruled the waves, and no nation could challenge her rule. And yet, before another fifteen years had passed. . . .

THE BATTLE OF CHESAPEAKE BAY, WHICH BROUGHT AMERICA HER INDEPENDENCE

Rebirth of the French Navy—the American colonists allied with France against Britain—clashes in the Channel—D'Orvilliers's squadron repulses Admiral Keppel's off Ushant (July 27th, 1778)—the terrific fight between the Quebec and the Surveillante—John Paul Jones, America's first naval hero—the battles in West Indian waters—Admiral Byron's defeat off Grenada—Rodney against De Guichen off Dominica (April 17th, 1780)— the Battle of Chesapeake Bay, and its fortunate consequences for George Washington—British victory of the Saints (April 12th, 1782) comes too late to affect the issue of the War of American Independence.

THE Seven Years' War was brought to an end by the Treaty of Paris on February 1st, 1763. French reverses had been so obviously due to insufficiencies in the navy that the lesson was at last borne home. Under the able administration of Choiseul and his cousin, Praslin, the fleet became strong and powerful again in a remarkably short period. For the first time, the whole country appeared to take an interest in her navy; each province paid for the construction of a ship and so had its name on her bows. The merchants of the capital subscribed for a fine three-master, the *Ville de Paris*. The building programme outlined by Choiseul provided for 80 ships-of-the-line and 44 frigates. By 1771 it had been more than three-quarters achieved for the ships (64) and even exceeded for the frigates (50). The arsenals were well stocked for the first time in many years. The Naval Academy and the "Gardes de la Marine" (School for Midshipmen) were re-established, and the gunnery branch of the navy was reorganized. In order to provide more competent ships'-surgeons, medical schools were founded in 1768 at the naval bases of Brest, Rochefort, and Toulon. This was the period in France, too, of great explorers and discoverers, such as Bougainville, Borda, and Fleurien.

When Benjamin Franklin signed a treaty of alliance with France, on February 6th, 1778 (a state of war already existed between the American colonies and Britain), the French Navy had as many warships in commission as the British. With Spain allied to France, the two had a combined naval strength of 90 ships-of-the-line against the 72 of the Royal Navy.[1]

[1] This was a period when the British naval administration, unlike the French, was in incompetent hands. Service morale was low. "Estimates were falsified, ships were

The first clash at sea between France and Britain occurred on June 17th, 1778. A French 30-gun frigate, the *Belle Poule*, Captain Chadeau de La Clocheterie, was keeping watch on British movements in the Channel when she was hailed by the 28-gun *Arethusa*, Captain Marshall, a frigate from Admiral Keppel's squadron, and was requested to explain her activities to the Admiral. The French captain indignantly refused, Captain Marshall put a shot across his bows, and he replied with a broadside. The fight lasted for five hours, from half past six in the evening, and at the end both vessels were in a bad way. The *Arethusa* had lost her mainmast, most of her rigging had been shot away, and there were 44 dead or wounded on board. The *Belle Poule* had 45 of her crew killed and 57 wounded.[1] She succeeded in making the coast of Brittany and anchored among the rocks off Plouescat, where two British ships endeavoured to get at her, but without success.

Six weeks later, Keppel's squadron of 30 ships-of-the-line and 16 frigates opposed a French squadron of equal strength under the command of Count D'Orvilliers. Action was joined at eleven in the morning, off Ushant, and lasted three and a half hours; but victory was denied to either side, and each missed an opportunity to work round the other's rear division. On the whole, the French had the better of it. Their ships received only minor damage, whereas six of Keppel's were a dismal sight, and one of these had been about to strike but a consort had gone to her aid just in time. Moreover, it was Keppel who broke off the action and withdrew, because—as he reported to the Admiralty —"the state of his ships gave him no choice".

Among D'Orvilliers's frigates was a new vessel, the *Surveillante*, of 26 guns and with 10 four-pounders mounted fore and aft. She had been fitted out at Lorient at the beginning of the year and her command had been given to a younger son of a landed but impoverished Breton family—the Chevalier du Couedic de Kergoualer. He had entered the Service at the age of sixteen, just as the Seven Years' War was beginning, and his long and distinguished service in the East had merited this new command. He was keenly aware of the honour, and told everyone that the *Surveillante* "would be his tomb or his triumphal chariot". She was more or less both, as it happened.

He had some success during the *Surveillante's* winter cruise, following the fight off Ushant, by sinking the 18-gun privateer *Old England* on March 12th, 1779; and, on April 19th, by capturing a 20-gun sloop

---

counted twice in the Weekly Progress Lists, and ships were put into commission to 'gratify' political supporters when there was no intention of fitting them out for active service" (*The British Navy in Adversity*, by Admiral Sir W. M. James). (*Tr.*)

[1] Figures given by Clowes, *op. cit.*, Vol. IV, p. 15.

that only struck her colours when three-quarters of her crew were casualties and every gun was out of action.

At the end of the 1779 campaign (to which I shall return later) the warring fleets were laid up for the winter, as was customary then, leaving a few small vessels to patrol the Channel and keep watch for any

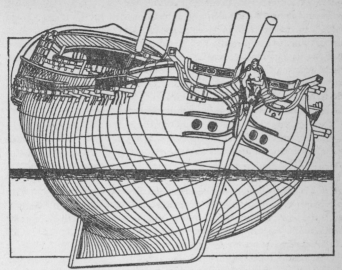

Eighteenth-century ship's hull (*from a contemporary drawing*)

enemy activity. Thus it was that the frigate *Quebec*, Captain George Farmer, set sail on October 4th to patrol the waters outside Brest, while on the same day the *Surveillante* put out from Brest with orders to keep watch on the Solent. The armament of the two frigates was about equal, and each was accompanied by a schooner as tender, the *Surveillante* by the 10-gun *Expedition*, Lieutenant De Roquefeuil, and the *Quebec* by the 10-gun *Rambler*, Lieutenant George. Captain Farmer, like Du Couedic, had learnt his business in the East; he had returned home a post-Captain, but had requested command of a fast frigate, which was more to his taste than a lumbering ship-of-the-line.

When the two frigates sighted each other they were about equal distance from their respective stations, some ninety miles east of Ushant. It was soon after daybreak on October 6th, a fine morning with a fresh breeze blowing down-Channel. The *Quebec*, with a good spread of canvas, was on the port tack and making to the south-west; while the

Surveillante was heading north-east on the starboard tack. Farmer took in sail and, receiving no reply to his recognition signals, stood on towards the enemy; and Du Couedic hugged the wind as closely as possible to get within range. The first shots were fired at eleven in the morning, and for six hours the fight was stubborn in the extreme, on both sides. It would be difficult to say which showed the greatest courage and the finest qualities. Let the account left by the Chevalier de Lostanges, the second officer on the *Surveillante*, speak for itself:

Du Couedic let loose the first broadside with his port guns as soon as he was within range, and Farmer came running down to pour in a reply with his starboard guns. For an hour the two pounded away at each other, tacking on a parallel course and keeping within musket-range. It was a murderous business. At one point the *Quebec* began turning into the wind with the object of bringing the port guns to bear and raking the *Surveillante*; but Du Couedic realized in time and parried the movement, and his gunners were ready with their starboard guns.

Both vessels had received so much damage that it had become impossible for either to sail close to the wind. They continued heading north-west, the *Quebec* to windward still; and so close together that ramrods of the gunners in one vessel banged against the other. A shot cut through the halyard of the French colours, but the shouts of triumph from the British were short-lived; the pilot unfurled another flag and held it to the mizzen-mast, miraculously surviving the hail of fire, until the French colours were flying from the poop.[1]

Shortly afterwards, the *Surveillante* lost all her three masts, leaving only the bowsprit with a few shreds of canvas dangling from it, and the flag-staff. Five minutes later the *Quebec* was dismasted, and with more damaging effect, for a number of her crew were killed or injured by the falling rigging, which crashed down on the guns aft and encumbered them so much that they could not be served.

But it took more than that to defeat Captain Farmer. His first lieutenant had lost an arm, and he was himself wounded, but he continued to encourage his men. "It's a close fight, lads. So we've got to put twice as much heart into it. We either win or die." But he had a worthy opponent. Du Couedic had already been twice wounded in the head, and was then hit in the stomach, but refused to go below. He gave orders to board the enemy. "Lay her aboard!" he cried heartily, and turned to his nephews who were serving under him as midshipmen. "Lay her aboard, my boys! It's up to you to set an example, and remember to uphold the honour of the family. . . ."

[1] One of the English said to him later that the *Quebec's* colours had been nailed to the mast; and the other replied, "Ours were kept there by honour".

But just then the *Quebec* suddenly burst into flames, and was soon blazing from stem to stern. Du Couedic ordered firing to cease and all boats and rafts available to be launched, putting as much energy into saving his enemies as he had in fighting them. But all the boats except one had been smashed by gunfire, and the surviving boat crashed on a gun muzzle while being lowered, and sank as soon as it touched the water.

The *Quebec* was a horrible sight. The fire had swept over the helpless wounded lying about the deck, turning them into human torches; the men clinging to the sides jumped into the sea as flames licked at them from the gun-ports. Even in the *Surveillante* the heat became so intense that the crew had to keep pouring sea-water over the bulwarks. In order to draw away, Du Couedic had to set his men to get out the oars. But no sooner had his ship made a little headway than the *Quebec* drifted on to her bowsprit, setting light to the tattered rigging. The crew quickly cut it free with axes; meanwhile, the loaded guns of the British frigate went off one after the other, as the flames reached them, and added to the ravages aboard the *Surveillante*.

Hardly had the one danger been averted than the *Surveillante* was found to be taking water. All aboard set to work at the pumps or made a bucket-chain. There was no human foe now; the seamen rescued from the *Quebec* joined the French in fighting the common enemy.

The *Quebec* had drifted off a little way, but now swung so close that the tar on the side of the *Surveillante* began to melt. The dangling rigging of the blazing frigate was seen to be still caught on the *Surveillante's* bowsprit, and some men ran to cut it loose—just in time, for a moment later the *Quebec* blew up, showering the other's deck with blazing debris. Captain Farmer went down with his ship. He was last seen sitting calmly on the anchor and gazing at the flag, which the flames had spared.

The two schooners, all this while, had been as closely engaged as their leaders. There were thirty casualties in the *Expedition*. The *Rambler* had suffered much damage, but when Lieutenant George saw the fire spreading in the *Quebec* he hastened to her aid. So did the *Expedition*, and rescued about a dozen of the *Quebec's* crew, including her first lieutenant, Francis Robert, who told of Captain Farmer's heroic fight and gallant death.

The *Surveillante* was in little better shape; the leaks were increasing, in spite of all efforts. Before having his wounds attended to, Du Couedic did what he could for the safety of the surviving men. The ship was lightened, all the remaining munitions being cast overside. The largest holes were thus brought above the water-line, and were hurriedly caulked as well as possible. British and French toiled with equal energy under the orders of the few remaining able-bodied officers. Lostanges had lost an eye, the first lieutenant had had his right arm blown off and had lost three fingers of his left hand. Towards six o'clock Du Couedic finally consented to hand over command to Dufresneau, an auxiliary officer.

The light wind had veered north-east, and with some makeshift sails to the jagged stumps of her masts the *Surveillante* was able to make one knot an hour towards Ushant, some forty-five miles away. Darkness had fallen, and a lantern was slung from the poop to guide the *Expedition* to the crippled frigate. The *Rambler* had already vanished from sight. Some forty French sailors and as many British[1] worked in relays at the helm and the pumps, snatching a little sleep or rest in between. The roar of the guns and the crackle of the blazing ship had given way to an almost complete silence, disturbed only by the moaning of the wounded and the dying.[2]

The *Expedition* came up with the labouring frigate at eleven that night, and took her in tow. There were then two dangers to be feared: bad weather getting up, and an enemy ship putting in an appearance; either would mean the end of the *Surveillante* in her present condition. But she was spared both, and late next morning was in sight of land. The first vessels met with were fishing-smacks from Ushant; they gave the exhausted sailors some of their catch, and helped to tow the *Surveillante* with such enthusiasm, pulling heartily at their oars to cries of '*Vive le Roi!*', that by sunset the frigate was at anchor off Camaret.

The naval authorities at Brest were informed by semaphore and despatched a corvette with all necessary aid. During the night a number of French and Spanish launches reached the *Surveillante* to tow her into Brest. At dawn, arranged in a double line with French and Spanish alternating, they began the long haul round to the naval base. And so the battered but proud frigate, preceded by the launches flying French and Spanish colours, passed through the combined fleet of seventy warships at their moorings in Brest roads, and was loudly cheered by the crews perched in the rigging.

A great welcome was given to the survivors, French and British alike. The latter, by the King's orders, were treated as guests, not prisoners. When Lieutenant Robert and his men were fit to travel they were repatriated, sailing from Brest under a neutral flag and with every help and kindness from the local population.

[1] Of the *Quebec's* complement of 195, about 70 were rescued. The *Rambler* picked up 17, the *Surveillante* had 38—of whom 2 died of their wounds—and the *Expedition* 10. A few others were very likely picked up by a passing Russian merchantman.
[2] The *Surveillante* had 30 killed and 85 wounded.

Du Couedic, alas, did not recover from his wounds. He was promoted Captain soon after his victory, but died at Brest on January 7th, 1780, aged forty, three months to the day after his great fight against the *Quebec*. George Farmer's death was just as great a loss to the British Navy. Nelson and Troubridge both served under him in their young days, and—as Clowes writes—"the master was worthy of his disciples!"

In St. Louis's church at Brest there used to be a marble slab (the church was destroyed in 1944) with an inscription that I often gazed at when a boy: "Young Naval cadets, admire and follow the example of brave Du Couedic."

Only a fortnight before that single combat in the Channel, an equally furious encounter had taken place off Flamborough Head—and one which gave the embryo American Navy a hero whose name is still revered: John Paul Jones. His career was short, and his heroic actions did not greatly influence the course of the War of American Independence; but his tomb in the crypt of the chapel at the Naval Academy in Annapolis is more magnificent than that of Nelson's in St. Paul's. I am not sure whether midshipmen at Dartmouth and at Brest are still reminded of the example set by Farmer and Du Couedic, but one of the first things that American naval cadets learn is the reply of John Paul Jones when called upon to surrender: "I have not yet begun to fight."

On November 1st, 1777, Jones sailed from America in command of an 18-gun sloop, the *Ranger*, and reached Nantes a month later with two prizes taken on the way. A few weeks later, on February 14th, 1778, he received from a French ship, the *Robuste*, the first salute given to the thirteen-starred flag of the Union by a foreign ship.

He put to sea again in April, sailing up the Irish Sea and making several raids on the west coast of England. He set fire to Whitehaven, and captured the *Drake*, the first British warship to be taken by an American. For his 1779 campaign the French gave him an old East Indiaman, the *Duc de Duras*. Jones renamed the ship *Poor Richard*, in honour of Benjamin Franklin's celebrated book *Poor Richard's Almanack*. She was fitted out at Lorient, and had a somewhat mixed armament— six 18-pounders on the lower gun-deck, twenty-eight 12-pounders on the upper gun-deck, and eight 9-pounders mounted fore and aft. The crew, too, was a mixed lot, with sailors of many nationalities. The *Poor Richard* sailed on June 19th, at the head of a small division This consisted of the *Alliance*, a 32-gun frigate commanded by Landais, a Frenchman who seems to have been something of a madbrain, more of a danger to his friends than to his enemies; and two armed merchantmen, the 30-gun *Pallas* and the 12-gun *Vengeance*, and an 18-gun cutter, the *Cerf*.

The cruise began badly; hardly had the ships cleared the coast than the *Poor Richard* and the *Alliance* came into collision and had to return to port for repairs. The little division sailed again on August 14th, picked up a few prizes in the Irish Sea, continued round the north of Scotland and attempted a raid into the Firth of Forth; but this was impeded by adverse winds and the lack of co-operation from Landais, who had ideas of his own. However, three more prizes were taken on September 21st, off Flamborough Head; and two days later the small force came upon a rich convoy from the Baltic, consisting of forty-one sail escorted by a powerful frigate, the 44-gun *Serapis*, Captain Richard Pearson, and an auxiliary vessel, the 20-gun *Countess of Scarborough*.

The encounter took place so close inshore that it was witnessed by a crowd of people on the cliffs between Flamborough and Scarborough; and they saw one of the fiercest combats in the history of sea warfare.

Captain Pearson's two ships had come between the convoy and its attackers, and the day was already well advanced when the fight began. The *Serapis* and the *Poor Richard* were running on a parallel course towards the shore, both on the port tack and within musket-range of each other; challenging cries and calls to surrender were passing from one ship to the other. The American opened fire first, at twenty-past seven. The *Serapis* at once replied, and an explosion occurred in the *Poor Richard*. It was not, however, the British guns that had caused the damage; two of the 18-pounders had burst, and the lower gun-deck was already out of action.

The *Pallas* and the *Countess of Scarborough*, meanwhile, were fighting it out; and the *Alliance* was circling the combatants and firing indiscriminately—and with little effect—on British and American. In short, the *Poor Richard* could not count on any help against an opponent who was a better sailer and had the heavier armament, and whose crew was decidedly better trained and disciplined than the motley crowd under Jones's orders. Before very long, the difference was making itself felt. The American ship was badly battered; her 12-pounders were put out of action, and Jones found himself with only three of his 9-pounders still serviceable and a crew completely demoralized, many of whom called on him to strike. "For the love of God, cap'n, strike!"—"No, I'll sink first!" he replied. "Strike, never!" And, seizing his speaking-trumpet, he shouted across at Pearson, "I haven't begun to fight yet!"

And, in fact, there was plenty to come. The *Poor Richard* was taking water in numerous places, and her captain realized that his only chance was to board and enter. The first attempt failed, but at the second Jones himself lashed the *Serapis*'s bowsprit to his own rigging, and the two ships swung together, bows to stern.

It was then half past eight. Pearson anchored, hoping that the current would drag away the other ship; about forty of her crew were fighting their way along his deck, cutting down the English amid the tangle of fallen rigging. His gunners were firing into the hull of the *Poor Richard*, smashing it to pieces but killing no one, for all the crew were up above, at work with musket and cutlass. One of them tossed a grenade down a hatchway and it exploded in the powder-store, causing frightful damage to men and guns.

When the smoke cleared, the British were seen to be still defending themselves aft—and unexpected help seemed at hand. John Paul Jones had released his prisoners, the crews of the prizes he had taken, as his ship was in danger of sinking; and their numbers could now sway the fight either way. He at once saw the peril, and with great resourcefulness and commanding presence ordered them to the pumps if they wanted to save their lives. They obeyed without a word.

Landais at last began to take a real interest in events. He brought the *Alliance* round to port of the *Seraphis*, his guns ready to rake that now defenceless ship. Pearson was obliged to strike his colours; just then— it was half past ten—his mainmast came crashing down into the sea.

Du Couedic was able to save the victorious *Surveillante* only with the help of his prisoners; John Paul Jones went one better and saved his victorious men with the aid of the captured ship. The *Poor Richard* was sinking fast, and all aboard her were transferred to the *Serapis*. A few days later, flying the Union flag, John Paul Jones proudly brought her to the Texel; eventually he reached Lorient with her, in spite of the British corsairs in the Channel.

Strange as it may seem, John Paul Jones received no recognition in America until long after his death; whereas Pearson was honoured and given a title for his heroic resistance. Jones never received another command, though he served for a while in the Russian Navy with the rank of Rear-Admiral. Catherine the Great eventually tired of him, and he returned to Paris where he died, almost forgotten, on July 18th, 1792.

It was not in European waters, however, that the War of American Independence was being decided, but across the Atlantic, in the West Indies and on the American mainland. The chief question was whether Britain could maintain command of the Atlantic approaches. Only the French were capable of disputing it—the Colonists had practically no real navy—and for once the French had a strong fleet and no war to sustain in Europe. On April 18th, 1778, a squadron of twelve ships commanded by Vice-Admiral Count D'Estaing sailed from Toulon, and by July 8th was off the mouth of the Delaware. The French chargé d'affaires to the Americans was landed there, and then D'Estaing sailed on to New York. He missed an opportunity of attacking Admiral

Conservation of standing wood for use in ship-building

Lord Howe, who had only a small squadron of nine ships; and a French naval victory at that point might well have settled the American issue. D'Estaing, though, had served in the army until he was forty-three, and probably lacked a sense of the sea and the necessary audacity. He took his squadron up to Rhode Island, where the Americans were besieging six thousand British in Newport. Howe went after him, and the decisive battle might still have taken place, but a north-easterly sprang up that scattered both squadrons and caused about the same amount of damage to each.

With the approach of wintry weather, the theatre of naval operations moved to the West Indies. But D'Estaing had no better luck there. He was unable to save St. Lucia, which capitulated to the British in November. When news of this reached France, the decision was made to send out strong reinforcements. The first to reach D'Estaing were four ships commanded by De Grasse; then the Marquis de Vaudreuil arrived with two more, and finally a division of six led by Lamotte-Picquet. On June 30th, 1779, D'Estaing sailed from Martinique with this strong squadron—twenty-five ships in all—and had little difficulty in capturing Grenada. But two days later a British squadron under

Admiral Byron hove in sight, with the obvious intention of recapturing the island. In the event, though, Byron met with a crushing defeat; seen in isolation, the most disastrous suffered by the British Navy—according to Mahan—since Torrington's defeat off Beachy Head.

Admiral Byron, flying his flag in the 98-gun *Princess Royal*, had twenty-one ships under his command. D'Estaing, in the 80-gun *Languedoc*, was supported by the best captains in Louis XVI's navy—Suffren, Boulainvilliers, De Grasse, Bougainville. . . . All were ready for Byron, though he was hoping to catch the French at anchor. He had signalled to engage the enemy, and the squadron bore down with the wind astern. The French were not yet in regular order of battle, nevertheless the British van was badly mauled—as much by the Kingstown shore batteries as by the guns of the ships. The *Cornwall*, the *Monmouth*, and the *Lion* soon had to draw out of the line, the last having lost her top-gallant and main-topmast.

It could have been a complete victory for the French if D'Estaing had followed up the advantage gained. But he stayed to consolidate his capture of Grenada, and Byron was able to withdraw to St. Kitts and patch up his damaged ships. At least D'Estaing had won the esteem of his captains, as he had that of the British. "D'Estaing acted with great courage," Suffren wrote later, ". . . . but if his tactical ability had been of the same quality as his bravery, four dismasted ships would not have escaped us." The naval historian, Geoffrey Calender, gives the following appreciation: "D'Estaing proclaimed himself the victor, and the most impartial enquirer would be obliged to agree. But why did Byron throw down the gauntlet? To recover Grenada? The damage he received obliged him to retire and abandon the island to D'Estaing. . . . Or to show that he held command of the sea? He failed there too, for although he was not brought to his knees, neither did he bring his enemy down; and in such circumstances the loser is surely the one who attacked."[1]

De Grasse suggested that he should lead an attack against the battered ships at St. Kitts. But they were found to be too well protected by shore batteries, and the idea was abandoned. D'Estaing at least had the satisfaction of defying Byron on two occasions, sailing close to the island with his line but not meeting any response from the British. Not long afterwards, Byron was relieved of his command, Sir Hyde Parker going out to replace him.

Encouraged by success, D'Estaing next attempted to deliver a great blow by attacking Savannah, which was still held by the British. But he was less fortunate on the coast of America. Repulsed with heavy losses,

[1] *Sea Kings of Britain*, by Sir Geoffrey Calender, Vol. III, London, 1911.

himself wounded, D'Estaing began to think of returning to home waters. His attempt against the mainland, however, was instrumental in helping the American cause. The British withdrew their forces on Rhode Island to reinforce New York, with the consequence that in July of the following year a French expeditionary force under Rochambeau was able to land there without opposition. And it was Rochambeau, supported by De Grasse's squadron, who did much to bring about an American victory in the autumn of 1781.

While D'Estaing had been active in West Indian waters, the Brest fleet had put to sea on June 3rd, 1779, under the command of Count D'Orvilliers, with the object of carrying the war to English soil. D'Orvilliers first sailed south across the Bay of Biscay to make rendez-vous with a Spanish squadron; then the allied fleet of sixty-six ships and fourteen frigates made for the Channel, where such a large enemy concentration had not been seen since the time of Tourville. England appeared to stand in as great a peril as then. There was panic in the south, and an order to the coastal population to send their horses and farm stock inland did not help to allay fears.

As it transpired, the Spaniards had been so late at their rendezvous that the French fleet had become weakened by disease and shortness of provisions, and D'Orvilliers was forced to put about after being at sea 104 days. He returned to Brest having only once caught sight of the smaller British fleet, commanded by Admiral Sir Charles Hardy, hovering off Plymouth and seeming as little inclined for action as the combined fleet.

Back at Brest, the commander of the Blue-and-White squadron, De Guichen, received orders to take sixteen ships-of-the-line and four frigates out to the West Indies. De Guichen was then sixty-seven, and had spent fifty years of his life at sea; he had fought under Duguay-Trouin, and had a better tactical sense than any other squadron commander in the French Navy. On arriving in the West Indies he was joined by De Grasse and his small division, and on March 22nd, 1780, they sailed for St. Lucia, where Sir Hyde Parker was at anchorage. But the British refused to go out and meet the French challenge; Parker was expecting the arrival of an important person—Rear-Admiral Sir George Brydges Rodney, with four warships.

Rodney had served with great distinction under Anson, Boscawen, and Hawke. He had left the Service after the Treaty of Paris, and had led such a high life that he was obliged to flee to France to escape his creditors. Although an inveterate gambler and lover of good living, when on active service with the navy the fine seaman in him predominated. As soon as war broke out again, he returned to England and was given a sea-going command, although his energies were somewhat impaired by poor health and frequent attacks of gout, due to his excesses.

On April 16th, 1780, De Guichen with twenty-one ships was beating to windward to reach the shelter of the island of Dominica when he sighted Rodney's squadron, of equal strength, coming up from the south-east with the wind abeam. For the rest of the day, De Guichen tried unsuccessfully to gain the weather-gauge. The following morning, when action was joined, the wind was still in the north-east; both squadrons were on the starboard tack, making course parallel to each other. Rodney signalled for each ship to engage the corresponding enemy ship. But did this mean the ship opposite, or the corresponding number in the enemy line? For the leading French vessels were well ahead of the remainder, whereas the British were in much closer formation. And so, instead of his ships concentrating in overwhelming force upon the rear half of the French squadron—to which the other half could have brought no immediate aid—Rodney was mortified to see his leading ship, the *Stirling Castle*, make for the leading Frenchman and not the ninth in the line, as was intended. Parker, commanding the van, saw nothing wrong in this movement, though; and when his flagship imitated it, the centre began to follow suit. Rodney, seeing that his plan of battle had gone overboard, found himself obliged to correspond with the general movement, and led the eleven ships astern of him in an attack on the French opposite.

The two squadrons pounded away at each other from a quarter to one to five o'clock. The *Ajax* in particular was gravely damaged and had to draw off, and similarly the French *St Michel*, whose captain had his right arm blown off. Rodney's flagship, the 90-gun *Sandwich*, fought De Guichen's flagship and two of her consorts for an hour and a half, and the *Sandwich* then had no less than eighty shot-holes in her hull, three of them below the water-line. With her main- and fore-masts gone by the board, and her rigging in tatters, she was in grave danger of sinking. Rodney shifted his flag to another ship.

Neither commander-in-chief could have been sorry when the battle ended. Yet back home, both Britain and France regarded it as a victory, in due course.

Rodney's despatch, however, contained the following:

"The French Admiral, who appeared to me to be a brave and courageous officer, had the privilege of being nobly seconded throughout the action. It is with unutterable concern mingled with indignation that I find myself obliged by my duty towards King and Country to report to Your Lordships that, on the occasion of this encounter of the 17th instant between the French fleet and His Majestys', the British flag was not properly supported."

That hardly smacked of victory. Nor did the letters sent "under the rose" to the Admiralty by some of Rodney's captains, replying to his charges against them by saying that "the Admiral was nothing but a gouty old fogy who did not know his business, and whom it was urgent to replace."

It is certain that Rodney was not in good form. He went after De Guichen, whom he believed had made for the coast of America, spent some time in New York having treatment for his gout—instead of attacking Rochambeau, who was landing his troops at Newport—then returned to the West Indies for the winter, and sailed for home the following August. This was all to the good of the American colonists, for by then the war was rapidly approaching its critical phase.

But first, let us go back several months, to just after the battle off Dominica. In May, 1780, the American land forces suffered a grave defeat with the loss of Charleston, in South Carolina. Their situation deteriorated still further during the winter. General Arnold went over to the British, who then held nearly all the bases on the Eastern seaboard. Washington had only a thousand men to stave off Cornwallis; and Rochambeau's expeditionary force, unable to move without support from the sea—and a strong naval force was just what was lacking—spent its idle days pleasantly enough, to the joy of the pretty young women and the moneylenders of Newport.

It was then that Admiral De Grasse arrived on the scene, and by his victory at the Battle of Chesapeake Bay swung the balance in favour of the Americans. This battle was no major engagement, and no outstanding feat occurred, but its effects had far greater importance for the history of the world than many a larger naval action.

De Grasse has already been mentioned on preceding pages. He had, like De Guichen, seen much active service and was an experienced seaman. François Joseph Paul de Grasse was born in 1722 in the small Provencal village of Bar-sur-Loup, the fifth son of an army captain. At the age of eleven he was sent to the Naval School at Toulon, and was a midshipman at the Battle of Toulon in 1744. As a lieutenant in the *Gloire* he took part in the heroic fight off Finisterre, on May 14th, 1747, when five French warships and two frigates put up a terrific resistance against fifteen British ships commanded by Admiral Anson. The *Gloire*'s captain had his head blown off, and De Grasse who was next to him received a serious head wound. Yet the ship fought on, and for three hours sustained the attack of Anson's flagship, the 90-gun *Prince George*, and of two other ships. Only when two of her three masts had gone, when the deck was littered with dead, the hold taking water, and the last shot and bullet spent, did the *Gloire* strike her colours.

After the Peace of Aix-la-Chapelle De Grasse took service for a time with the fleet of the Knights of Malta, to whose Order he belonged, like Tourville before him. On the outbreak of the Seven Years' War he returned to his King's service, did a tour of duty in the Indian Ocean and was then sent to the West Indian station as captain in the *Protée*. In 1776 he obtained his flag and commanded a division of the Blue, under D'Orvilliers, at the battle off Ushant. Later he was again in the West Indies, with four ships, and served with distinction under D'Estaing and De Guichen.

He was back in France in 1780, after the battle off Dominica. On March 22nd, 1781, he sailed from Brest for the West Indies once again, this time as commander-in-chief of a fleet of twenty line-of-battle ships and a proportionate number of frigates and corvettes, and with many transports and supply ships. He made a remarkably quick crossing for the times, reaching Martinique on April 29th. Avoiding a squadron commanded by Rear-Admiral Sir Samuel Hood, De Grasse captured St. Lucia, then made for San Domingo to embark the garrison there— these troops being intended as reinforcements for General Rochambeau.

While still at San Domingo, De Grasse received the latest news of the situation in America, brought in record time by the frigate *Concorde*; she had left Boston with despatches from Rochambeau on June 20th, and reached San Domingo on July 6th. De Grasse learnt that the small squadron, commanded by Count Barras de St. Laurent, had arrived at Newport on May 8th with more reinforcements for Rochambeau, and that the latter—having consulted Washington—left it to De Grasse to decide the best way in which the naval forces could support the land operations. The British, Rochambeau reported, were then advancing through Carolina and Virginia towards Chesapeake Bay, while Rochambeau was crossing Connecticut to join up with Washington.

The alternative before De Grasse was whether to make for the region of New York, which was the chief British base, or for Hampton Roads (the mouth of the Chesapeake) where he would be able to give closer support to the Franco-American armies, He decided in favour of the latter and sent the *Concorde* back to Newport to inform Rochambeau, while he set sail, keeping to leeward of the Bahamas and then stealing up the coast of the mainland.

Hood, meanwhile, had been searching for the French squadron

since missing it off St. Lucia, and had sent off a corvette, the *Swallow*, to inform Rear-Admiral Thomas Graves, who was in command of a strong force then moored in the mouth of the Hudson. But the *Swallow* was intercepted by four American corsairs, and Graves never received the despatches.

Hood took the shortest route across to the Chesapeake, while the French were creeping up the coast, and arrived in Hampton Roads on August 25th to find the anchorage empty. Having satisfied himself that no enemy ships were in the neighbourhood, Hood continued northward and three days later cast anchor off Sandy Hook, at the entrance to the Hudson River, well satisfied at having got ahead of De Grasse and barred the way to him.

However, five days after Hood had sailed from Hampton Roads, De Grasse arrived at the Virginia capes, and anchored without any hindrance in Lynnhaven bay, inside Cape Henry. He put his troops ashore, conferred with Washington, and sent two pairs of ships to blockade the rivers James and York. The British under Cornwallis were thus invested by land and sea, and shut themselves up in Yorktown.

Rear-Admiral Graves was still unaware of the movements of De Grasse's squadron, which he believed to be somewhere off Cuba! Now that Hood had joined him, Graves was in command of more than twenty warships. They sailed south, with the object of helping Cornwallis. Hood had the van and was flying his flag in the 100-gun *Barfleur*, Graves commanded the main body in his 108-gun *London*, and the rear was under the command of Samuel Francis Drake in the 82-gun *Princessa*. In this formation, with the wind almost dead astern, they were approaching the entrance to the Chesapeake when the presence of a few suspicious sail was signalled. Graves, believing he had to deal with a small division at most, crowded on sail. . . .

It was ten in the morning of September 5th, 1781. The French, too, were so little expecting to see a strong enemy squadron that many of their ships' crews were ashore or ferrying boats across the bay with supplies for the army. Altogether some eighteen hundred seamen and ninety officers were away from their ships.

When some sails were sighted low down beyond Cape Charles they were at first thought to belong to Barras's division, which was expected with troop reinforcements from Newport. But then the guard frigates came scudding back, firing their guns to announce the strength of the enemy force—ten, twenty-five, ultimately twenty-seven vessels, of which nineteen were men-of-war . . . the British, obviously. There was no time to spare. If the French remained at their moorings they would have to fight under the worst possible conditions, and be unable to give any help to Barras should he appear on the scene. However, there was an off-sea wind, the tide was still coming in, so that in order to stand out to sea the French ships had to beat about interminably in the three-mile-wide channel between Cape Henry and the Middle Ground shoal. To gain time, De Grasse ordered the ships to slip their cables; in those days, weighing the anchor was a long, man-handling process.

Never before had French sailors been so quick and adept at getting their massive vessels under weigh. In a quarter of an hour all were beginning to wear out to sea, though it was impossible to hug the wind very closely; there was little room to manoeuvre, and the ships had to remain on the short tack. A great sigh of relief must have gone up when, just before one o'clock, the great *Ville de Paris*—the largest man-of-war in the world at that time—rounded Cape Henry and stood out to sea. She was the eleventh in the French line; Admiral Graves had missed a golden opportunity, one "beyond all dreams of any naval commander".[1] If, as Hood suggested to him, he had attacked each ship as she came tacking slowly out of the bay—and the British had the wind in their favour—he could have destroyed the French van before the rest of the squadron was out. Instead, he gave the French all the time they needed, until they were formed in line abreast, though in the order in which the ships had cleared the bay, not in their theoretical stations in the line, and with the van well ahead. Graves, meanwhile, was deploying to port, so that the squadrons should face each other in two long lines. His intention was to engage the enemy in the dignified, orderly manner of van against van, centre against centre, rear against rear. He still had the weather-gauge, and therefore the initiative, but unfortunately the sacrosanct "Fighting Instructions" contained no signal corresponding exactly to the situation; and the signals he made to remedy matters somewhat baffled his captains. It was unfortunate, too, that the movement had brought Drake's division into the van— "an officer with a great name but of moderate worth"[2]—and left Hood's in the rear, where he was unable to influence the main action.

When Graves signalled "Prepare to attack", the commander of the French van, Bougainville, veered away instead of continuing to tack into the wind; this had the effect of delaying the beginning of the action and enabling De Grasse and the rest of the squadron to get into proper station. Moreover, Hood had continued in line ahead, maintaining

[1] Admiral W. M. James, *op. cit.*
[2] Samuel E. Morison, "The Naval campaign of Yorktown"; a lecture given at Washington, October 18th, 1956.

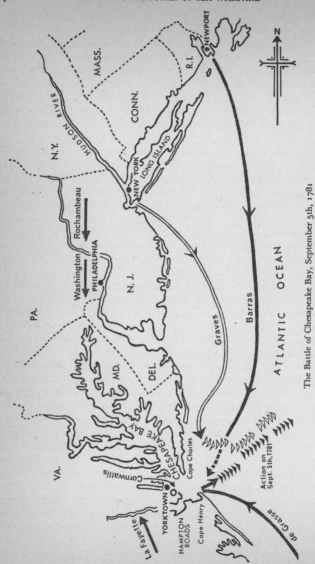

The Battle of Chesapeake Bay, September 5th, 1781

that the signal was still hoisted in the *London*, instead of bearing down on the French centre.

In short, it was four in the afternoon before action was joined, the fifth ship in the French line, the *Réfléchi*, being hit first, and her captain killed. The first few minutes were the worst, in fact, for the four or five leading French ships, which came under fire from seven or eight of the enemy van. Drake's flagship, the *Princessa*, set the *Diadème* on fire and was about to board her when the *St. Esprit* came to her aid, "opening fire with such terrible effect that the English backed and drew away".

Bougainville, in the *Auguste*, was engaged in a duel with the *Terrible*, which got so much the worst of it that she had to be abandoned four days later. During these exchanges, a shot from the *Terrible* carried away the bowline of the *Auguste*'s fore-topsail. Two sailors who tried to restore it were killed one after the other by sharpshooters in the fighting-tops of the *Princessa*. "My purse to whoever fixes that bowline!" cried Admiral Bougainville. A young seaman darted forward through the hail of fire and began scrambling up the rigging. "You haven't to pay me for doing my duty, Admiral!" he shouted down; and repaired the damage.

After the opening clash, the French soon gained the ascendancy, and Graves eventually drew off. The French were still to leeward, and so unable to continue the action. For five days the two squadrons remained within sight of each other. Then came a sudden shift of wind, and De Grasse, convinced by now that Barras had safely reached the Chesapeake, returned to his anchorage.

The French casualties amounted to 220, and the British to 336, but the damage to British vessels was greatly disproportionate to the French. The *Terrible* was burnt on September 10th, after her crew were taken off completely exhausted by four days at the pumps. The *Princessa* had lost her main-topmast, the *Shrewsbury* her main and foretopmast, the *Intrepid* had her topsail-yards splintered and her lower masts in a bad state; the *Ajax* was holed and taking almost as much water as the *Terrible* had, while the *Montagu*'s rigging looked likely to collapse at any moment. But only two of the French ships, the *Diadème* and the *Caton*, had suffered any serious damage.

The real outcome of the battle, however, was that the whole strategic situation of the war had definitely swung in favour of the French and the Americans. Barrass had indeed reached the Chesapeake with reinforcements. De Grasse, moreover, now had thirty-six warships under his command and could confidently withstand any further sea offensive; but none came. Freed of threats from the sea, Washington and

Rochambeau tightened their grip on Yorktown, and Cornwallis capitulated on October 19th. The War of American Independence was practically lost to the British, and chiefly due to De Grasse having gained command of the sea at the right moment. As an American historian recently wrote, "without De Grasse's victory off the Virginia capes, it is not Cornwallis's capitulation but Washington's that history would have recorded at Yorktown".[1]

There are some trends in history which could never have been stemmed. The American colonies would have undoubtedly won their independence eventually, but if Washington had been defeated at Yorktown it might well have been delayed for a generation.

"It was not the Declaration of Independence that brought the United States into being," wrote Geoffrey Calender (*The Naval Side of British History*), "neither was it the alliance with France, nor the defeat of Burgoyne at Saratoga. It was the Battle of Chesapeake Bay which decided the final issue of the war, crowned the work of Washington, and reduced to ashes our grandiose ambition to keep North America under the Crown."

In that year, 1781, the French flag was victorious in many seas. In the Mediterranean, De Guichen landed troops on Minorca unopposed, and the British garrison on the island was forced to capitulate some four months later. In the Atlantic, a small division of five ships-of-the-line, a frigate, and a corvette, commanded by Suffren, was on its way to the Cape with reinforcements for the Dutch colony, when it surprised a British division under Commodore Johnstone at anchor in the Cape Verde islands; after a sharp action, Suffren reached the Cape first, then crossed the Indian Ocean, raised the siege of Trincomalee, and repulsed a British force larger than his own in the Bay of Bengal. Finally, at the end of the year, Rear-Admiral Kempenfelt was lying in wait for a French convoy off Ushant when De Guichen hove in sight with a squadron twice the strength of his own, and he rightly refused to give battle. But the British public was still waiting to hear of great victories as in the days of Hawke and Boscawen, and so was "deeply concerned at seeing British squadrons in all corners of the globe so unwilling to engage the French".[2]

It is easier to reach the summit of power than to stay there. If the War of American Independence had ended with the surrender at Yorktown, the French Navy would have emerged from the conflict

[1] "The Battle that Set Us Free", by S. E. Morison, published in *Saturday Evening Post*, July 7th, 1956.
[2] *The United States and World Sea Power*, ed. Potter, published by Prentice Hall, 1955.

triumphant all along the line. But the war continued because France and Spain saw the opportunity to obtain their revenge for past defeats and to seize British possessions. De Grasse, having captured or recaptured a number of islands in the West Indies, sailed from Martinique on April 8th, 1782, with 35 warships, 6 frigates, and 150 store ships, with the intention of attacking Jamaica. However, Rodney appeared on the scene with 36 ships and 15 frigates. De Grasse ordered his store ships to make for Guadeloupe, and turned to engage part of Rodney's fleet, which was still dispersed. The French more than held their own, but then the luck turned against them. Two ships in the van had been considerably battered, and during the night another was damaged in a collision and had to be taken in tow. De Grasse refused to abandon these crippled ships, and so Rodney came up with him again on April 12th, in the channel between the islands of Dominica and Guadeloupe. The battle that followed takes its name from the Saints Islands, a small archipelago in the channel.

De Grasse was encumbered with the three damaged ships, and six others had been sent to guard the convoy, but the wind was in his favour and morale was high among his crews, due to the series of successes since leaving Brest the year before. Matters were going well for the French when, about mid-morning, the wind shifted four points to the south. This threw the French into some confusion, as they endeavoured to keep their proper stations. But gaps appeared in their line; and the British, who could now turn to starboard, sailed through them. Rodney broke the French line not far from the *Ville de Paris*, De Grasse's flagship, and was followed by the five ships immediately astern, all raking the French as they passed. A similar movement took place in the rear. The French line was thus broken into three, with the *Ville de Paris* and other ships of the centre being isolated. The action developed into a furious mêlée, with the British getting the best of it owing to their initiative and the more telling fire of their guns. Recent technical improvements in British gunnery had not so far been adopted by the French, and the firing from Rodney's ships was far more precise in its aim. The *Ville de Paris* was running short of powder and shot, too; and by five in the afternoon, assailed on all sides, her gunners were stuffing whatever came to hand into their muzzle-loaders, including the Admiral's silver. Instead of shifting his flag, De Grasse continued fighting his ship, putting up a most gallant defence until half past six, when he surrendered.

Four other French ships had struck their colours during the afternoon. However, this British victory of the Saints came too late to affect the result of the war. The Americans had obviously won, and a separate treaty between them and the British was being negotiated. A peace settlement was signed in November, 1782.

Rodney received a barony on his return to England, where his old enemy, De Grasse, was treated with every respect and sent to France with proposals for a peace treaty. The outcome was the Peace of Paris, signed in January, 1783.

General La Fayette was given a triumphal welcome on his return to France from America, but no thought was given to the sailors and sea-captains who had borne most of the burden of the war, and whose endeavours had enabled the military to bring it to a successful con-clusion. Not until a century and a half after the death of De Grasse was his name thought fit to be given to a French warship.[1] And the best biography of him was recently published, appropriately enough, by an American naval historian.[2]

[1] The *De Grasse* was on the slips at Lorient when the Germans invaded France in 1940, but she was still far from complete; because of this, she remained there through-out the war, miraculously escaping damage from Allied bombing. She was completed after the war, and put into commission as an anti-aircraft cruiser. The *De Grasse* took part in the U.S. Naval Review at Norfolk in 1957, in waters where the Admiral had so distinguished himself; and the ship's company visited Yorktown, seeing the com-memorative monument which bears the names of Washington, Rochambeau, and De Grasse too.

[2] *Admiral de Grasse and American Independence*, by Charles Lee Lewis, United States Naval Institute, Annapolis, 1945. My acknowledgements are due to this author, whose work has been of great help to me in writing this chapter.

XI

THE FIRST ACTIONS OF THE RUSSIAN NAVY

A Russian victory over the Turks, off Greece, with Scottish assistance (July 5-7th, 1770)—the Russo-Swedish War of 1788—the Swedish Fleet is defeated—an Admiral's gallant gesture brings disaster to the Russians—the last battle between galleys, in Svensksund fjord on July 9th, 1790.

IN 1768 Russia declared war on Turkey. Admiral Count Alexis Orloff received orders from Catherine the Great to sail for the Levant with the Kronstadt fleet. The Turks could not believe that the Russian ships would ever reach the Mediterranean, and so took no precautions. They were mistaken; Orloff set sail with twelve warships and twelve frigates, called in at Portsmouth—where friendly relations between Russia and Britain enabled him to take in fresh supplies—then crossed the Bay of Biscay, and so passed through the Straits of Gibraltar. He anchored for a time in the Balearics to allow crews and ships to recover from the long voyage.

The Mediterranean Powers were less enthusiastic about the venture, especially the Republic of Venice, whose ships were sent to deny the Russians access to the Adriatic. Orloff was not particularly concerned; he made for the Ionian Islands with his small fleet and established a base in the bay of Navarino, in March, 1770.

A one-time slave was then at the head of the Turkish Navy. Hassan, as he was called, had done so well in the service of the Dey of Algiers that the latter had made him Admiral. But as the result of a quarrel, he had offered his services to the Sultan, Mustapha III. Hassan was a redoubtable foe; and Orloff wrote to Catherine the Great expressing his concern. Catherine cast around for help, and sent Orloff another Russian admiral, Spiridoff, to assist him, and also two Scottish volunteers from the British Navy, Admiral Elphinstone and Commodore Greig.

During May, 1770, Hassan came through the Dardanelles with a squadron composed of 15 warships—one of them mounted 100 guns—8 galiots, 5 xebecs, and 2 corvettes. On July 5th he came upon the main body of the Russians, 10 warships and 5 frigates under Admiral Spiridoff, off the island of Chios. Hassan at once attacked Spiridoff's ship, the 108-gun *Rotislav*, and boarded her. So furious was the fight that both ships caught fire and blew up. Neither of the admirals, however, was injured.

The other ships on both sides had watched this single combat without much attempt to imitate it; and now its frightful end made such a fearful impression upon the Turkish squadron that Hassan broke off the action before nightfall, taking his ships to shelter in the Bay of Chesme.

The engagement ended in a British victory under the Russian flag! For the best means of attacking the Turks in their refuge was with fireships, and the Russians neither knew how to manage them nor, apparently, had any great desire to learn. This mattered little, as the British officers were quite prepared to take charge of the business; and Spiridoff had the good sense to leave it all to Elphinstone.

During the night the Russian ships took station outside the bay, to prevent any Turkish attempt to escape. Commodore Greig then took command of six ships to cover the assault of four fireships, which were in the charge of two more Scottish naval officers named Dugdale and Mackenzie. Three of the fireships went aground, however, because their terrified Russian crews jumped overboard before reaching the Turks. Considering what a dangerous business it was, one can hardly blame these Russian novices. But Dugdale succeeded in grappling the fourth to a Turkish ship, and in setting light to the "sausage".[1]

The fire spread from the one blazing ship to almost all those anchored in the bay, so close together were they, and only a 62-gun ship and a few hulks survived. Thus did a handful of Scottish volunteers enable the navy of Catherine the Great to gain its first major victory.

Admiral Orloff, encouraged by this success, might then have captured Constantinople. But the Turks there had a Frenchman in their service—De Tott was his name—who was as clever at building fortifications as Greig and Dugdale were adept at setting fire to ships at their moorings.

Nearly twenty years later, Russia was at war with another of her neighbours, one to the north this time: Sweden. The two navies were at almost equal strength in the Baltic; and each had British naval officers as trainers and advisers. Sidney Smith, who later distinguished himself during the British occupation of Toulon, was then with the Swedish Fleet; while Commodore Greig had become Admiral of the Russian fleet in the Baltic, but was killed at the siege of Sveaborg soon after the outbreak of hostilities.

[1] A fireship was usually a light vessel crammed with powder, resin, pitch, and other combustibles, all well moistened with turpentine; it was set on fire by means of a long "sausage" filled with saltpetre and powder. A captain of a fireship needed to have steady nerves and be very experienced at grappling enemy ships. As soon as the fireship was securely attached to her victim, the crew hurriedly got into a boat astern, the captain set a light to the "sausage", and everyone rowed for dear life. It was a speciality in which few of its practitioners lived to a ripe old age.

Though the galley had long disappeared from the fleets of the Western powers, it was still in service in the Baltic; and continued so until 1809. But the last occasion that two flotillas of galleys figured in a battle was during this Russo-Swedish War of 1788-90—2,270 years after Salamis.

In July, 1788, the Swedes sailed up the Gulf of Finland to attack St. Petersburg, but were intercepted by the Russians. The result was hardly favourable to the latter, yet they did succeed in saving their capital.

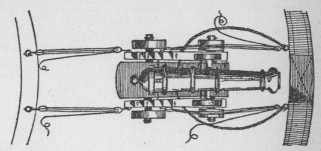

Eighteenth-century cannon with breeching to restrict the recoil, and tackle for return to firing-position

Two years later the Swedes appeared in the same waters in far greater strength. Prince Carl had 22 warships and 12 frigates under his orders, and King Gustavus III in person commanded the "oar-propelled fleet" comprising 19 transports, 27 galleys, and 236 gunboats. This numerous force had set out from Karlskrona on April 30th, 1790, and a fortnight later met with serious resistance from Russian ships under the command of the Prince of Nassau-Siegen. A Swedish warship was captured, and another sank during a gale. King Gustavus had nevertheless succeeded in forcing his way into Frederikshamen, seizing 29 Russian coasters and destroying the arsenal. He then put his troops ashore at Viborg, which was to be his base for operations against St. Petersburg.

Prince Carl should have made rendezvous at Viborg, but on June 3rd he was attacked by Admiral Kruse with 17 warships and 7 frigates from Kronstadt. It was an indecisive battle, though costly to both sides. Then Kruse was joined by 13 ships and 11 frigates under Admiral Tchitchagoff, which gave the Russians overwhelming superiority. Prince Carl considered himself fortunate to be able to reach Viborg and take shelter there.

The Russians blockaded the bay, and at the end of a month the Swedes were running short of food. An attempt to force the blockade

became imperative, and the Swedes began by sending down a fireship; but it was carried back by the current on to the vessel following, which caught fire and then·collided with a neighbouring frigate. Both vessels soon blew up, and the Swedish Fleet was thrown into tangled confusion. Several ships came into collision; others began firing at one another. Those which managed to extricate themselves had a hot reception from the Russian guns, and two of the Swedish ships-of-the-line were captured.

Such was the Battle of Viborg on July 3rd, 1790, at which the Swedish sailing fleet was practically wiped out, and which some historians have called "the Baltic Trafalgar". There was, however, a sequel to it a week later, when the Russians paid dearly for their earlier victory.

King Gustavus had taken advantage of the general confusion to escape from Viborg Bay with almost his entire force of galleys and other vessels, and they were sheltering in an arm of Svenksund fjord.

The Prince of Nassau was so elated by his recent victory that he expected to make short work of this flotilla—which consisted, nevertheless, of 195 vessels of various kinds, with 1,124 guns, and a fighting force of 14,000. But Nassau, counting his chickens before they were hatched, had accommodation prepared in his flagship for his prisoner-to-be, the King of Sweden. If only Nassau had attacked at once, before the Swedes had time to recover from their hurried flight! But instead he made the gallant gesture towards his Sovereign of waiting until her birthday, July 9th, before attacking the enemy, in order to present her with a victory on that day.

King Gustavus had made good use of the six days respite. His force

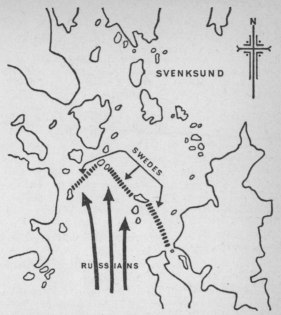

Svenksund, the last Battle of oar-propelled ships, July 9th, 1790

was in a strong position behind the low rocks in Svenksund fjord; and a deadly, concentrated fire took heavy toll of the Russian galleys, which advanced arrogantly to the attack without any thought of tactics or safety. This swaggering display cost them dear—9,500 in dead, wounded, or captured, and a third of their flotilla destroyed. The Swedes had fewer than three hundred casualties. The Prince of Nassau narrowly escaped the fate he had intended for the King of Sweden; as it was, his flag-captain was made prisoner.

This victory removed the threat of a Russian attack on Stockholm, and Sweden seized the opportunity to sign an honourable peace treaty, on August 14th, 1790.

Hostilities between the two countries broke out again in 1808, when oar-propelled galleys and gunboats were in action, in the headwaters of the Baltic, for the last time in history.

XII

THE GREAT NAVAL BATTLES OF THE NAPO-
LEONIC WARS

The new fleet of the French Revolution—the "Glorious First of June", and the legend of the Vengeur—*Jervis and the Spithead mutineers—Nelson's audacity at the Battle of Cape St. Vincent—Napoleon's army is conveyed to Egypt—the Battle of the Nile—the intercepted despatches.*

THE theorists of the French Revolution so undermined the authority of the regular navy officers and disheartened them, that three-quarters of those who had not been sent to the guillotine or hanged from lamp-posts either left the Service or emigrated. Then the same theorists suddenly woke up to the fact that they were at war with two of the greatest naval Powers of the time, Britain and Holland, and that they had no one to command what remained of Louis XVI's fine fleet. Thirty ships and twenty frigates were built—not before it was time! But who was there to take them into battle?

There was no lack of brave sailors prepared to die a hero's death. But naval battles are not won by being killed, rather by killing others. And, with very few exceptions, the new commanders of the Republican Navy knew little more than how to die fighting.

In such circumstances, how could the Republic undertake a well-planned naval campaign or defend its Colonies? All that the Convention dared ask of its navy in 1794 was to protect a grain convoy anxiously awaited from America. The shortage in France was due to a disastrous harvest brought about by political troubles and civil war as much as by bad weather.[1] On April 2nd, 1794, one hundred and seventeen cargo-ships had left Chesapeake Bay escorted by a small force under Rear-Admiral Vanstabel (two 74-gun men-of-war, two frigates and a brig); these were to be joined by five ships and a few frigates which sailed from Rochefort on May 6th, commanded by Rear-Admiral Nielly, recently promoted by the new régime—he had been a Sub-Lieutenant just before the Revolution! But this combined force would not be nearly enough if the British appeared on the scene—as they undoubtedly would.

[1] The convoy was supposed to bring more sugar than corn, but quite a lot of the sugar had been sold to pay for the long delay in harbour. What most interested the Convention, though naturally this was not divulged, was a group of rebels and witnesses of the revolt in San Domingo, who were being shipped to France to appear before the Revolutionary Tribunals.

Somehow or other, twenty-five ships were fitted out at Brest and their command was given to Captain Villaret de Joyeuse, promoted Rear-Admiral for the occasion by members of the Convention who were on mission at Brest. He replaced Vice-Admiral Morard de Galles, an old sea-dog whose fifteen battles and eight wounds had not saved him from prison. The new Admiral—"General Villaret", as he was called—was closely supervised aboard his 120-gun flagship, the *Montagne*, by a People's Commissary whose function was to see that the Convention's orders were carried out to the letter. This man, Jean Bon, who called himself Saint André—after a fashion of the time—had been a Calvinist minister; he now hunted down Royalist and Catholic officers "with the grim ferocity of a vendetta". When the guns roared, however, his ardour perceptibly diminished; and if scandal-mongers are to be believed he suddenly found imperative reasons for disappearing into the bowels of the ship, well away from the fire of British muskets.

Only one of the captains of the thirty-six warships engaged in protecting the grain convoy had been in command of a ship-of-the-line before 1789. The others had then been Lieutenants or Sub-Lieutenants, dockyard officers, master mariners, or skippers of coasters—there was even a seaman from the lower deck among them. Most had never sailed in squadron formation. They had to learn while in action, just as the gunners did—most of the latter being young recruits from the army, whom it had been thought fit to send to replace the regular gunners after the Quiberon insurrection.

Such were the men sent to fight the Channel fleet, which was led by Lord Howe, a veteran of sixty-eight who had commanded ships for half a century. Villaret had not been born when Howe won promotion to post-captain by a successful action against a superior enemy force. All his senior officers had won renown during the War of American Independence, while Revolutionary France had deprived itself of the services of the French captains who had fought against them. The proven worth and experience of the British constituted a severe handicap for the novices fighting under the new French flag.[1]

Lord Howe had been at sea since May 2nd. He had sailed from Spithead with a squadron of thirty-four ships to ensure the safe passage down-Channel of a large convoy destined for the East Indies. Once

[1] Only the *Montagne* was flying the Tricolour, for when Villaret's squadron sailed from Brest there had not been enough bunting available to supply new flags to all the ships. The decree making the Tricolour (three vertical bands of blue, white, and red) reglementary for the navy had only just been passed, on the First of Prairial (May 20th), 1794. But the fanatical Jean Bon had not even waited until then to hoist the new flag in Villaret's flagship. All the other ships fought under the white Bourbon flag with one quarter tricolour, which had been reglementary since 1791.

clear of the Channel, Howe had detached six ships to continue escorting the convoy, then headed into the Atlantic to seek the French grain
convoy. Meanwhile, Villaret had set out from Brest on May 16th,
which in itself was something of a triumph. Howe spent a week searching for him, but in vain, until put on his track by an American merchantman. Howe eventually sighted the French on May 28th, some
four hundred miles west of Ushant.

There were twenty-six ships in each squadron.[1] A fresh south-
westerly was blowing. The French, more or less in formation, were on
the port tack and in three columns when the British were sighted ahead
and to leeward, at about eight on the morning of May 28th. Villaret
had been informed of the convoy's position by a frigate from Nielly's
division three days earlier. Having the advantage of the wind, he endeavoured to draw the enemy away from the convoy's route by sailing
in the opposite direction to the rendezvous. With a rising wind and a
mounting sea, the French had some difficulty in getting into order of
battle, in line ahead; and in order to help matters, Villaret first cast on
the starboard tack, then half an hour later brought his line round
nearer the wind.

The task for Howe was straightforward enough; he had first to engage and destroy the French squadron, then nothing would be easier—
at least in theory—than to round up the defenceless convoy. His opening move was to detach a division of six ships under Rear-Admiral
Pasley in the 78-gun *Bellerophon* to attack the French rear.

When Pasley, hugging the wind, arrived within gunshot of the end
of the French line, he found that the 114-gun *Révolutionnaire*, Captain
Vandongen, which had been despatched by Villaret to aid the smaller
ships, was determined to carry out her task beyond the commander-in-
chief's wildest hopes. A duel between the *Révolutionnaire* and the *Bellerophon* began at six in the evening, and they pounded away at each other
to such effect that the British flagship had to draw off an hour or so
later. But by then five of her consorts, all 78-gun ships, had joined in
the attack on the *Révolutionnaire*, which was unable to run out her
lower-deck guns against the enemy to windward because of the heavy
seas. First her mizzen-yard went, then her fore-topsail-yard, and soon
she was lying helpless before the wind. Vandongen was killed at nine-
thirty; his First Lieutenant had already been badly wounded, so it was
the next senior officer, Renaudeau, who took over command. Then he,
too, was wounded, and handed over to Lieutenant Dorré. The deck
was littered with dead and wounded. Against such overwhelming
odds, the ship would certainly have fallen into the hands of the enemy;

[1] A ship from Nielly's division had joined Villaret at sea.

but Howe signalled to disengage. Dorre managed to make off towards the north-east with a following wind, but during the night both the mizzen- and main-masts went. Next day he had the luck to meet with two of Nielly's ships. One of these towed him into Aix roads, off Rochefort.

On the British side, the *Audacious* had to seek shelter at Plymouth, in almost as bad a condition as the *Révolutionnaire*. This first day of the running fight had ended without advantage to either side, but neither had been fully engaged. Villaret felt more confident, as he still had strength equal to the British.

All that night the two squadrons were about six miles apart, both on the starboard tack, with the French still to windward. Next morning, the 29th, Howe resumed his attack on the French rear. The *Queen Charlotte* succeeded in breaking their line, passing astern of the *Eole*, the sixth ship from the end, and so getting to windward of her. Four other British followed suit—the *Bellerophon*, the *Leviathan*, *Orion*, and *Barfleur*—cutting out the *Terrible*, the *Tyrannicide*, and the *Indomptable*, and engaging them closely. The French ships put up a determined resistance, but received a good deal more punishment than they inflicted. The *Tyrannicide* and the *Imdomptable* were reduced to their bottom masts, and had to be escorted from the scene of action by two consorts.

When the firing died away, towards five in the evening, Villaret had lost the advantage of the wind through protecting the withdrawal of his crippled ships to a friendly anchorage. This handicapped him for the fighting on the following days, as critics were quick to point out afterwards. Nevertheless, the French admiral's manoeuvre drew the enemy still farther away from the route of the convoy, which next day passed safely through the area of the earlier fighting.

On May 30th a sea mist gave the French time to reform. Nielly had joined with three ships, and another arrived from Cancale, near St. Malo. These reinforcements filled the gaps left by the previous day's battle, whereas there were quite half a dozen British in a damaged condition.

The sun was shining brightly on the morning of June 1st, and a fresh south-westerly had swept away the mist and whipped up the sea. Lord Howe, who might have been expected to be tired out, considering his age, suddenly recovered the dash and eagerness of his earlier days. At eight o'clock his whole squadron sailed in to the attack.

Howe had briefed his captains on his intention to pierce the centre of the French line, and left them full liberty to choose the most convenient enemy ship to attack. The British cut through the line without much difficulty, and there ensued a fierce, close engagement in which the faster succession of broadsides and more accurate fire of the British prevailed over the inexperience of the French gunners. Moreover, the British directed their fire at the hulls of the enemy instead of at sails and rigging, and this "shooting to sink" proved better policy than the

The French flagship, the *Montagne*, in action during "The Glorious First of June"

French "shooting to dismast". And while the battle was raging in the French centre and rear, the van remained regrettably aloof in spite of repeated signals from its commander-in-chief, which may not have been seen, however, because of the smoke from the gunfire.

Towards midday, the *Montagne*[1] managed to disengage from the persistent attacks of the *Queen Charlotte*, and Villaret was then able to take stock of the situation. A dozen of his ships were still in action, though nine of them were completely dismasted. He succeeded in saving five, and having them towed away by corvettes or frigates. But Howe cut him off from the other seven, six of which remained in British hands. The seventh, the *Vengeur du Peuple*, went down fighting; and the circumstances of her end were seized upon by the French régime to create a glorious legend—stories of heroism being badly needed to boost French morale at home.

[1] When she got back to Brest, the *Montagne* was found to have no less than 230 shot-holes in her hull above the water-line. Among the 300 dead and wounded on board was her flag-captain.

The strange thing is that the story was as readily accepted and applauded abroad as it was when described to the French Convention. The truth was that the *Vengeur*, Captain Renaudin, had put up a great fight in a duel with the *Brunswick*, whose starboard anchors had become firmly hooked in the other's hull. So closely were the two ships locked together that the *Brunswick*'s gunners had to widen their gunports; and the French lacked room to use their ramrods. The *Brunswick*'s masts went one after the other, and her captain was wounded.

The duel had been going on for three hours when the two ships suddenly parted company. But the *Vengeur* was no sooner free of the *Brunswick* than she found herself attacked at close range by the *Ramillies*, which poured a broadside into her. Riddled with shot, the *Vengeur* began to sink.

In those days, when a ship was obviously lost and incapable of further defence, there was no shame in surrendering in order for the surviving crew to be saved. The *Vengeur* struck her colours, and immediately every effort to save her crew was made by the enemy ships. But, badly damaged as these were, it took time to rescue them all; and the *Vengeur* went down while a hundred or so poor wretches were still on board—some of whom shouted *"Vive la République!"* as they disappeared beneath the waves.

It had indeed been an heroic fight, and there was no need for imaginary details to be added, as in Barère's vivid report to the French Assembly: the *Vengeur* had sunk three enemy ships before disappearing beneath the waves; the captain and the whole crew had gone down with the ship, flag flying and firing to the last. . . . So that when Captain Renaudin (who had certainly not been one of the last to leave the ship) returned to France from the English prison-hulks with some of his men, he was almost looked upon as a clumsy idiot who upsets an elaborate performing-trick.

Villaret might well have recovered the six captured ships if he had made the slightest attempt, for with eleven of his own in like bad shape Lord Howe was in no position to defend and tow them. But the French admiral was prevented from making any such move; when the action was broken off, Jean Bon recovered his wits and his authority, and reminded Villaret that the grain convoy was of primary importance.

The convoy reached port quite intact, anchoring in Brest roads on June 7th near Villaret's squadron, which had arrived the previous day. So the main object had been achieved; Howe had failed to capture the convoy, and the French could therefore claim a victory. However, when Howe returned with his six prizes he was received with wild rerejoicing; and this battle which is known in France merely as "the

Fight on the Thirteenth of Prairial" is celebrated in British naval history as "The Glorious First of June".

Nevertheless, it gave the Admiralty much food for thought. As neutral historians have noted, the French squadron had been competently directed and handled—far better than could have been expected in the circumstances prevailing. There might well have been no need to despair for the new Republican Navy if it had received the support and attention necessary. But France had eyes only for her armies. The result of neglecting her navy was soon to have dire consequences, at the time of General Bonaparte's expedition to Egypt in 1798.

Yet the French Navy still had some advantage over the British. The seeds of insubordination that had earlier affected French ships, were now germinating among British crews. On December 3rd, 1794, six months after "The Glorious First of June", there was mutiny in the *Culloden*, at Spithead, which took more than a week to quell. A few months later the whole fleet at Spithead refused to cast off moorings. The mutiny spread to the Nore, and even to units at sea. Whole divisions hoisted the red flag; blood was shed, for guns had to be brought to bear upon the mutineers in some ships. It was not unknown for crews to murder their officers and then take their ships over to the enemy. There was the instance in March, 1800 (which gives an idea of the length of the crisis), when the frigate *Danae* deserted her station with the blockading force outside Brest, the lower-deck having taken over the ship. However, when the men took her into the French port, expecting a triumphal reception, they were greatly disillusioned when the Naval authorities clapped them into irons and treated their officers with every consideration.

The mutinies in the English Fleet, unlike those that had occurred at Brest and at Toulon, were not a revolt against authority. Indeed, the British mutineers proclaimed themselves faithful and loyal subjects of the King. They were demanding improvements in their wretched conditions—and their grievances were very real.

Britain had been engaged in almost continuous war at sea for the past century, yet during that long period there had been no improvement in conditions for the lower-deck. It is difficult today to imagine how hard and wearing were the long cruises, for instance when keeping watch and ward off Brest or Toulon. The men's food and living conditions were bad; and although sailing in Mediterranean waters did not perhaps aggravate matters, it was very different when ships were pounded by the south-westerly gales sweeping across the Bay of Biscay.

No doubt the seamen gained much experience from sailing the rough seas and reef-strewn waters . . . but there were intolerable delays in their pay, which was in any case inadequate. It was often not received until the ship was laid up—and the men "paid off". A sailor wounded in action had no claim to any pay while unable to serve; and widows received at most one year of their husband's pay, and nothing further.

The morale of the British Navy was therefore very low just at the moment when the safety of the country depended on its fleet. Holland and Spain had made an alliance with the French Republic. The Spanish Navy, admittedly, was not what it had been. Nelson expressed himself in no uncertain terms on that subject: "The Dons make fine ships—they cannot, however, make men. . . . Their fleet has nothing but bad crews and officers who are still worse!" And again: "It is stated that Spain has agreed to supply the French Republic with fourteen ships-of-the-line ready to put to sea. I can only suppose that they are ships without crews; for to accept them with such a company would be the surest and quickest way for the Republic to lose them." There were in fact only sixty to eighty seamen in each Spanish ship, the rest of the crew consisting of peasants recently pressed into the service or convicts taken from the prisons.[1]

These circumstances should be borne in mind when considering the famous Battle of Cape St. Vincent on February 14th, 1797, when Admiral Sir John Jervis commanding the British Mediterranean squadron of fifteen ships defeated the Spanish who had twenty-seven. The Spanish admiral, Don Jose de Cordoba, was making for Cadiz when the British, sailing in two close columns of seven and eight, came upon him. The Spanish force was in loose formation, and the half a dozen ships in the van were far ahead of the rest.

"A victory is very essential to England at this moment," Jervis murmured to one of his captains when the Spanish were first sighted. Their numbers went on increasing. "Never mind," he exclaimed. "Even if there are fifty sail I will go through them!"

"Very good, Sir John," said the captain. "We'll give them a damned good licking!"

This was the spirit in which Jervis decided to cut through the huge gap in the Spanish fleet; and on his signal, the British moved into line formation with remarkable speed. Troubridge, in the *Culloden*, was the first to attack, heading straight for a three-decker; his First-Lieutenant, with the greatest respect, expressed some anxiety about the imminent collision. Troubridge kept on, and it was the enemy that swung away. Commodore Nelson, flying his pendant in the *Captain*, should have

[1] *French Naval Battles*, by O. Troude, Vol. III, p. 14.

tacked in succession. But, his ship being the last but two in the line, he could see that the leading ships would arrive too late to keep the gap open. Nelson at once wore the *Captain* out of the line, turning her before the wind in a direction heading at first away from the enemy; then, his movement completed, sped into the fast-closing gap, engaging half a dozen Spanish ships single-handed.

Jervis's flag-captain frowned on seeing this disregard of orders, and remarked upon it. "Yes," said the Admiral, "and if you always disobey orders in like manner, you'll be forgiven in advance."

For a short time, Nelson fought alone, but he was quickly supported by Troubridge and then by Collingwood, whose *Excellent* had been astern of Nelson and the last in the line. Collingwood took his ship between Nelson's and the *San Nicolas*, and ranged so close alongside the Spaniard that, to quote his own expression. "you couldn't have put a pin between them". As the *San Nicolas* retreated before his fire, she fell under the guns of one of her consorts. Nelson finally captured both. He himself was with the boarding party that took the *San Nicolas*. "And on the quarter-deck of a Spanish First-rate," he wrote in his memorandum of the battle, "extravagant as the story may seem, did I receive the Swords of the two vanquished Spaniards."

Four prizes in all were taken by the British. But the tangible result of this victory was as nothing compared with its psychological effect: British morale at home shot up.

Nelson was promoted to Rear-Admiral and made a Knight of the Bath. Jervis was created Earl of St. Vincent. The new peer had still a difficult task before him. From April, 1797, to May, 1799, he was blockading Cadiz with his creaking ships and weary crews, and the only reinforcements sent out to him were ships that had mutinied in home waters. Courts of enquiry were in almost continuous session, with the squadron lying not far from an enemy harbour! St. Vincent pursued his task with untiring vigour, but he was often sick at heart and discouraged. "Why do they go on sending me these shiploads of mutineers? Do they take me for the fleet's executioner?"

Even so, he forged from this weary fleet a tool for victory. He heard of French preparations at Toulon. For the past two years the Royal Navy had been driven from one Mediterranean base after another by Bonaparte's conquest of Italy. The British admiral decided to send a dozen ships into the Mediterranean, and gave the command to the young Rear-Admiral who had lost his right eye in the siege of Calvi in 1794 and his right arm in the assault on Santa Cruz, in the Canaries, in July, 1797.

A man lacking one eye and one arm . . . but certainly not lacking in moral fibre! By his daring action at the Battle of the Nile he was soon to regain naval supremacy in the Mediterranean for his country—which she was to maintain until the Second World War.

The expedition being prepared at Toulon was undoubtedly the most amazing and wildest of all that Napoleon conceived. He had shelved the idea of invading England, because he lacked the sea-power, and was instead mustering a force of thirty thousand to invade and conquer Egypt, and then attack British interests east of Suez, possibly even India.

He swept aside all objections and difficulties. Transports were to be requisitioned in conquered Italy; escort ships could be provided from the Eastern Mediterranean squadron—the few, that is, which had escaped destruction by the British at Toulon in December, 1793—and from those in ports along the Italian Riviera. The sum total was thirteen ships and half a dozen frigates, "old and rotting, not even able to support the firing of their own guns if it became at all heavy". In fact, some of the guns had to be unshipped, as it was doubtful whether the decks would continue to bear their weight. The crews were not much better than the ships. A report made a few days before the battle, while the fleet was moored in Aboukir Bay, said that "On the whole our ships are very poorly manned, and in my opinion it needs much courage to command such an ill-prepared fleet."

The seamen of the Republic were badly fed, badly paid, and were without even a change of clothes. Admiral Sercey, writing in 1796, complained that his men had to go naked while they washed their clothes. Five years later, similar conditions still existed; in 1801 the captain of the *Sans Pareille* gave as an excuse for the poor showing of his men under fire that "they were all wet through after twenty-eight hours with nothing to change into, for I could only get ten lots of spare clothes for the whole crew".

The Toulon squadron was commanded by Pierre Martin. At forty years of age he had been a naval officer without a future when "elected" Rear-Admiral by the People's Representatives at Fort National (Fort de France), the capital of Martinique. The Paris Convention had not made a bad choice in appointing him to the Toulon command, for he was not without firmness and skill, and had held his own against a British squadron off Corsica in 1795. It was a misfortune for the French, however, that he should have failed to intercept four British ships in the Gulf of Genoa, that same year, for one of the four was the 64-gun *Agamemnon*, Captain Horatio Nelson.

Pierre Martin, however, was not liked by Truguet, the new Minister of Marine appointed by the Directory. Martin was relieved of his command and replaced by François Paul Brueys d'Aigalliers. The new commander had been a mere lieutenant in 1789, but the dearth of naval officers due to the Revolution had brought him promotion to flag rank, although he was in no sense qualified to lead a squadron, especially against Nelson; yet his courage was equal to the Englishman's, as was to be shown by his heroic death in action. Brueys had come to the notice of the young General Bonaparte at Ragusa, during the Italian campaign, and the General had praised him highly to the Directory. He could not have been a bad organizer, for he achieved the feat of escorting the four hundred troop transports safely to Egypt. He sailed from Toulon on May 19th, 1798, captured Malta, just missed being sighted by Nelson, who was searching for him all over the Eastern Mediterranean (neither knew they had been so close at the time), and on July 1st arrived at Alexandria. Nelson had looked in there two days before, and then left to seek the French elsewhere—in the direction of Constantinople!

Three weeks later, Napoleon won the Battle of the Pyramids and made himself master of Egypt. But he was not sufficiently aware of the vital importance to him of even a third-rate fleet. He gave no further thought to it, beyond ordering Brueys to return to Alexandria; the execution of the order was left entirely to him.

Now Brueys was haunted by a fear of running aground. There was little likelihood of it, as his largest ship only drew twenty-two feet, and nowhere in the harbour of Alexandria was there less than twenty-seven feet of water. However, he preferred the more doubtful shelter of the anchorage at Aboukir, about nine leagues east of Alexandria.

Aboukir Bay extends in a large semi-circle from Aboukir Point to the Rosetta mouth of the Nile. The coast shelves very gradually, so that Brueys had to moor his squadron three miles from the shore. The only natural protection was the small island of Aboukir a few cable-lengths off the western tip of the bay, and some rocks and sandbanks.

The squadron anchored in a single line with the van headed towards Aboukir island. The 74-gun ships, *Guerrier*, *Conquérant*, *Spartiate*, *Peuple Souverain*, and *Aquilon*, formed the van, with the 80-gun *Franklin* wearing the flag of Rear-Admiral Blanquet du Chayla. Then came Brueys's flagship, the powerful 120-gun *Orient*, seventh in the line of thirteen, followed by the 80-gun *Tonnant* and the 74-gun ships, *Heureux* and *Mercure*.

The rear, commanded by Villeneuve in the *Guillaume Tell*, included the *Généreux* and the *Timoléon*.

Four frigates of 36 to 40 guns, the *Diane, Justice, Arthémise*, and *Sérieux*, commanded by Rear-Admiral Decrès, were moored inshore of the larger ships.

Brueys was so haunted by the fear of running aground that he had given himself a generous margin of safety. Far too generous a measure,

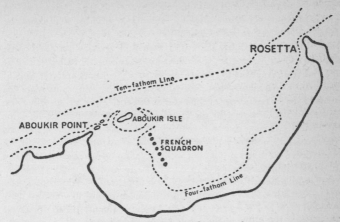

Aboukir roads. French squadron at anchor

as events were to prove; the *Guerrier* could have been much nearer the island, and the whole line a good thousand yards farther inshore.

As was to be expected, it was not long before Nelson learnt of the French landing in Egypt. Brueys was well aware that the British admiral would not rest until discovering his whereabouts even if it meant exploring every harbour along the coast. All that Brueys could do was to arrange to give him a suitable reception.

But the French could not agree among themselves, and the councils held by Brueys were remarkably similar to those of Quieret, Béhuchet, and Barbavera just before the Battle of Sluys. Brueys, who had never commanded a squadron in battle, could not see that his best chance was to take the initiative instead of waiting passively in the bay. Du Chayla urged on him the advantage of choosing the place and time of battle, of trying to take the enemy by surprise, and having the wind in his favour. Du Chayla was one of the most experienced officers in the fleet, with twenty-three years service at sea; he had taken part in thirteen battles and been wounded several times. "Our only chance is to fight under sail," he declared. And the captain of the *Tonnant*,

Dupetit-Thouars, backed him up. "We've no hope if we wait for Nelson in this awkward situation. We must weigh at once!"

Brueys did not know what to do. His Chief-of-Staff, Gauteaume, held the entirely opposite view; he pointed out the bad state of the ships and how impossible it was for them to fight on the open sea—which was true enough. Finally, Brueys decided to remain on the defensive. If they had to fight, it would be while at anchor; they would be prepared, but would not seek battle.

It would be thought, therefore, that they quickly installed some shore batteries, or at least made a strong-point of Aboukir Island. But all that was done was to mount five or six 6-pounders and a couple of mortars on the island—not enough even to command the passage between it and the *Guerrier* at the head of the line. The days sped by. The squadron was lying so far off-shore that getting supplies to the ships presented quite a problem. Every day there was much ferrying of boats between ships and shore, in search of food and water. Almost half the crews were occupied in digging wells or going as far as Rosetta in the hope of obtaining supplies of food.

Then the inevitable occurred. Nelson appeared off Alexandria, saw there was a bustle of transports in the harbour, but no warships, and scouted eastward in search of them. At one in the afternoon of August 1st, 1798, the lookout in the *Heureux* signalled a dozen sail to the north-north-west. It was the British squadron in line ahead, under full canvas with a following wind. The afternoon was fine and sunny, the sea barely ruffled by the freshening wind.

Brueys sent a couple of gunboats on reconnaissance. It was rather late to think of that; for the past three weeks no guard frigates had been sent out. Brueys hurriedly had hawsers slung between the ships to deter the enemy from breaking through the line. Pinnaces were sent off, to bring back as many men as possible from the working parties ashore; but more than four thousand men did not reach their ships in time, and were sorely missed.

Neither Nelson nor his captains were well acquainted with the coast, and the charts they had were not very good. But Nelson reasoned that where there was room for an enemy to swing at moorings there was room for him to pass. Hood in the *Zealous* led the line, and kept sounding as he stood in. The *Goliath* passed between the *Guerrier* and Aboukir Island, and was followed to an inshore position by the *Zealous* and the *Theseus*. The *Audacious* penetrated the French line from seaward, passing between the first two ships of the van. Nelson in the *Vanguard* attacked the French from the seaward side, followed by the rest of the squadron, though Troubridge's *Culloden* ran aground.

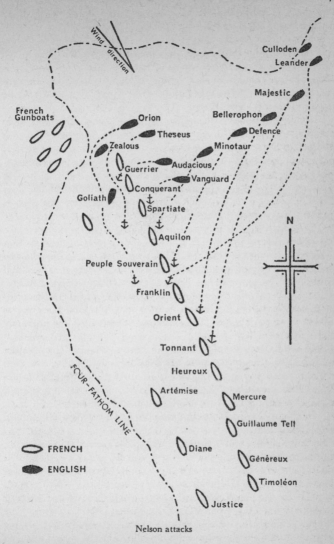

Wind direction

Culloden
Leander

Majestic

French
Gunboats

Orion
Theseus
Zealous
Minotaur
Bellerophon
Defence
Guerrier
Audacious
Vanguard
Conquerant
Goliath
Spartiate

N

Aquilon

Peuple Souverain

Franklin

Orient

Tonnant

FOUR-FATHOM LINE

Heuroux
Artémise
Mercure
Guillaume Tell
Diane
Généreux
Timoléon
Justice

⬭ FRENCH
⬬ ENGLISH

Nelson attacks

Troubridge was furious at being out of the action, for he did not manage to refloat his ship until the following morning. But at least he served as a marker-buoy and so saved others from his own misfortune.

It was five-thirty in the afternoon when Nelson signalled for close action. The small guns mounted on Aboukir Island had no effect on the British manoeuvre, their shot falling short of the ships passing to leeward of the *Guerrier*. She and the next in line, the *Conquérant*, bore the full brunt of the British van. They were attacked on both sides at once, yet had barely enough men to fire the guns on one side; and their anchored consorts were unable to give them any assistance.

The leading British ships had anchored by the stern, and were directing a devastating fire upon the two Frenchmen. The *Guerrier* was soon dismasted by the *Zealous* but she fought on until nine o'clock before surrendering. The *Conquérant*, after being attacked by the *Goliath*, was given a broadside by the *Orion* and then by the *Theseus* as they passed inshore, was raked by the *Audacious* as that ship crossed her bows, and in less than a quarter of an hour was put out of action.

In the meantime the British had brought pressure to bear on the French centre from the seaward side. The *Bellerophon* and the *Majestic* opened fire on the massive *Orient*, but the first was so roughly handled by the French flagship that she cut her cables and began to drift slowly down the French line. The *Tonnant*, the *Heureux*, and the *Mercure* in turn subjected her to fierce fire, hoping to finish what the *Orient's* gunners had so well begun. The *Bellerophon's* masts went one after the other; her captain was wounded, and he shouted that he surrendered.[1] But the ship continued drifting until she was out of range. The *Majestic* was dismasted too, and her captain was killed.

The *Alexander* had in the meantime penetrated the French line between the *Orient* and the *Tonnant*, and anchored inshore, sending broadside after broadside into the flagship, which was soon reduced to a shambles. Brueys had been wounded twice and was almost cut in half by a cannon-ball, but refused to be taken below to the cockpit. "A French admiral dies giving orders."

If only he had been able to give orders to the rest of his squadron! "For four fatal hours the rear had seen nothing but the fire and smoke of the battle. It had remained at its moorings without firing a shot, waiting for signals that were not made, for the Commander-in-chief had long lost the power to make his desires known."[2]

Yet what orders could Brueys have given to his rear? Placed as they

[1] Clowes asserts that it is not true. "There is no evidence that anyone in this ship ever thought of surrendering—but obviously the crew was making a lot of noise!" (*op. cit.* Vol. IV, p. 366).
[2] Diary of Rear-Admiral Decrès, commander of the frigates.

were to leeward of the battle, how could Villeneuve's ships "moored by two large anchors, a small one and four cables, have weighed and tacked about to get within range of the fighting before the ships engaged had been disabled ten times over?"[1] Villeneuve was later accused of looking on while the other ships were battered and destroyed. But if he had weighed, and the wind and current had carried him still farther from the battle, he would have been accused of flight. The only way of bringing the squadron together, to present a unified defence, was for the ships engaged to cut their cables and drift down towards Villeneuve's division. That was what Captain Racord in the *Peuple Souverain* did in order to give assistance to the *Orient*, to leeward of him. But this movement left a gap in the line, ahead of the *Franklin*, into which the *Leander* placed herself. The *Franklin* was soon beset by five ships, all firing at close range. Her captain, Du Chayla, was wounded in the head and lost consciousness. When he came round, the *Franklin* was no longer firing. On asking the reason, he was told that only three guns were still serviceable. "Never mind, go on firing," he said. "The last shot may be the one to bring victory."

Night was falling. All the ships of the van were out of the action. The *Peuple Souverain* and then the *Conquérant* had struck their colours, half their crews being killed or wounded. The *Spartiate*, third in the line, had put up a great fight against the *Vanguard*. "Her captain, Emeriau, directed his broadsides with the utmost effect," wrote Guérin, the historian. "They caused havoc on the enemy's decks." Nelson felt the effect of it. He was hit in the forehead by a piece of iron-shot and the skin hung down over his blind eye. It was thought in the *Vanguard* that he would stay below, but once the wound had been dressed he made his way back to the quarter-deck. The *Spartiate* was soon overwhelmed; with forty-nine shot-holes below the water-line on the port side, and twenty-seven on the starboard side, she was taking water everywhere. Her powder-magazines were flooded, the guns were put out of action one after the other. When her captain was finally forced to surrender, Nelson refused to take the sword of such a brave opponent. "Return it to him," he told the officer who brought it. "He has used it so well."

The drama in the *Orient* went on until far into the night. Most of her guns were out of action, and in any case only enough unwounded men were left to serve the stern guns. Then the rigging caught fire; the enemy ships drew off, closed their gun-ports, and hastily assembled buckets of sea-water on their decks. The *Orient*'s First-Lieutenant had ordered the powder-magazines to be flooded—but too late. At about ten o'clock a terrific explosion shook the air, and the great ship

[1] Letter from Villeneuve to Du Chayla, November 12th. 1800.

vanished beneath the waves, taking with her the unfortunate Admiral, the captain, Luz de Casabianca, and his ten-year-old son, and most of the officers and crew. The shower of burning debris caused small fires on two British ships. The shock was so great that firing ceased and a strange silence fell upon the scene of the battle.

The *Franklin* had lost first her main-mast, then her mizzen-mast; and when Du Chayla struck his colours, towards midnight, only about a quarter of the crew was still uninjured. The soft Egyptian night continued to be lit by the flash of guns. Nelson had earlier ordered his ships to make ready four horizontal lanterns at the mizzen peak, to avoid them fouling or firing on each other. The British wasted not a shot, always finding a target amid the glare of the blazing French ships. Only the *Tonnant*, razed to her deck and low in the water, was still firing. Her captain, Dupetit-Thouars, was still frenziedly urging on his men from the quarter-deck. His right and then his left arm had been hit, and another shot took away a leg. But even that did not silence him. To arrest the bleeding he had himself placed in a tub of bran, and continued shouting his orders; the last, just before he died, was to direct the colours to be nailed to the mast and to scuttle the ship rather than surrender.

So died Aristide Aubert Dupetit-Thouars at the age of thirty-eight, in what British historians have called one of the most outstanding episodes in a day which saw so many acts of heroism.

At two in the morning the *Mercure* and the *Heureux* had to be beached, and two British ships slipped into the gap and began to bombard Villeneuve's division; his ships had still not moved, and this was the only time they became involved in the battle. Dawn on August 2nd revealed the French squadron as smouldering hulks at their moorings or gone aground. During the night, Decrès's frigates had managed to stand out to sea, but the *Arthémise* had gone aground and the *Sérieux* had been sunk by a British ship. Two of Villeneuve's ships had also escaped, but the third—the *Timoléon*—had broken her fore-mast, been beached and set on fire by her crew. Only the gallant *Tonnant* was still flying the French colours. She had reached a less-exposed position by her crew hauling on the cables. Lieutenant Briard, who had succeeded to her command on the death of the senior officers, rejected a demand for surrender. The *Theseus* and the *Leander* then battered her into subjection. But first the crew carried out the last wishes of Dupetit-Thouars and committed his body to the deep before giving up the struggle.

Villeneuve's two ships and the two surviving frigates safely reached Corfu, then sailed for Malta. On the way, they intercepted the *Leander*, which was taking despatches from Nelson announcing the victory. After a sharp engagement, the *Leander* was captured.[1]

The Battle of the Nile was a heavy defeat for the French. They had lost eleven out of the thirteen major ships. Their casualty figures were 1,700 dead, 1,500 wounded, and 3,000 were prisoners. Whereas the British had 288 killed and 677 wounded, and had not lost a single ship.

The strategical consequence of the destruction of the French Mediterranean squadron was that Napoleon's army could not return to France; nor, with its lines of communication cut, could it advance farther east from Egypt. Napoleon himself was lucky enough to slip through the British blockade in the *Muiron*, which landed him at Fréjus on September 9th, 1799.[2]

The final word to the Battle of the Nile was given some eighteen months later, when the *Guillaume Tell* tried to escape from Malta, which was closely blockaded by the British. The *Guillaume Tell* had been Villeneuve's flagship, but Decrès was commanding her when, at eleven on the night of March 30th, 1800, she slipped out to sea with a strong wind blowing from the south. Immediately set upon by a 44-gun frigate, then by a 64- and an 86-gun ship, Decrès fought valiantly from midnight until half past eight in the morning before being forced to surrender. His ship was completely dismasted, but he had meted out such punishment to his opponents that neither of the two ships was in a fit state to secure the *Guillaume Tell*, and it was the frigate that towed her into Syracuse. Clowes has given the following account of the end of the engagement:

"At half past six the *Guillaume Tell* lost her main and fore-masts, and the *Foudroyant* (British), having cleared away the rigging cluttering her deck, resumed the action. At eight o'clock the Frenchman's mizzen-mast came down; at eight-twenty, with the 80-gun *Foudroyant* on her starboard quarter, the 64-gun *Lion* to port, and the *Penelope* close under her bows, the *Guillaume Tell* struck her colours after a most magnificent defence which had lasted nearly eight hours."[3]

---

[1] Nelson had sent off two sets of despatches. The other was safely carried to Naples by the brig *Mutine*, and this was the means by which news of the triumph was spread through Europe. (*Tr.*)

[2] Captain Muiron had sacrificed his own life to save Napoleon's at the fight for the bridge at Arcole, during the Italian campaign. Napoleon had renamed this frigate, captured during the campaign, after his saviour.

[3] *Op. cit.*, Vol. IV, p. 424.

XIII

COPENHAGEN, THE BATTLE WHERE DIS-OBEDIENCE PAID

The League of Armed Neutrality—the Freja *incident—Nelson versus Parker—a fortunate change of wind—Nelson attacks the Danish line (April 2nd, 1801)—the commander-in-chief is anxious—"I really do not see the signal"—an unnecessary battle.*

THE heartening news of the Nile victory had been received with every satisfaction in England, but there were nevertheless some spiteful or jealous tongues to point out that Nelson had really been very lucky. Astonishing as it may seem from this distance of time, Nelson's reputation was finally established among his contemporaries by a victory against ships of a country that was not at war with Britain, and which represented no military danger for her. A victory in a battle which, moreover, proved to have been unnecessary, for the British obtained satisfaction through diplomatic channels soon afterwards. And a victory that was won in circumstances bordering on indiscipline!

This Battle of Copenhagen [1] is so often mentioned by naval historians because of the famous incident when Nelson disobeyed his cautious commander-in-chief's signal, in order to continue and win the battle.

Some British naval historians, perhaps with the desire to prevent over-zealous Royal Navy captains from believing they may do as they please about their commander-in-chief's signals, have advanced the theory that Nelson did not really disobey Sir Hyde Parker's signal to break off the action, as it was not an order but merely gave an excuse to retreat to captains whose ships were in difficulties. But Nelson himself destroyed all basis to such a theory by his remark to the officers who drew his attention to the signal that was being flown. "I have only one eye—I have a right to be blind sometimes." Then, putting the glass to his blind eye, he exclaimed, "I really do not see the signal!"

Neutral shipping usually feels some repercussions of naval warfare between great powers. One has only to think of the number of innocent cargo ships that were sent to the bottom during the two World Wars.

[1] There was another Battle of Copenhagen in 1807, when the British destroyed the Danish Fleet to prevent it giving aid to Napoleon—much as they destroyed the French Mediterranean fleet in 1940, to prevent it giving aid to Hitler.

In earlier times, it was not submarines that they had to fear, but corsairs, or ships of the warring Powers who claimed the right to search their cargoes, and under this well-worn pretext took them into port, often holding them indefinitely on some trumped-up charge.

The maritime nations of northern Europe—the Baltic countries—became exasperated over this interference with their shipping, and in 1780—during the War of American Independence—formed the League of Armed Neutrality. This was revived during the Napoleonic Wars, when the neutral countries realized the profits to be made from evading the British blockade and running cargoes into French ports. Their merchant ships were given armed escort, which naturally brought about dangerous incidents—such as that off Ostend on July 25th, 1800, when the Danish frigate *Freja*, escorting six merchantmen, refused a British request to heave to and allow the cargo ships to be searched. The British had five warships, so the *Freja* had no chance in the fight that ensued. Denmark made a strong protest; and the British Government—which had been involved in more than one incident of this kind—thought it wise to send Lord Whitworth on a diplomatic mission to Copenhagen, but accompanied by a squadron of ten warships.

Ten were too many for a diplomatic mission; and too few for a demonstration of force, as the Danish Fleet was twice as strong. All that Whitworth succeeded in obtaining was agreement from the Danes to take part in a conference to study the means of applying the right to search, provided that Britain agreed to pay reparations for the damage caused to the *Freja* and the merchantmen she had been escorting.

But a year later, nothing had been settled; on the other hand, Russia had formed with Prussia, Sweden, and Denmark a new Armed League of neutrals. This time, the British Government decided to make a real demonstration of force, and on March 12th, 1801, sent Sir Hyde Parker to the Baltic with twenty-one ships-of-the-line and thirty smaller vessels.

Parker had been a dashing frigate captain during the War of American Independence, but with the passing years he had become prudent and cautious. So he was given Nelson as his second-in-command. If matters went well, the Admiral would bring the moderation of age to the discussions; if action became necessary, Nelson would provide the energetic leadership.

The two were vastly different in character, as soon became evident. Parker saw only difficulties. He hung about in the North Sea for a week, worried over the long dark nights and the ice-floes in the Baltic; while Nelson was seething with impatience, and urged his chief to enter the

Baltic before the Russian and Swedish Fleets joined the Danish. Eventually, on March 21st, the British Fleet dropped anchor in the Kattegat, about eighteen miles above Kronenburg and the narrow entrance to the Sound; and Parker waited to hear from Vansittart, whom the Foreign Office had sent ahead of the fleet with instructions to allow Denmark forty-eight hours to withdraw from the Northern Coalition, or else take the consequences. Parker learnt on the 23rd that the terms had been rejected, and that Copenhagen was feverishly strengthening its defences. Over a week went by, however, before Parker decided to weigh and pass into the Sound. A fresh north-west wind on March 30th gave every help. Nelson was commanding the van in the 74-gun *Elephant*, a ship that was better suited than his 98-gun *St. George* for manoeuvring in the shallow and tricky waters ahead.

The Danish fortress at Kronenburg opened fire on the ships as they passed, but they were out of range, keeping well over to the Swedish shore; and the batteries there, at Helsingborg, remained silent. The missiles from the British bomb-ships, however, inflicted considerable damage to the shore batteries and caused a number of casualties.

Copenhagen stands on the east coast of the island of Zealand and is protected by the islet of Amager from approach by sea. The straits are divided by a shoal called the Middle Ground, and are narrowed even more by the sandbanks along each shore. The two channels, the Kongedyb and the Hollaensdyb, give no room for a ship to tack, and Nelson's ships could only negotiate these narrow waters one at a time, in line ahead. In other words an enemy squadron would seem to have little chance of success against the Danes, especially as their ships obviously had no intention of leaving their moorings.

The Danes had eighteen ships and floating batteries concentrated in a line extending from Amager islet to the great Trekroner fort commanding the entrance to the harbour of Copenhagen. This line was about two miles long and was supplemented at the southern end by batteries mounted on Amager itself. There were a few frigates and fireships at the entrance to the harbour, under the protection of the guns of the citadel.

This description of the Danish defences brought back by Vansittart had given Sir Hyde Parker much to think about, and at the council of war held in the *London* most members were inclined to abandon the operation. Nelson was not one of them. But he had a difficult and delicate task—to avoid offending his irresolute superior, yet dissipate an atmosphere of gloom and rouse the ardour of the younger captains, some of whom did not conceal their jealousy of him. Instead of the "band of brothers" of the Battle of the Nile, Nelson was faced by men

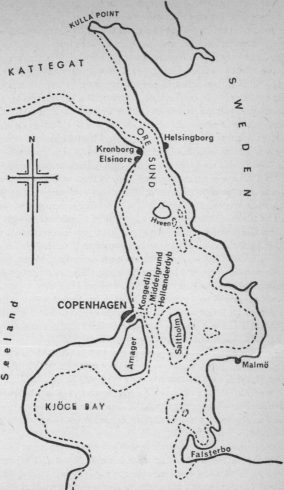

The approaches to Copenhagen (April 2nd, 1801)

who still thought of him as the Earl of St. Vincent's favourite. It could be said that Nelson had to win a psychological battle in his own camp before engaging in the real fight.

However, he carried opinion with him, and by midday on the 30th the whole fleet had passed the Elsinore batteries and anchored in the lee of the little Swedish island of Hveen, in the middle of the Sound and about fifteen miles above Copenhagen. Towards nightfall, Sir Hyde, Nelson, Rear-Admiral Thomas Graves (Nelson's second-in-command), and the Captain of the fleet, made a reconnaissance of the Danish line of defence in a schooner. Parker returned looking despondent. The defences were formidable. Another council was held, at which opinions were again divided. Then Nelson proposed that he should lead a detachment of ten ships-of-the-line, some frigates, and other small vessels in a tactical assault on Copenhagen. To this, Parker agreed; and Nelson hastened to make a closer examination of the whole Danish position. It was a wise precaution, for the Danes had removed all the buoys! Those of Nelson's officers most skilled in surveying employed most of the night in laying down fresh buoys. Nelson's plan was to pass along the Outer Deep with his detachment, gain the southern end of the Middle Ground, then return by the Kongedyb or King's Deep to attack the line of Danish ships, which were more vulnerable than the Trekroner fort. But he would have to anchor off the southern end of the Middle Ground until a change of wind enabled him to carry out the assault. Parker would remain in reserve to the north of the Middle Ground, some six miles above Copenhagen—a position the whole fleet had reached on March 31st. There was little Parker could do to help, for most of his ships were of deep draught. He not only left all the tactical details to Nelson, but generously gave him two more line-of-battle ships.

Nelson accomplished the first part of his design on April 1st. The wind being still in the north-west, he weighed at one o'clock that afternoon and by five the *Elephant* and the other eleven ships, the frigates, bomb- and gun-vessels, some thirty in all, were safely anchored to the southward of the Middle Ground. With the wind in its present quarter, there was no possibility of tacking up the narrow King's Channel, especially at night. But was there enough depth of water to sail up it at all? Nelson was not sure until eleven that night, when Captain Hardy —who was flag-captain in Nelson's *St. George* but had asked to be allowed to accompany him on this adventure—returned in a rowing-boat from taking soundings, having actually been round the outermost Danish ship, the *Provesteen*.

Fortune favours the brave. The wind changed round during the night, and was blowing from the south-east at daybreak on April 2nd. It was a fair wind to take Nelson's ships north, and all passed into the King's Channel except two that failed to clear the Middle Ground and got stuck on the west side. The action began as soon as the leading ship

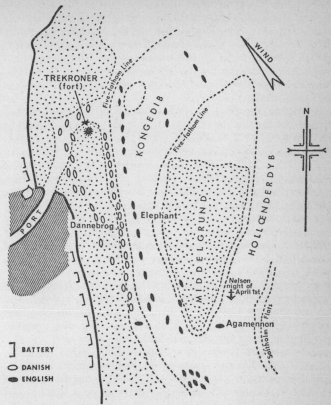

Positions of English and Danish fleets (from Clowes's *History of the Royal Navy*)

was within range of the *Provesteen*, and continued with great violence for three hours. The Danes put up a fierce and determined resistance. At one o'clock all their batteries were still in action, while three British ships stuck on the Middle Ground had hoisted distress signals.

Sir Hyde Parker had weighed at the same time as Nelson, but wind and current prevented him from giving direct support. He was in the worst of situations for a commander-in-chief—near enough to know that all was not going well, yet too distant to follow the intricacies of the fighting; and in any case unable to give any aid. So it was that Signal No. 39 was made—to discontinue action—and was received by Nelson in the manner already described. He still had No. 16, for close action, hoisted in his flagship, the *Elephant*, and kept it flying. He merely acknowledged his commander-in-chief's signal, but did not repeat it. Those of his captains who could see the *London*'s signal acted according to the situation they were in; only those in very real difficulties hauled off, while the others continued in action, like Nelson . . . fortunately, for soon afterwards the Danish fire weakened and some of their ships struck their colours.

Nevertheless, the situation was most confused. The ships that had struck were being fired at by shore batteries, and there was spasmodic fire from the ships themselves whenever British boats approached; other ships were on fire, and rescuers were being hampered by shots from the shore. "Either I must send on shore and stop this irregular proceeding," Nelson exclaimed, "or send in our fireships and burn them." He thereupon wrote a note to the Prince of Denmark, suggesting that firing should cease, otherwise "Lord Nelson will be obliged to set on fire all the floating batteries he has taken, without having the power of saving the brave Danes who have defended them." The note was headed "To the brothers of Englishmen, the Danes." It was delivered under a flag of truce by one of Nelson's staff. He was back at three o'clock, accompanied by the Danish Adjutant General, who wished to know more of Nelson's intention in sending the letter. Nelson sent another messenger ashore to explain that his only aim was to save human lives, and that any further negotiation should be conducted with his commander-in-chief, whose flagship could be seen four miles away and who alone had power to conclude an armistice.

The firing ceased. It was a good thing that it did, for although Nelson's ships had inflicted great damage on the enemy, they had suffered much themselves. The shore batteries and the guns of the Trekroner fort were still capable of battering any ship that came within range. Nelson had been fortunate; if the Danes had refused to negotiate, he would have found it difficult to extricate his squadron. As it was, his most damaged ships were able to withdraw while Sir Hyde Parker was arranging a continuance of the armistice with the Danish envoy.

Next day, the armistice was formally ratified. The battle had taken a heavy toll, and the casualties were high. The British had 350 killed, and some 6,000 Danes were dead, wounded, or prisoners. More than half of the Danish fleet had been destroyed or taken as prizes by the

British. And not long afterwards it was learnt that the battle had been unnecessary; for belated news arrived of the murder on March 24th of Paul, Czar of Russia, who had been the leader of the Northern Coalition. His successor, Alexander I, soon reversed the pro-French policy of his government.

XIV

THE CAMPAIGN OF TRAFALGAR

Napoleon threatens to invade England, and plans the naval campaign like a military one—Pierre Villeneuve, the new French Vice-Admiral, gives Nelson the slip—the "Fifteen-Twenty" battle off Finisterre—Napoleon is furious—Villeneuve gives his successor the slip—Trafalgar, and the death of Nelson (October 21st, 1805)—the gale after the battle brings destruction to victors and defeated alike—the unsolved mystery of Villeneuve's death.

IT was a fine, calm October day, and the north-west breeze was barely enough to fill the sails of the Franco-Spanish Fleet that had left Cadiz the evening before and was now making for the Straits of Gibraltar. A swell was already causing the ships' timbers to creak, presaging the gale which would be on the fleet by nightfall. But there was more than a gale blowing up for Vice-Admiral Villeneuve, the commander-in-chief of the fleet. . . . The reefs of Cape Trafalgar could be seen on the port bow, ten or twelve miles to the south-east. . . .

On this twenty-first of October, 1805, one sharp naval action was soon to bring to a conclusion a drama which had been played out over several years—ever since the young French Republic had declared war on England and decided to invade her.

It was in 1798 that the Directory, finding General Bonaparte's reputation to be "excessive and inopportune", and wishing to get him away from Paris, had given him the command of the "Army of England". Seven years later, this "Army" had still not crossed the Channel. In the meantime, Napoleon had conquered Egypt, returned to France and made himself master of that country as well as much of Europe; and now, after the uneasy Peace of Amiens, the Emperor of the French was encamped at Boulogne and waiting for his fleet to appear—to give him, if only for twenty-four hours, a mastery of the narrow seas which would enable him to throw his Grand Army on to English soil.

It is a matter for speculation whether he really intended to invade England, whether all his preparations were not a cover for other projects. In any case, it was not the Battle of Trafalgar that decided Napoleon to strike his camp at Boulogne; he had already done so. Nor, in England, was Nelson's victory considered, at the time, as a deliverance from the threat of invasion. It might even be said that the victory was not fully appreciated, as the English were more concerned with the news of the French triumphs at Ulm and Austerlitz, which created dismay among the government and the people.

There is no doubt, however, that the preparations at Boulogne were thorough. If Villeneuve or Ganteaume had appeared off Calais they would certainly not have had to send off messengers as Medina Sidonia did to seek the Duke of Parma.

Nelson

It is probably true that Trafalgar did not save England in as obvious a manner as the victory at South Foreland had in 1217. But, ten years before Waterloo, Nelson's victory at sea settled once and for all the old quarrel which had divided French and English for six centuries. It closed what might be called the Third Hundred Years' War, demonstrated the importance of sea-power, and left England—with her eight hundred years of naval tradition—undisputed mistress of the seas.

When Villeneuve put to sea on October 19th, 1805, there was indeed a heavy burden on the shoulders of this forty-two-year-old Vice-Admiral. Yet many fortuitous circumstances had brought him to this position of great responsibility. Seven years previously he had been Rear-Admiral at the Battle of the Nile, unable—for reasons already mentioned—to give any support to his commander-in-chief. He was bitterly attacked on that account, but the hasty judgment on him was reversed when he reached Malta, and he was acclaimed as the clever, wily admiral who had given Nelson the slip. His conduct during the siege of Malta, moreover, finally cleared his name. He was the very spirit of the island's resistance, and was defeated only by overwhelming forces. His reliability and powers of imagination might be doubted, but not his physical courage.

He was appointed to the Mediterranean command after the death of Latouche-Tréville, one of the finest seamen of the time, who died of fever at Toulon in August, 1804, on board the *Bucentaure*. Bruix had first been considered to succeed him, but was too valuable at the head of the flotillas at Boulogne. The commander of the Brest squadron, Ganteaume, one of the survivors from the *Orient*, had never been able to get out to sea with his squadron. His second-in-command, Missiessy, was only a Rear-Admiral. Rosily was never even considered, as he had been away from sea for too long; though, as will be seen, his name was put forward later.

So it was Villeneuve, then in his forty-first year, who was given command of the Mediterranean squadron. He hoisted his flag in the *Bucentaure* on October 26th, 1804. The plans for the invasion of England were still beset with the same problem—how to obtain a passage across the Channel for the troops. The Brest squadron was being blockaded by Cornwallis; the Rochefort squadron—commanded by Missiessy, who had succeeded Villeneuve on his appointment to the Mediterranean—was also contained by the British, as was Rear-Admiral Gourdon's division at Ferrol; and the Toulon squadron was being watched by Nelson.

Napoleon had never fully understood that naval squadrons cannot be moved like regiments. He devised a plan with the ultimate object of uncovering Brest, so that Ganteaume could proceed up the Channel and obtain temporary command of the Straits of Dover. This was to be brought about by creating a diversion on the other side of the Atlantic. First, Villeneuve would embark General Lauriston's troops at Toulon and set sail for Senegal, capturing St. Helena on his way to the West Indies; there he would be joined by Missiessy with troops under the command of General Lagrange. This combined force was to recapture Guiana, aid the garrison on San Domingo, and then return to Rochefort after freeing Gourdon's ships at Ferrol from the British blockade. It would be surprising if this large-scale manoeuvre did not draw off the British and so disperse their strength that Ganteaume would be able to come out of Brest. He would then land Marshal Augereau's army of 18,000 men in Ireland, and sail up the Channel to the Straits.

The plan, as can be realized, was far from simple; and, naturally, things happened very differently. Instead of leaving Toulon in October, 1804, as planned, Villeneuve did not get away until January 18th, 1805. He had 11 ships, 7 frigates and 2 brigs, and transports with Lauriston's army corps. But he was beaten back to port by adverse winds. Not until March 30th was he finally on his way, and by then it was too late for the diversion to Senegal. However, on April 9th he was joined off Cadiz by 3 Spanish ships under Admiral Gravina, for Spain had declared war against England on December 4th, 1804.

Villeneuve reached Martinique on May 14th, and was there joined by more Spanish vessels, bringing the strength of his squadron up to 18 ships, 7 frigates, and 4 corvettes.

The circumstances which had enabled Villeneuve to slip out of Toulon were extraordinarily like those in which Brueys had escaped in May, 1798. Nelson's squadron was off the southern end of Sardinia when, on March 21st, he heard that troops were being embarked at Toulon. He weighed at once, but bad weather forced him into Pula, where he had to stay until April 3rd. On the 4th, one of his scouting

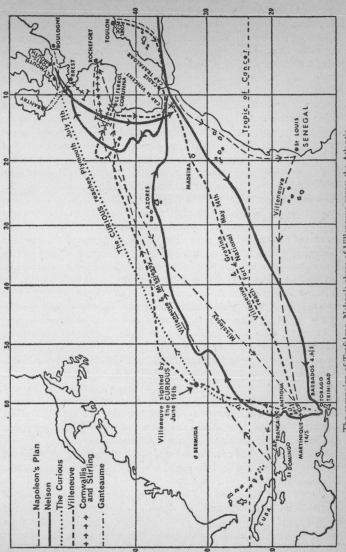

The campaign of Trafalgar. Nelson's chase of Villeneuve across the Atlantic

frigates brought news of having seen Villeneuve's squadron at eight-thirty on the morning of March 31st, sixty miles south-west of Toulon. Nelson thought that his opponent's destination was eastwards, and he took up position midway between Sardinia and Tunisia, thus barring the way to Naples, Sicily, and Egypt, which Nelson believed to be the most gravely threatened of British interests. That Villeneuve might have steered west to leave the Mediterranean never seemed to have occurred to him.[1] It was only on April 16th that he heard the news—a week after Villeneuve and Gravina had stood away from Cadiz and begun their long voyage across the Atlantic. Then all news of them was lost.

Villeneuve had a minor success soon after his arrival at Martinique. On June 4th, Captain Cosmao-Kerjulien captured a fortified rock six miles out to sea from the entrance to Fort-de-France—H.M.S. *Diamond Rock*, as the British called it. The garrison had been holding out ever since the French had recaptured Martinique.[2]

Villeneuve then decided to attack Barbados, and on the way he captured a convoy of fourteen merchantmen escorted by a corvette, which was the only vessel to escape him. Luck was certainly on his side, for the prisoners revealed that a British squadron of fourteen ships (actually, there were only ten) had just reached Barbados.

Nelson had arrived.

He had lost a fortnight by not hearing that Villeneuve had sailed into the Atlantic, and had then been locked up in the Mediterranean by adverse winds for another three weeks. It was not until May 7th that he passed Gibraltar and shaped course for the West Indies.[3] He dropped anchor at Barbados on June 4th, and was there joined by two more ships; however, the talkative merchant skippers had removed all hope of catching Villeneuve. For the latter, as might have been expected, had abandoned his plan to attack Barbados and had sailed for Europe. It was not until June 14th that Nelson learnt of his opponent's departure. He was only four days behind him now, but that was sufficient start for Villeneuve. By July 17th Nelson was in sight of Cape St. Vincent, but without any knowledge of the course that Villeneuve had taken. Nelson took in fresh supplies at Gibraltar, then put to sea

[1] See *The Campaign of Trafalgar*, by Julian S. Corbett.
[2] Missiessy, who had managed to get away from Rochefort, had passed near the "Diamond Rock" three months earlier without making any attempt to capture it, to Napoleon's extreme annoyance. "That rock," he said to Decrès, then his Minister of Marine, "will be a memorial of everlasting shame to the expedition."
[3] On May 6th Nelson had news from Commodore Donald Campbell, a British officer in the Portuguese service, that Villeneuve's destination was the West Indies. Nelson decided, in spite of the long French start, to go in pursuit. (*A Portrait of Lord Nelson*, by Oliver Warner.) (*Tr.*)

again on July 24th. On the following day, a brig just arrived from England gave him the latest gazettes which had been bought when she put in at Lisbon.

Nelson was glancing through them when an item of news caught his eye. The *Curieux* had arrived at Plymouth on July 7th. Now the *Curieux* was the brig that Nelson had speeded home from the West Indies in advance of his squadron to give the Admiralty the latest information about his movements. So the *Curieux* had arrived safely. But the gazette also announced that a week after the brig's departure it had sighted the French Fleet in the Atlantic, standing to the northward, about three hundred miles to the north of Antigua. This made the situation clearer to Nelson. Villeneuve had not, then, made for Cadiz, but had sailed on a course farther to the north and was heading for some port in the Bay of Biscay. Nelson had been looking for him too much to the south; so, without wasting a moment, he took advantage of a fresh easterly wind and headed into the Atlantic.

It was not Nelson who was then destined to encounter the French Fleet. His quarry had again eluded him, though Villeneuve as will be seen—had indeed been brought to battle. Nelson, again meeting adverse winds, tacked his way across the Bay of Biscay and joined Cornwallis, still on station blockading Brest. Leaving most of his ships with Cornwallis, he proceeded in the *Victory* and accompanied by the *Superb* to Portsmouth, where he went ashore on August 19th. Nelson believed he had failed in his mission, and felt anxious about the reception he would receive in London. But he found he stood even higher in the estimation of the public, for the worth of his long watch was fully realized, as was his achievement in keeping his force at sea for two long years.

Nevertheless, it was only too true that Nelson had missed his opportunity. According to Corbett, he missed it on July 26th. On that day, baffled by northerly winds when off Cape St. Vincent and prevented from shaping course, he had decided to head out into the Atlantic, instead of beating up the coast towards Ferrol. He took this decision because of his conviction that Villeneuve had gone northwards, and he wanted to arrive as quickly as possible at what he considered the danger spot—Cornwallis's station at the western approaches to the Channel.

If only Nelson had known what had happened a week before off Cape Finisterre! "If only he had met with Calder, what a world of anxiety would have been spared! What a success would have been in store! The battle of Trafalgar would probably never have taken place, for Barham's great plan would have completely succeeded."[1]

[1] Corbett, *op. cit.*, p. 211.

Barham was the First Sea Lord. He was in bed when Captain Bettesworth of the *Curieux* reached London at eleven o'clock on the night of July 8th with news of Villeneuve's movements. At that time Villeneuve was five or six hundred miles west of Finisterre; with a good wind in his sails he could hope to be off Ferrol in a week or ten days, and was in sufficient strength to attack Sir Robert Calder who, with only ten ships, was still blockading Gourdon and the Spanish. Barham was not given the news from the *Curieux* until the following morning, which made him furious; but he acted at once, and his orders were on the way to Portsmouth that morning, the 9th. A fast frigate reached Cornwallis, off Brest, on the 11th; and Stirling, watching Rochefort, on the 12th. The orders were for Cornwallis to cruise some thirty leagues out to the south-west for a week, with his flagship, the *Ville de Paris*, and most of his squadron, leaving only a few frigates to keep watch on Ganteaume; and for Stirling in the *Malta*[1] to move south with his division to reinforce Calder, who was then to stand out to sea. There was thus a strong force ready to intercept Villeneuve—by Cornwallis, who had twenty of the finest ships-of-the-line, if he made for Brest or the Channel; by Calder, who now had fifteen ships, if he made for Ferrol or Corunna.

On the other hand, Rochefort and Brest were left uncovered. The diversion which the French had been seeking for months past now seemed in sight, and Napoleon's plans about to be brought nearer fruition. "Imagine the excitement in Paris when news of Cornwallis's disappearance reached there, and was followed shortly afterwards by the raising of the Rochefort blockade."[2]

With favourable winds[3]—and with any other Admiral but Ganteaume—the complicated plan might have succeeded. Napoleon was beside himself with impatience. "I do not understand Ganteaume's inactivity," he wrote to the Minister of Marine on July 18th. Messenger after messenger sped along the road to Brest. Ganteaume must get away! He must engage any enemy force of less than sixteen ships, and if the enemy has moved off towards Ferrol or anywhere on the high seas, he must head direct for Boulogne, where everything was ready. "Hold command of this passage for three days, and you will give us the means of putting an end to British pretensions. . . ."

[1] The *Ville de Paris* was not De Grasse's flagship which had been captured at the Battle of the Saints in 1782, but a similar 110-gun ship built at Chatham in 1795. The *Malta* was the renamed *Guillaume Tell*, which had put up such a magnificent fight off Malta in 1800, and which had been Villeneuve's flagship at the Nile.
[2] Corbett, *op. cit.*
[3] For the first three weeks of July they remained constant in the north-east—to Villeneuve's despair. But it was just what Ganteaume needed to enable him to leave Brest and stand out to sea, then wait for westerly winds to sail up the Channel.

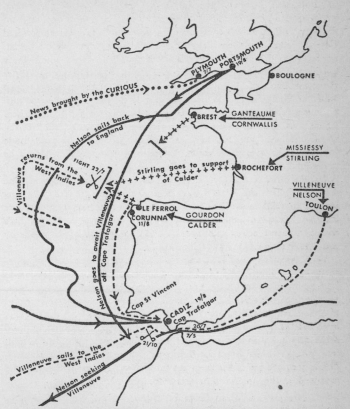

The strategical situation after Villeneuve's return to Spain

Whether Napoleon was as ready as he pretended to be is irrelevant, for when Ganteaume finally put to sea it was much too late; the way was barred again. It was not until August 21st that Ganteaume poked out of the Bertheaume inlet, the narrow entrance to Brest roads, and found Cornwallis back at his station. Ganteaume returned to his moorings, which caused the naval cadets to circulate a lampoon about him:

> *Here lies Admiral Ganteaume,*
> *Who went from Brest to Bertheaume,*
> *And helped by a wind from the west,*
> *Went back from Bertheaume to Brest.*

Cornwallis had been back for a month, having returned on July 22nd—the very day that Villeneuve and Calder had fought their action 120 miles off Cape Finisterre. It was almost exactly the area foreseen by Lord Barham in his orders. Unfortunately, the results were disappointing.

Calder's fifteen ships were opposed by twenty French and Spanish, so the engagement became known as the "Fifteen-Twenty Battle" on their side. A "blind fight", Corbett called it. The day had dawned misty, and the opposing squadrons only caught a sight of each other when the haze cleared from time to time. Smoke from the guns did not help matters, and neither commander-in-chief endeavoured to make a close action of it. Calder succeeded, however, in cutting out two Spanish ships from the rear, and captured them after a strong resistance. But this proved to be a disadvantage; encumbered with his two prizes, and the squadron being somewhat disorganized, Calder was unable to resume the action next day. Villeneuve, for his part, had 1,200 of his men sick, most of his ships were short of food and water, so he was not anxious to renew the fight either. On July 28th he reached the shelter of Spanish waters.

"Leave at once," Napoleon wrote to him, as though moving another army corps about. "You have only to sail up the Channel to ensure our becoming masters of England!" But Villeneuve had first to take in supplies and put the sick ashore. Then the "army" set sail for Ferrol, but was refused entrance, went on to Corunna, and was there joined by five French ships from Gourdon's division and eleven Spanish. Villeneuve then had some thirty ships-of-the-line under his command, but was not greatly enthusiastic.

"When I leave here with twenty-nine ships," he wrote to Decrès on August 7th, "I'm supposed to be capable of fighting about the same number. I don't mind telling you that I shouldn't like to meet twenty."

Of those twenty-nine ships, Corbett writes scornfully, at least a dozen were nothing more than floating barracks!

North-east winds once again prevented Villeneuve from reaching the Channel. Besides, he was convinced that, now the opposing forces were concentrated, the Emperor's plans were no longer feasible; and he returned to Cadiz on August 19th.

"What a navy! What an admiral!" Napoleon's fury on receipt of this news is well known. So the opportunity to conquer Britain had been missed; some other plan was needed—and that very evening Napoleon dictated to Daru the outline of his Austerlitz campaign.

As for Villeneuve, he was finished as far as Napoleon was concerned. There was even talk of a court-martial; but in the end a successor was chosen—Rosily, who had been passed over the previous year. But before he could take over the command, before he had even reached Madrid, Villeneuve had weighed and the fateful encounter on October 21st, 1805, had taken place.

The long pursuit, which had begun with the departure from Toulon, was inexorably drawing to its dramatic close. Villeneuve, penned up in Cadiz, with the British increasing their blockade and the Spanish arsenals having nothing for the repair of his ships, Villeneuve was being harassed by urgent instructions from the Emperor. He had not yet been told of his disgrace. Rosily himself was to be the bearer of the news when he came aboard the *Bucentaure* with his letter of appointment. Meanwhile, new ideas had germinated in Napoleon's fertile brain. During the Austrian campaign, Villeneuve's combined fleet was to transport to Naples the troops which he had embarked in the spring, in order for them to create a powerful diversion. Villeneuve was to leave as soon as possible, seizing the first favourable opportunity to pass through the Straits of Gibraltar. He must not hesitate to attack any enemy force equal or inferior to him in strength. The Emperor wished the enemy fleet to be annihilated. "He reckons the loss of his ships as nothing, provided they go down in glory," Decrès wrote on September 17th. It was reminiscent of the eve of the Battle of Barfleur, a hundred and thirteen years before.

Villeneuve was no Tourville, but he was as brave and as obedient to orders: "As the Emperor thinks that only boldness and determination are necessary for success at sea, I shall satisfy him on that score."

By October 5th there were thirty British ships cruising off Cadiz. But Nelson stood away with the bulk of his fleet, well out of sight, some fifty miles to the westward, leaving his frigates to keep close watch on Cadiz. Then six ships were ordered to Gibraltar to water and provision, as the

French soon learnt; and another ship left for England. Thirty minus seven—that left twenty-three. Villeneuve had thirty-three ships, although fifteen were Spanish, and Napoleon had allowed that two of them should only count as one French. Even so, that still made twenty-five against twenty-three; and the orders were to attack any inferior or equal force.

So he decided to leave port, especially as he heard that Rosily was on the way; he strongly suspected the reason, though he had still not been told anything. He would be "delighted to hand over the command to him", but did not intend to wait to do so. The squadron would weigh at the first opportunity.

That opportunity came on October 18th. Rosily had still not arrived; the orders given to him by Napoleon were far more moderate than those received by Villeneuve. Perhaps the latter had not been informed of the change because Napoleon was convinced he would not leave port anyway. If so, it was a great error of judgment—which was to cost the Emperor his fleet in a day or two, and his throne in ten years time.

There were twenty-seven ships-of-the-line waiting for Villeneuve to come out, hoping that he would come out. Nelson had left Portsmouth in the *Victory* as soon as news of Villeneuve's presence at Cadiz had reached the Admiralty, and was again in control of the Mediterranean fleet. Calder had been ordered home for an enquiry into the circumstances of his summer action against Villeneuve, but his departure had not grieved Nelson, even though he had sailed away in a fine 90-gun man-of-war. Nelson had Collingwood with him again, and the "band of brothers". During the three weeks since his arrival, Nelson had done everything possible to ensure that the battle would be a British victory. He had his captains to dine with him aboard the *Victory* and expounded his plans, which were the subject of a tactical memorandum that he issued on October 9th. The business of getting into a long line of battle, in view of the enemy, was considered outdated. In future, the order of sailing was to be the order of battle, and this would be in two columns

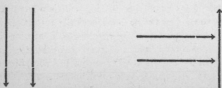

Classical formation of opposing fleets   "The Nelson touch"—his attacking order at Trafalgar

heading for the enemy line to break it up and cause a general mêlée. This was "the Nelson touch". The enemy would be presented with the highly desired opportunity to "cross the T", and doubly so, with the British advancing in two columns in line ahead; and there would be some unpleasant minutes for the leading ships, when the enemy guns would be able to rake them before they could bring their own fire to bear. But it was a risk worth taking. The French gunners still fired to dismast rather than to sink; and the swell was likely to make their aim erratic.

The tactics to be employed were thoroughly gone over, so there would be little need of signals. And besides, Nelson's Memorandum contained that magnificent phrase: "but in case signals cannot be seen, or clearly understood, no captain can do very wrong if he places his ship alongside that of an enemy". Once Nelson's intentions had been made known, his second-in-command, Collingwood, would have entire direction of his line. If possible he was to cut through the enemy about the twelfth ship from the rear; while Nelson would see that no interference was encountered from the van. There was only one outcome to be sought in the battle—the capture or destruction of the entire enemy fleet.

Nelson's ideas were received with enthusiasm. Some captains had tears in their eyes, such was their joy. If only Villeneuve could have relied so confidently on his own captains! But he had no illusions: "All we know is how to form a line, which is what the enemy wants us to do; I have neither the time nor the means to adopt other tactics, nor is it possible with the captains commanding the ships of the two navies. . . ." Yet he concluded his instructions with words that Nelson would have approved: "Captains must rely upon their courage and love of glory rather than upon the signals of the Admiral, who may already be engaged and wrapped in smoke. . . . The captain who is not in action is not at his post."

On the morning of October 18th Nelson noted in his Diary: "The enemy could not have better weather for putting to sea." The combined fleet was in fact doing so. But there was so little wind that only eight ships were able to get out of harbour, and not until the 20th were all thirty-three clear of the Bay. The previous day, at nine-thirty in the morning, the hoped-for signal had been made by the frigate *Sirius*, the nearest to Cadiz, and been relayed to the *Victory*, fifty miles to the westward. It was No. 370 of Admiral Popham's new Signal Book, of which fifty copies had reached the fleet: "The enemy ships are coming out of port or setting sail." At four o'clock, Nelson made sail and stood away in the two columns in which he would give battle. But another two days were to pass before then.

Not the least of Villeneuve's difficulties and handicaps was the need to go carefully with the Spanish commanders. History had shown that having ships of allied nations within one fleet usually gave rise to difficulties. In this particular instance, the French were heartily detested by the Spanish. The latter's admiral, Gravina, who had been following Villeneuve around for the past six months, had fought against the French twelve years previously, at Toulon, alongside Admiral Hood. Gravina, moreover, was not directly under Villeneuve's orders. His instructions were to give the French every assistance, but his was an independent command; and Villeneuve had had to use the utmost tact to obtain his agreement on the order of battle—which was far from respected, anyway. The general plan was that the Spanish admiral, Don Alava, commanded the allied van in his 112-gun *Santa Anna*; the French admiral, Dumanoir-Lepelley, in the 94-gun *Formidable*, commanded the rear, and Villeneuve led the main body with a Spanish rear-admiral, Don Balthazar Cisneros Vicente, as his second-in-command, the latter flying his flag in the 130-gun *Santissima Trinidad*, a powerful four-decker that carried a greater weight of armament than any other ship of the time. As for Gravina, he was commanding the twelve ships in reserve, his flagship being the *Principe de Asturias*, and he was supported by the French rear-admiral, Magon, in the 86-gun *Algesiras*.

About six in the evening of the 20th Villeneuve's frigates signalled that the enemy had been sighted to windward. Villeneuve ordered his fleet to reform on a course of south-south-west, which threw it into some disorder, and the ships of the two nations became intermingled. Throughout the night, the combined fleet continued standing to the southward, with the British about fifteen miles to windward. Soon after daybreak on October 21st the opposing fleets were in clear view of each other, with the British steering in two groups for the centre and rear of the French and Spanish. Villeneuve made a signal to form a single line of battle, on the starboard tack. Confusion resulted. The swell was increasing, but the westerly wind was still light. At eight o'clock Villeneuve made another attempt to get his ships into line, and then to reverse their direction—to turn together to the northward—maintaining a cable's length between each ship. It was not an easy manoeuvre for a well-trained fleet, let alone for the herd that Villeneuve was leading into battle! Not until eleven o'clock, with the enemy drawing near, was the combined fleet in anything approaching orderly disposition.

Collingwood described it, in his despatch, as "forming a crescent, convexing to leeward". It stretched from north to south, and was some twenty-seven miles south-south-west of Cadiz.

Nelson had hoisted the signal to form order of sailing in two columns. Now that he had the enemy in sight at last, he could not get at him

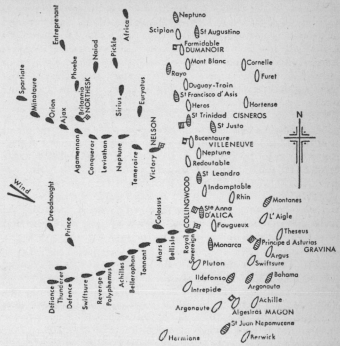

Trafalgar, October 21st, 1805. Nelson (to the north) and Collingwood attack the Franco-Spanish line (from Corbett's *The Campaign of Trafalgar*)

quick enough; the pace was stately, the wind still slight. Collingwood, in the *Royal Sovereign*, was in no less of a hurry. "Make more sail," he signalled to his line. And Nelson, goaded by this, ordered such a press of sail as none of the crew could remember having seen on a ship going into action. The two old friends seemed to have no other thought than to race to be the first to engage the enemy. Neither of them was, of course, keeping his proper station in line, which should have been third or fourth; both were at the head of their column.

The *Victory* was leading the left-hand column, the one to the north, as the British fleet was heading east. Captain Blackwood, the commander of the frigates, having failed to persuade Nelson to transfer to a frigate, had then suggested that he should allow two or three ships to precede the *Victory* into action. Nelson half-heartedly consented, and ordered one ship to go ahead—the *Temeraire*, which was immediately astern of him. But he then took an almost childish delight in refusing to give way, and when the *Temeraire* at last ranged upon the flagship's quarter, Nelson ordered her back.

The *Victory* (right) bearing down on the *Bucentaure*

At eleven, the *Victory* was still three miles from the centre of the enemy line. Not being sure which was the opposing flagship—Villeneuve did not hoist his flag until the first shots were fired—Nelson stood towards the *Santissima Trinidad*, as for some unknown reason he believed that Decrès himself was commanding the combined fleet and that he would naturally be in the heaviest-armed ship. When Nelson was able to identify the enemy flagship—the tenth in the line—he shifted a little to starboard, and pierced the line between the *Bucentaure* and the *Redoutable*.

Collingwood had then been in action for fifteen minutes or so. By hoisting the studding-sails, the *Royal Sovereign* had gained a little extra speed and got ahead of her squadron—and thus gained the privilege of being the first to open fire on the enemy, and to be for some minutes without close support! Raked by shot from the *Santa Anna* and her neighbouring ships, the *Royal Sovereign* had continued straight on course; sixty men were killed or wounded, but then she broke the enemy line just astern of the *Santa Anna* and poured in broadside after broadside, inflicting two hundred and fifty casualties in Don Alava's ship.

The *Victory* had a similar opening duel with the *Bucentaure*, and the number of victims in each ship was in similar proportion to that in the

Royal Sovereign and the *Santa Anna*. There was no doubt that the British gunners could fire faster and more accurately than the French or Spanish.

The British Fleet was nevertheless in a risky situation, due to its plunge into the enemy line—which, being in the form of a crescent, gave Dumanoir and the van an opportunity to tack and bear down to encircle the *Victory* and the leading ships before those in the rear could make sail and arrive within range, because of the slight wind. But the French rear-admiral proved incapable of such initiative, merely signalling that the ships of his division—which meant, in fact, all those ahead of the *Santissima Trinidad*—had no one to fire at! It was then one in the afternoon, and the battle had been in progress for nearly an hour. By the time Dumanoir's signal had been relayed to Villeneuve, and the latter had ordered him to execute the necessary movement, it was a quarter to two; and there was so little wind that, even by ordering his boats out, Dumanoir took nearly two hours. And by half past two, the battle was virtually over. The general mêlée that Nelson had brought about had given great advantage to the British . . . but he was no longer on his quarter-deck to follow the course of the action.

When the *Victory* was bearing down on the French flagship, to pass astern of her, the next ship in the French line had been driven to leeward, and there was a considerable gap between the two ships. The *Redoutable*, Captain Lucas, tried to fill it, and in order to avoid a collision Nelson gave the order to port the helm earlier than he had intended. The *Victory* not only lost way, but her mizzen-and fore-top-masts went, falling on to the *Redoutable* as the two ships ranged close alongside. They were soon locked in death-grips, muzzles nearly touching. The firing from the *Redoutable*'s fighting-tops almost cleared the decks of the *Victory*, and there was some danger that she would be boarded. But then the *Temeraire* ranged up on the starboard side and poured such a fire into the *Redoutable* that two hundred of her crew were killed or wounded.

The battered *Victory* was able to draw off, but Nelson had received his death wound. His uniform and decorations had attracted the fire of a sharpshooter from a fighting-top in the *Redoutable*; the ball had penetrated Nelson's chest and lodged in his spine. He was carried down to the cockpit, and died about three hours later, "at thirty minutes past four o'clock".

The battle had continued under the direction of Collingwood; though in truth no direction was needed, for Nelson had made all necessary signals. It was reported that Collingwood had shown some impatience, just before the action began, on seeing various flags being hoisted in the *Victory*. "What is Nelson signalling about? We all know what we have to do." It was the now celebrated signal, "England expects that every man will do his duty."

The *Santa Anna*, completely dismasted by the guns of the *Royal Sovereign* and the *Belle Isle*, struck her colours at a quarter past two. She had, however, done much damage to Collingwood's ship, which had lost her main- and mizzen-masts. A little later, the *Fougueux* surrendered; she had gone to the assistance of the Spanish ship, been attacked by the *Royal Sovereign*, the *Mars*, and the *Tonnant*,[1] and was finally boarded by the *Temeraire*. Her captain was killed while trying to repulse the boarders from the *Temeraire*, and his first-lieutenant was soon forced to accept defeat. The *Monarca*, too, had struck. In the *Algesiras*, Rear-Admiral Magon was killed, his flag-captain wounded, as were the two officers who successively took over command; dismasted and on fire, her colours were hauled down. The captain of the *Aigle* was killed too, and his first-lieutenant badly wounded; with all her masts gone and her rigging swept away, after a terrific duel with the *Defiance*, she struck her colours at half past three. By then, three more French ships had surrendered: the *Swiftsure*, with nearly four feet of water in her hold and three masts gone by the board; the *Berwick* which had lost her two senior officers; and the *Redoutable*, which was so entangled with the *Temeraire* that the latter did not manage to free herself until seven in the evening.[2]

The *Bucentaure* and the *Santissima Trinidad*, the two ships which had borne the full fury of the enemy attack, fought side by side until completely dismasted. The French flagship was in danger of sinking, and Villeneuve wished to shift his flag to another ship and endeavour to save what remained of the combined fleet. But not one of the *Bucentaure*'s boats was seaworthy. The *Santissima Trinidad* was hailed, but she was about to surrender. Villeneuve abandoned the fight, and the *Bucentaure* was secured by the *Conqueror*.

The most tragic end of any ship in the combined fleet was that of the *Achille*. For two hours she was assailed by four British ships in turn. Nearly all her officers were killed or wounded, but Sub-Lieutenant Cauchard con-

Villeneuve

---

[1] The *Tonnant* and the *Belle Isle* had both been French ships, the former having been captured at the Nile. The British had repaired her, and retained the name.

[2] The *Swiftsure* had been captured from the British in July, 1801, in the Mediterranean; the *Berwick* in March, 1795, off Corsica.

tinued to fight the ship and gave her namesake, the British *Achilles*, half a dozen broadsides that caused considerable damage. Then her foremast caught fire and was brought down by the guns of the *Prince*, which had joined in the attack. Unluckily, the blazing mast and rigging fell to the deck instead of in the sea, and the flames spread with frightening rapidity. The bravest tried to put out the fire, the others jumped overboard and many were picked up by boats from the British ships. It was half past five when the *Achille* blew up and sank, flag still flying, taking four hundred and eighty of her crew down with her.

Five more Spanish ships surrendered; and the *Neptuno*, one of the van, was captured at a quarter past five, by which time the battle had practically ended. There were dismasted and disabled ships of both sides scattered over a wide area of sea. The *Redoutable* and the *Temeraire*, lying together, had five of their six masts hopelessly entangled. But Nelson could die content; not a single British ship had struck, and seven French and twelve Spanish were in their enemy's possession. The remainder of the combined fleet, some seven or eight ships, were retreating towards Cadiz led by the *Principe de Asturias*, in which Admiral Gravina had been mortally wounded. Dumanoir drew off to the west with four of his ships; although they had taken little part in the fighting, it had been enough for them to be in need of some repair.

Collingwood was left with his prizes and with another enemy to face—the gale, which the swell had been heralding since early morning. Few of the British ships were capable of bearing sail. They rode out the storm with much difficulty, the south-westerly threatening to drive them on to the sharp reefs of Cape Trafalgar a few miles to leeward. Fortunately the howling wind shifted a little to the north, else all the prizes and the dismasted British ships would inevitably have foundered. The prisoners under hatches were released to help the depleted crews in their struggles against the elements. The battered *Redoutable*— which was being towed by the *Swiftsure*—went down with 156 men on board; and the *Fougueux* was driven ashore and wrecked, though 120 men were saved from her.

The *Algesiras* became separated from the rest of the fleet. Her prize crew of fifty made great efforts to keep the disabled ship from being swept on to the jagged reefs, but at daybreak on the 22nd she was only two miles off shore and drawing closer every minute. There were two hundred and seventy French prisoners in the hold. The officer in charge of the prize crew sent for the senior French officer, Lieutenant Labretonnière. The latter agreed to help save the ship and all their lives, but said that he and his fellow-prisoners no longer considered themselves bound by their surrender. "We're quite resolved to capture the ship from you, even without weapons, if you don't accept our conditions. Give us back our ship and our freedom, and we'll guarantee that you and your men will go free if we all reach port safely." The British officer agreed; and by strenuous and united effort, sufficient sail was set to get the *Algesiras* into Cadiz.

The *Aigle* was abandoned by her prize crew, and the French remaining on board managed to keep the ship afloat throughout two stormy days, lightening her by casting some of the guns into the sea, and they finally beached the ship at the entrance to Cadiz Bay. The *Conqueror* was obliged to cast off the *Bucentaure*, which she was towing, and the prize crew had to call upon the French prisoners, much as had the crew aboard the *Algesiras*. But they were less fortunate, as the *Bucentaure* was driven on to the reefs and began to break up; five hundred men were rescued from her by the *Indomptable*, then she in turn foundered, and all except a hundred and fifty of those on board were lost.

On the morning of the 22nd, Captain Cosmao in the *Pluton* made a sortie from Cadiz with the intention of seizing some of the captured ships from the British. He had three other French ships with him, two Spanish, and a few frigates. In face of this unexpected sally, the British cut two of their prizes adrift, the *Santa Anna* and the *Neptuno*; but Cosmo's little force lost the *Rayo*, which was attacked by a British ship that had just reached the scene from Gibraltar.

Collingwood realized that it was impossible to retain all the captured ships, and sank or burnt the worst damaged among them. Only four were brought safely into Gibraltar—the French *Swiftsure*, and the Spanish *Bahama*, *San Ildefonso*, and *San Juan Nepomuceno*.

Four other prizes were brought into Plymouth several weeks later. These were the four ships of Dumanoir's division; they were caught off Finisterre on November 4th by Commodore Strachan, who was in command of four ships-of-the-line and four frigates, and were captured after Dumanoir had put up as decided a fight as his showing at Trafalgar had been timid. "The French fought magnificently," Strachan said in his report, "and surrendered only when their ships had become completely disabled."

So ended Villeneuve's attempt, begun a year previously when he took over the Toulon command. The unhappy man did not long survive his victor at Trafalgar. Villeneuve was a prisoner in England for four months, and was then freed and returned to France. A few days later, on April 21st, 1806, he was found dead in an hotel at Rennes. Whether he committed suicide or was the victim of a political assassination is not known; the mysterious circumstances of his death have never been satisfactorily explained.

NAVARINO—THE LAST FLEET ACTION
WHOLLY UNDER SAIL

The Greek War of Independence—British, French, and Russian intervention with a combined fleet—who fired the first shot?—destruction of the Turkish fleet—Greek ingratitude.

TWENTY-TWO years after Trafalgar—and only twelve after Waterloo—British and French sailors fought on the same side for the first time since the Battle of Sole Bay, a century and a half previously. This was at the battle of Navarino, where the British, French, and Russians were aligned against the Turks and Egyptians. This multi-national battle was fought in extraordinary confusion, but resulted in the complete destruction of the Turko-Egyptian Fleet, which greatly out-numbered that of the Western Allies. What is more, not one of the five nations involved was officially at war with another. Neither is it known who fired the first shot; and one of the governments on the winning side—the British—refused to recognize the actions of its admiral and relieved him of his command!

All in all, from both a political and tactical point of view, Navarino presents a picture of utter confusion.

The Greeks had finally risen against their Turkish overlords, in 1821, and were at first successful. But then Mehemet Ali, the Khedive of Egypt, placed his army and fleet at the disposal of the Sultan, and things began to go badly for the Greeks. Enthusiasm for their cause spread throughout Europe. Nicholas I, who had just succeeded to the Russian throne, saw an opportunity to harass his country's traditional enemy, which was barring access to the Mediterranean. Russia joined France and Britain in an attempt at mediation in this Greek War of Independence, and the three Powers backed up their efforts by sending an allied naval force to Greek waters.

The ships of the three nations joined forces, in October, 1827, off the island of Zante in the Adriatic. The Russian division was commanded by Rear-Admiral de Heyden, the British by Vice-Admiral Sir Edward Codrington, and the French by Rear-Admiral Gauthier de Rigny. Codrington happened to be the senior in rank and took command of the combined fleet consisting of ten ships-of-the-line, ten frigates and some half a dozen brigs and schooners.

The confused fighting at Navarino, October 26th, 1827

Philippe Augustus embarking at Genoa in 1190 for the Third Crusade.
There were no great sea-battles on that crusade, but many stirring naval
episodes.

2. The invention of gun-ports early in the sixteenth century (the ship shown was built in 1514) considerably increased the firing-power of warships and changed the tactics of sea warfare.

Oar-propelled galleys still predominated at the Battle of Lepanto (1571), where the combined fleets of the Holy League crushed the Turks.

4. The invincible Armada, sent against England by Philip II of Spain in July 1588, was to his mind a crusade against the 'infidels' in the north.

5. The 'Four Days' Battle' in the Channel, June 11-14th, 1666, at which the Dutch under Ruyter got the better of the English fleet commanded by Prince Rupert and Monck.

6a. The Battle of Barfleur, on May 27th, 1692, was without doubt the most magnificent and the most thrilling of all the battles fought by the French Navy until present times.

6b. Rodney's victory at the Battle of The Saints, off San Domingo, on April 12th, 1782. The French were beaten by Rodney's dashing tactics and the technical improvements in British gunnery.

7. The Battle of Navarino, on October 20th, 1827, was the last naval action fought under sail. A combined squadron of British, French, and Russian ships completely destroyed the Turko-Egyptian fleet.

8. The second half of the nineteenth century saw rapid changes in war-ships. In 1878 the British corvette *Comus* was still fully-rigged; but the cruiser *Magician* (inset), built in 1888, had only a sail or two in case of need.

9. Torpedo-boats greatly contributed to the French victory at Foochow. Here one of the boats, towing its torpedo, is about to attack the Chinese flagship.

10. At the Battle of the Falkland Islands (December 8th, 1914) the battle-cruisers *Inflexible* and *Invincible* sank the two German cruisers *Scharnhorst* and *Gneisenau*, whose 8-inch guns were no match for the 12-inch of the British warships. The *Inflexible* is seen here picking up survivors from the *Gneisenau*.

11. Above: *The Indomitable,* another battle-cruiser, built in 1908.
Below: The armoured cruiser *Warrior* at Jutland. She sank in rough seas soon afterwards.

12. The aircraft-carrier *Formidable,* whose planes greatly contributed to the victory at the Battle of Matapan.

13. An Atlantic convoy reaches home waters. From the very beginning of the war, the threat of the U-Boat packs made it necessary for merchant ships to sail in convoy, with Navy escort.

14. The elements were an additional enemy for the convoys to Russia. Snow and
    ice frequently covered decks and superstructure; and the waves were
    sometimes high enough to sweep over the flight-deck of a carrier.

15. The *Tirpitz*, a grave menace to the Russian convoys.

16. While the *Tirpitz* was anchored in a Norwegian fjord, British midget-submarines made a daring incursion and torpedoed her. She was finally sunk by RAF bombers.

The Allied force was vastly outnumbered by the Turkish and Egyptian ships, which totalled sixty-five; but only three of these were line-of-battle ships. There were, however, nineteen frigates, and the weight of metal amounted to 1,962 guns against the 1,294 of the Allies.

The Turkish commander-in-chief, Ibrahim Pasha, had anchored his fleet in the Bay of Navarino, on the west coast of Greece—not far from where the battles of Actium and Lepanto had been fought. His ships were drawn up in three lines in a horse-shoe formation extending from the Navarino fort on the mainland to the battery on the island of Sphacteria. On September 25th, 1827, Codrington and De Rigny had a meeting with Ibrahim Pasha to inform him of the Allied offer of mediation, which had already been accepted by the Greeks.

The Turkish commander gave a verbal agreement that his squadron would not leave Navarino until a reply to the Allied proposition had been received from the Sultan. The Allied fleet therefore withdrew, leaving two frigates to keep watch on Navarino.

A settlement might have been reached had it not been for the untimely arrival in the Gulf of Patras of a Greek naval division—commanded, incidentally, by a British officer, Lord Cochrane. Ibrahim Pasha objected to the presence of these Greek ships and sent part of his force, under the command of Petrona Bey, to demand their withdrawal. But Codrington, with three or four ships, intercepted the Turks not far from Lepanto and signified his intention not to let them proceed. Whereupon Petrona Bey turned back. But another Turkish detachment of some fifteen vessels was met with later, proceeding with the same purpose; these, too, withdrew when Codrington barred their way. In the meantime, the Turkish forces had been devastating the mainland. The Allies therefore decided to put pressure on Ibrahim Pasha, and stood into Navarino Bay with their fleet; as the Turks had already given way before a small demonstration of force, there was no reason to suppose that they would provoke a full-scale action.

It was midday on October 20th when, aided by a following wind, Codrington led the fleet into the bay in his flagship, the 84-gun *Asia*. There was no reaction from the Turkish and Egyptian ships. At two o'clock the *Asia* dropped anchor near the Turkish vessels, and De Rigny's flagship, the *Sirène*, within pistol-shot of the Egyptian flagship. The rest of the Allied ships anchored within the horse-shoe formation of the Turko-Egyptian Fleet.

Shortly afterwards, the British frigate *Dartmouth*, which had been ordered to watch the Turkish fireships, sent off a boat with an officer to request one of the fireships to draw off a short distance. The boat was fired upon and the officer was killed. The *Dartmouth* at once gave covering fire to her boat's crew. Then, like an echo spreading round the bay, firing broke out from ship after ship. The Egyptian frigate *Irania* opened fire on the *Sirène*. The Turkish shore batteries pounded the French ships *Trident* and *Breslaw*. The Russians had not yet reached their mooring positions, as the wind had suddenly dropped, and their ships tried in vain to get within range.

The *Scipion* (centre) and the *Dartmouth* endangered by two Turkish fireships

A thick haze of smoke was soon hanging over the bay, making it difficult for the gunners to know whether they were hitting an enemy or not.

The discipline and training of the European crews told in the end; in spite of their courage, the Turks and Egyptians were overwhelmed in an hour or so. Not that they surrendered; rather, they set fire to their ships in the hope of destroying any enemy ship that drew near. In this way the *Irania*, which had fought the *Sirène* for an hour, blew up before the French ship had drawn off, and the shock of the explosion brought down the latter's mizzen-mast. The *Scipion* was almost set on fire by a Turkish fireship, that had just been warded away from the *Trident* . . . and then it drifted down to the *Daphne*, which directed it into a cluster of Turkish and Egyptian vessels.

A single Turkish ship struck her colours—the frigate *Sultane*, which had been disabled by the *Armide*. The *Albion* attacked and boarded another Turkish ship, but she was already on fire and in danger of blowing up; the boarding-party scrambled back, the *Albion* cut herself free and stood off—only just in time.

The battle was so confused that no coherent description of it has ever been possible. The casualties among the Allies were not heavy

(75 British were killed, 59 Russians, and 43 French, and the total wounded was just under 500), but much damage was caused to their ships. All the French, except the *Trident*, had to return to a home port for repairs, as did most of the British ships.

As for the Turks and Egyptians, they seemed set on continuing the destruction of their own ships; the following day they were beaching

Ibrahim Pasha

and burning those that were still afloat, and Admiral Codrington sent envoys to explain that it was not his intention to destroy or capture their fleet. The Allies had been fired upon first, and had replied . . . and would do so again, if necessary. But not if the Turks respected the agreement and kept the truce.

The final touch to the whole affair was when the Greeks—for whom, after all, the European Powers had been fighting—sent their corsairs to stop and search European merchant ships that came within sight. British and French cargo vessels were captured in this way—at a time when ships of their nations were fighting at Navarino for Greek independence!

What folly it all was! Codrington was disowned by his Government and recalled to London. He was not long in disgrace, however, and was later given command of the Home Fleet. On the other hand, De Rigny met with nothing but honours in France; he was promoted to Vice-Admiral and given a title, and became a most popular Minister of Marine. While Russia exploited the destruction of the Turkish Fleet by continuing hostilities which ended to her advantage in 1829.

XVI

THE MASSACRE AT SINOPE

General Paixhans demonstrates his new shell-gun—its great success at Vera Cruz—the first instance of the reduction of a fortress by warships—the Russians adopt the new weapon, and blow the Turkish Fleet out of the water, at Sinope (November 30th, 1853).

CASUALTY figures of thirty-seven killed on one side and two thousand nine hundred and sixty on the other as a result of a naval battle is not a discrepancy which would astonish people today, for many instances have occurred of one or two lucky hits securing a victory before any damage has been caused to the opposing side. But a hundred years ago this was not the case; and when the Russian Fleet blew the Turks out of the water at Sinope, in November, 1853, with the resulting casualties given above, the whole world was aghast and amazed.

The new death-dealing weapon of this "massacre", as it was called then, was the invention of a Frenchman.

In the days of wooden ships, explosive shot had been fired by mortars mounted in bomb-ships—such as had been employed by Nelson at the Battle of Copenhagen—which had to get within close range of their objective. In 1821 the French General Paixhans had tried firing explosive shot from guns of longer range and with a low trajectory which had previously been used for solid cannon-balls. Three years later he successfully demonstrated his new weapon by sinking an old 80-gun ship, the *Pacificateur*, which the French Minister of Marine provided for the purpose. By 1837 the new "shell-gun" had been adopted by the French Navy, and was used in action the following year, when Admiral Baudin attacked the fortress of San Juan d'Ulloa, which was believed to be impregnable.

The property of French nationals had suffered during an army mutiny in Mexico,[1] and the French Government was unable to obtain reparations. So a small naval force was sent out, as a means of applying pressure on the Mexican Government. But it had no effect; and a blockade of the coast proved more exhausting for the French crews, who were soon suffering from a shortage of food and weakened by yellow fever, than it did for the Mexicans. Stronger measures were obviously re-

---

[1] The mutineers had plundered, among other places, a baker's and pastrycook's shop; this caused the episode to become known in America as "The Pastry War".

quired, and the French Government sent reinforcements under the command of Rear-Admiral Charles Baudin. He was off Vera Cruz on October 26th, 1838, with three heavily gunned frigates, two corvettes, two steam-powered tugs, and several brigs and bomb-ships.

LA VERA CRUZ

Foreign ships at anchor

SACRIFICE ISLE

Fort St Jean d'Ulloa

CRÉOLE

GALLEGA REEF

GLOIRE
NÉRÉIDE

ORESTE   MÉDÉE   IPHIGÉNIE
ALCIBIADE   LAPÉROUSE   VOLTIGEUR
ECLIPSE   DUPETIT-THOUARS   VULCAIN   CYCLOPE
          ZÉBRE
GREEN ISLE   PHAÉTON
                    I. BLANQUILLA   MÉTÉORE   GALLEGUILLA

One nautical mile

Reduction of San Juan d'Ulloa fortress by Admiral Baudin's squadron, November 27th, 1838

He tried for a month to obtain satisfaction through talks with the Mexican Government, then decided to take offensive action.

Vera Cruz was defended by the fortress of San Juan d'Ulloa, built on an islet about a thousand yards off shore and itself protected from approach by a large reef—the Gallega Reef—which was completely uncovered at low tide. Admiral Baudin sent the Prince de Joinville, one of King Louis-Philippe's sons and captain of the corvette *Créole*, on a reconnaissance of the reef with a view to spiking the lower guns of the fortress by that means of approach. This did not appear possible, however, and Admiral Baudin then planned to bombard the fortress into subjection.

The three frigates, the 60-gun *Iphigénie*, the *Néréide* (the Rear-Admiral's flagship), and the *Gloire*, were towed by the steam-tugs close to the reef, to positions where they were out of reach of most guns of the fortress. The *Créole* was given a station ahead of the frigates, nearer the shore; she was to remain under sail during the shoot, because of the shallows.

At midday on November 27th Admiral Baudin sent a final message to the military commander of Vera Cruz; and at two thirty-five the bombardment began. It had a most telling effect. The thick smoke from the fortress's guns hindered the French at first, for there was no wind to sweep it away; but the ships gradually increased their rate of firing, and after an hour or so had blown up the powder magazines of the fortress. The bombardment continued until five o'clock, by which time the Mexicans had ceased firing. When darkness fell, a boat came away from the fortress with an officer who requested a suspension of hostilities to enable the dead and wounded to be evacuated. Admiral Baudin refused, saying that he required a formal surrender, otherwise he would renew the bombardment next day and blow the fortress to bits.

The French ships returned to their positions the following morning, and were about to open fire when the Mexican Chief-of-Staff came out to the *Néréide* to surrender the fortress.

One of the witnesses of this impressive demonstration of the new weapon was an American naval officer who later earned a high reputation—Admiral Farragut—and he submitted a detailed report to his superiors. But it was not given the attention it deserved; nor did the European Naval Powers attach great significance to the episode, probably because the ships had been firing on a fortress and not on other ships.[1] Fifteen years passed before the shell-gun was used to great effect in a purely naval engagement. The Russian victory at Sinope, on November 30th, 1853, gave the signal for the contest between metal-piercing missiles and protective armour.

Sinope is a small Turkish port on the southern coast of the Black Sea. Turkey and Russia were again at war, for reasons that were not very clear—actually, because the Czar wanted to seize the Dardanelles, which the Russians have always coveted. A small Turkish squadron commanded by Osman Pasha was caught in a storm when returning

[1] "It is the only instance I know of a land fortress being reduced purely by a naval force," the Duke of Wellington said in the House of Lords.

from the Circassian coast of the Black Sea—the supply area for Turkish guerillas in the Caucasus—and took shelter in Sinope harbour. Its presence was soon discovered by the Russian admiral, Nakhimov. He had three line-of-battle ships, whereas Osman Pasha had only frigates; but the former was taking no chances and sent to Sebastopol for reinforcements. He was joined by three 120-gun three-deckers, whose main armament consisted of 68-pounders that fired the new shell, which had only been introduced into the Russian Navy the previous year.

A thick mist hid the approach of the six Russian ships until they were within half a mile of Sinope. There were seven frigates and a few smaller vessels at anchor in the harbour, protected by coastal batteries which were, however, very ancient. It was ten in the morning when the Russians appeared out of the mist. After twenty minutes gunfire the *Grand-Duc Constantin* had put a shore battery out of action and had sunk one frigate. . . . By four o'clock, when Admiral Nakhimov withdrew, there was not a single Turkish ship still afloat in the harbour.

The Turks had fought hard, opening fire first as soon as the Russians emerged from the mist. But what could cannon-balls do against shells? And the eighty-four hits that the Turkish gunners registered on the Russian flagship, the *Imperitritza Marie*, did no serious damage.

The Western Powers protested, for no obvious reason . . . though one can guess. Britain and France had openly favoured Turkey and sent warships to cruise in the Sea of Marmara, as a means of intimidating Russia.[1] Their failure to do so made a greater impression upon the French and British Governments than had the deaths of three thousand Turks at Sinope—many of whom had been killed, contrary to the finest traditions of sea warfare, while escaping from their sinking ships. This loss of prestige was a factor in the decision of Britain and France to send forces to the Crimea, the following year, in active support of the Turkish cause.

The victory of the Russians at Sinope therefore proved to be detrimental rather than helpful to their war effort. But it was nevertheless a "surprise attack brilliantly conceived and executed",[2] and the lessons to be drawn from it gave the naval Powers much to reflect upon for several years.

[1] The French squadron, under Vice-Admiral Hamelin, alone consisted of nine ships and eight frigates and steam-powered corvettes.
[2] *The Imperial Russian Navy*, by Fred T. Jane, London, 1899.

XVII

PRIVATEERS AND IRONCLADS IN THE AMERICAN CIVIL WAR

The blockade-runners from Bermuda—success of the Confederate raiders—the
Alabama's seventy-one victims—the Alabama and the Kearsage fight a duel
off Cherbourg (June 19th, 1864)—the first Ironclad is built by the Confederates
—the Federals reply by constructing the Monitor in six months—the Battle
of Hampton Roads (March 8–9th, 1862)—the Monitor arrives on the scene—
the first fight between Ironclads.

AT the outbreak of the American Civil War in 1861 the United States'
Navy was still small and had little relation to the size of the merchant
fleet, which was already carrying the star-spangled banner to all
corners of the world. The Southern States possessed hardly any of the
naval forces, so the war seemed certain to be fought out entirely on
land. However, events proved otherwise. In spite of the Federals' great
superiority in naval strength and industrial power, they were unex-
pectedly harassed by the privateers and blockade-runners of the
South; and for a time their sea communications were seriously threatened. When Virginia went over to the Confederates, the frontier between the two sides was in the region of Chesapeake Bay; and the huge
arsenal at Norfolk—still the largest in the world today—fell into the
hands of the Confederates.

The first incident in the Civil War was, moreover, one in which a
ship was involved: the shore batteries at Charleston had opened fire on
a Federal ship, the *Star of the West*.

The curious thing was that the Federals made no apparent attempt
to prevent the Confederates from building up a small fleet, which later
proved to be most troublesome. One of the most successful naval commanders of the South, Captain Raphael Semmes, was still on active
service with the United States Navy in February, 1861. He resigned
before going over to the Confederates, but continued to move freely
about the Northern States; President Davis had given him the mission
of placing orders for machinery and munitions for the Confederates
with factories in the North, even with State arsenals if possible.

In April, 1861, the Confederates came into possession of their first
warship. The *Merrimack*, a heavily armed, steam-powered frigate and
a prototype of a new class of warship, was undergoing repairs in the

naval dockyards at Norfolk, and the Federals were arranging to have her towed away to Philadelphia before the State of Virginia went over to the Confederates. But events moved too fast for them; Virginia made the decision to join the South on April 12th, 1861, while the *Merrimack* was still in the Norfolk dockyards. She was scuttled by a demolition squad that arrived in the U.S.S. *Pawnee* and set fire to the workshops and installations of the arsenal. But the Confederates later raised the frigate, built armoured-plating on to her, and renamed her *Virginia*; under this name she was a powerful asset to the South, as we shall see.

However, in the meantime the Federal Navy was maintaining a close blockade of the Southern ports. It was a matter of life or death for the Confederated States to force the blockade; having little industry, they had to import nearly all their arms and ammunition, and export their cotton in order to pay for them. The number of blockade-runners eventually reached a high figure, as can be gathered from the fact that eight hundred and fifty were captured by Union ships during the first two years of the war. The chief centre of this activity was the Bermudas, and the vessels employed were long, lean paddle-steamers which could produce a turn of speed of up to seventeen knots; they burnt anthracite because it gave little smoke, and were painted grey to be inconspicuous at sea.

It was not only arms and ammunition that the blockade-runners took on in the Bermudas. Luxury goods and spirits were well worth carrying—anything, in fact, which was in short supply in the Southern States as a result of the war. The speed of the blockade-runners enabled them to outdistance the Union ships; they made port at night, quickly discharged their cargo, and were off again, loaded with cotton, before the blockading ships at anchor outside the port had time to weigh and put to sea.

It was a risky business, but exceedingly profitable. Freight charges were so high that three successful voyages paid for the cost of a ship. Some of the captains made five thousand dollars a month, whereas their normal pay in peacetime would have been between a hundred and forty and a hundred and sixty dollars.

The Confederates' reply to the blockade was to send privateers to attack the sea-borne trade of the Union. The results far exceeded the most optimistic hopes, although only a few privateers were employed. In the first six months of the war, some sixty Union merchant ships were captured. The Confederates, heartened by these successes with ships that had been fitted out in their own poorly equipped yards, placed orders with British shipbuilders. Although the British Government was officially neutral, assistance was given almost openly to the Confederated States, whose ships were allowed to use British ports of call. The extent of this assistance can be gauged by the fact that a Neutral Commission, sitting at Geneva in 1871, called upon Britain to pay the United States fifteen and a half million dollars as compensation for the damage caused by Confederate privateers fitted out with British complicity. The Americans had also claimed damages for indirect losses due to the rise in maritime insurance rates and to the transfer of merchant ships to the flag of another nation in order to avoid capture; but these claims were rejected.

The privateer most often cited in the course of these judicial proceedings was the *Alabama*, which had a total of seventy-one seizures of Union ships to her credit.

The *Alabama*'s captain was the Raphael Semmes already mentioned. When he joined the Confederates he was first given command of the C.S.S. *Sumter*,[1] a mail-packet that had been on the New Orleans–Havana run, when she was known as the *Havannah*. This 500-ton ship had been converted and was the first unit of the Confederated States' Navy—the only unit, in fact, when Captain Semmes joined her. Armed with an 8-inch swivel-gun and four 24-pounders, and with her bunkers made larger to increase her range of action, the *Sumter* succeeded in slipping out of New Orleans on June 29th, 1861, and in reaching the West Indies, in spite of the vigilance of the U.S.S. *Brooklyn*, a faster and more heavily armed ship, which was cruising off the mouth of the Mississippi. Six and a half months later, the *Sumter* put in at Gibraltar having destroyed seventeen Union merchantmen during her long cruise in the Atlantic. But she was in such great need of a refit that her captain finally sold her to a British ship-owner—who later employed her as a blockade-runner, to the further advantage of the Confederates.

This cruise of the *Sumter* was a good augury for that of the *Alabama*. The latter was one of three ships built at Birkenhead in 1862 for the Confederated States, whose agents did not conceal their intentions to arm and use the ships as privateers. However, the proper form was observed. . . . The British Government, having proclaimed its neutrality, could not consent to warships for one or other of the opposing sides being constructed in English shipyards; so the contracts were purported to be on behalf of the French Government, or of the Khedive of Egypt. And then one day the crew arrived to take over the *Alabama*—a pack of adventurers, picked up in ports around the Irish Sea. "A hundred and ten of the most reckless boozers from the Liverpool pubs," was how

---

[1] C.S.S. stood for Confederate States' Ship. The Federal Navy continued to use U.S.S. (United States' Ship).

Captain Semmes described his crew when he wrote his Memoirs. Needless to say, they were a tough lot to manage.[1]

The ship was still known as "No. 290", a three-masted barque with an auxiliary engine giving a maximum speed of thirteen and a half knots, and had no armament as yet. Her trials were quietly taking place under a captain acting as stand-in for Semmes, until one evening he forgot to return to port—probably having had wind that the ship was about to be seized by the port authorities on directions from the Government, and at the demand of the Federals. A gay party was in progress on board the "290", the guests having been invited as a screen to the preparations for putting to sea; but a tug arrived by pre-arrangement to take off the men and women before the ship was very far out. Some days later, the ship put in at the Azores; and on August 18th, 1862, the barque *Agrippine* of London reached her there, bringing the guns and ammunition—which had been loaded in secret—and a great quantity of coal. Captain Semmes arrived two days later to take over his command. The Portuguese authorities turned a blind eye on the conversion of the ship into an armed raider; and on August 24th, a Sunday, Captain Semmes took her out to sea and read out to the crew his Commission from the President of the Confederate States to the command of the steam-sloop C.S.S. *Alabama*.

The whole of the Atlantic was her hunting-ground, and in the next two months she captured twenty enemy ships—or rather, burnt them, after taking the crews prisoner, for there was no means of securing the vessels.

Another rendezvous with the faithful *Agrippine* had been arranged for the middle of November, this time in Martinique. But an intruder appeared in the shape of the U.S.S. *San Jacinto*, which was larger and had heavier armament than the *Alabama*; luckily, she was not so fast, and the *Alabama* managed to evade her during the night, after having fixed a meeting with the *Agrippine* in Venezuelan waters. All went well on that occasion, and as soon as fresh supplies had been taken on, off Blanquilla Island, the raider put to sea again and soon added another victim to the list—a big packet-boat, the *Ariel*, out of New York.

The *Alabama* had run no great risk so far, but it was a different matter when off Galveston on January 11th, 1863, she met with a

---

[1] "My seamen are playing the very devil as usual," Captain Semmes wrote in his Diary on August 13th, 1863, when the ship was at Capetown. "They manage to get liquor on board, and the drink makes them insubordinate and impossible to deal with. We are obliged to put some in irons."

September 19th—"The men on shore leave are all drunk. Only a few have returned."

September 23rd—"A score of men still absent. Some have been picked up by the Simonstown police, who are hoping for some reward."

division of Union ships which was supporting a landing of their troops. However, the raider was disguised as a British cargo-vessel, the *Petrel*, and, when the Union gunboat *Hatteras* came to investigate, succeeded in drawing her off some twenty miles from the rest of the Union force. Then, suddenly revealing her true identity and unmasking her guns, the *Alabama* opened fire at close range and in eleven minutes put paid to the smaller vessel, which went down in flames just after the last of her crew was taken off.

The *Alabama* transferred her activities to the South Atlantic, then to the Indian Ocean and the China Sea, but her score increased much less rapidly than in earlier months: Union merchant ships were being trans-ferred to foreign flags at an alarming rate, because their owners dared not send them to sea under their own flag. In the summer of 1864, after twenty months of scouring the seas and having had hundreds of adven-tures—for which much more space would be required to recount here— Captain Semmes brought the *Alabama* back to Europe, capturing two more ships in the Atlantic and bringing his total to seventy-one. On June 11th he was off Cherbourg, where he asked permission to enter harbour for a much-needed overhaul.

The news caused great agitation among the Union representatives in Europe. Semmes had always evaded his pursuers because communi-cations were so poor and slow, and Union warships had been much too late in reaching the scene of his latest activity. But telegraphic com-munications existed in Europe, and the United States Consul was able to get a message to the U.S.S. *Kearsarge*, which was then at Flushing. Three days after the *Alabama* had tied up at Cherbourg, the *Kearsarge* appeared outside the harbour.

Captain Winslow of the *Kearsarge* had been a colleague of Semmes in the days before the Civil War, but there was no thought of friendship in his mind now! He sailed his ship near to the *Alabama*, as though in defiance, then cruised beyond the harbour mole. Semmes did not keep him waiting for long. Faced with the alternative of internment or going out to fight, he sent a challenge to his adversary, gave his ship's papers and forty-five chronometers (souvenirs of some of his victims) into the safe-keeping of the Port authorities, and left harbour on Sun-day morning, June 19th.

The imminent prospect of this sea-fight had naturally caused great excitement on both sides of the Channel. An English yacht, the *Deer-hound*, chanced to appear in the area; what was more, an excursion train brought twelve hundred Parisians to watch the spectacle from the heights of Cherbourg. They were not disappointed.

The two American ships were fairly evenly matched. The U.S.S.

Kearsarge had a complement of 163 to the C.S.S. *Alabama*'s 149 and 7 guns to the latter's 8, though the *Kearsarge*'s broadside of 432 pounds was 72 pounds the heavier. The Union ship was escorted outside territorial waters by a French warship, and then the *Alabama* put to sea. The latter opened fire first, at 2,000 yards, as soon as she was 3 miles out.

It was a curious sort of fight, for each ship endeavoured to rake the other; they moved in two concentric circles for an hour or so, firing at each other and drawing ever closer, until they were little more than 600 yards apart. The shooting from the *Kearsarge* was the more effective—hardly surprisingly, considering the composition of the *Alabama*'s crew. Moreover, Captain Winslow had improvised some protection for his engines by spreading the anchor-chains over the side. Only 14 of the 370 shots from the *Alabama* made hits on the *Kearsarge*; and one of those, a 100-pounder, failed to explode.

After an hour of this roundabout, a lucky shot from the *Kearsarge*'s 11-inch put the privateer's engines out of action. Semmes tried to get under sail, but it was no use. His ship was sinking. . . . He struck his colours and hoisted a white flag. At half past twelve the *Alabama* went down by the stern.

Semmes and about forty of his crew were rescued by the English yacht and some French boats that had quickly put out from Cherbourg. The remainder, except for a dozen or so killed, were taken prisoner aboard the *Kearsarge*. The Union ship had only one man killed and two wounded. Among those who met their death in the *Alabama* was the ship's doctor, a Welshman named David Herbert Llewellyn; he refused to leave the wounded, and was drowned with them.

The *Alabama* was not the last of the Confederate raiders. The *Shenandoah*, which was fitted out in October, 1864, succeeded in destroying thirty-six Union ships, most of them after the cessation of hostilities; for the news was a long time in reaching her. She wreaked such havoc among the American whaling fleet in the North Pacific that it has never recovered.

Incidentally, the *Shenandoah*'s crew continued to draw a rum ration long after the custom had been suppressed in American warships. News of the defeat of the Confederated States also brought prohibition to the raider's crew.

The American merchant navy suffered severely from the Confederate privateers. Nevertheless, the Civil War gave American naval engineers and officers unique opportunities to experiment with and develop new armaments, and to play a leading part in the evolution of sea warfare, which had recently seen great changes with the introduction of the shell-gun and the advances in steam-power.

In 1861, as previously mentioned, the Confederate States had no navy with which to oppose the Federal ships only a few miles away across the Chesapeake. The Navy Secretary in the Confederate Government, Stephen R. Mallory, considered that what was needed was not wooden ships but an ironclad, a ship cased with plates of protective armour, which would be able to eliminate the enemy's wooden frigates one after the other and so put an end to the blockade. Early in July, 1861, he gave orders for the scuttled *Merrimack* to be raised from Norfolk harbour.

The work which was done on her would amuse or horrify a modern engineer. The Norfolk dockyards, with their limited means, delivered a monstrosity that had a draught of twenty-three feet and only two feet of free-board, and which could make no more than five knots. On the other hand, what protection it had, and what a weight of armament! The *Virginia*, as the ironclad was named, had three 8-inch guns from Dahlgreen[1] and two 6-inch, two 7-inch swivel-guns, and a heavy steel beak or lance at the stem. It was not surprising, therefore, that her deep draught—most unusual at that period—made her navigation difficult among the shoals of Hampton Roads.

Her command was given to Captain Buchanan, who had been the first Commander of the Naval Academy at Annapolis before going over to the Confederates. He had some difficulty in completing his crew; eventually, eighty seamen were discovered in a New Orleans regiment in the field, outside Yorktown, and with a few local sailors and some volunteers from the army the ship's complement was brought up to three hundred and fifty.

The Confederates' hopes of using this ugly but powerful vessel to destroy the five Federal ships which were blockading the Chesapeake and the river approaches to Norfolk received a blow when it was learnt that a formidable adversary was in course of construction at New York. This was the *Monitor*, the first ship to be conceived and built as an ironclad; whereas the *Virginia* had been converted from a wooden frigate.

The father of the *Monitor* was John Ericsson, a Swede by origin, who had won an international reputation as a marine engineer, and was especially known for his new type of steam-driven screw-propeller. The *Monitor* was laid down in mid-September, two months after work had begun on the ex-*Merrimack*, and represented a revolution in shipbuilding. The superstructure was reduced to a minimum, so that the

[1] One of the largest manufacturers of naval guns in the U.S.A. today.

ship's shortened outline gave little help to enemy gun-layers; and there was hardly more than one foot of free-board. But the ship drew only twelve feet of water, as compared with the *Virginia's* twenty-three. Her armament consisted of two Dahlgreen 11-inch guns—the largest calibre of the time—both in a turret nine feet high and twenty feet in diameter and which revolved on a circular brass rail inserted in the deck; its pivot went right down to the keel. The turret was protected with one-inch iron plates and its roof covered with iron rails. It weighed one hundred and forty tons, and was turned by an auxiliary steam-driven engine.

The *Monitor* was launched at the beginning of March, 1862, less than six months after her construction had begun—no mean feat for a young industry engaged on a completely new type of ship. The *Monitor* left New York on March 6th under the command of Lieutenant-Commander John L. Worden and towed by two wooden steamships, the *Currituck* and the *Sachem*; there was no question of the ironclad sailing the open sea under her own power. This maiden voyage was almost her last; the very next day, when off the mouth of the Delaware, she met bad weather and was soon in difficulties. She was shipping water everywhere, through the funnel and the air-vents; conditions became so bad in the engine-room that men were fainting and had to be brought up to the roof of the gun-turret until they revived. Time and again Worden doubted if he could keep his ship afloat. The nightmare voyage ended, however, on the afternoon of March 8th when the *Monitor* rounded Cape Charles and reached the sheltered waters of Hampton Roads—to be greeted by the thunder of cannon-fire.

That very morning Captain Buchanan had cast off at Norfolk and the *Virginia* had been towed down the River Elizabeth to attack the blockading ships on the other side of the bay. These were the 50-gun, screw-driven frigates *Minnesota*, *Roanoke*, and *Congress* (of the same class as the ex-*Merrimack*), the 52-gun sailing frigate *St. Lawrence*, and the 24-gun sloop *Cumberland*, all under the command of Admiral Goldsborough, U.S.N. Once out of the river, the *Virginia* headed across the bay under her own power—for the first time. Her crew had had no firing practice, either; so both ship and crew were to be tried out while under fire. The *Virginia* quickly proved herself a clumsy ship to handle; the most simple manoeuvre took half an hour to carry out! But the Union ships anchored off Newport News were not expecting to have to fight that day; washing was hanging out to dry on the decks, and the *Cumberland*'s captain was ashore. The *Virginia* opened fire on the *Congress* at fifteen hundred yards, and her superiority at once became obvious. The shot from the *Congress*'s 25-pounders ricocheted off the

Virginia's armoured plating, whereas the latter's fire smashed the oak hull of the Union frigate. Buchanan then turned his attention to the *Cumberland*, ramming her on the starboard bow and crushing the hull like an egg-shell, at the same time firing his bowchaser and killing ten men. The *Cumberland* began to sink so quickly that she threatened to drag the *Virginia* down with her. The crew fought their ship to the very end. The water was pouring in through the hole made by the ironclad—a hole large enough for a carriage and four to pass through—

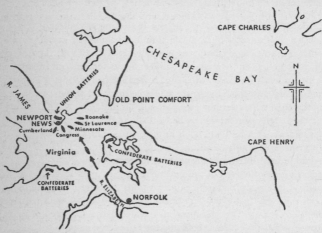

The Battle of Hampton Roads, March 8th, 1862 (from Potter's *The United States and World Sea-Power*)

but her crew kept firing the remaining guns at the *Virginia*, which was moving round the sloop and raking her deck. "Sailors of steel in a ship of wood!"they have remained an example for the United States Navy. There was so little depth of water that when the sloop settled on the bottom her flag was still visible at the mast-top.

The *Virginia* turned to finish off the *Congress*, but she managed to beach herself at a point where the ironclad could not get close enough to board her. But from a distance of one hundred and fifty yards Buchanan sent in shell after shell. The captain was killed, all the guns were put out of action, and the first-lieutenant was forced to strike his colours. The *Virginia* was in process of securing her prize and taking the prisoners aboard, when Union troops arrived and opened fire from the shore, being soon supported by their shore batteries. Buchanan hurriedly recalled the prize-crew and pounded the *Congress* with red-hot shot to set her alight. Then he was badly wounded in the leg, and Lieutenant Jones took over command.

The other three Union ships had gone aground while trying to reach the scene of the action. After endeavouring for three hours to get within range of one or the other, the *Virginia* returned across the bay as darkness was falling and anchored under the protection of the Confederate batteries on Sewel Point. She had scored an overwhelming victory, having destroyed two enemy ships and damaged a third, and inflicted two hundred and fifty casualties; yet only twenty-one of her crew had been killed or wounded, and the sole damage was a gash in her bows from ramming the *Cumberland*. No shot had penetrated the ironclad, which was quite capable of continuing the battle next day. The news of the victory was joyfully telegraphed all over the Southern States.

However, the battle was not yet over. Soon after the *Virginia* had withdrawn across the bay, the *Monitor* steamed into Hampton Roads and stopped in a position where she could protect the stranded *Minnesota*. The flames from the burning *Congress* were casting a flickering light over the scene. She blew up just before midnight, and then an uneasy silence settled over the dark waters.

As day was beginning to break, at about half past six, the men on watch in the *Monitor* made out the *Virginia* heading across the bay towards the *Minnesota*. The Union ironclad was so low in the water that at first the *Virginia*'s crew took her turret to be just another buoy. They soon realized their mistake, and that they had to deal with the enemy ironclad about which there had been so many reports in the Norfolk papers. Battle was joined at once, and the *Virginia* found it a very different proposition from the previous day. The superiority of the *Monitor* quickly became evident; she was much the more manageable ship, especially in these shallow waters. But neither ironclad suffered

The fight between the *Monitor* and the *Virginia*

from the gunfire of the other; even the *Monitor*'s 11-inch made no impression on the *Virginia*'s protective armour. Lieutenant Jones then decided to ram his adversary as Captain Buchanan had done so successfully the previous day to the *Cumberland*, and headed at full speed towards the *Monitor* with the intention of striking her amidships. But Lieutenant-Commander Worden swung his ship away just in time, and the *Virginia* only caught her a glancing blow which was more harmful to the already-damaged bows of the aggressor.

Finding he could do nothing to the *Monitor*, Jones turned his guns on the *Minnesota*, which eventually caught fire. But while manoeuvring to avoid the *Monitor*, which had come to the help of the Union frigate, the *Virginia* became stuck and seemed at the mercy of the enemy ironclad. However, a lucky shot struck the slits of the *Monitor*'s armoured control-cabin, temporarily blinding her captain. The helmsman was left without orders for a while and continued on course, which took the ship away from the *Virginia*. Churning up the mud, the latter succeeded in getting into deeper water and promptly retired across the bay. The *Minnesota*, seeing her own ironclad making off, was just then preparing to blow herself up rather than fall into the hands of the Confederates.

Thus ended the first battle between ironclads, in which protective armour had the advantage over missiles. Both ships had received a great many hits; but the only damage caused to the *Monitor* was by the hit on her control-cabin, while the *Virginia*—on which the marks of forty-one hits were counted—had only a few armoured plates fractured. On the other hand, the repairs to the *Virginia*'s buckled bows kept her in dock for a long time.

It was not the first occasion that armoured ships had been engaged. Seven years earlier, during the Crimean War, three French vessels with protective armour—the *Tonnante*, the *Lave*, and the *Dévastation*—had greatly contributed to the reduction of Russian fortresses, having been able to approach with impunity and shatter them with shell-fire. But the duel between the *Monitor* and the *Virginia* was the first time that one ironclad had fought another, and it therefore marks a date in the history of sea warfare.

Both contestants eventually met with an inglorious end. The *Virginia* was still in dock at Norfolk when Union troops advanced on the town, in May, 1863, and she was scuttled by her crew just before the Confederates withdrew. The *Monitor*, which had shown her unfitness for the open sea during her first voyage, went down in a gale while off the Carolina capes at the end of 1863.

The Ironclad was not the only innovation on the naval side during the American Civil War. Torpedoes were tried out, and Lieutenant William B. Cushing of the United States Navy sank the C.S.S. *Albemarle* with one, in October, 1864. Submersible warcraft, too, were experimented with; but after the Confederates had lost half a dozen volunteer crews in them, the naval command used them only for surface attack. In February, 1864, the Union ship *Housatonic* was sunk in this way, but took the attacker and its crew down with her.

XVIII

LISSA, WHERE RAMMING—OR MORALE—WON THE DAY

Admiral Tegetthof is prepared to do without guns—the Italian Fleet lacks a real leader—the attack on the island of Lissa (July 18–20th, 1866)—ramming tactics by the Austrian ships.

"If you haven't any guns, let me have the ships anyway, and I'll do the best I can with them."

So said Rear-Admiral Baron Wilhelm von Tegetthof, to whom the Emperor Francis-Joseph gave command of the Austrian Fleet at the outbreak of war against Prussia and Italy, on May 9th, 1866. The Admiral's intention was simply to ram the Italian ships, to pierce their hulls with a strong pointed beak, and send them to the bottom at once, instead of destroying them gradually with gunfire.

This period, the mid-nineteenth century, was when the transition of sail to steam had almost been completed. The first armour-plated warships had come into service, but practically nothing was known of their behaviour in battle on the high seas. The contest between armour and metal-piercing missiles had begun, and the results of the battle of Hampton Roads caused some experts to believe that armour would prevail.

Prussia had no real navy, so the war at sea would be fought out between the Italian and Austrian Fleets. The former was the larger and equipped with the more modern weapons; in fact, the Austrians were still in process of re-organizing their navy. Several of their armour-plated frigates had been awaiting delivery of latest-type guns from Krupps when war had broken out with Prussia, and so had to make do with old, smooth-bore guns. This had led Admiral Tegetthof to make his witticism.

The Austrian Fleet certainly had in him a determined Commander. Tegetthof was thirty-eight—the same age as Nelson at the Battle of the Nile—and came from an old military family. His grandfather had gained the title during the Seven Years' War; his father had been promoted Major on the battlefield of Austerlitz. He himself had made his mark at the beginning of his naval career, but it was an episode in the war on Denmark, in 1864, which had brought him into prominence.

He was then captain of the armoured frigate *Schwarzenberg* and in command of a small division comprising two other vessels, the *Radetsky* and the gunboat *Seehund*. Ordered to proceed from the Mediterranean to the North Sea, he surprised three Danish ships off Heligoland, on May 9th, 1864. He attacked at once, but encountered a stiff resistance from Commodore Svenson, the commander of the small Danish division. Although three Prussian ships arrived on the scene (but gave little fight), the Danes succeeded in withdrawing safely to their base, after inflicting considerable damage on the Austrians. Tegetthof's frigate had received ninety-three hits and was on fire.

He was subsequently given his flag, at the age of thirty-five, and revealed himself an ardent believer in offensive action. The young Rear-Admiral proclaimed the advantages of ramming tactics, in spite of the fact that no Austrian ship had a pointed beak or ram; at most, there was only a sort of cutwater formed by the joining of the armour-plating at the bows.

Italian warships, however, had projecting rams that were more than six feet in length. The latest ship, newly received from a British ship-yard, had been given a ram thirty feet long, and was aptly named the *Affondatore* (literally, the "Sender-to-the-bottom").

Tegetthof

The Italian Fleet was much the larger, with thirty-three ships totalling 87,000 tons against 27 Austrians totalling 54,000 tons, and with 695 guns and 11,425 officers and ratings against the Austrians' 523 guns and 7,492 personnel. But the Italians lacked what the best of weapons could not compensate for—a determined commander-in-chief prepared to take the offensive.

Their admiral, the Conte Carlo Pellione di Persano, had been a brilliant naval commander in the past. He was twenty years older than the Austrian commander-in-chief, and had taken a prominent part in the capture of Ancona,[1] Gaeta, and Messina for King Victor-Emmanuel, supporting the army with his frigates and gunboats. But the high administrative functions that he had been called upon to exercise since then, and the honours conferred upon him, had separated him from the serving naval officers at a time when, Italy still not being united, they thought of themselves primarily as Piedmontese, Sardinians, Neapolitans . . . and were in need of an energetic and determined leader capable of forging a national navy from the various provincial

[1] It was he who received the sword of General Lamoricière, the commander of the Papal troops.

elements. Admiral Di Persano, senator and ex-Minister, took command of the Italian Fleet at Tarento on May 16th, 1866, but without the slightest enthusiasm. If the King had not insisted, he would have declined the honour and pleaded incompetence.

Meanwhile, Tegetthof, with the fleet at Pola on the Adriatic, was being restrained by the Austrian authorities from embarking on some risky enterprise. The Italian ships were assembled at Ancona on June 27th, but the High Command could not prevail upon Persano to put to sea. He did not even chase off six Austrian ships, under the command of Tegetthof, which came on reconnaissance and for two hours remained within sight of the eleven armoured Italian ships, and then regained their base at Pola in their own good time.

The morale of the Austrian sailors shot up. . . . "The effect on our crews was excellent," Tegetthof wrote on July 4th. "To be practically within range of eleven enemy warships (without counting the others), of which at least half were ready to put to sea . . . and yet remained under the protection of their shore batteries! What our neighbours on that side of the Adriatic thought of our sudden appearance, I cannot say. But Admiral Persano himself was astounded and completely flustered, there can be no doubt of that. He could have utterly crushed us. . . ."

Yet Italy greatly needed a victory at sea to compensate for the defeat by the Austrian army at Custozza on June 24th, only four days after the declaration of war. In vain did the Minister, Deprettis, and the Parliamentary delegate, Boggio—who embarked in the flagship, *Re d'Italia*, as a kind of political commissar—urge Admiral Persano to take some action. On July 14th, however, he received a letter that concluded with the following words: "At the Minister's request, I have to inform you that if the Fleet remains inactive he will be obliged to remove you and appoint another Commander-in-chief, one better able to make use of an offensive force for which so many sacrifices have been made and on which high hopes are fixed."[1] The Minister in person arrived in Ancona the following day. Persano agreed to put to sea! Though not in the direction of Pola and the Austrian Fleet, but to carry out a minor operation against the island of Lissa . . . "chosen because its defences were strong enough to give some military importance to the operation, without there being any likelihood of defeat with the force to be deployed".[2]

The island of Lissa, thirty miles from the Dalmatian coast, had been

[1] *Storia della Marine Militari Italiana* (Vol. II), by C. Randaccio; quoted by Lt. Moreau in *Lissa*, French Naval College, 1928.
[2] From the despatches of Lt. d'Ancien of the *Eclaireur*. (French National Archives, BB 859.) The *Eclaireur* was in the Adriatic at the time of the battle.

an Austrian possession since 1815. It had a garrison of 1,893 men commanded by Colonel von Margina, and the batteries numbered 88 guns.

Admiral Persano sailed from Ancona at three in the afternoon of July 16th. His fleet of twenty-nine ships included eleven ironclads.[1] The *Affondatore* was to join the fleet at sea, bringing a landing-force of

---

[1] The *Re d'Italia* and the *Re di Portogallo* had 7-inch side-armour and carried respectively 36 and 28 guns, some of which were 10-inch. The *Affondatore* had two 10-inch in gun-turrets.

a thousand troops from Naples. The despatch-boat *Messagero* went ahead and made a reconnaissance of the island on the 17th, sailing close inshore and flying the British flag—which later brought strong protests from the Austrian Government. But no disregard had been shown of the customs of sea warfare, as warships may fly false colours provided they hoist their proper flag before opening fire.[1]

The Italians met with a stiff and unexpected resistance from the Lissa garrison. For two whole days Persano's ships bombarded the island, and it was a sheer waste of ammunition. One ship in particular, the *Formidabile*, which fought a duel with a shore battery, retired badly damaged and with sixty casualties among her crew of three hundred and fifty.

Meanwhile, news that the Italian Fleet was at sea had been brought to Tegetthof, at Pola, by a vessel which had slipped away from Lissa after the reconnaissance made by the *Messagero*. At first, Tegetthoff thought the Italians were carrying out a diversionary movement and that their real intention was to attack Trieste or the coast of Istria. But when he learnt, on the 19th, that the attack on Lissa was continuing and that more than twenty ships were engaged, there was no longer room for doubt. That afternoon Tegetthof's flagship, the *Ferdinand Maximilian*, led the Austrian ships out to sea. The squadron sailed in three divisions: the *Ferdinand Maximilian* was in the lead with six other armoured frigates; then came the *Kaiser* and five frigates and a corvette, under the command of Kapitan von Pets; and seven gunboats brought up the rear. There were six despatch-boats acting as scouting vessels.

At daybreak on July 20th an Italian scouting vessel, the *Esploratore*, found herself in the midst of the Austrian squadron, which was making slow headway against a strong south-easter. Rain and mist were reducing visibility, and the *Esploratore* was able to slip away, heading south at her maximum speed of twelve knots to warn Admiral Persano. It was said later, in Austria, that the Italian commander-in-chief replied to the signals made by the *Esploratore* that the suspicious vessels she had sighted could only have been a fishing fleet. If Persano really did so, he was soon disillusioned; for by eight in the morning the Italian ships were all at action stations.

At ten o'clock the ironclads were in line ahead five miles to the north of Lissa and heading towards the Austrian squadron which had been sighted six miles to the north-north-west. Rear-Admiral Vacca's division was in the van, then came Persano's flagship, the *Re d'Italia*,

[1] There were several instances of this during the Second World War, on the part of both British and German ships.

followed by six other ships; the *Affondatore* was on a parallel course east of the line, on the *Re d'Italia*'s starboard quarter. The smallest of these ships was of 2,000 tons; the largest, 5,700, and had 36 guns.

Soon afterwards, Admiral Persano left the *Re d'Italia* and was taken

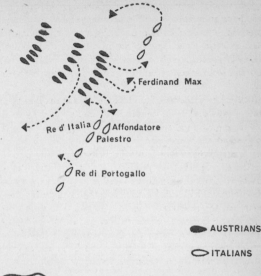

Ferdinand Max

Re d' Italia   Affondatore
Palestro

Re di Portogallo

AUSTRIANS

ITALIANS

L I S S A

The Battle of Lissa

to the *Affondatore*, for a reason that has never been quite clear, but omitted to inform the fleet of the change in flagship; the only evidence was the flying of a vice-admiral's flag in the *Affondatore*—a full admiral's not being available—and the hauling down of the flag in the *Re d'Italia*. This caused a certain amount of confusion among the

Italians; and the *Re d'Italia*, having heaved to for the Admiral to get away, found herself isolated when the action began.

The Austrians were already in order of battle, as they had been since leaving port, and as soon as the Italians were sighted Tegetthof had made the signal "Head straight for the enemy and sink him." The Austrian ships ploughed forward at maximum speed—which was not very much. Their commander realized that his plan to ram the ships of the enemy van would not work, and veered towards the *Re d'Italia*. It was then, just after half past ten, that Vacca's three ships opened fire at one thousand yards; their guns made so much smoke that the Austrians were blinded by it and passed right through the enemy line without succeeding in ramming a single ship. However, the gunfire had done them little harm; and, like a line of cavalry, they returned to the charge, damaging four Italian ships this time, though not seriously enough for any to leave her station.

In the course of a second mêlée, three Italian ships were cut out by a stronger group of the enemy and severely punished. The *Re d'Italia* had her helm put out of action, and the *Palestro* received two broadsides in quick succession and was set on fire.

Tegetthof was determined on his ramming tactics. His flagship had already given two Italians a glancing blow astern, but not hard enough to be decisive; he had, however, a trophy in the shape of the *Palestro*'s mizzen-mast and flag which had fallen across his deck. His flag-captain, Von Sterneck, who had clambered into the rigging, caught sight of an ironclad, through the smoke, which was passing across his

course; and he at once ordered full speed ahead.

The intended victim was the *Re d'Italia*, still unable to answer to her helm. But her captain tried to avoid the shock by going hard astern. It was too late. The *Ferdinand Maximilian* rammed him on the port side, just at the place intended, making a hole six feet deep and twelve feet wide, through which the sea poured as soon as the *Ferdinand Maximilian* backed away. The Italian ship went down in less than three minutes, colours flying, and her crew on deck firing muskets and pistols at the Austrian.

Tegetthof at the moment of boarding (*from a caricature*)

One ironclad sunk, two others burning fiercely (the *Palestro* blew up a little later), and four more damaged . . . the Italians had had enough, and the remainder of the action had no influence upon the final result. There were, however, other attempts at ramming by Austrian ships, making the Battle of Lissa almost unique in the history of sea warfare.[1]

The *Kaiser* made several runs at the *Re di Portigallo*, and finally succeeded in giving her such a blow that some fifty feet of her armoured plating was ripped off; but the *Kaiser* was damaged even more, and had to withdraw from the action.

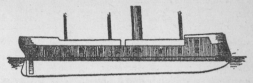

Outline of the *Ferdinand Maximilian*, the Austrian flagship
at the Battle of Lissa

At one moment the *Affondatore*—the one ship deliberately equipped with a long pointed ram—was well positioned to run down the damaged *Kaiser*. In fact, the shock seemed so imminent that the men on deck were ordered to lie down as a safety precaution, one of her officers said later. But Admiral Persano would not permit the tactic, perhaps from fear of sinking his own ship, and the *Affondatore* veered away, being fired upon by the Austrian ship.

The battle had to all intents ended. The main action had lasted about fifty minutes. At two o'clock the Italian Fleet withdrew to the west, and was back at Ancona by three the following afternoon.

The Austrians had scored a notable victory. They had not lost a single ship, and their casualties amounted to 38 killed and 138 wounded, whereas two Italian ships had been lost and 611 men killed. But Lissa had no influence upon the outcome of the war, which was definitely lost to Austria after the defeat of her army by the Prussians at Sadowa on July 3rd that same year.

The tactical and strategical lessons to be drawn from the Battle of Lissa caused many arguments between advocates of ramming and those of gunfire. But the truth of the matter was that once again victory had gone to the bravest and most daring.

---

[1] Ramming and boarding was a favourite tactic in the time of sail, as we have noted; but the ships had relatively little speed and their bows were not strong enough for a decisive result to be obtained from ramming alone. In modern times, there have been many instances of submarines being run down, but although the opportunity is one not to be missed it is never considered the chief means of destruction.

XIX

THE FIRST TORPEDO ATTACKS

The Russians send torpedo-boats to the Black Sea by train, for use against the Turks—torpedo attacks in the Danube (May 25th, 1877)—the first self-propelled torpedoes—French against Chinese—the Battle of Foochow (August 23rd, 1884)—French torpedo-craft play a decisive role—destruction of the Chinese squadron.

AFTER the shell-gun at Sinope and the ram at Lissa, the torpedo was put to the test—first by Russian sailors, who were again fighting the Turks. Most naval powers had been experimenting with and making torpedoes, or explosive mines, but none would have put their faith in a weapon that had not yet proved itself in battle conditions. The moment came, however, in 1877, when war caught the Russians with only one old ironclad in the Black Sea, against a strong Turkish fleet. Some bright person in St. Petersburg had the idea of sending by train a few of the "torpedo-boats"—small steam-launches that could be armed with one torpedo or explosive mine—then being tried out at the naval base of Kronstadt. They did not seem much to be feared by the Turkish naval commander, Hobart Pasha (who had seen service with the British Navy), and he thought he had done sufficient when ordering strong defensive precautions to be taken against these mosquitoes; though he would have done much better to have attacked and destroyed them in their nest. Although the Russian torpedo-boats did not inflict serious damage on the Turkish squadron, they were successful enough to show that they had a future as an offensive arm.

The first attack took place during the night of May 25th, 1877, and was directed against two Turkish river-gunboats, the *Seife* and the *Fethul Islam*, which were moored in the mouth of the Danube. It consisted of four torpedo-boats, under the command of Lieutenant Doubasoff, each armed with a stick-torpedo or explosive mine. As the boats could do five knots at most, and the torpedoes had to be exploded against the enemy ships at night, it was a dangerous mission with a strong possibility of being cut to pieces by enemy fire or blown up by the torpedo exploding too soon.

One of the boats, the *Tsarvitch*, only just escaped disaster. It had got to within seventy yards of its target, the *Seife*, before being detected, but then came under fire from the Turks' heaviest guns. However, either the aim was poor or the torpedo-boat had got underneath the guns; it safely reached the Turkish ship and fired its torpedo against the stern. The *Tsarvitch* was thrown about by the explosion and seemed in danger of sinking; as it slowly drew away a hail of fire was directed at it from the gunboat. But just then another torpedo-boat attacked, and its torpedo exploded beneath the gunboat's turret; some of the debris thrown into the air damaged the gunboat's screw as it fell. When daylight came, the *Seife* was seen to be sinking, but was still firing on her aggressors and put one out of action.

Not one of the Russians had been even wounded, and the Turkish casualties were negligible; yet this small night-action on May 25th, 1877, is memorable in the history of sea warfare as the first successful use of a weapon destined to make great ravages when developed and perfected. The towed torpedo became obsolete in a very short while, though it was used with success by the French seven years later, in their war against the Chinese.

When Lieutenant Doubasoff was trying it out at the mouth of the Danube, Admiral Makharoff was attempting to attack the Turkish squadron at the far end of the Black Sea, at Batoum, with another kind of torpedo—one that was towed towards its objective but was sent on its way at fairly close range. This proved unsuccessful; but there did exist a self-propelled torpedo at that time, the result of research and development by an Austrian, Lupis, and an Englishman, Whitehead. It still had a limited performance, having a speed of eight knots and an effective run of two hundred yards at most. The Russians tried out several in action against the Turks at Batoum; after a few unsuccessful attempts, a combined attack on January 26th, 1878, by two torpedo-boats which fired their torpedoes at eighty yards range succeeded in sinking a 2,000-ton Turkish gunboat.

It was not so much the results achieved by all these small torpedo-boats that was so remarkable, as the intelligent use made of them. The Russians had held off the much greater naval force of the Turks in the Black Sea by improvised use of a hitherto untried weapon. The harassing tactics employed and the bravery shown in driving home the attack constituted examples which have been continually followed by the crews of torpedo-craft in later wars. Proof of this was given by French sailors only seven years later, and thousands of miles from the Black Sea, during the Second Tonkinese War.

The French had been gradually securing control of Indo-China for the past twenty years, but the mother empire of China had refused to recognize the treaties concluded between the French and the Annamites. The situation was particularly delicate in Tonkin, where the

French representative, Rivière, a naval officer, had captured Hanoi but was defeated and killed in 1883 by the "Black Flags"—Annamite troops who were agents of the Chinese. However, the Treaty of Tientsin was concluded between the governments of Paris and Pekin in May, 1884, by which the Chinese agreed to evacuate their troops from Tonkin; and the Treaty of Hue, signed on June 6th, 1884, acknowledged Indo-China to be a French protectorate. But it was one thing to conclude a treaty with the Chinese and quite another to get them to keep the terms. A French military force of a thousand men under the command of Lieutenant-Colonel Dugenne was attacked up-country in Tonkin by a superior Chinese force and obliged to withdraw.

It fell to the French Navy, led by Admiral Courbet, to avenge this insult and insist on the Chinese respecting the terms of the Treaty of Tientsin. Courbet, one of the most popular of French naval commanders, was born in 1827 at Abbeville in northern France, and had entered the navy as an engineer. His career had followed a normal course, with little to distinguish it; and not until he was fifty-three did he attain flag-rank. He had just returned to France after filling the unenvious post of Governor of New Caledonia, when he received orders to sail at once for Indo-China, shortly after news of the death of Rivière had reached Paris.

Courbet

Rear-Admiral Courbet sailed from Quiberon Bay in the cruiser *Bayard* and arrived at Saigon on July 12th, 1883. He was at Hue for the signing of the treaty; then, only three weeks later, while returning to his squadron anchored in the Gulf of Tonkin, he learnt of the "ambush" of Dugenne's column.

Courbet was appointed commander-in-chief of the "China and Tonkin Naval Divisions", and at once went to Shanghai to confer with the French Minister, Patenôtre. The two agreed to advise the French Government to send a strongly worded Note to Pekin, demanding implementation of the Treaty of Tientsin, immediate evacuation of Chinese forces from Tonkin, payment of an indemnity of 250 million francs, and the handing over of the arsenals at Foochow and Nankin. Prime Minister Jules Ferry was unable to obtain support for such strong demands; having difficulties at home, the most he could authorize Admiral Courbet to do was to maintain a close blockade of Foochow, provided he did not engage in hostilities without the sanction of the Government.

Foochow, the capital of the Chinese province of Fokien, is situated on the River Min and thirty-four miles from the coast. The river is quite narrow halfway between Foochow and its mouth, but then opens out to form a natural anchorage, called the Pagoda anchorage. The Chinese there had a number of batteries on the northern shore, controlling the sea approaches to the estuary. There, too, stood the

The *Triomphante*, one of the French warships
at Foochow

Arsenal, which had been built between 1869 and 1873 under the direction of two French naval officers.

Courbet did not delay long before carrying out his instructions. He meant to keep a very tight blockade, and sent his available ships as far up the river Min as their draught allowed. The *Bayard* drew too much water, so he flew his flag in the 1,200-ton *Volta* and took the most dangerous station, as close inshore to the arsenal as the ship could get; astern of him were anchored six gunboats and the cruiser *Triomphante*. The remainder of the squadron were at their moorings off Matsou island, outside the river.

The situation was a highly explosive one, with the eight French ships —ten, rather, for the two torpedo-boats, Nos. 45 and 46, have not been mentioned (they were so small! but were to be the heroes of the action) —ten units, then, were under the guns of the Chinese batteries, only a few miles from an enemy city of half a million inhabitants and a garrison of twenty thousand regular troops, and facing an enemy squadron which, although Chinese, could not be discounted; it consisted of eleven warships, the largest being of 1,600 tons and five others of more than a thousand tons. There were also nine war-junks armed with old-fashioned, smooth-bore guns, but which in the event were used to better effect than those of the warships. The forty-seven guns of the nine junks included two 10-inch; but the great defect of these gallant little ships was that they were built entirely of wood, without any protective armour.

The French ships were at the mercy of the slightest incident. It would have been so simple for the Chinese to have made a surprise attack, to have blocked the river downstream by sinking a few junks loaded with stones and boulders, and so trapped the French within a narrow area where they would have found manoeuvring difficult. What was the Chinese naval commander, Admiral Ting, thinking about? And the Governor of Fokien Province? It was not as though Courbet's ships remained there for only a few days, or that he suddenly opened hostilities. The French division remained there in the anchorage for six weeks! For six weeks Courbet waited for a reply from Paris, for permission to take offensive action. His men were kept on the alert, his ships with steam raised, and the guns trained. The crews slept by their guns—not once did they unsling their hammocks.

In Paris, however, Jules Ferry finally lost patience with the evasive replies of the Chinese. He obtained a majority vote in the Chamber and sent Courbet the long-awaited authority to open fire. Probably never before in history had an attack been delivered after such a long warning!

On August 22nd, 1884, a signal was made from the *Volta* summoning all captains for a council of war at eight in the evening. By then, night had fallen, and there was a howling wind and beating rain. Captain Baux of the *Triomphante* was unable to get to the flagship, but was later sent a note informing him that the ships would open fire at two the following afternoon.

Why not at daybreak? Why wait until two in the afternoon? There were two reasons. Courbet was waiting for the ebb tide, so that the Chinese warships would swing round at their moorings and have their stern facing the French instead of their bows. Secondly, the French admiral, as in the grand old days, intended to give the enemy due warning. At ten in the morning the French Vice-Consul, Monsieur de Bezauce, called on the Governor of the Province to inform him of Admiral Courbet's intentions, then similarly informed the other Consulates, and returned to his own to haul down the French flag, thus

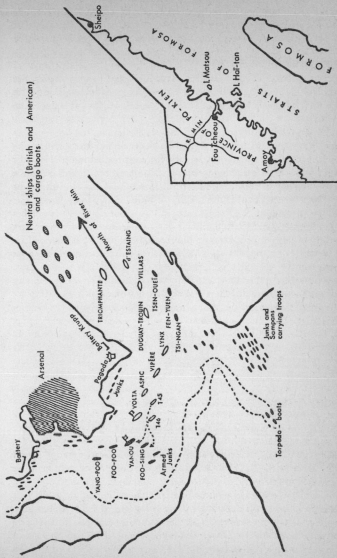

Destruction of the Chinese fleet and the Arsenal of Foochow by Courbet, August 23rd, 1884. (Inset—Formosa and the Fo-Kien coast)

signifying the rupture of diplomatic relations. Courbet, meanwhile, had informed Admiral Dowell, who was in a British warship in the estuary, and the captain of an American corvette, the *Enterprise*.

It was all reminiscent of the French commander of the leading troops at the Battle of Fontenoy, bowing to the English commander and requesting him to fire first: "After you, gentlemen." But the English did fire first. What were the Chinese waiting for, with the tide about to turn and put their ships at a disadvantage? Admiral Ting took no action; perhaps he had little confidence in his crews, who were good sailors but poor fighters.

The French were at action stations. The crews had eaten, and at half past one had been quietly given their final orders, without whistles or bugles being sounded—the enemy could not expect to be told of the exact time that hostilities would begin! In any case, that time could be easily discovered from the tides, and was indicated by the yellow waters of the Min as surely as a ship's clock.

There—the tide was on the turn! A signaller standing by the *Volta*'s main-mast had his eyes fixed on the Admiral; a sign from him, and up fluttered the flag for the ships to open fire. Almost at once, the guns began to roar.

But let us leave the gunners to their task and turn to a couple of small craft about to go into action—torpedo-boats Nos. 45 and 46, each of 32

Foochow: in foreground, *left to right*, the *Saone*, *Duguay-Trouin*, and Chinese junks; in background, Chinese gunboats, the *Lynx* (hidden by the *Duguay-Trouin*), *Aspic*, and *Volta*. On the right, the pagoda. (Sketch made at the time by Commander Jourdan)

tons, 90 feet long, and with a crew of nine. They were heading at sixteen knots towards the Chinese ships, each with its torpedo in tow—30 lbs. of guncotton![1]

Lieutenant Douzans, commanding No. 46, had only a short distance to cover. His objective, Admiral Ting's flagship, the *Yanou*, was only four hundred yards away; before her gunners had time to take any action, the torpedo had exploded amidships and No. 46 was going

---

[1] At the outbreak of the Second World War, torpedo-warheads contained 550 lbs. of explosive.

astern as fast as possible. The damaged *Yanou* struggled to reach the shore, under fire from the *Volta*, and suddenly burst into flames.[1]

One gone!

Lieutenant Latour had made for the gunboat *Foo-Sing* with his No. 45. His towline got caught up in the gunboat's screw when the torpedo went off, and this brought a hail of grenades and small-arms fire in his direction. But he got free, and sped back to the French line; while the *Foo-Sing* limped towards the arsenal. . . .

Courbet's ships had been continuing their shoot in the meantime. The *Volta* had turned her guns on the junks, which returned her fire with some effect; three sailors near the Admiral were badly wounded. But then the other French ships concentrated their fire on the junks, which were soon drifting in flames and sank one after another. The three largest Chinese ships had made little attempt to return the French fire. They were pounded at close range and soon became "floating wrecks speedily abandoned by their panic-stricken crews".[2]

There can be no doubt that the early elimination of Admiral Ting's flagship was a cause of the panic that descended upon the Chinese squadron, thus proving the high value of the attack carried out by torpedo-boat No. 46. However, the success of Lieutenant Douzans and his crew was due in considerable measure to the support from the guns of the French ships, and it is difficult to apportion the worth of one arm or the other in this action—much more so, as far as the torpedo is concerned, than in the case of the *Tsarvitch* in 1877.

Courbet had no difficulty in pressing home his opening success. The remaining Chinese ships were soon set on fire or sunk; their crews could not abandon ship and make for the shore quickly enough. The honour of the Celestial flag was saved by two gunboats, the *Kien-Sheng* and the *Fon-Shing*, which fought it out until carried by the current close to the larger French ships, when they were disposed of with a few broadsides.

There was still the *Foo-Sing* limping towards the arsenal. . . . Lieutenant de Lapeyrère went after her with some launches, whose crews boarded her and drove the remaining Chinese overside. Lieutenant de Lapeyrère hoisted the French flag; but it was too late, the fire aboard had gained too great a hold. The French just had time to put off in their launches before the *Foo-Sing* went down "sizzling and spluttering like a red-hot iron plunged into water".[3]

Nothing then remained of the Chinese squadron but some burning

---

[1] Admiral Ting survived the disaster. He commanded the Chinese Fleet at the Battle of the Yellow River during the Sino-Japanese War in 1894.

[2] *Courbet, marin légendaire*, by Marc Benoist, Paris, 1946.

[3] *Vagues Sanglantes*, by R. de Pirey; quoted by M. Benoist, *op. cit.*

wreckage and corpses drifting on the murky waters. The French ships turned their guns on the shore batteries and put them out of action one after the other. The following day, after a disturbing night on the watch for fireships, the arsenal was bombarded. Admiral Courbet then took his ships down the river and out to sea again, relieved at being in open waters once more. He had certainly avenged the treacherous ambush of Dugenne and his men: a Chinese squadron had been utterly destroyed at its moorings and all the shore installations of military worth rendered useless—and for the loss of ten men killed and forty-eight wounded. Such a small casualty list was the best satisfaction for a commander who cared for the safety and lives of his men, even in the most risky situations.

The day of the torpedo-boat trailing a torpedo to its objective seemed to be over. . . . The self-propelled torpedo was being perfected, notably by the French scientist, Augustin-Normand. But Courbet, eight thousand miles from home, had to use what was to hand. In February, 1885, his squadron was off Sheipoo, where a Chinese frigate and a gunboat had taken refuge from him. The only way of getting at them was with torpedo-boats, but there were none with the squadron.

However, where there's a will there's a way. Commander Gourdon of the *Bayard* had two of the launches fitted with torpedo-carriers, gave command of the second launch to Lieutenant Duboc, and at midnight they made for the harbour. They were not showing any navigation lights, and it was four hours before they reached their objectives. In a matter of seconds, both ships had received their death-blow. The Chinese contributed to the French success, for in their panic the frigate's gunners fired on the gunboat and sank her. Still, the result was what mattered.

Such were the forerunners of the courageous and dashing motor-torpedo-boat crews in the two World Wars. The weapon had been greatly developed—the torpedo was no longer towed to its objective, as the *Tsarvitch* had done, nor even fired at a range of eighty yards. But getting within fifteen hundred yards of a warship like the *Scharnhorst*, as British and Norwegian torpedo-boats did at the Battle of the North Cape, was quite as dangerous an undertaking.

Courage, skill, and . . . luck are still, as in 1878 and 1884, the first conditions of success.

XX

AMERICAN VICTORIES AT MANILA AND SANTIAGO

The Maine *incident and the Spanish-American War—Uneasiness along the East coast of the U.S.A.—Dewey's division annihilates the Spanish squadron at Manila (May 1st, 1898)—Admiral Cervera reaches Cuba—the Americans blockade him in Santiago—how General Shafter's troops unwittingly caused the Spanish sortie—American naval victory at Santiago (July 3rd, 1898)—regrettable disputes between the victorious admirals.*

EARLY in 1898, when the Cubans' revolt against their Spanish overlords was at its height, the American cruiser *Maine* was sent to Santiago to safeguard the lives and interests of U.S. nationals. An explosion resulted in the loss of the ship and two hundred and sixty of her crew. There was a great outcry in America, and a Commission of Enquiry was set up. Its preliminary findings did not preclude the possibility of the disaster having been due to an exterior cause, and the Americans therefore accused the Spanish of exploding a mine under the ship. Without waiting for the final result of the Enquiry (which showed that the explosion might equally have been caused within the ship), the United States declared war on Spain, on April 25th, 1898.

The two countries being separated by a vast ocean, it seemed that the war would be decided at sea. The relative strength of the naval forces bore no relation to the industrial resources of the two nations, although the American Fleet was decidedly greater than the Spanish. Nevertheless, the American public was most uneasy, especially along the Eastern seaboard, where people were expecting the Spanish Fleet to appear at any moment and were obviously in a state of jitters. The Navy Secretary was inundated with letters and telegrams demanding "guns everywhere and mines in all the estuaries and harbour approaches". In order to boost morale, the Navy Department dug out some of the obsolete cannon which had been peacefully rusting away in arsenals since the Civil War, and they were sent to end their days equally peacefully guarding a coast that never saw the smoke of a single Spanish warship.

Much more to the point were the measures taken to reinforce the Atlantic squadron. The armoured cruiser *Oregon* made the long voyage from the Pacific, round Cape Horn, in sixty-six days at an average speed of twelve knots—a considerable achievement in those days. This brought the strength of Admiral Sampson's Atlantic squadron up to five armoured cruisers, two light cruisers, and a few smaller ships; and he wisely kept them together, ignoring demands for each ship to be affected to the defence of a port.

On the Spanish side, Admiral Pasquale Cervera had left Cadiz on April 8th with half a dozen ships and orders to destroy the American naval base at Key West and then to blockade the coast. But his force was hardly adequate for the purpose, and there was no well-appointed base available to him in the West Indies. He was doubtful about the outcome of his mission, so made for the Cape Verde Islands to await

events. It was the news of his departure that had sent the East-coast Americans into such a state of nerves—a state that was quite unjustified, as events would show.

Hostilities first broke out in the Pacific. The Navy Department had already had an eye upon the Spanish Philippines, and some months previously had sent a capable and energetic officer to take command of the small naval division in the Far East. In December, 1897, Commodore Dewey had hoisted his pennant in the *Olympia*, which was then at Nagasaki. He concentrated his small force of four cruisers and two gunboats at Hong Kong, and started an intensive training programme. His crews were at maximum efficiency when the Navy Department informed him that the United States were at war with Spain.

Commodore Dewey

Four days later, on April 30th, Dewey's division reached Luzon, the chief island of the Philippines, found Subic Bay empty of the enemy, and continued towards Manila.[1] The Spanish squadron commanded by Rear-Admiral Don Patricio Montojo was at anchor there, for his ships were in no state to fight at sea. At daybreak on May 1st Dewey was in sight of the anchorage, and soon put paid to the whole Spanish squadron. Two runs past the anchorage, and the American gunners had put every one of Montojo's ships out of action; they were either in flames or sunk, or had been beached and abandoned by their crews. All that remained was for American troops to be sent from San Francisco, and the occupation of the Philippines was completed by August 13th, with the capitulation of Manila.

"The naval battle of Manila was won at Hong Kong," Dewey wrote in his despatch. Thanks to their training and to a greatly superior

[1] The Philippines had been in revolt against Spain since 1896, and had asked for American aid. (*Tr.*)

firing-power, Dewey's gunners had scored 171 hits on Montojo's ships, while only 15 Spanish shots had reached their target. The Spaniards had 381 killed or wounded, the Americans only 7 wounded.

So right from the beginning of the war the American Navy was relieved of all anxiety in the Pacific, and could concentrate on the West Indies campaign. That, too, was soon over.

On war being declared, Admiral Cervera had left the Cape Verde Islands for the Caribbean. The American naval commander in that area, Admiral Sampson, was not then at full strength. The *Oregon* was still on her way, and his second-in-command, Admiral Schley, was at Norfolk with a light division, retained there to calm the fears of the public. Sampson's plan to attack Havana was turned down by the Navy Department, and instead he sailed for Porto Rico with the *Iowa*, the *Indiana*, the *New York*, and two monitors, hoping to take the enemy squadron by surprise. He was off San Juan on May 12th, but there was no sign of Cervera. After a few desultory exchanges with the shore batteries, the American ships withdrew towards Cuba without having inflicted or suffered much damage. Cervera had correctly guessed the Americans' intentions and had avoided Porto Rico. He had instead made first for Martinique, but the French were anxious to maintain their neutrality and refused him entrance. The Dutch at Curacao, however, had fewer qualms, and he was able to refuel there. He then proceeded direct to Santiago, on the southern coast of Cuba, while Sampson was looking for him at Havana on the north of the island.

In the meantime, Schley had sailed from Norfolk with his light division. He lingered rather longer than was necessary, taking in supplies at Key West and then nosing round Cienfuegos, and it was not until May 28th that he arrived off Santiago. Three days later he was joined by Sampson, who had been reinforced by the *Oregon*.

The Spanish ships were at anchor behind a thickly sown minefield, and shore batteries prevented any attempt at sweeping it. Admiral Sampson first tried to bottle up the Spanish by sinking a cargo boat in the narrow entrance to the harbour. But the enemy was on the watch. A shore battery destroyed the vessel's rudder, and she drifted off to sink harmlessly away from the channel.

The minefield had to be cleared before the Americans could get within gun-range of the Spanish squadron; and as the shore batteries had first to be rendered harmless, the only way was to attack them by land. Now the American army was becoming restive; all the laurels in this war were being won by the navy. The military were only too eager to send an expeditionary force to Cuba, and in mid-June 16,000 troops commanded by General Shafter sailed from Tampa in cargo ships escorted by the navy. They landed unopposed at Daiquiri, some fifteen miles east of Santiago. This amphibious operation, which had been hastily mounted and laboriously carried out, had a surprising result. After a few days the troops became alarmed at their isolated position, and called for assistance from the sailors they had come to support. Admiral Sampson therefore sailed in the *New York* in response to the request from General Shafter. Before the Admiral reached him the naval Battle of Santiago had begun.

The wreck of the cruiser *Oquendo*, after the Battle of Santiago

The Spanish sailors had become even more alarmed than the American troops. Cervera was convinced that the fall of Santiago was only a matter of days, and had decided to stake all on forcing his way out to sea rather than be trapped in harbour. During the morning of July 3rd he led the way through the channel in his flagship, the *Maria Teresa*, followed by his three cruisers and two torpedo-boats. Schley was waiting for them with the squadron he temporarily commanded; but Admiral Sampson, on learning of the situation, was mad at being absent from the action he had tried so hard to precipitate, and made all speed to return to Santiago in the *New York*.

But the battle had practically ended before he reached the scene. As at Manila, the Spanish squadron was soon overwhelmed. The *Maria Teresa* came under the concentrated fire of the *Oregon* and four other ships; she was hit about thirty times, her boiler burst, her wooden deck was set on fire, and finally she went aground about six miles west of the harbour entrance. Then it was the turn of the *Oquendo* and the *Vizcaya*, which also went aground in flames. The two torpedo-boats were hotly engaged by the armed yacht *Gloucester*, then came under the fire of the *Indiana*; one was sliced through by a shell and the other surrendered to the *Gloucester*, but sank soon afterwards.

There remained only the *Cristobal Colon*. She was the one ship that succeeded in getting out to sea. According to one account, the stokers had been primed with spirits and shovelled on the coal at such a rate that the cruiser exceeded her maximum speed. But then reaction set in; torpor overcame the stokers, the cruiser's speed dropped, and the *Brooklyn* and the *Oregon* caught up with her after a chase of fifty-five miles. And before long the *Cristobal Colon* was disabled, and was beached by the crew.

The Spaniards had lost their entire squadron; one hundred and sixty of them had been killed, and eighteen hundred were prisoners, including Admiral Cervera. The Americans had but one man killed and one wounded. Santiago capitulated a fortnight later. Porto Rico was taken at the end of July; and then the American Navy began to plan an expedition against the coast of Spain itself. But the Spanish Government was not eager for the experience and preferred to open negotiations instead. The result was a peace treaty, signed on December 10th, 1898, which gave Cuba its independence, and Porto Rico, Guam, and the Philippines to the United States. The Americans were not then opposed to colonialism.

This first major victory of the United States Navy was marred by a stupid squabble. The American Press praised Admiral Schley to the skies as the man responsible for the victory. He gallantly asked his commander-in-chief to correct this impression, and Sampson thanked him. But at the same time Sampson submitted a most unfavourable report on his second-in-command, and the latter demanded an enquiry. Its findings went against him, so the quarrel broke out afresh. Finally, after two years, President Theodore Roosevelt intervened personally to put an end to the dispute, of which the real underlying cause has never been made clear.

The most important outcome of the battle was that the United States Navy had shown that it was a force to be reckoned with at an international level. Nevertheless, a warning was given by the eminent strategist, Mahan, who was then a captain in the Navy Department at Washington. He wisely reminded the Navy and the American public that they would not always come up against an enemy so ill-prepared as the Spanish had been. Forty-three years later, at Pearl Harbor, the Japanese gave point to Mahan's warning, which may have been forgotten during the intervening years.

XXI

THE RUSSIANS' LONG HAUL TO TSOU-SHIMA AND DISASTER

Surprise attack by the Japanese on the Russian squadron at Port Arthur (February 8th, 1904)—Admiral Makaroff takes over—but goes down with his ship six weeks later—the Battle of the Yellow Sea—Port Arthur falls to the Japanese—the odyssey of the Russians' second Far East squadron—the Dogger Bank incident—refuelling difficulties—troubles at Madagascar—the Japanese on the watch—they inflict a crushing defeat on the Russians, on the anniversary of the Czar's coronation—Nebogatoff surrenders to save the lives of his crews—the consequences of it all.

THE Imperial Russian Navy, which had been the first to make successful use of the shell-gun and then of the torpedo, was slowly moving towards the most crushing and decisive defeat ever recorded in history, including even those suffered by the French at Sluys and at Trafalgar.

At the beginning of the twentieth century, Russia's age-long quarrels with Sweden and Turkey seemed to have ended, but she then found herself in difficulties with her neighbours in the Far East, the Japanese. The causes were many, but the principal Japanese objection was to the Russians' presence at Port Arthur and to the territorial concessions they had obtained from Manchuria in order to complete the Trans-Siberian railway. Talks between the two powers had been in progress for some time when, on February 6th, 1904, the Japanese suddenly broke them off; and, without any ultimatum or other procedure to signify that a state of war existed between the two countries, the commander-in-chief of the Japanese Fleet, Admiral Heichiro Togo, was given a free hand to attack and destroy the Russian squadron at Port Arthur.

The military and naval forces of the Czar were greatly superior numerically to those of the Emperor. But they had far vaster territories to defend. The Russian Fleet was divided into three squadrons of about equal strength: the Far East squadron, based on Port Arthur and Vladivostock; the Black Sea squadron, which under the Treaty of London of 1870 was not allowed to pass through the Dardanelles; and the Baltic squadron, which was free to pass through the Skagerrak but was nevertheless separated from the Russian naval bases in the Far East by a distance equal to three-quarters of the earth's circumference. So that to have parity with the Japanese in the Pacific, the Russians ought to have built a fleet three times the size or else ceased to maintain any naval forces in Europe. But the latter solution was prevented by the attitude of Britain, which was allied with Japan, and by Turkey, which in spite of her decline was still capable of attack.

The Far East squadron, commanded by Admiral Stark, was comprised nevertheless of seven battleships—the flagship *Petropavlosk* was one—and six cruisers, and a couple of dozen destroyers and torpedoboats. It was not greatly outnumbered by the Japanese Fleet, except in cruisers and destroyers. Admiral Togo had the following ships under his command: a battle group of six 12-inch battleships; a light squadron of four fast cruisers, nineteen destroyers and eight torpedo-boats; and a squadron of six heavy and four light cruisers.

Togo's mission, moreover, required a force superior to that of the Russians. His ships had to give cover to troops landing on a defended coast, and then support them against enemy attack. It was in order to eliminate the most likely intervention as quickly as possible that the Japanese High Command had decided on a surprise attack before a state of war had been officially declared—just as it did thirty-seven years later, in the attack on Pearl Harbor.

Togo had every hope of putting most of the Russian squadron out of action with one swift attack. And it must be said that the Russians gave him every help! Their commander-in-chief and Governor of Eastern Siberia, Admiral Alexeief, was an irresolute person whose capabilities were in question; his chief aim was to take no risks and husband his resources. Still, even that was a policy—provided it was accompanied by stringent precautionary measures. But he had taken none whatever. The squadron was slumbering peacefully at its moorings in the roadstead, and its commander was still unaware that the diplomatic talks had been broken off, when the Japanese attacked on the night of February 8th, 1904. What was more, an exercise by the Russian torpedo-boats due to take place that night had been cancelled, without the rest of the squadron being so informed; no one felt any alarm, therefore, when the watch reported torpedo-boats approaching, at eleven that night. One of them was displaying the identification number of a Russian torpedo-boat that would have taken part in the night exercise, it was said later.[1]

Two battleships and one heavy cruiser were torpedoed by the Japanese. None of the three was sunk, but the *Tzesarevitch* limped into harbour with a list of eighteen degrees, and the *Revitzane* and the *Pallada* had to be beached, near the harbour entrance. The results would have been more disastrous if the Japanese torpedo-boats had

[1] *L'Escadre de Port Arthur*, by Captain Semenoff.

been equipped with radio and could have reported the success of their attack. As it was, Admiral Togo let precious time pass before arriving on the scene with his ships; by then, the Russian shore batteries—whose hydraulic recoil system had been drained for the winter—were again ready for action and opened fire on the Japanese.

The surprise attack had brought no decisive result, especially as the Russians soon managed to repair their damaged ships by hauling them on to slipways. Some days later, a Japanese attempt to block the harbour entrance was repulsed. The twenty-seven blockships sent in were either destroyed by the shore batteries or went aground because the crews were blinded by the Russian projectors. Such was the situation between the opposing forces when, on March 8th, Vice-Admiral Stefan Ossipovitch Makaroff arrived at Port Arthur to take over command of the squadron.

The blame for the state of unpreparedness on the night of February 8th had fallen upon Stark; and there could have been no better choice to replace him than Makaroff. He was, without doubt, the most capable and efficient of the Russian senior naval officers. A fine sailor and clever tactician, he had a European reputation as a hydrographer; and, moreover, he was an inspiring leader. The news of his arrival to take command gave a great zip to the morale of the ships' crews. Their enthusiasm knew no bounds when, a few days after his arrival, the new commander-in-chief put to sea in a light cruiser and raced to the assistance of a flotilla of torpedo-boats in action against the enemy. He was given a triumphal greeting on his return. "There were thousands of men jostling together on the quays, on the parapets of the shore batteries, and hanging from the rigging or leaning over the ships' sides, all closely watching the small cruiser as she came through the narrow channel and into harbour. . . . Everyone wanted to see for himself that Makaroff's flag was flying from her mast." [1]

He infused a new energy into the squadron; repairs were quickly carried out, training was stepped up, and security precautions were overhauled. The Japanese soon realized that the time was past when they could cruise leisurely off Port Arthur. A change had obviously taken place!

It did not last for long—the Russians were out of luck. Makaroff met his death about six weeks after his arrival at Port Arthur. On April 12th, he and 32 officers and 600 ratings were lost in the *Petropavlosk* when she struck a mine two miles out; she was returning to harbour after chasing off some Japanese cruisers that had been protecting minelayers. Another Russian ship, the *Pobieda*, was also damaged by a mine,

[1] Semenoff, *op. cit.*

but not seriously. The material losses were as nothing compared with the disappearance of "Old Whiskers", as the squadron affectionately referred to the Admiral. "What do the ships matter," said an old sailor to his officer. "A couple could have been sunk, and even a few gun-boats as well. . . . You don't realize, your Honour! We've been guillo-tined, that's what's happened. . . ."

The governor of the region took temporary command, flying his flag in the *Sevastopol*; and then Admiral Witheft succeeded Makaroff. The squadron remained strictly on the defensive, until obliged to make a sally on August 10th. The anchorage had come under artillery fire from the Japanese land forces; and when this news of the enemy closing in had reached the Czar, he had personally telegraphed orders to Witheft to make a sortie with all his forces and reach Vladivostock. But it ended in a hurried retreat back to Port Arthur after the sharp action known as the Battle of the Yellow Sea, in which Admiral Witheft lost his life; a shell burst on the bridge of his flagship, the *Tzesarevitch*.

The fate of the Russian ships at Port Arthur was now sealed. Rein-forcements were on the way, but before they had covered half the distance Port Arthur fell to the enemy The ships that had not been sunk by the Japanese siege-guns scuttled themselves the day before, the first of the New Year, 1905.

It would have been better for Russia to have cut her losses, and not prolonged a war that had begun so badly for her. That was very likely what Admiral Sinovie Petrovitch Rojesvensky often thought during his long voyage from the Baltic with the second Far East squadron. It was what all logical persons and naval officers everywhere thought. However, the planners in St. Petersburg thought otherwise. The Czar, Nicholas II, and his Government dreaded losing face, feared a loss of prestige in the eyes of the world. It was known everywhere that Ad-miral Rojesvensky had sailed with his ships for Vladivostock, and the navies of all countries took a deep interest in this extraordinary endeavour.

The really amazing thing about this odyssey is not that the Russian squadron was practically wiped out by Admiral Togo when it did reach Japanese waters, but that it arrived at all, and complete. That was a feat which threw great credit upon the Russian sailors and their commander. It was an exploit worthy of better reward; but their High Command had already condemned them by sending the ships three-quarters of the way round the world to fight an enemy who had months in which to prepare, and who was fresh and rested—not worn out, like the Russians—and who was within easy reach of his bases.

The dramatic circumstances of Admiral Rojesvensky's long voyage made it akin in some measure to that of Medina-Sidonia and the Great Armada, which reached the Straits of Dover in spite of the efforts of the English—a not inconsiderable feat in the era of sail. Rojesvensky led his squadron of "colliers" from the Baltic round to the Sea of Japan, being denied access to neutral ports and forced to all manner of subterfuges to take in supplies and to refuel, and having to cope with despondency among the crews. Both the voyage of Medina-Sidonia and of Rojesvensky ended in defeat; the former being beaten by the elements more than by enemy gunfire, the latter battling through high seas and stormy weather only to go down within sight of his destination, which was barred to him by a superior enemy force.

It was on April 30th, 1904, eighteen days after the death at sea of Admiral Makaroff, that the Czar's Minister of Marine, the Grand-Duke Alexis, announced the formation of the second Far East squadron. The programme was for it to sail from the Baltic at the end of July and reach Vladivostock four or five months later. The command of this squadron, which included five 12-inch battleships still being completed at Kronstadt, was given to Rojesvensky, then Deputy Chief of Naval Staff; and he was allowed a free hand to chose his own staff, so he should have had the pick of the Russian naval officers.

Rojesvensky was an excellent staff officer, intelligent and firm, but he had little experience of command at sea He was a taciturn man who rarely confided in his staff and who lacked imagination—the type of commanding officer who could be utterly relied upon to do everything possible to carry out the most exacting orders, yet who was without that spark of brilliance which often decides the successful outcome of a battle. When he found his way blocked he had no thought of manoeuvring, but advanced headlong into the narrows where the enemy was barring his way to Vladivostock; and when, badly wounded after two hours of battle, he regained consciousness for a few moments it was to repeat his order "head for Vladivostock" as though nothing had happened in the meantime.

The squadron sailed from the Baltic not at the end of July but on October 14th; the ships were not ready for sea before then. Even so, one of the new battleships had to be left behind, for she was still months from being completed. The crews had received no training—but they would be given it during the voyage! Most difficult of all was to get rid of the ingrained ideas which were prevalent among the naval High Command and which had little relation to reality. When Captain

Semenoff, who had been at Port Arthur and taken part in the Battle of the Yellow Sea,[1] got back to Russia and gave his report, he was listened to with an absent ear, for it all went against the official doctrines of the "Technical Committee". It was only after much effort, too, that Rojesvensky succeeded in discarding a group of old ships which the High Command wanted to add to his squadron. (It was only a temporary respite; they were sent to join him later.) Rojesvensky saw them as so much dead weight—the "sink-by-themselves class" was what their crews called them—and he would have much preferred going into battle with a smaller but better-balanced squadron.

When the squadron finally sailed, however, it numbered forty-five ships including store ships. The two smallest battleships, three light cruisers, and the destroyers were to take the route via Suez, under the command of Admiral. Felkersam. It was feared that the other ships drew too much water, and they were to go round by the Cape. A rendezvous was fixed at Madagascar, and from there the whole squadron would cross the Indian Ocean together.

It is almost 18,000 miles from the Gulf of Finland to Port Arthur by way of the Cape of Good Hope; and there was not a single Russian base in the whole distance. There were French bases, and France had just concluded a pact with Russia; but France was not at war, and under international conventions neutral powers were forbidden to give shelter for more than twenty-four hours to the warships of belligerent nations. And the British and Japanese Governments would certainly put pressure on the French to ensure that the conventions were observed. Germany possessed a few useful ports of call on the route, and would have been pleased for the Russians to make use of them, if only in the hope of thereby weakening the Russo-French alliance. But the Germans, too, were bound by the international conventions. However, they gave valuable help to the Russians. The Hamburg-Amerika Line agreed to the Russian Government chartering seventy of its freighters to keep the squadron supplied with coal in the course of its voyage.

Nowadays the refuelling of warships at sea presents little problem. It is almost a common occurrence for a tanker to pump fuel-oil into a ship's bunkers—or into two ships at once, one on either quarter—while proceeding at twelve or fifteen knots. But in 1904 it was a different matter. Coal was the fuel needed, and thousands of sacks of it had to be transhipped—an operation that could be carried out only in a sheltered anchorage, or at least when the sea was calm and both ships were

[1] His ship, the cruiser *Diana*, had escaped to Saigon after the Battle of the Yellow Sea and was interned by the French. Semenoff reached Marseilles in a French passenger ship, and from there returned to Russia overland—just in time to join Rojesvensky's staff before he sailed.

hove-to. Rojesvensky, under the stress of necessity, was to be the first to succeed in carrying out the operation while under way.[1]

The voyage began badly. The squadron had hardly cleared the Denmark Straits and turned into the North Sea than the maintenance-ship *Kamtchatka*, which had fallen behind with engine trouble, signalled that she was being attacked by torpedo-boats! It was fantastic. The only Japanese torpedo-boats that had ever been in the North Sea were those built by the British on Tyneside, and the last of them had been sent out East a year previously. And yet there were certainly suspicious shapes to be seen in the darkness, all among the squadron; and the numbers were being increased by the imagination of the nervous men on watch.

The ships began firing their light guns at random—it was never known where the order came from, if there was one. A few of their own vessels were hit—the *Aurora* had four holes on the water-line, and the priest on board had his hand shot away—and a fishing vessel out of Hull was sunk and her crew drowned. For the "suspicious shapes" were the trawlers of a British fishing fleet on the Dogger, all showing regulation riding lights.

Relations were already strained between Britain and Russia, and this latest incident almost brought Rojesvensky up against the Royal Navy. The British Press carried indignant articles calling for the destruction of "the mad dog". A cruiser division was sent to escort the Russian squadron and remained with it as far as Gibraltar, by which time the Russian Government had agreed to the matter going to The Hague and to pay whatever damages were ordered by the International Court.

On October 26th the squadron dropped anchor outside Vigo Bay, where five German colliers were waiting as arranged. But there were also representatives of the Spanish Government waiting to inform Rojesvensky that no transhipment of coal would be allowed in Spanish territorial waters. This also applied to the Russian supply ship *Anadyr*, whose 7,000 tons of coal would have just sufficed to refill the squadron's bunkers. However, on this occasion an exchange of telegrams between Madrid and St. Petersburg arranged matters; and the Russians continued their voyage, bunkers full again and their ships attended by cruisers from Gibraltar commanded by Admiral Sir Baldwin Walker.

The next port of call was Tangiers, where the ships that were going through the Suez Canal were to part company from the rest of the

[1] While in the China Sea in May, 1905, a week before the battle of Tsou-Shima, Rojesvensky stopped a British cargo vessel suspected of carrying contraband, and put a prize-crew aboard to take her into Vladivostock. As the ship did not have sufficient coal left in her bunkers, one of the Russian transports drew alongside and coal was transhipped while both vessels were under way.

squadron. The only difficulty at Tangiers was caused by the strong east wind, which made refuelling in the open roadstead almost impracticable. The Sultan of Morocco (Tangier had not yet become an international zone) was officially unaware that a state of war existed between Russia and Japan, and so could but respect the commands of Mohamet and welcomed in the traveller as an honoured guest. It was a different matter at Dakar, where Rojesvensky arrived with the larger ships on November 12th. A French naval officer went aboard the Russian flagship and with some embarrassment requested the Admiral to be kind enough to refuel outside territorial waters . . . off the Cape Verde Islands, for instance—where there was a very rough sea! And the telegraph wires began to hum between Dakar, Paris, and St. Petersburg. But as the Russian ships were anchored some distance out, Rojesvensky had the German colliers come alongside and deliver their supplies without waiting for permission to arrive from Paris. When it came, it merely put the record straight. And this time the Russian ships had taken a double helping of coal; not only were their bunkers full, they had a deck cargo too—there was coal "not just up to the neck, but over our ears".

They met with similar opposition at Libreville on December 1st, being refused permission to enter the Gabon estuary. However, they were able to refuel in a calm sea off Cape Lopez, just south of the Equator. Then came the turn of the Portuguese to demonstrate their respect for international conventions. Rojesvensky's ships had hardly dropped anchor off Mossamedes, on the coast of Angola, than a small gunboat proudly flying a huge Portuguese flag put out to inform the Russians that they must continue their voyage without delay. Rojesvensky tried to convince the captain in the most polite terms, that although the ships were anchored in a bay they were nevertheless three miles out—which was probably not true. In any case, the gunboat's captain refused to cede the point, and returned to port looking most irritated—while the jeering Russians continued to replenish their stocks from the colliers as though nothing had been said.

The Governor of Angra-Pequena, in German South-West Africa, where the Russians arrived four days later, had hit upon an excellent solution and a very simple one: there were no Russian ships, so there could be no question of them using or not using the roadstead. At least, he could not see them from his Residence; and as for going out beyond the reef in a canoe to inspect the roadstead—there was certainly no question of that!

Unhappily for the Russians, wherever they were given friendly assistance it was the elements which proved unkind. The German

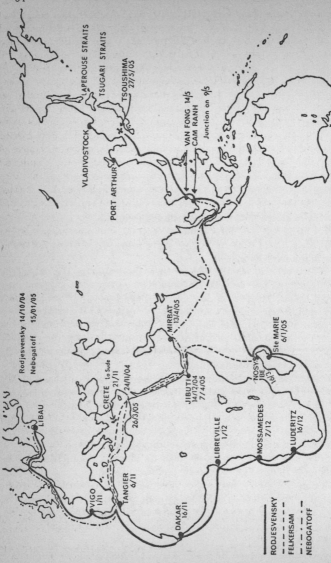

LAPEROUSE STRAITS

TSUGARI STRAITS

TSOUSHIMA 27/5/05

VLADIVOSTOCK

VAN FONG 14/5
CAM RANH
Junction on 9/5

PORT ARTHUR

Rodjesvensky 14/10/04
Nebogatoff 15/01/05

MIRBAT 13/4/05

Ste MARIE 6/1/05

CRETE la Sude 21/11
24/11/04
26/3/05

JIBUTI 14/12/04 7/4/05

NOSY BE 16/3

LIBAU

LIBREVILLE 1/12

MOSSAMEDES 7/12

LUDERITZ 16/12

TANGIER 6/11

VIGO 1/11

DAKAR 16/11

RODJESVENSKY
FELKERSAM
NEBOGATOFF

The way to Sacrifice; routes taken by the Russian squadrons from the Baltic to Tsou-Shima

governor was right not to go beyond the reef. The sea was so rough that a collier alongside the *Souvaroff* was swept against one of her guns, and the work had to be interrupted for a time. It took six days for all the coal to be got aboard the Russian ships to enable them to make the next stage, one of the longest of the whole voyage, round the Cape to St. Marie Island just off the north-east coast of Madagascar. They were soon to meet the Roaring Forties, and with a deck cargo that set them low in the water. Those latitudes maintained their reputation, and between December 20th and 25th the wind howled and the ships rolled through waves more than thirty feet high. Boats were carried away, superstructures swept loose, and there was a long succession of mechanical breakdowns which brought despair to the engineers.[1] Nevertheless, all the ships reached St. Marie, only to learn that they had to continue for another six hundred miles, round to the west coast of Madagascar. The other ships, commanded by Felkersam, had reached the island but been refused permission by the French authorities, officially at least, to remain in their waters. So Felkersam had taken his ships round to Nossi-Be Island, just off the north-west coast; it was a long detour, but the island gave the only good anchorage without a telegraph service in the vicinity, so the squadron's presence would not be too quickly reported to the world.

In any case, this was a minor drawback compared to the other troubles and difficulties which descended upon the squadron. First came the news of the fall of Port Arthur and the end of the first Far East squadron; this removed all reason from the odyssey of the second squadron. Then Rojesvensky found that Felkersam's ships were all in bad shape and would have to remain at the anchorage for at least a fortnight, whereas he wanted to press on and attack the Japanese before they had time to recover from the Port Arthur campaign. There was worse to follow—the freighters of the Hamburg-Amerika Line refused to accompany the squadron across the Indian Ocean.[2] And to crown all, news came from St. Petersburg that the old, worn-out ships which Rojesvensky thought he had seen the last of, all the "sink-by-themselves", were on their way to join him, under the command of Rear-Admiral Nebogatoff.

From one cause and another, the squadron remained off Madagascar more than two months, finally sailing on March 16th, 1905, for

[1] "Our long voyage was a prolonged and despairing struggle with boilers that burst and engines that broke down. On one occasion, practically every ship's boilers had to be relit in the space of twenty-four hours," Semenoff wrote in his book, *Sur la voie du sacrifice*.

[2] The reason given was fear of being seized by Japanese cruisers. But it seems to have been connected with the pressure that the German Government was putting on Russia to separate her from France.

its long stage across the Indian Ocean. The crews were more despondent and anxious than when they had first reached Madagascar. Everyone had lost faith in the mission. Many had fondly hoped that the squadron would now return to Russia. Felkersam was suffering from some incurable disease (he died before the end of the voyage), and Rojesvensky had to take to his bunk for several days. One can imagine how stifling it must have been in the cramped conditions between-decks, with the hot damp steam and the coal-dust everywhere; sleep was practically impossible.

But far from recalling the squadron, the Russian Government had sent the old ships as reinforcements. The ancient cruiser *Nicolas I* and three armoured coastguard vessels of 4,000 tons armed with 9- and 10-inch guns had sailed from the Baltic on January 15th, and were nearing Suez. In the hope of giving them the slip, Rojesvensky had sailed as soon as he could, and while Nebogatoff was still in Suda Bay, Crete.

The German freighters sailed with the squadron after all—the matter had been arranged after two months of negotiations—and refuelled the ships in the course of the long stage to the coast of Annam, which took almost a month. On April 14th Rojesvensky reached Cam Ranh with his forty ships, after a voyage of 4,500 miles—the longest ever made between one port and another by a coal-fuelled squadron. This brought the total distance covered to 16,628 miles.

For three weeks the world had been without news of the Russian squadron, wondering which route Rojesvensky would take and whether he intended sailing round Australia to the Pacific. But he was eventually sighted in the Malacca Straits—where he could hardly be missed—only five days after a Japanese cruiser division had left those waters to go and seek him off North Borneo.

Cam Ranh is one of the best anchorages in the South China Sea. The Russians were at first given a friendly welcome there by Rear-Admiral De Jonquières, the second-in-command of the French Far East squadron, but he soon received peremptory orders to inform Rojesvensky that he must quit Indo-Chinese waters within twenty-four hours. And at the same time Rojesvensky received strict instructions from St. Petersburg to await Nebogatoff and his ships before proceeding any farther.

Thus began a fortnight or so of aimless and wearisome cruising about, dropping anchor in a deserted bay one day, drifting along at three knots the next; and losing what little morale the crews still had. At last, on May 9th, Nebogatoff's ships were sighted . . . Togo would have been more welcome! Rojesvensky's men wanted only to see the end of it all. Death or captivity seemed to matter little now. As for victory, only a few of the youngest officers still had any hope of that. In any case, the sooner they fought the Japanese the better, for whichever route they took to Vladivostock the enemy would be waiting for them.

But first they had to wait another five days while Nebogatoff's ships were provisioned and a few boilers repaired. This was done at Port Dayot; and French ships tactfully refrained from putting in an appearance until May 14th, by which time the whole Russian squadron was in sailing order and starting on the final stage of its lon; haul . . . to the disastrous finish a few days later—thirteen, to be exact.

Admiral Togo would have been victorious even if the Russian squadron had equalled him in numbers, gun-power, and fitness. He was kept fully informed of all his enemy's movements, and knew Rojesvensky's destination. Whichever route the Russian admiral chose in order to penetrate the Sea of Japan and reach Vladivostock, Togo could bar the way with all his available forces, thanks to his short lines of communication.

The Paris magazine Le Monde Illustré carried in its number dated May 20th, 1905 (a week before the Battle of Tsou-Shima) an announcement that Rojesvensky had sailed from Indo-China and an article on the different routes he could take to reach Vladivostock. There were three: by the southern entrance to the Sea of Japan, the Straits of Korea, which are divided by the island of Tsou-Shima; by the eastern entrance, the Tsugari channel between the two main Japanese islands of Nippon (or Honshu) and Yeso (or Hokkaido); and by the Laperouse Straits, between Yeso and Sakhaline. The last meant a long and perilous voyage, and there was the line of the Kurile Islands to pass through first. Moreover, the Laperouse Straits had been mined by the Japanese, as had the Tsugari channel; and the Japanese ships cruising off either entrance to the Inner Sea would soon inform Admiral Togo if Rojesvensky decided to attempt one or the other in spite of the longer distance. As for the Straits of Korea, the Japanese Fleet had been based there ever since the capture of Port Arthur—the heavy cruisers at Masampo, the light cruisers and other ships at Takeshii, on the island of Tsou-Shima itself. The large arsenal at Sasebo, on the Japanese mainland, was close at hand and facilitated the repairs and fitting-out of the fleet.

Since putting to sea on May 14th the movements of the Russian ships had been constantly reported during their passage through the busy China Seas; but trace of them was lost on May 25th and 26th. On the night of the 26th, however, a Japanese auxiliary cruiser, the

Sinano Maru, almost ran down one of the Russian hospital ships in the thick mist. It seemed probable that the main Russian force was in the vicinity. And at 5 a.m. the *Sinano Maru* signalled by radio: "Enemy fleet in sight in square 203. Is apparently making for the eastern channel."[1] An hour and a half later, the Japanese Fleet was putting to sea. At 7 a.m. patrolling vessels reported the Russian Fleet on a north-easterly course, twenty-five miles north-west of the island of Uku-Shima. Rojesvensky had tried to trick his adversary by detaching two cruisers towards the east coast of Japan, in an attempt to make the enemy believe the whole squadron was intending to take one of the northern passages. But this had failed.

The first contact was made by the *Idzumi*, of the Japanese Third cruiser squadron, which followed the Russians through the thinning mist for more than an hour; at one time she was within 9,000 yards of the Russian flagship, the *Souvaroff*, but promptly turned away when the 12-inch guns of the battleship were trained on her. Then at nine o'clock all four cruisers of Admiral Katakoa's division appeared out of the mist on the Russians' port side, and steered on a parallel course for a while, then withdrew after making this reconnaissance. At eleven o'clock the four ships of the light cruiser division appeared on the Russians' port beam. Rojesvensky had to be sparing with his ammunition and so had not yet opened fire. But one of the ships of the division he was leading, the *Orel*, inadvertently fired a shot; this was followed by the guns of other ships. The small Japanese cruisers returned the fire, then made off.

By midday the Russians were near the southern point of Tsou-Shima, and so far had maintained their estimated rate of progress.[2] The signal "Steer North twenty-three degrees East" went fluttering up the halyards of the *Souvaroff*. It was to remain flying until the end.

Aboard the flagship, the officers hurriedly finished a meal and the mess-president gravely gave them a toast to the anniversary of the Czar's coronation, which happened to fall that day, May 27th. A previous royal anniversary—Catherine the Great's birthday—had not been auspicious for the Prince of Nassau at the Battle of Svensund. One wonders whether any of the officers thought of that occasion as they raised their glasses and drank to the toast.

A few minutes later everyone was at action stations. Japanese cruisers and destroyers had been sighted on the port bow, and seemed about to pass across the course of the Russians. Rojesvensky signalled

[1] Of the Straits of Korea, between Tsou-Shima and the Japanese mainland.
[2] Rojesvensky had decided against passing through the Straits at night for fear of a torpedo attack in the narrow waters.

to form line abreast by all ships turning ninety degrees to starboard and then simultaneously to port, still on the same course. But the manoeuvre was badly carried out, due chiefly to an error by the *Alexandre III*, astern of the flagship; and the only result was to bring the squadron into two unequal columns. However, it caused the Japanese cruisers and destroyers to turn away, for fear of being caught between the two columns. But at twenty-past one, when Rojesvensky had just reformed in line ahead, Togo and his main battle group appeared to starboard and heading south-west—six battleships followed by six armoured cruisers.

Admiral Togo

Since midday Togo had been slowly cruising ten miles north of Okino-Shima, waiting for the Russians. He now turned eastward to "cross the T" to the Russians, while his light forces swung south to attack their rear. Soon afterwards the *Souvaroff* opened fire, followed by the whole of her line. Togo waited until within 6,000 yards, and then his ships concentrated their fire on the flagships of the two leading divisions, the *Souvaroff* and the *Osslyablia*.[1] The Japanese gunners soon found their aim, with disastrous consequences to the *Osslyablia*. Blazing from stem to stern, and with a gaping hole from three hits close together, she began to sink and disappeared just after three o'clock.

The Japanese then turned their guns on the *Alexandre III*, though still not neglecting the *Souvaroff*. By half past two their line was curved across the head of the Russians'; but in spite of this dangerous situation which exposed his ships to a cross-fire, Rojesvensky continued on his course. The distance between his flagship and the Japanese line was rapidly decreasing, but at last the *Souvaroff* turned away to starboard. By then, she had one turret out of action and no longer replied to her helm. The ship turned a complete circle, but her captain managed to get on course again by steering with the propellers. However, her foremast had gone, and both funnels had collapsed; fire was spreading rapidly through the ship, which had a list of eight degrees to port. . . . The *Alexandre III* took her place at the head of the line, but she

---

[1] The *Osslyablia* was still flying Admiral Felkersam's flag, although he had been dead for two days. Rojesvensky had given orders for it not to be hauled down, to keep the news from other crews.

continued to fight on. At half past four a torpedo attack was beaten off, and then the *Buiny* —which had saved two hundred of the *Osslyablia*'s crew of eight hundred—managed to get alongside the stricken ship. Rojesvensky, who had been wounded four times and was unconscious, was taken off, as well as some of his staff. The gallant *Souvaroff* stayed afloat until past seven o'clock, her last gun still firing, when another torpedo attack sent her to the bottom.

The *Alexandre III*, which had taken over direction of the squadron and vainly endeavoured to break out of the ring of fire, was mortally hit and sank just before the *Souvaroff*. There were only four survivors out of the 830 men on board. Shortly afterwards, one of Togo's battle-ships, the *Juji*, scored a direct hit on the magazines of the *Borodino*, the third ship of Rojesvensky's division, which blew up. Her keel re-mained above the water for a few minutes, then suddenly disappeared. There were no survivors.

It was the beginning of the end for the Russians. Admiral Nebogatoff, leading the third division in the old *Nicolas I*, signalled "Follow me" and tried to gather the scattered ships and make towards the south-west. Night was beginning to fall. The main body of Japanese ships withdrew to the north, leaving the battle area free for their torpedo-boats to operate in. Four of them attacked and sank the *Navarin*, from which there were but three survivors. The *Sissoi* was hit astern and limped along throughout the night, only to sink at daybreak. The *Nakhimoff* had her bows shattered, and was scuttled off the island of Tsou-Shima to prevent her falling into the hands of the enemy; and a similar fate befell the *Monomakh*, which had been torpedoed in the engine-room.

Daybreak on the 28th found Togo's big ships to the north of the battle area, still barring the way to Vladivostock, and Nebogatoff steaming towards them with five ships which had been relatively little engaged in the battle, but were nevertheless incapable of holding their own against the enemy ships that were beginning to surround them.[1] Nebogatoff did not hesitate for long. He hoisted the international signal of surrender.

"I'm an old man of over sixty," he said to his crew just before going to surrender his sword to Admiral Togo. "I shall be shot for this, but what does that matter? You are young, and it is you who will one day retrieve the honour and glory of the Russian Navy. The lives of the two thousand four hundred men in these ships are more important than mine!"

[1] The battleships *Orel* and *Nicolas I*, the cruiser *Izumrund*, and two of the armoured coastguard vessels.

One of the five ships, the cruiser *Izumrund*, managed to slip away in the confusion and make at all speed for Vladivostock. But it was only a short reprieve, for she went aground in Vladimir Bay, south of Vladivostock.

The remaining units of the squadron tried to escape from the net, but few succeeded. The badly damaged *Ushakoff* was sighted by Togo's ships while they were occupied with the surrender of Nebogatoff's little force. Two of the armoured cruisers were sent after her. Called upon to surrender, the *Ushakoff* replied with her guns that were still serviceable; the two cruisers then poured their fire into her, and she went down just after eight that evening. Two other Russian ships were beached; four destroyers were caught and sunk, two others were captured—one being the *Biedovy*, which had the still unconscious commander-in-chief on board, for the *Buiny* had broken down during the night and had transferred him to the sister ship.

The battle had certainly ended in utter disaster for the Russians. Six of their eight battleships had been sunk, and the other two captured. Of the thirty-seven ships that had sailed towards the Straits of Korea and met the Japanese Fleet, twenty-two had been sunk or had gone aground, six had been captured, and six had managed to reach a neutral port, where they were interned; only three finally arrived at Vladivostock.

The Japanese had one armoured cruiser, the *Azama*, and two light cruisers badly damaged. Three torpedo-boats had been sunk; and six or seven destroyers were in need of repairs. The number of Japanese killed was something under six hundred, but six thousand Russian sailors had perished in this battle which determined the outcome of the Russo-Japanese War.

The Russian Government accepted an American offer of mediation, and peace was soon signed. Japan obtained Port Arthur and the southern half of Sakhaline, the long narrow island off the coast of Siberia and just north of Japan.

The territorial cost to Russia was as nothing compared to what the defeat cost her navy. The material losses at Tsou-Shima were great, but even more disastrous was the effect on morale. After the disappearance of the two Far East squadrons, the Russian High Command found itself faced with an enemy more to be dreaded than the Japanese Fleet—mutiny. In July, 1905, the Black Sea naval base of Odessa was the scene of much bloodshed; the officers of the battleship *Potemkin* were killed by the crew, who then seized the ship and hoisted the Red flag.

It was not just the defeat at Tsou-Shima that rankled; the number of ships that had surrendered was a great blow to Russian pride. On their return to Russia after the war, Nebogatoff, Rojesvensky, the captain of the *Biedovy*, and many others were court-martialled at Kronstadt. Rojesvensky was acquitted—although he claimed the entire responsibility was his—as he had been unconscious when the *Biedovy* surrendered. But several officers were condemned to death; the sentences, however, were never carried out.

Tsou-Shima created a precedent which made a deep impression on navies the world over; henceforth, sea warfare became more implacable. It was still known for troops or a besieged garrison to surrender, with their guns or tanks . . . whereas a warship, a squadron, no longer struck to the enemy. Yet many great sea-captains in the era of sail had done so, without their future career or reputation suffering; it was not then considered dishonourable to strike one's colours after putting up a valiant fight. But since Tsou-Shima, and although the seven seas have been the scenes of battle in two World Wars, few indeed are the captains who have surrendered their ship or even tried to save their crew by taking to the boats after scuttling a vessel no longer capable of fighting. That, perhaps, is what Admiral Nebogatoff should have ordered, instead of surrendering without firing a shot. Yet Togo allowed him to keep his sword, thereby showing understanding of his decision. But between the surrender of that old sailor, who thought more of the lives of 2,400 men than of his own honour, and the awful end of the *Bismarck*, and of the *Scharnhorst*, there ought surely to be some more reasonable solution!

Five years after Tsou-Shima, a young French naval officer—now a Vice-Admiral on the retired list—was in Crete and there met some Russian officers who had taken part in the battle. He found them still marked by the fatalism which had enabled them to make their long voyage, and by the determination or stubbornness with which they had overcome all difficulties, continuing towards almost certain defeat and possible death like sheep going to the slaughter. There is something terrifying in this aspect of the Slav character, and a great reserve of strength too, as was shown in a later war.

XXII

FROM CORONEL TO JUTLAND

British apprehensions over Kaiser Wilhelm II's new fleet—first skirmishes at sea in the 1914 War—Von Spee's victory at Coronel (November 1st, 1914)— the British hit back hard in the Falklands—Jellicoe and Beatty—the Battle of the Dogger Bank (January 24th, 1915)—Scheer takes command of the German High Sea Fleet—the Grand Fleet puts to sea—the Battle of Jutland, the greatest naval battle ever—the fight between the battle-cruisers—Jellicoe "crosses the T" to the enemy—the High Sea Fleet escapes during the night— heavy losses on both sides.

BRITISH naval supremacy was not seriously challenged either by the American naval victories or by the Japanese Navy's brilliant performance at Tsou-Shima. But a rival appeared in an unexpected quarter—just across the North Sea, where Britain had held undisputed sway since her epic struggles against the Dutch fleets.

By 1914 more than a century had passed since a naval action had taken place in the North Sea; during that long period there had been no interruption in the shipping between the Baltic and Western Europe. The last set battle had been fought off the Dogger Bank on August 3rd, 1781, between a Dutch division under Admiral Zoutman and a British under Sir Hyde Parker. Then the theatre of naval operations had moved westwards, and little had troubled the peaceful activity in the North Sea. But now Admiral von Tirpitz was building a brand-new navy for Kaiser Wilhelm II, who had suddenly come to the conclusion that "his future was on the water".

There was no apparent reason for this urge to go to sea. Germany was traditionally a continental power. She had only a short coastline on the North Sea, and her access to the Atlantic was by way of narrows guarded by the British Isles, moored like a great ship opposite the German Bight.

Nevertheless, in the space of a few years Wilhelm II's navy assumed such proportions that one day in 1907 the First Sea Lord, Admiral Sir John Fisher, warned King Edward VII of the danger. He declared that it was highly necessary to "Copenhagen" the German Fleet at its bases, to apply the same treatment that had been meted out to the Danish Fleet exactly a century earlier.

But in the twentieth century that kind of thing was hardly feasible.

However, it is certain that the existence of the powerful Imperial German Navy largely influenced the British decision to ally herself with France and Russia. Tirpitz has even been blamed for causing anxiety in Britain by building his huge fleet. On the other hand, once the Germans had embarked on their naval programme they could not be satisfied with half-measures. Being certain to meet the British once they ventured out to sea, they had to gain and maintain the lead in the naval arms race. Otherwise, there was no point in having started. So Tirpitz had no other choice but to forge ahead with his programme.

The British gained a great advantage in 1906 when a battleship of a new type, which had been built in the utmost secrecy, was brought into service. This was the Dreadnought, which outclassed all previous battleships. Her main armament was of one and the same calibre, which simplified the supplying of ammunition; she had ten 12-inch guns mounted in five twin-turrets, of which four could be trained in the same direction and thus gave a broadside two and a half times heavier than other battleships. She had been given a displacement twice as great to allow better armoured protection, and with greatly improved turbine-engines she could produce a speed of 21·5 knots, which was outstanding at that time for a vessel of 18,000 tons.[1]

Any other navy wishing to maintain its place was obliged to revise completely its shipbuilding programme. Germany at once did so, and by the beginning of 1914 had built a dozen Dreadnoughts as well as eight large battle-cruisers,[2] and had overcome the problems they created by making larger dry-docks and widening the Kiel Canal. So when war came, Britain had not a great lead over Germany in spite of having accelerated her own naval programme. The enemy was difficult to attack in his harbours, and for four long years the Grand Fleet maintained a remote blockade over him from Scapa Flow. Most of the British Navy was thus kept practically tied to its moorings in the Orkneys, apart from exercises and a few skirmishes. It never managed to entice the High Sea Fleet between its jaws; yet in the few encounters that occurred—scarcely a dozen during the fifty-one months of the war—the upstart German Navy proved very dangerous. This new navy, with no traditions behind it, inflicted more losses on the British than it suffered itself. And after the long-awaited clash occurred, at Jutland on May 31st, 1916, opinions differed—and still do—as to who

[1] *Dreadnought* was a name which had been borne by a long line of ships, the first in 1573. The latest is a nuclear submarine which joined the Fleet in 1963.
[2] The battle-cruiser, which Britain brought into service two years after the Dreadnought, was not so heavily armed and had only four twin-turrets with 12-inch guns; but these could all be trained in the same direction, thus giving a broadside as powerful as the Dreadnought's. And her speed of 26 knots equalled that of the fastest cruiser.

had gained the victory; unless it was, as some have said, Admiral Death. The British ships destroyed amounted to 115,025 tons against the Germans' 61,180; and 6,094 British sailors were killed, against 2,551 Germans. But the High Sea Fleet hardly ever again showed itself at sea, so that the strategic victory was with the British.

Nevertheless, the Battle of Jutland was the greatest naval battle ever fought. Not even the Battle of Leyte Gulf in the Second World War can compare with that titanic struggle—28 battleships and 8 battle-cruisers opposed to 22 battleships and 5 battle-cruisers, without counting the cruiser squadrons and the flotillas of destroyers.

Britain declared war on Germany on August 4th, 1914, but the Great War had already broken out on the 2nd. The French naval forces were concentrated in the Mediterranean in order to protect communications with North Africa against possible attacks by Italian or Austrian warships. All that was left in Channel ports were the few old cruisers of the Second Light Squadron at Cherbourg, the destroyers based on Dunkirk and the submarines based on Calais.

On the night of August 2nd Admiral Rouyer, commanding the Second Light Cruiser Squadron, received two communications; the first informed him that German squadrons had passed through the Kiel Canal from the Baltic, and the second contained the following orders:

"No. 2700, August 3rd, 00.30 hours. Put to sea forthwith and forcibly intercept the German Fleet, anywhere except in British territorial waters."

Rouyer and all his squadron were only too well aware that the German Fleet under Admiral von Ingenohl would make short work of them. So it was in a state of exaltation and apprehension that the crews left port for this sacrificial mission.[1]

However, when off Dover, a British destroyer came out to inform the French admiral that Britain was now in the war. Henceforth the Royal Navy assumed responsibility for the North Sea and the Straits of Dover. The French were understandably greatly relieved—even those who, in view of the imminent battle and the risk of fire, had taken advantage to throw overboard such inflammable material as the flagship's account-books and the chairs and piano from the wardroom!

The entry of the British Navy reduced the role of the French to one

[1] Before leaving, the captain and other officers of the *Dupetit-Thouars* had posted their Wills and farewell letters to their families. Luckily, these mournful epistles did not reach their destinations until after news was received of the squadron's safe return to Cherbourg.

of subsidiary importance. Although French warships took part in no major action, the Navy lost half of its tonnage and eleven thousand men in the course of the war. France played the larger role in the land battles, while the British Navies predominated at sea.

Less than a month after the outbreak of war the British scored an opening success by sinking three light cruisers off Heligoland, before German battle-cruisers at Wilhelmshaven were able to intervene, being held up by the tide in the Jade estuary. But the Germans soon hit back. On September 5th the *U-21* sank the cruiser *Pathfinder* at the entrance to the Firth of Forth; and on the 22nd the *U-9* accomplished a remarkable hat-trick by sinking the old cruiser *Aboukir* off the Dutch coast, then her sister ships *Hogue* and *Cressy* which had gone to her assistance.

But the Germans won their most spectacular victory thousands of miles from the North Sea. The encounter took place off the coast of Chili, between Vice-Admiral Graf von Spee's squadron and a British cruiser division under Rear-Admiral Sir Christopher Cradock.

A few months before the war, Admiral Tirpitz had very unwillingly allowed two modern battle-cruisers, the *Scharnhorst* and the *Gneisenau*, to join the Pacific squadron. These ships of 12,000 tons had a speed of 23 knots and were each armed with eight 8-inch guns. In August, they and a few light cruisers were in the Carolines under the command of Von Spee. Fearing that he would soon find himself outnumbered by a combined Allied force, Von Spee detached one of his light cruisers, the *Emden*, to prey on Allied merchant shipping, and then set course with the rest of his ships for the coast of Chili, where the existence of an influential German colony made him reasonably sure of a friendly welcome.

On his way across the Pacific he shelled the French port of Papeete, on the island of Tahiti, and several other Allied bases, and was then reinforced by two cruisers, the *Dresden* and the *Leipzig*, when off Easter Island in mid-October. This brought his strength to two battle-cruisers and three light cruisers, as he continued towards Valparaiso.

Rear-Admiral Cradock was hurrying to intercept the Germans with a heterogeneous force of almost obsolete cruisers which had already had a long cruise in the Atlantic. Both Admirals were out for battle. Cradock, in the Nelson tradition, sought to destroy an enemy who was within reach; and the reverses of the first weeks of the war had roused the Navy to seek action at any price—a state of mind hardly conducive to considered judgment. Spee was eager for the encounter because once he eliminated this enemy force he would be free to raid the Allied shipping lanes in the South Atlantic as he wished. It should be added that communications were unreliable, with long delays. Cradock had gone hurrying off as soon as he heard of Spee's presence in those waters, although he had little information concerning the enemy strength, and while his one battleship, the *Canopus*, was still three hundred miles away.

When he met Spee off Coronel on November 1st his force only consisted of three old cruisers—the *Good Hope* (his flagship), the *Monmouth*, and the *Glasgow*—and the auxiliary cruiser *Otranto*. To make matters worse, the sea was so rough that it broke over the main deck-guns of the British cruisers, thus increasing the German superiority in fire-power even more.[1]

Action was joined at half past six in the evening. Spee had held his fire until sunset, as the British were steaming towards him from the west, so that his own ships were half hidden in the twilight while the British were clearly outlined against the glowing horizon. The *Scharnhorst* opened fire on the *Good Hope*, and the *Gneisenau* on the *Monmouth*, astern of the flagship. The *Leipzig*'s mark was the *Glasgow*, and the *Dresden*'s was the *Otranto*. The *Nurnberg* was still some way off, but approaching at full speed.

The German gunners were soon on target; the *Scharnhorst*'s gun-crews were particularly good, having won many gunnery competitions during the previous four years. Helped as they were by the clarity with which their targets stood out against the setting sun, they scored hits on the *Good Hope* and the *Monmouth* with their third salvo. The flames lit up the darkening horizon, giving a mark to the German gunners still, and after an hour of murderous fire the *Good Hope* was listing heavily and with her engines stopped. She went down shortly afterwards. One of the *Monmouth*'s gun-turrets had exploded; the ship was still afloat, but had only one gun in action. The *Nurnberg* came up and soon finished her off.

The *Glasgow* and the *Otranto* had vanished into the gathering gloom, and Von Spee decided not to pursue them. He knew that the *Canopus* was in the vicinity; and he had to be sparing with ammunition, for there was no possibility of further supplies before returning to Germany. He put in at Valparaiso, and he and his crews had a great welcome from its large German colony.

Coronel was a bombshell to the British. The war on land was going badly, too. Belgium had been over-run, and the Allied armies were in retreat. And it was not only at far-away Coronel that the Germans were having success at sea, but even in attacks on the English coast.

---

[1] The twelve 8-inch guns which formed the combined broadside of the two German armoured cruisers were mounted on the upper deck, thus securing them an additional advantage in such weathers. (*Tr.*)

On November 3rd, only two days after Von Spee's victory, three battle-cruisers commanded by Admiral Hipper had shelled Yarmouth and slipped away again before the Navy could intervene. There was an immediate outcry in the country. What was the Navy doing? How came it to be caught at a disadvantage at Coronel? Why had it not attacked this "baby-killer" whose shells were the first enemy missiles to fall on English soil for centuries?

The Admiralty said nothing, but acted promptly. On suggestions from Sir John Fisher, Churchill instructed Admiral Jellicoe, who was in command of the Home Fleet, to detach two of his latest battle-cruisers "for a secret mission of the highest importance". Command of the two battle-cruisers, the *Inflexible* and the *Invincible*, was given to Vice-Admiral Sir Doveton Sturdee, who as Chief of Naval Operations had been partly responsible for the Coronel disaster, and so would be all the more eager to retrieve the situation. Events moved swiftly. The two battle-cruisers, their bunkers filled to capacity, cleared the Channel and proceeded at full speed to their destination a quarter of the way round the world. They refuelled at the Cape Verde Islands on November 19th; by the 28th they were off the coast of Brazil, where they were joined by the South Atlantic squadron commanded by Rear-Admiral Stoddart, which had been reinforced by the two cruisers that had escaped after the battle of Coronel. Some colliers were waiting at the Falklands with supplies for them, in the event of a long hunt for the enemy.

The colony in the Falklands, where the *Canopus* had remained in its defence, was expecting Von Spee to appear at any moment. There were watchers at every vantage-point. At Port Darwin, two elderly ladies were relaying each other on the roof of a farmhouse and telephoning their reports to the *Canopus* on the other side of the island, at Port Stanley.

The colony's anxiety was quite justified; the Falkland Islands were, in fact, Von Spee's next objective. While Sturdee was combing the South Atlantic, his ships spread along a line fifty miles long, the Germans were rounding Cape Horn and meeting with the usual foul weather. On December 6th they made rendezvous with a supply ship in the empty waters off Picton island. At noon the following day, the elderly lady on the farmhouse roof saw smoke on the horizon, then picked out two, three . . . eight ships in formation.

Eight—but Von Spee had only six. It was Sturdee, with his two battle-cruisers, the three armoured cruisers, *Carnarvon*, *Cornwall*, and *Kent*, and the light cruisers *Glasgow*, *Bristol*, and *Orama*. The colony was greatly relieved.

However, the Germans were not far distant. For at eight the follow
ing morning the smoke of two of their ships appeared on the horizon;
and they might well have been the first to reach the Falklands if the
Inflexible and the *Invincible* had been delayed in the Channel at the
beginning.[1]

The two German ships were the *Nurnberg* and the *Gneisenau,* which
Von Spee had sent in to attack the islands, believing them to be undefended. The *Gneisenau's* lookout reported smoke over Port Stanley.
This was thought to come from stocks of coal being destroyed before
the island was evacuated. . . . But then the mastheads of warships were
distinguished; and a cruiser was nosing out of the harbour. The
Gneisenau and the *Nurnberg* broke their ensigns and speeded to the
attack.

The *Scharnhorst,* out at sea, had distinguished the characteristic
topmasts of British battle-cruisers, revealed by the rays of the rising
sun. This was a different matter; here were ships that had a nominal
speed of twenty-six knots and were armed with eight 12-inch guns.
Von Spee promptly recalled his two cruisers and wisely made off to
the south-east. But his speed was kept down to fifteen knots by his
slowest ships.

The British were finishing coaling when the alert was given. But in
record time they raised steam and proceeded to sea. The *Glasgow* was
the first away from her moorings, and joined the *Kent* which had been
patrolling outside the harbour. An hour later, at half past ten, the two
battle-cruisers and the *Cornwall* had cleared the harbour. The enemy
was no longer in sight; but the *Glasgow,* farther out, signalled that she
could see their mastheads twelve miles to the south-east. This was
fortunate, as the wind was driving the smoke from the battle-cruisers
in the direction taken by the Germans, and a dense cloud of it was
shrouding the horizon.

The chase was on. Sturdee had all the advantage; with his greater
speed, the enemy could not now escape him. By one o'clock the
Inflexible had drawn sufficiently near to open fire on the rear German

[1] This almost happened, for there was thick fog in the Solent, and the battle-cruisers
could not rely on their magnetic compasses as they had not been checked since the
recent work done on the ships' armour. It seemed that the ships would be unable to
sail that day, but someone at the Admiralty suddenly thought of Elmer Sperry, a
young American engineer who had invented a gyro-compass and had offered it to the
Admiralty—where it had been politely declined. He was quickly found at his hotel,
put into a train to Southampton with his "Yankee device", and a few hours later this
was fitted to the bridge of the *Invincible* under the disapproving look of her captain.
Followed by the *Inflexible,* she made her way down the Solent through fog that was
thicker than ever. The two ships reached open water and clear weather without accident, and proceeded down the Channel; while a delighted Sperry returned in the
pilot's boat, convinced that his invention would be adopted by the British Navy—as
indeed it was, and by all others.

ship, the *Leipzig*; out-gunned and out-ranged, the latter had no chance. Von Spee ordered his three light cruisers to scatter, while he tried to hold off the enemy with the *Scharnhorst* and the *Gneisenau*. But Sturdee's two battle-cruisers were quite enough to deal with them, and he sent his other ships in pursuit of the fugitives. At half past one the *Inflexible* was in action against the *Scharnhorst*, which succeeded in registering a hit on the battle-cruiser although firing at extreme range. Sturdee turned away to open the range and obtain full advantage from his heavier armament; the enemy's fire then fell short, while the *Inflexible*'s guns were still effective.

Meanwhile, the *Invincible* had engaged the *Gneisenau* and inflicted considerable damage; the German cruiser had to flood one of her magazines. Matters were going badly for Von Spee, and he endeavoured to slip away behind the smoke. Sturdee rapidly closed the range to finish him off. The *Scharnhorst*'s armour was of little protection against the 12-inch guns of the *Inflexible*, and flames and smoke were soon pouring from the German cruiser. The *Gneisenau* might have escaped behind this thick black cloud, but she remained doggedly by the sister ship, firing her remaining guns.

Soon after four, the blazing *Scharnhorst* was seen to swing round and head towards the *Inflexible*. Had her steering jammed? Was she going to try to ram the enemy or to loose a torpedo? It will never be known, for her guns suddenly stopped belching fire, "like a candle blown out", and she sank quickly by the bows, her engines still turning. The last seen of her was the ensign of the Imperial German Navy. There was not a single survivor.

The *Gneisenau* fought on for another hour before she, too, began to sink. But twenty of her officers and one hundred and sixty-seven ratings were picked out of the water. Meanwhile, Stoddart's cruisers had put paid to the other German ships with the exception of the *Dresden*, which managed to escape altogether. Later, the two German supply ships, the *Baden* and the *St. Isabel*, were caught and sunk.

The defeat at Coronel had been more than avenged, and the Germans had not even been able to sell their lives dearly. The British squadron was intact; the *Inflexible* had been hit—twenty-three times in fact—but no real damage was caused, her armour having withstood all those stings. Not a man had been wounded.

The disappearance of Von Spee's squadron meant an end to the raiding of Allied merchant shipping by large surface vessels, in which the German Navy had placed great hopes. Three lone raiders had already been destroyed. The *Kaiser Wilhelm der Grosse* had been sunk off the coast of Spanish Morocco in the first month of the war; a mysterious explosion aboard the *Karlsruhe* had sent her to the bottom of the Atlantic in November, 1914; and the end of the *Emden* came a few days later. There remained the *Dresden*, but she was destroyed off Juan Fernandez Island in March, 1915; and the *Kronprinz Wilhelm*, which put in at Norfolk the following month, her bunkers empty, was duly interned. The U-boats had not yet begun to cause great anxiety to the British. For the moment there was nothing, not even the disputable Dardanelles expedition, to turn the Admiralty from its major concern —the powerful High Sea Fleet in its well-guarded harbours of the German Bight.

Admiral Sir John Jellicoe had assumed command of the Grand Fleet at the outbreak of war, flying his flag in the *Iron Duke*. Jellicoe, fifty-five years old and a typically curt navy man, had filled a variety of appointments in his career, both ashore and afloat. Since 1912 he had been Director of Supplies at the Admiralty, Third and then Second Sea Lord; and in the summer of 1914 he had become second-in-command of the Home Fleet, but in his pocket was a letter of appointment to commander-in-chief in the event of hostilities.

Twenty-one years previously his career had almost been cut short by an extraordinary accident at sea. This was in 1893, when he was commander in the *Victoria*, the flagship of Admiral Sir George Tryon, commanding the Mediterranean Fleet. Tryon, who had a high reputation as a tactician, sailed from Beirut on June 22nd with thirteen battleships and cruisers for a short run to Tripoli. The weather was fine and clear, and the Admiral decided to carry out a few fleet exercises. To begin with, he formed his ships into two columns sailing on a parallel course; the *Victoria* was leading one column, and the *Camperdown*, wearing the flag of Rear-Admiral Markham, the other. Each column was then to wheel round, one to port and the other to starboard —but towards each other. Now this was only possible if the distance between the two leading ships were greater than the aggregate of the space each needed to make the turn, a space that could vary from 550 to 730 yards, according to the angle of the turn.[1] But the distance between the ships was only six cable-lengths—1,110 yards, much too short. At the suggestion of Tryon's flag-captain and his chief-of-staff, it was agreed that the distance would be increased to eight cable-lengths, 1,480 yards.

However, when the moment came, the Admiral ordered a distance

---

[1] Unless it was Tryon's intention, as a British naval historian has suggested, to have one column pass round the other, as in the diagram below. But if so, the Admiral made no mention of it to anyone.

of only six cable-lengths. Everyone was aghast. Markham, in the *Camperdown*, did not complete his acknowledgement of the signal, to show he had not understood. But it was of no avail. Tryon insisted; Markham had to make the signal to his own line. And the two flag-captains obeyed the order.

The inevitable occurred. The *Camperdown*'s bows sliced into the

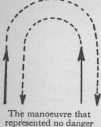

The manoeuvre that represented no danger	The manoeuvre that led to the collision

Victoria and she went down in a few minutes, taking the stubborn Admiral with her and also 359 officers and ratings. Among those rescued was Commander Jellicoe; he was ill and in his bunk when the collision occurred, and just had time to fasten a life-jacket over his pyjamas before diving overboard.[1]

This tragic incident is mentioned not only to show that Jellicoe's career might well have ended there, but also because it made a deep impression on the Navy. Its lessons were not lost on the Admiralty, and improvements in naval design and construction followed; while in some naval circles it was thought that a limit should be set to blind military obedience, that at least a more flexible interpretation ought to be allowed of what had been "the corner-stone of discipline and a refuge for the weak".[2]

In short, by the time Jellicoe became commander-in-chief of the Grand Fleet and "the one Allied Commander who could have lost the war in a single afternoon", he carried prudence to extremes—excessively so, said some people. He would take no unnecessary risk, and had a respect for mines and torpedoes that led him to adopt a strategy which seemed contrary to the best traditions of the Navy.

Though refraining from risking his ships in the minefields of the German Bight or exposing them to torpedo attacks at night, Jellicoe made every effort to keep the Fleet at a high standard. Exercises were

[1] One of the best scenes in the film "Noblesse Oblige" was based on this tragic accident.
[2] *True Stories of Ships and Ghosts*, by Hanson W. Baldwin.

constantly carried out, and the battleships and cruisers were manoeuvred with the same ease as the destroyers—as witness the success of the *Dreadnought* which on March 18th, 1915, ran down and sank the *U-29*, an unusual feat for a battleship!

Yet Jellicoe felt that all was not as it should be. "His team was not one, as in Nelson's day." The real trouble was that his relations with his second-in-command had little in common with those that had existed between Nelson and Collingwood. The career of David Beatty, who commanded the battle-cruisers, had been as rapid as it was unusual. He had been promoted commander over the heads of 395 officers senior to him, then achieved the rank of captain at the age of 29, when the average age was 43. In 1910 he had been given his flag, despite the regulations. He married a wealthy American and took extended leave of absence, but in 1911 Churchill appointed him to the command of the battle-cruiser squadron. He was a flamboyant character, something of a "show-off", and given to wearing irregular dress. He aimed at being popular with the general public; and ever since he had had the occasion to save Tyrwhitt's destroyer flotilla from a dangerous situation in the Heligoland Bight, and then to sink three German light cruisers with his powerful battle-cruisers, his popularity had reached a height from which nothing could shift it. Besides, the country needed a hero; and Beatty fitted the book. But this did not mean he was a Collingwood, much less a Nelson.

There were no comparisons to be found among the Germans, for they had no naval traditions. Both ships and men were new—and mostly of a high quality. The Imperial Navy had first-class equipment and used it admirably; the gun-crews, with their excellent direction-finding instruments, were considered the best in the world. The war had not interfered with training, for the ships were able to pass through the Kiel Canal into the Baltic, where they were quite safe; whereas the moment Jellicoe's ships left harbour they risked being attacked by some prowling U-boat. But the German Navy had no strategic precedents to refer to, and each successive commander-in-chief cherished the fanciful idea of succeeding in drawing a portion of the British Fleet into a trap.

When news of the Battle of the Falklands reached Admiral von Ingenohl, then commanding the High Sea Fleet, he seized the opportunity provided by the absence of two British battle-cruisers to repeat the raid on the English coast. Hartlepools and Scarborough were bombarded on December 16th, and Beatty failed to intercept the German ships as they withdrew. There was a great outcry, and to satisfy public opinion the Admiralty based the battle-cruisers and the

First Cruiser Squadron at Rosyth, where they would be nearer the scene of possible operations than at Scapa Flow.

The first important clash occurred off the Dogger Bank on January 24th, 1915. Admiral Hipper had sailed from Schillig the day before with three battle-cruisers, the *Seydlitz*, the *Moltke*, and the *Derfflinger*, one armoured cruiser, the *Blücher*, four cruisers, and a destroyer flotilla, though with no other intention than to scatter the East Coast fishing fleet, which the Germans believed the Admiralty to be using for reconnaissance purposes.

The Admiralty, in any case, had no need to rely on trawlers for information of enemy intentions, for it was now in possession of the German Navy's code-book (a copy had been salvaged by the Russians from the wrecked cruiser *Magdeburg*, which had struck a mine while in the eastern Baltic); and a network of radio-goniometer listening posts had been established along the East Coast, which represented a great technical advance in fixing the direction and position of ships from their radio-signals. So Admiral Hipper's force was soon known to be at sea; and Beatty went to meet him with a strong force from Rosyth—four battle-cruisers and the Third Cruiser Squadron—which was joined at sea by the light cruisers from Harwich under Commodore Goodenough and by light cruisers and destroyers under Commodore Tyrwhitt.

Contact with the enemy was made quite by chance. The light cruiser *Aurora* sighted a ship ahead and asked for her recognition signal—and received a salvo for reply, the ship being the German cruiser *Kolberg*. There then began a chase across the North Sea, with Beatty's battle-cruisers making twenty-five, twenty-six, and even twenty-nine knots in an attempt to bring the Germans to battle before they reached the safety of their home waters.

It was a near thing. The 13·5-inch guns of Beatty's *Lion* scored a hit on Hipper's flagship, the *Seydlitz*, and set two of her gun-turrets ablaze; she was only saved from disaster by the bravery of three of the crew who succeeded in flooding the magazines. Then the *Lion* was put into a similar plight by the 12-inch guns of the *Derfflinger*.

Success seemed within reach of the British, when Beatty was obliged to shift his flag to a destroyer. While doing so, his second-in-command, Sir Archibald Moore, made a mistaken manoeuvre due to imperfect reading of signals; and all the German ships except the *Blücher* managed to escape. The *Blücher* came under fire from the battle-cruisers, and was finally sunk by the *New Zealand*. Admiral Hipper could consider himself lucky, even with his *Seydlitz* badly damaged.

The British failure to clinch their advantage was due chiefly to poor communications; signals were difficult to read, and wireless, still in its infancy, proved practically useless during the action. Moreover, the gunners were far from being at their best. In spite of superior fire-power, they had only registered three hits apart from sinking the *Blücher*—two on the *Seydlitz*, and one on the *Moltke*. Whereas the *Lion* had received eleven hits, and the *Tiger* one.

Neither side was satisfied with the result. The German High Command took the opportunity to replace Ingenohl by Admiral von Pohl. The Admiralty, however, said nothing of Moore's unfortunate man-oeuvre, for to do so would have revealed the poor state of communica-tions in the battle-cruiser squadron . . . and Beatty's reputation could not be allowed to suffer. Nothing was said of Jellicoe, either; and he continued with unshaken resolve to bring the Grand Fleet to a high pitch of readiness.

Nothing of importance occurred in the North Sea area during the rest of 1915. Matters were going badly for the Allies in the Dardanelles, and the heavy naval losses were increased during the withdrawal;[1] and among other consequences were the departures of Fisher and Churchill from the Admiralty. Jellicoe, however, recovered the battle-ships he had been obliged to detach for the campaign; and by 1916 the Grand Fleet was stronger than ever. Jellicoe then had under his command 24 Dreadnoughts mounting 12- or 13·5-inch guns, 4 super-Dreadnoughts of the Queen Elizabeth class with 15-inch guns, 9 battle-cruisers, 8 armoured cruisers, 26 light cruisers, 77 destroyers, and 2 seaplane-carriers.

The Germans succeeded nevertheless in carrying out another quick raid on the East Coast. Lowestoft was bombarded on April 24th, 1916. Beatty was too late to catch the German ships with his battle-cruisers, but Commodore Tyrwhitt was better placed and tried valiantly to get within range of the raiders, though without success. The Navy was not very popular with the people living on the East Coast!

However, the time was coming. . . .

Admiral von Pohl had not lasted long in command of the High Sea Fleet. He fell ill and was replaced in January, 1916, by Reinhard Scheer, whose aggressive character marked him out from his pre-decessors. He wanted to make use of every means at his disposal—the U-boats against Allied merchant shipping, the Zeppelins for recon-naissance duties, and the Fleet to draw the enemy towards the mine-fields and within range of torpedo attacks by his destroyers. It had been

[1] In capital ships alone, the Allies had lost the old French battleship *Bouvet* and the British *Irresistible* and *Ocean*.

Scheer's idea that had led to the raid on Lowestoft; his plan had been for the ships to sneak along the Frisian Islands, thus remaining un-

detected for as long as possible and then causing consternation among the merchant shipping in the Downs and the Thames estuary. Bad weather had caused the attempt to be postponed until April.

Scheer then had under his command 22 battleships of which 15 were Dreadnoughts, 5 battle-cruisers, 11 light cruisers, and 62 destroyers. It was not a powerful enough force to oppose the whole of the Grand Fleet, but could be a great danger if Jellicoe were led to divide his strength.

Scheer

At this time, the spring of 1916, the German Armies were being held up before Verdun by the heroic defence of the French and were batter-

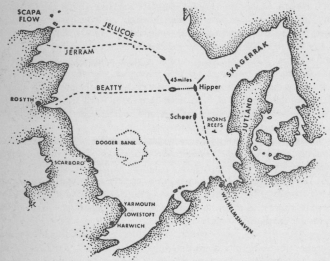

The Battle of Jutland. The British and German Fleets put to sea

ing themselves unavailingly against the Allied lines. The time had come to seek a decision at sea. . . .

In the afternoon of May 30th the Admiralty was informed that a coded message from the German High Command to its ships had been intercepted. The decoding experts were unable to break the message—

which read "31 Gg 2490"—but it seemed to indicate that something important was afoot.

The Grand Fleet was alerted, and at half past nine that evening Admiral Jellicoe sailed from Scapa Flow in the *Iron Duke*, with sixteen battleships and three battle-cruisers. Vice-Admiral Sir D. Beatty, in the *Lion*, put to sea from Rosyth with six battle-cruisers and four fast battleships. Six more battleships left Invergordon under the command of Vice-Admiral Sir Martyn Jerram to join Jellicoe at sea. All made course to be off the entrance to the Skagerrak by morning. At 14.00 hours Beatty was to reach the position 56 degrees 40 North, 5 degrees East, and if the enemy had not been sighted was then to turn towards Jellicoe, who would be about seventy miles to the north. The twenty-six battleships and the nine battle-cruisers would then together extend their reconnaissance towards the Horns Reef, off the west coast of Jutland, which could be said to mark the northern limit of the German Bight.

Beatty's force[1] reached the position and, not having sighted the enemy, turned north; and everyone began to think another sally had been made without result. After all, the mysterious message "31 Gg 2490" might be no more than a routine signal of no interest, especially as a misleading telegram from the Admiralty had informed Jellicoe that directional wireless signals placed the German fleet flagship, the *Friedrich der Grosse*, in the Jade river. But for all the Intelligence reports, the Admiralty was not aware of Scheer's latest ruse—when his flag-

Jellicoe

ship put to sea, he exchanged radio recognition signals with a shore transmitting station.

In fact, the mysterious message was a signal to all units of the German Fleet that Top Secret Order No. 2490 was to be put into effect on May 31st. This meant a reconnaissance in force towards the Norwegian coast by Admiral Hipper's battle group,[2] with the main body of the High Sea Fleet in support some fifty miles to the south. Scheer was hoping that Hipper's presence would provoke a hurried sally by various elements of the Grand Fleet, and that he would be able to

---

[1] Beatty had under his command the battle-cruisers *Lion, Princess Royal, Queen Mary, Tiger, New Zealand,* and *Indefatigable*; the Fifth Battle Squadron (Rear-Admiral Evan-Thomas) consisting of the battleships *Barham, Valiant, Warspite,* and *Malaya*; the First Light Cruiser Squadron (Commodore Alexander Sinclair), the Second (Commodore Goodenough), and the Third (Commodore Napier); and four destroyer flotillas.

[2] Hipper had under his command the five battle-cruisers *Lutzow* (his flagship), *Derfflinger, Moltke, Seydlitz,* and *Von der Tann*; the four light cruisers *Frankfurt, Wiesbaden, Pillau,* and *Elbing,* commanded by Rear-Admiral Boedicker; and three destroyer flotillas under Commodore Heinrich in the *Regensburg*.

snap up some before being confronted by the whole force. He was far from suspecting that the entire Grand Fleet had put to sea four to five hours before he had himself.

Jellicoe's appreciation of the enemy's intentions was correct, and with a little luck his dispositions would have proved perfect. Hipper had almost reached the same latitude as Beatty by 14.00 hours, but was to the east of him and below the horizon. If Hipper continued on course, in compliance with his orders, he would be caught between two

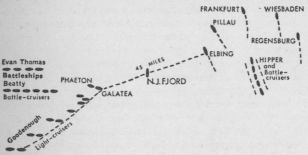

The *N.J. Fjord* sails between the enemy fleets, and so leads to their reconnaissance ships sighting each other

fires; and Scheer, speeding towards the sound of the guns, would come up against the combined Fleet—which was not at all what he wanted.

But luck brought an old Danish tramp into the picture. The *N.J. Fjord* was sailing on a course that took her between the forces of Beatty and Hipper, at about equal distance from both. She was sighted by light cruisers on the wing of each force, which were out of sight of each other. The *Galatea*, on the eastern wing of the light cruiser screen, stood on to the south-east to examine her. Simultaneously, the *Elbing*, on the western wing of the German scouting force, made towards her. The Danish ship was thus the unwitting cause of the *Elbing* and the *Galatea* sighting each other and exchanging salvoes, at the same time as their aerials began to crackle with the all-important news. The *Galatea* had opened fire first but the *Elbing* was on target the quicker, though the first shell that hit the British cruiser failed to explode. A sailor went to throw it overside. "Hell—the blasted thing's hot!" he exlaimed, snatching his hand away.

Such was the opening shot in the greatest naval battle the world has ever known.

It can be seen that the new means of reconnaissance adopted by either side—under water and by air—had not produced any results. The U-boats sent to patrol off the Scottish naval bases had only sent back fragmentary or incomplete reports; the Zeppelins had provided no information at all. Beatty had sent off one of the seaplanes carried in the *Engadine*, as soon as the *Galatea* reported sighting the enemy. The seaplane was forced down by engine trouble, but took off again, found Hipper's battle-cruisers and reported their position and course. Unfortunately, no one picked up the message. So that each commander-in-chief had to rely on what he himself could see and what his subordinates reported to him as well as possible—which was not very well, on the whole. In fact, the entire action took place in considerable confusion.

To begin with, the commander of the light cruiser squadron to which the *Galatea* belonged, Commodore Sinclair, turned away to the north in the hope of drawing the enemy after him and so towards Beatty, whose battle-cruisers would then be able to cut Hipper's line of retreat; but because Commodore Sinclair had not continued towards the enemy, the information he had of Hipper's strength and disposition was far from complete. While on the German side, the signals made by the *Elbing* were badly interpreted and gave the impression that twenty four or twenty-six battleships had been sighted!

Nevertheless, the courses of the rival forces were swiftly converging. But the signals made by Beatty's flagship, the *Lion*, had not been at once understood by the Fifth Battle Squadron (Rear-Admiral Evan-Thomas), which continued for about ten minutes on a course that was taking it away from the battle-cruisers. And as Evan-Thomas's big ships needed more time to get up to their maximum speed—which was only twenty-four knots—they eventually found themselves about ten miles astern. Although Evan-Thomas managed to decrease the distance, he was still six miles astern and to port of the *Lion* when the action began, a little after three-thirty.

Beatty was then trying to pass astern of the German battle-cruisers' and cut off their line of retreat; but Hipper was aware of the danger, recalled his light cruisers, and did a right-about turn to bring his force on a south-easterly course almost parallel to that of the British.

The sky is never very clear in the North Sea; and the billows of smoke from the destroyers as they circled the big ships did not help matters. The gun-control officers were not having an easy time on either side.

At 15.48 the *Lützow* (Hipper's flagship) opened fire on the *Lion* at 18,000 yards. Twenty seconds passed before the British battle-cruisers replied, and then they were more than a thousand yards over target. The Germans were easily the first to find their mark. After three minutes they had made eight hits on the *Lion*, the *Tiger*, and the *Princess Royal*, whereas it was seven minutes before the British registered a hit, when the *Queen Mary* put one of the *Seydlitz*'s gun-turrets out of action. In fact, it almost caused the end of the *Seydlitz*; the ammunition caught fire and, as at the battle of the Dogger Bank, the ship was saved only through her magazines being quickly flooded.

Meanwhile, the range had decreased to 12,000 yards; but for five minutes the British did not register a single hit. Moreover, due to some confusion in the distribution of fire, no ship was engaging the third battle-cruiser in the German line, the *Derfflinger*. "They've jumped over us," the gun-control officer, Lieutenant-Commander von Hase, said over the communications system. This was welcome news to the gun-crews, who applied themselves to their task as though on manoeuvres.[1] Eventually, at 15.58 hours, the *Queen Mary* turned her guns on the *Derfflinger* and soon had her under accurate fire.

At 16.00 hours, the *Lion* and the *Lützow* obtained a hit on each other; the German flagship was not seriously damaged, but the *Lion* had her midship turret knocked out, the shell exploding near the magazine. But for the presence of mind and devotion to duty of Major F. W. Harvey of the Royal Marines (awarded a posthumous V.C.) who, when mortally wounded, saw to the flooding of the magazine, the flag-ship would doubtless have been destroyed. However, in the next few minutes the *Lion* was hit six times and had to draw out of the battle-line; there were fires raging everywhere, and several compartments were taking water. The *Princess Royal* had her after-turret put out of action. And then, at 16.05 hours, three shells from the *Von der Tann* crashed into the *Indefatigable* and exploded in her magazines. Another salvo burst all round the ship, which blew up and quickly sank. A German destroyer picked up two of her crew; they were the only survivors from the ship's company of one thousand and seventeen.

Matters were going badly for Beatty. But Evan-Thomas was coming up with his four powerful battleships, which could be expected to turn the balance in favour of the British. For the past hour they had been steaming at high speed to reach the scene of action. The *Von der Tann* had barely time to rejoice over the sinking of the *Indefatigable* before a 15-inch shell crashed into her on the water-line; six hundred tons of water poured into her, but she managed to stay in the battle-line.

The British battleships were firing much more accurately than the battle-cruisers, except the *Queen Mary*. But owing to the poor quality,

[1] *The Battle of Jutland seen from the "Derfflinger", by Von Hase.*

their 15-inch shells were bursting without penetrating the enemy's armour. Hipper thus escaped disaster. Not only that; the *Derfflinger* and the *Seydlitz* concentrated their fire on the *Queen Mary*, and an explosion rent her asunder. She went down so rapidly that the *Tiger*, astern of her, had to turn sharply to avoid running on to the sinking ship. Only eight of her crew of 1,274 were saved.

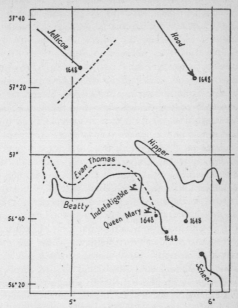

The action between the battle-cruiser squadrons

"There seems to be something wrong with our damned ships, Chatfield," remarked Beatty to his flag-captain. No comment was necessary. There was indeed something wrong with the battle-cruisers —their magazines were insufficiently protected against fire spreading from the gun-turrets. The Admiralty endeavoured to remedy this fault when new battle-cruisers were built, but twenty-five years later the *Hood* met with disaster through the same weakness.

There were still eight British ships against five Germans, and they had great superiority in fire-power. Hipper had plenty to worry about, yet he was expected to hold the enemy until the arrival of Scheer— whose ships were only just beginning to show their topmasts above the horizon. So the German destroyers dashed in to attack without even waiting for the order. The British destroyers counter-attacked and, with the big ships firing their secondary armament, there was a great, confused mêlée over the churned-up, shell-spattered sea, and many brave deeds were performed on both sides. Not one torpedo struck, but the British destroyers under Commander Bingham in the *Nestor* sank two of the German destroyers. Then the *Nomad* and the *Nestor* herself were mortally hit, the latter by the concentrated fire of the *Regensburg*, the German flotilla-leader, and all the battle-cruisers. A second wave of British destroyers was about to go in, when the *Lion* signalled their recall and turned to run north.

It so happened that Commodore Goodenough, commanding the Second Light Cruiser Squadron in the *Southampton*, had been far enough south to sight the enemy battleships—whose presence at sea was still unknown to the British—and had made a signal direct to Beatty. The *Southampton* stood on to the south, followed by the rest of the squadron, until within 12,000 yards of the German battleships. They had not opened fire on the British squadron, which was well within their range, as the cruisers were difficult to identify while in line ahead. But when they began to wheel round, having seen that Scheer was out in full force, the shells started to fall all around them and they needed all their speed and dodging tactics to escape the hail of murderous steel.[1]

The first part of the battle was now over, and Beatty's idea was to draw Scheer's battleships towards Jellicoe, whose presence was still unknown to the Germans. That was the reason for him suddenly turning to run north, a move which had seemed surprising at first, and which was not accomplished without a further exchange of broadsides with the German battle-cruisers as the rival forces passed on opposite courses. Hipper was heading south towards Scheer as Beatty steered north towards Jellicoe. Between the two, Evan-Thomas continued on his easterly course, covering Beatty's withdrawal with his big ships until receiving the order to follow the movement. His four battleships then had to wheel in succession round the same point—a dangerous moment, for the German line was drawing ever nearer to it and could concentrate fire upon it.[2] Evan-Thomas's squadron thus came under the combined fire of Hipper's battle-cruisers and of Scheer's leading battleships. The *Barham* was the first to be hit, sus-

---

[1] The *Southampton*, which was the rear ship when her division had turned, was straddled by fifty or sixty shells, while the range was too great for her own guns to reply. When Commodore Goodenough was later asked what tactics he had employed to escape, he said he was content to "steer by the last enemy salvo".

[2] *Jutland*, by Captain Donald Macintyre.

taining considerable casualties; and then the *Malaya* was straddled almost continuously for a good half-hour, being twice hit below the water-line. The enemy did not escape hurt, though; the *Lützow* and the *Derfflinger* were hit, and the *Seydlitz* in particular was damaged still further, while hits were also registered on two of the leading battleships, the *Grosser Kurfürst* and the *Markgraf*.

The time had come for the opposing commanders-in-chief to take control of the battle, after this prologue directed by their subordinates.

Scheer, in the High Sea Fleet flagship *Friedrich der Grosse*, was highly satisfied. He had no idea that the Grand Fleet was at sea, and certainly not that it was so near, but thought he had a portion of it at his mercy. Everything appeared to be going according to plan, and the information he had just received of the presence of the Fifth Battle Squadron only increased his satisfaction. His own three battle squadrons made a splendid spectacle as they sailed majestically north-west. In the van went the Third Squadron commanded by Rear-Admiral Behncke, the seven battleships *König*, *Grosser*, *Kurfürst*, *Kronprinz*, *Markgraf*, *Kaiser*, *Kaiserin*, and *Prinzregent Luitpold*. Then came the First Squadron led by Vice-Admiral Schmidt in the *Ostfriesland*, astern of the Fleet flagship, and comprising the *Thüringen*, *Heligoland*, *Oldenburg*, *Posen*, *Rheinland*, *Nassau*, and *Westfalen*. Astern of them was the Second Squadron under Rear-Admiral Mauve—the five battleships *Hessen*, *Pommern*, *Hannover*, *Schlesien*, and *Schleswig-Holstein*. The battleships had a screen of four destroyer flotillas commanded by Kommodore Michelsen in the *Rostock*. The only annoying fact was that the slowness of Mauve's older-class ships prevented the Fleet from exceeding fifteen knots. To gain time, Scheer had swung dead north when the battle-cruisers were engaged; and then, confident in his superiority over this enemy force, had ordered a general pursuit.

Hipper, whose ships had been badly battered, was not so convinced as his commander-in-chief. He endeavoured to communicate his impressions, but the signalling was ineffective; so he resigned himself to join in the pursuit, although for the moment he was still under heavy fire from Evan-Thomas's battleships, which had closed to 11,000 yards. The *Derfflinger* was in a bad way; while the *Seydlitz* was down by the bows and only keeping afloat because of her watertight compartments. Hipper was forced to stand off a little to the east.

Meanwhile, in the *Iron Duke*, Jellicoe had learnt very little since receiving the *Galatea*'s signal "enemy battle-cruisers sighted". He had shaped course for the Horns Reef, increasing speed from eighteen to

twenty knots, his twenty-four battleships sailing in six columns; he was
waiting for further reports before deploying in the requisite battle
formation. Some of the most glorious episodes in British history were
evoked by the names of his battleships, which were in three Battle
Squadrons:

> Second Battle Squadron: First Division (Vice-Admiral Sir
> Martyn Jerram), *King George V*, *Ajax*, *Centurion*, *Erin*; Second
> Division (Rear-Admiral Leveson), *Monarch*, *Conqueror*, *Thun-
> derer*.
> Fourth Battle Squadron: Third Division (Admiral Sir John
> Jellicoe), *Iron Duke*, *Royal Oak*, *Superb*, *Canada*; Fourth Division
> (Vice-Admiral Sir Doveton Sturdee), *Benbow*, *Bellerophon*,
> *Temeraire*, *Vanguard*.
> First Battle Squadron: Sixth Division (Vice-Admiral Sir Cecil
> Bruney), *Marlborough*, *Revenge*, *Hercules*, *Agincourt;* Fifth Division
> (Rear-Admiral Gavot), *Colossus*, *Collingwood*, *Neptune*, *St.
> Vincent*.

The Fourth Light Cruiser Squadron was giving close protection
against U-boat attacks. The First and Second Armoured Cruiser
Squadrons formed a screen eight miles ahead of the Battle Fleet.
While some miles to the east the Third Battle Squadron (the *Invincible*,
Inflexible, and *Indomitable*) under Rear-Admiral Horace Hood was
speeding at twenty-two knots to cut off the enemy's line of retreat into
the Skagerrak; but when Jellicoe was informed that Beatty was in
action he ordered Hood to make at full speed towards the sounds of
gunfire.

Jellicoe was receiving little information from his squadron commanders to the south, with the exception of Goodenough; he was the
only one during the whole of the battle to give importance to the
mission of sending back reports. His signal from the *Southampton* at
16.38 hours that Scheer was in sight and proceeding north had caused
great surprise in the *Iron Duke*. The news had been at once transmitted
to the Admiralty, with the announcement that battle was imminent
and the request for all dockyards and arsenals along the East Coast to
be put on the alert.

The leading battleship of the starboard column, the *Marlborough*,
first reported gun-flashes ahead—at 17.30 hours—and then that she
had sighted the battle-cruisers. Jellicoe at last knew the exact position
of the forces engaged; at the same time he became aware that he was
eleven miles nearer the High Sea Fleet than he had believed, and that

consequently battle would be joined twenty minutes sooner than fore-seen.[1] It was high time to deploy his fleet for action.

After due consideration, the commander-in-chief ordered the fleet to deploy on the port (or easterly) column, on a course south-east by south. The manoeuvre was a vital one. It delayed making contact with the enemy, but it effectively barred him from entering the Skagerrak. Moreover, had Jellicoe followed his natural inclination to deploy to starboard—on the side towards the enemy—the ships on that wing would have found themselves at grave disadvantage.

It was then 18.16 hours, and Scheer was alarmed at the dangerous situation he was in, as he saw that interminable line of battleships stretching back into the mist that shrouded the end of it. . . . This was a case of the biter bit, and the High Sea Fleet would undoubtedly have been swallowed altogether were it not for "magnificent tactical skill and the perfect firing-discipline of its ships".[2]

And now the great confused mêlée was beginning.

Hipper's battered ships had retired towards Scheer. The *Lützow*, hit for the twentieth time, was completely disabled; and Hipper was obliged to leave her and go aboard a destroyer. For the next three hours his battle-cruisers were commanded by Captain Hartog in the *Derfflinger*. But the Germans soon sank another enemy ship—the *Invincible*, which had her midship-turret shattered. A violent explosion followed, and the ship broke in two. Rear-Admiral Hood, who had just complimented the gunnery officer, and the crew of nearly a thousand went down with the ship. There were only five survivors.

At almost the same instant British light cruisers had attacked and dis-abled the *Wiesbaden*. Two armoured cruisers, the *Warrior* and the *Defence*, approached to finish her off, but came under heavy fire them-selves from the *Derfflinger* and four of the most powerful battleships. The *Defence* blew up, and the *Warrior* only escaped complete destruc-tion because the enemy guns were turned on the *Warspite*, one of the battleships of the Fifth Battle Squadron.[3]

In spite of these isolated successes, Scheer's situation was becoming more dangerous with every minute that passed. Jellicoe was about to "cross the T" to the enemy, and in a more perfect manner than any squadron commander would have dared imagine. In a short while, heavy fire from his battleships was being concentrated on the German

---

[1] The navigation officers in the battle-cruisers had great difficulty in keeping a correct estimated position because of the continual manoeuvring and the incidents during the action. There was a story that the navigating officer of the *Lion* had his map snatched away by the blast of an exploding shell, and the hapless "pilot" saw it fluttering over the waves "like a frightened seagull".

[2] Captain D. Macintyre, *op. cit.*

[3] Her steering-gear had been damaged by a shell from the *Kaiserin*.

van, and only one or two of Scheer's ships were in a position to reply. Two hits were made on the *König*, which was soon listing badly; the *Markgraf* had her speed reduced by a hit in the engine-room. But visibility was worsening all the time. As Jellicoe wrote in his report, "the ships were firing on what they could see, when they could see".

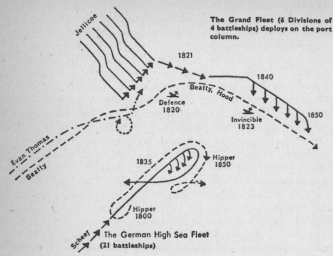

Deployment of British Battle Fleet and first retirement of the German Fleet

Scheer took advantage to extricate his fleet from the dangerous situation. At 18.35 hours he made the signal for the *Gefechtskehrwendung nach Steuerbord*—an emergency retirement which had been practised dozens of time during manoeuvres. The German destroyers dashed out, fired their torpedoes "into the brown", and put up a smoke-screen while each battleship did a right-about turn, beginning with the rear ship and followed in succession by those ahead. The manoeuvre was executed with perfect precision, and by 18.45 the German battleships had pulled out of range of the British, who ceased firing. None had thought to warn Jellicoe of the enemy manoeuvre, and he had continued on his easterly course, thus increasing still more the distance between the opposing fleets; he might well have lost contact completely if the vigilant Commodore Goodenough had not headed towards the retreating enemy in spite of the great risk to his light cruisers. It was not until 18.50 that Jellicoe altered course to the south; while Scheer, who was then twelve miles to the south-west of the Grand

Fleet, also altered course—but it brought him nearer the enemy. This was a most surprising manoeuvre; it not only placed his hard-pressed battle-cruisers in the van, within 10,000 yards of the enemy, but it also enabled Jellicoe to "cross the T" for a second time.

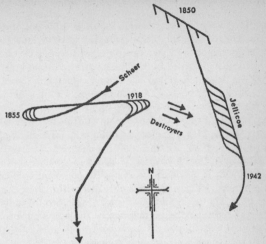

Jellicoe crosses the T, and Scheer turns away. The German destroyers launch a torpedo attack

One should remember that the German commander-in-chief was not in the best position, in the centre of his formation. Nevertheless, his manoeuvre was difficult to explain, and as the Official History of the German Navy has it, "went against all the rules". Scheer soon realized the fact. At 19.15 he ordered another right-about turn, this time leaving his battle-cruisers to protect the withdrawal, making a signal which has remained as celebrated in the annals of the German Navy as the order to charge given to the Light Brigade in the annals of the British Army. "Order to the battle-cruisers to make straight for the enemy. Charge and ram!"

Make for the enemy . . . but the battle-scarred ships were already under his fire. The *Derfflinger* had her two after-turrets knocked out; while in the *Von der Tann* the control-turret had been hit and everyone killed, and only one gun was still firing. Jellicoe was closing the range, bearing to starboard in order to concentrate the fire from his most powerful ships. The retirement of the German battleships—more hurried on this occasion, though the manoeuvre was miraculously executed without accident—was again aided by the destroyers dashing out to fire their torpedoes, from 7,000 yards, and then making a smoke-screen. Six of the destroyers were put out of action, and a seventh was sunk by a direct hit. The torpedoes—twenty-eight in all—either ran clear or fell short of their mark; but the attack saved the High Sea Fleet.

The best means of evading a torpedo is for the ship being attacked to turn on to a course parallel with the running torpedo; but obviously the ship has a choice between turning towards or away from the attacker. Jellicoe had turned his battleships two points and then again two points—45 degrees in all, which a rapid calculation showed to be sufficient—but 45 degrees *away from* the enemy. He thus widened the distance from an adversary who was in his power. "Twenty-eight torpedoes, and the firm determination to run no risk with his fleet, had robbed Jellicoe of the chance of gaining a decisive victory."[1]

Actually, Jellicoe was unaware that his enemy had turned about. Several of his subordinates had seen Scheer's manoeuvre, but none of them had thought it necessary to inform his commander-in-chief. In the circumstances, Jellicoe had reckoned that with Scheer remaining on course he would lose about 1,600 yards, which could easily be regained. But, Scheer having turned about, the opposing forces were moving away from each other at a speed of twenty knots; so that, when Jellicoe returned to his south-westerly course at 19.45, he had lost some 4,000 yards.

The Germans began to breathe again. The damage had been restricted to three battleships, the *Markgraf*, *Grosser Kurfürst*, and *König*; and they were still able to maintain their stations in the line, with all their guns serviceable. The last two, though, had shipped 800 and 1,600 tons of water respectively. Scheer had no thought of seeking to renew the action; instead, he shaped course for the Horns Reef, trying to avoid being driven westwards by the enemy, the bulk of whose forces were to the east of him. The sun was sinking swiftly to the horizon; in half an hour it would disappear, and in an hour darkness would have fallen. The British, coming from the east, now had the light in their favour; it was high time to take advantage of the fact. Jellicoe ordered a course converging on the enemy's; contact could be made in twenty-five minutes, and there would be thirty left in which to deal with the Germans.

Beatty had only just lost sight of the enemy battle-cruisers, and a little before eight o'clock he asked Jellicoe to detach the leading battle-ships, affirming that he would then be able to cut the line of retreat of

[1] Captain D. Macintyre, *op. cit.*

the enemy fleet. And it was not impossible for Beatty, if he had been joined by a squadron of battleships, to have "crossed the T" for a third time. But his request was impossible to give effect to, for the leading battle squadron (the Second, under Jerram) was not even in sight of Beatty and would have taken two hours to join him. So the action was renewed, at 20.00 hours, by Beatty's force alone. The *Derfflinger*'s remaining turret was put out of action, and more damage was inflicted on the *Seydlitz*. Mauve went to their assistance with his old battleships, but these could not withstand even the now reduced firing-power of the British battle-cruisers. The *Schleswig-Holstein*, the *Pommern*, and then the *Schlesien* were damaged, and Mauve was forced to break away to the west. Scheer regretfully altered course a few points to the west, too, realizing that he would be confronted with the whole of the Grand Fleet if he stood on to the south. Firing ceased at 20.45. Once again, Jellicoe had known nothing of it; but this time Beatty had a good excuse—the *Lion*'s wireless was out of action. As for the faithful Good-enough, he had been too busily occupied in the rear, beating off the destroyers attempting to make torpedo attacks on Evan-Thomas's squadron.

At nine o'clock Jellicoe altered course to the south, and twenty-five minutes later Beatty did the same, thinking he would thus head off the Germans from the west. So the three forces were speeding through the night on almost parallel courses, Beatty ahead and about eight miles in advance of Scheer, and Jellicoe about nine miles to the east of Scheer and abeam of him. But with none of the three very sure of his position in relation to the others.

The night was short; first light would be soon after three. Jellicoe decided, rightly, that Scheer was making for his base through the swept passage just west of the Horns Reef, and he sent the fast minelayer *Abdiel* on ahead to bottle it up. Scheer, too, had made a correct appreciation of his enemy's intentions. But he had no choice. There was no question of renewing the action in the morning; he had to make for his base during the night, come what may. And at 21.30 hours he ordered his fleet to steer south-east by south.

He did succeed in reaching his base; but to describe in detail how he managed it would require many pages. In short, his course converged on Jellicoe's, but he was astern of the British battleships; he smashed through their light cruiser screen when Jellicoe was less than six miles ahead.

It was a sharp, running action, with losses on both sides. The *Castor* was hit about ten times, the *Southampton* and the *Dublin* were both severely damaged, and the *Tipperary* was set on fire. Three British destroyers ran into each other at full speed, and one of them sank shortly afterwards. The Germans lost the *Frauenlob* and the *Rostock*, both being torpedoed; and the *Elbing* crashed into the *Posen*, damaging herself so badly that she had to be sunk.

The latter incidents occurred within sight of the two rear battleships of the Grand Fleet, the *Malaya* and the *Valiant*. But both captains

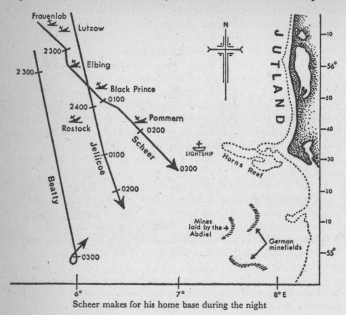

Scheer makes for his home base during the night

seemed to think that it would be more appropriate for their Divisional commander to signal the incidents, and so Jellicoe remained unaware of what was happening!

At about midnight Scheer's battleships sank three destroyers—the *Ardent*, *Fortune*, and *Turbulent*—and a little later the armoured cruiser *Black Prince* was brought under concentrated fire and blew up, with the loss of all her crew. Just before dawn the British retaliated by sinking the *Pommern*, the attack being carried out by destroyers of the Twelfth Flotilla; she was the last ship to be sunk at the Battle of Jutland.[1] There was a brief exchange between the light cruiser *Champion* and four German destroyers at 03.30 hours; but the destroyers soon

[1] The Germans described the attack as "a model of its kind".

made off, being hampered by having survivors from the *Lützow* on board—she had been scuttled earlier, being much too crippled to make port.

The mines laid by the *Abdiel* did no harm to the German ships, but the *Ostfriesland* struck a mine farther south and only just managed to limp into port. The battered *Seydlitz*, weighed down by 5,000 tons of water in her hold, went aground not far from the Horns Reef lightship

The *Warrior* at the Battle of Jutland

but a salvage vessel from Wilhelmshaven got her away by eleven in the morning.

When Jellicoe turned north at 02.20 hours, in order to be off the Horns Reef at dawn, the sea ahead of him was empty of the enemy. His destroyer flotillas were scattered; fearing an attack by U-boats, he remained well out—missing the chance of finishing off the *Seydlitz*—and cruised until midday, when he set course to return to base. At that moment, Scheer's flagship was dropping anchor in the Jade estuary.

The wind got up, the sea was running high. . . . The damaged British ships struggled to make port, some still fighting fires or taking water. The *Warrior* never managed it. . . .

The losses were heavy on both sides, but the British had lost twice as much tonnage as the Germans, and had three times as many casualties. The German ships, better built and skilfully handled, had proved themselves individually to be the more effective and the stouter.

They had also been very fortunate in twice escaping the dire consequences of the crossing of the T, to which Scheer had deliberately exposed himself on the second occasion. But the withdrawal during the night, when the battleships had smashed their way through the British screen, was undoubtedly a triumph for the Germans; and the German newspapers had some reason for their headlines on the evening of June 1st—"Great Naval Victory". Although fighting five against eight—roughly the proportionate strength of the opposing fleets— the Germans had inflicted losses of eight to their five. On the other hand, it was the British who had remained in command of the scene of the action.

But the result of the battle should be measured in its after effects, rather than by its momentary losses. After Jutland, the High Sea Fleet hardly ever put to sea again. A raid on the East Coast on August 19th, 1916, ended in a quick trail back; and afterwards the ships remained at their moorings, with a consequent gradual decline in the morale of the crews. Moreover, the mounting U-boat warfare was draining away the best of the officers and ratings. On two occasions in 1917, on October 17th and December 22nd, the cruisers ventured forth and made successful raids on the convoys to Narvik, sinking nine cargo ships the first time and fourteen the second. But a third attack, in April, 1918, was a failure.

In the final stages of the war, Admiral Hipper, who had succeeded Scheer (appointed Chief of Naval Staff), tried in vain to get the Fleet to sea. He came up against mutinous crews. . . . The spirit had gone out of the High Sea Fleet, which was as dead as if it had been destroyed at Jutland. Nevertheless, right until the end, it continued to weigh heavily upon British naval strategy by obliging the Grand Fleet to remain watchful at Scapa Flow.

The Royal Navy may still feel bitter at not having gained the crushing victory over the German Fleet, on May 31st, 1916, which would have assured it of supremacy at sea for a long time—a supremacy which, as the American historian, Frost, has written, rests as much on moral qualities as on material strength. And the British lost some of that precious advantage at Jutland.

Still, the question will always remain—what would have resulted that last afternoon in May, 1916, if Jellicoe—the only Allied commander who could have lost the war in an afternoon—had turned 45 degrees *towards* the enemy instead of *away*, when the German destroyers made their torpedo attack.

XXIII

THE CRUISE OF THE *EMDEN*

The German raider makes the first capture of the war—at large in the Indian Ocean—British merchant shipping suffers heavily—the dummy funnel proves effective—dawn raid on Georgetown—a gallant fight by the French Mousquet *—Müller's luck fails in the Cocos Islands—the Australian cruiser* Sydney *is sent to intercept the raider—the last of the* Emden *(November 9th, 1914).*

THE cruiser *Emden* was mentioned in the previous chapter as having been detached by Admiral von Spee from his Pacific squadron in August, 1914. This ship, which had been launched at Dantzig in May, 1908, was obviously designed to serve as a commerce raider when war broke out. She had ten 4-inch guns, a displacement of 3,650 tons, and with her two engines could attain a speed of twenty-four and a half knots. Her armament was not powerful enough for her to have a place in a battle squadron, but her range of action was considerable for those days; by cruising at an economical speed she could cover 6,000 miles, which was an excellent performance for a coal-burning ship.

After a year in service the *Emden* had left Germany to join the Pacific squadron. From 1913 onwards she was commanded by Kapitan von Müller. Even before the outbreak of the First World War the ship was in action, silencing a Chinese shore battery on the Yangtse which had opened fire on her. However, the World War gave Von Müller an opportunity to embark on a raiding cruise that was short but glorious, and which earnt him the admiration of sailors everywhere, not least the British, one of whom even wrote that "he was worthy enough to have served under the British ensign".

The *Emden* had been into Tsing-tao for careening (Tsing-tao was a naval base on the China coast that Germany had acquired in 1890), and was sailing out into the Yellow Sea when Müller received the news that his country was at war with France and Russia. He assembled his crew and told them that his intention was to shape course for Vladivostock and raid the shipping in spite of the risk of meeting Russian or French warships.[1] The *Emden* had not far to go before making her first

[1] The French Far East Squadron consisted of two cruisers, the *Dupleix* and the *Montcalm*, each more powerful but slower than the *Emden*, and of a few destroyers based on Saigon. The *Montcalm* had not yet arrived on the China station, but the *Dupleix* was placed under command of Rear-Admiral Jerram and on August 5th joined the cruisers *Yarmouth* and *Triumph* at Hong Kong. This force was responsible

capture. Soon after passing the island of Tsou-Shima she came upon the Russian liner *Rjesan*, during the night of August 2nd. This steamer was almost certainly the first of the Allied merchant shipping to be captured in the First World War. The *Emden* took the *Rjesan* into Tsing-tao, where she was converted into an armed auxiliary cruiser and given the name *Kormoran*, which had been that of a scrapped German cruiser.[1]

The *Emden* just got away again from Tsing-tao in time to avoid Rear-Admiral Jerram's cruisers, on August 6th, and in company with her supply ship, the collier *Markomannia*, sailed for the Marianas, where they made a secret rendezvous with Von Spee's force of raiders on August 12th.

In the weeks preceding the outbreak of the war Müller had thought out the best way of employing the *Emden*, and Von Spee agreed that the cruiser would have more success alone than incorporated in his own force. The ships put to sea the following day, Von Spee sailing east and having made the signal from the *Scharnhorst: Emden entlassen, Wünsche guten Erfolg* . . . Müller was a free agent, and had Von Spee's best wishes for success.

The raider took four weeks to reach the Indian Ocean, which had been assigned to Müller as his particular area of operations. During the voyage, through the Flores Sea and skirting the Dutch East Indies, a dummy funnel was added to the *Emden*'s three real ones, at the suggestion of Müller's first lieutenant, Von Mücke. This fourth funnel gave the raider an outline similar to British cruisers of the *Yarmouth*-class. At the end of the first week in September the *Emden*, still accompanied by the *Markomannia*, was crossing the Bay of Bengal to prey on the shipping lanes into Calcutta.

The fourth funnel worked wonders! On the night of September 10th a Greek cargo vessel, the *Pontoporros*, was captured; she was found to be carrying coal, so Müller put a prize-crew on board. The following day a British ship, the *Indus*, on her way to Colombo to transport troops, was stopped and sunk after the crew had been transferred to the *Pontoporros*. On the 12th came the capture of the *Kabinga*, a British ship with a cargo of American goods; but Müller released her after forty-eight hours, having put the crews of the two previous victims on board her and ordered the captain to take them into Calcutta. The 13th

---

for the blockade of Tsing-tao. Between August 16th and 22nd the *Dupleix* captured two of Von Spee's supply ships.

[1] After the destruction of Von Spee's squadron at the battle of the Falklands, and then the end of the *Emden*, the *Kormoran* was the only remaining commerce raider in the Pacific. But she had no success, and put in at Guam on December 15th, 1914, to be interned by the Americans.

brought two more victims, the *Killin* and the *Diplomat*, the latter a fine ship of 7,600 tons carrying a rich cargo of tea. The *Clan Mattheson*, loaded with tractors and locomotives, was sunk on the 14th, and another British cargo ship, the *Trabbock*, later the same day.

By then, something akin to panic had spread among the shipping in the Indian Ocean. The Australian Government held up the departure of troop transports for Britain. Müller, in the meantime, having stopped the Italian ship *Loredano* but allowed her to proceed, deemed it wise to make for other waters. On the evening of September 22nd he appeared off Madras, and at a range of 3,000 yards fired 130 shells at the storage tanks of the Burma Oil Company. A thousand tons of fuel was set ablaze. A shore battery opened fire on the *Emden*, but without effect. The raider withdrew, deliberately showing her port navigation lights, as though shaping course to the north; but then made to the south, with not a light showing. On the night of the 25th she was off Colombo, and Müller had the audacity to take advantage of the searchlights from shore to sink a large merchant ship with a cargo of sugar, after taking off her crew and clamping them into the hold of the *Makomannia*. During the next forty-eight hours four

The *Emden*

more names were added to the *Emden*'s list of victims, and on the 28th a collier, the *Buresk*, carrying 7,000 tons of Welsh coal, was captured. This prize could not have come at a better moment, for the supplies in the *Markomannia* had all been used and the coal in the *Pontoporros* had proved to be poor quality. And it was time for the raider to disappear once again. There were sixteen Allied warships—British, French, Russian, and Japanese—looking for Müller; though they were also searching for Von Spee, whose whereabouts only became known when he shelled Papeete. There was no lack of bases for the Allies in the Far East—Colombo, Singapore, Georgetown, at the head of the Malacca Straits, Hong Kong, and others. Müller could tell from the increase in wireless traffic that there were many enemy warships patrolling the area, though he had not the directional apparatus which would have enabled him to plot their positions. So he moved south, making for the island of Diego Garcia in the Chagos archipelago, a remote British possession in the middle of the Indian Ocean, 10 degrees below the Equator. He arrived there on October 10th.

At that time the islands' only link with the outside world was a twice-yearly steamer from Mauritius. Her last call was prior to the outbreak of war, so the *Emden*'s crew was welcomed with open arms by "their English cousins", whom they naturally did not disillusion. Müller decided to take advantage of the situation to beach and scrape his ship's keel, just as in the days of sail when it became necessary to clean the barnacles from a three-master.

While his men were thus occupied, and were rendering what service they could to their hosts in exchange for this facility, the British Navy took some revenge. On October 15th the cruiser *Yarmouth* found and sank the supply ship *Markomannia*, and recaptured the *Pontoporros*, which was sent to Singapore.

However, the *Emden* was soon heard of again—this time in the shipping lanes to the west of Cape Comorin, the southern point of India. In a matter of hours, on October 20th, the raider sank four British steamers and a dredger, then stopped another ship and put the crews of the first five on board her, and captured a seventh. This last was a British collier, the *Exford*, and she now succeeded the *Markomannia* as the raider's supply ship. Altogether, 26,477 tons of shipping had just been lost to the Allies.

The British Press and public opinion were now thoroughly roused. Until then, people had seen the sporting side of the *Emden*'s progress; all the crews of the raider's victims had spoken of the good treatment and fairness received from her captain. But there were limits! The value of the ships and cargoes lost had reached millions of pounds; maritime insurance rates were soaring, and merchant shipping in the Indian Ocean had been brought almost to a standstill. Even *The Times* printed a leader censuring the Admiralty in no uncertain terms.

There was little their Lordships could do, except issue a statement explaining that eight or nine commerce raiders were at large in the Atlantic, Pacific, and Indian Ocean, that seventy Allied warships were hunting them, and that the public must be patient.

Four days later, on October 28th, the *Emden* excelled even her own past achievements. She attacked naval vessels at their moorings at Georgetown,[1] on the west coast of Malaya, entering the roadstead before daybreak and sailing right into the sheltered bay. The *Emden* was showing no lights and had her dummy funnel in position. Müller loosed a torpedo at the Russian cruiser *Jemstchoug*, swept her with his guns as he passed, turned and fired another torpedo which caused an

---

[1] The French naval commander there, Captain Daveluy, had the *Dupleix*, the *D'Iberville*, and three small destroyers under his orders, as well as a Russian cruiser, the *Jemstchoug*.

explosion aboard the cruiser; she broke in two and sank in a matter of seconds. It was then about half past five.

Müller was about to deal in similar manner with the French gunboat *D'Iberville*, which was moored farther in, when his lookouts reported what they took to be a large British destroyer standing off the entrance to the bay. Müller at once made for the open sea, in order to fight it out with more advantage, but discovered that he had been the victim of a trick of light. The ship was the liner *Glenturrit*, which was waiting for a pilot to come out to her. All right—she would be given several pilots, but not to take her into Georgetown!

Just then the small French destroyer *Mousquet* arrived on the scene, returning from a patrol in the Malacca Straits. She had been too far off for any of the crew to have heard the gunfire and the explosion that had sunk the Russian cruiser. Lieutenant Théroine, the *Mousquet*'s captain, took the four-funnelled cruiser for a British ship and hoisted his recognition signal.

It must be admitted that the roadstead was badly guarded. Commander Audemard, the *D'Iberville*'s captain, had raised the matter several times with the British authorities. His ship was unable to put to sea because the engines were being repaired. In any case, he and his crew had also taken the *Emden* for an Allied cruiser—the *Yarmouth*, or perhaps the Japanese *Chikuma*, which the Russians in the *Jemstchoug* had once before been accused of firing on by mistake. . . . During the night some of the *Jemstchoug*'s crew had returned from shore leave in a very boisterous state—and the more drunken must have let off a few rounds. That would not have been surprising, and was no doubt the explanation of the firing heard earlier in the morning.

The other two small French destroyers, the *Fronde* and the *Pistolet*, were moored alongside the jetty. Their crews, however, had soon realized what was really happening. The *Pistolet* had trained her torpedoes on the *Emden*, but the raider had passed no nearer than 1,700 yards, and the maximum range of the *Pistolet*'s torpedoes was only 600 yards. Her captain raised steam as quickly as possible (unlike the *Fronde*, the *Pistolet* had already been getting steam up), but it was a good hour before she was ready to put to sea. Meanwhile, her captain had gone aboard the *D'Iberville* for orders. Everyone was so bewildered and confused that he was told the *Mousquet* had just been sunk; and he returned quickly to his ship to go and search for survivors.

The *Pistolet* sighted the *Emden* in the distance as soon as she cleared the bay. Appearing much larger in the shimmering light, and with her four funnels, the raider was taken for the *Scharnhorst* at least! Great efforts were made to get up more steam, but the *Pistolet* was unable to reach the scene in time to help the *Mousquet* fight the raider. Which was just as well, for she would only have gone the same way as the *Mousquet*—not yet sunk, but soon to be, after a gallant but hopeless action.

The *Mousquet* was taken completely by surprise. Her captain knew nothing of what had happened in the bay—by the time the *D'Iberville*'s batteries were charged and her radio able to transmit, the *Mousquet* was thought to be sunk. It was only when the German flag was unfurled that Lieutenant Théroine realized he had to deal with the notorious raider. By then, his ship was being straddled by the *Emden*'s 4-inch guns. Before his own guns were trained, the third salvo knocked out the forward gun, destroyed the wireless cabin (as the operator was sending out the news of the *Emden*'s presence), and smashed the after boiler-room. Another salvo put the forward boiler-room out of action. The *Mousquet* lost way and began to go down by the bows, but with her remaining guns still firing.

It had been a minute or two before seven when Müller first opened fire; by a quarter past the hour the *Mousquet* had gone down, firing to the last, taking forty-three of the crew with her. The *Emden* picked up thirty-six, five of whom died later.[1]

The raider then made off at full speed, steering north-west to clear the Straits as quickly as possible. The *Pistolet* and the *Fronde* tried to keep her in sight, but by midday she had disappeared below the horizon.

The cruise of the *Emden* was, however, drawing to a close. On October 29th Müller stopped the British cargo ship *Newburn*, but sent her into Sabang with the survivors from the *Mousquet*. The *Newburn* marked the end of the raider's activities at sea. By then, Müller had sunk or captured 70,000 tons of Allied shipping, not reckoning the ships he had released after capture, nor the *Pontoporros* which had been recovered by naval action. But now there were Allied warships on his heels, and strenuous efforts were being made to hunt him down, especially as thirty thousand Australian troops were then in convoy crossing the Indian Ocean. The Admiralty was striving to reinforce Jerram's squadron. However, a lucky chance was soon to remove all worries over the *Emden*.

Müller decided to withdraw to the south again, as his presence in the shipping lanes between Ceylon and Sumatra—where the *Newburn*

[1] Three died aboard the *Emden* and were buried at sea, wrapped in a French flag. A fourth died after being transferred to the *Newburn*, and the fifth in hospital at Sabang. All the *Mousquet*'s officers perished, including Sub-Lieutenant Carissan, who although badly wounded had refused to be attended to before the men.

had been hailed—was becoming known. He ordered his two supply ships, the prizes *Buresk* and *Exford*, to make rendezvous with him in the Cocos Islands. His intention was to destroy the radio station and telephone cables there, as a preliminary to raiding shipping using the Sunda Strait between Sumatra and Java.

In the early morning of November 9th the *Emden* appeared off Port Refuge, a bay on the north coast of Direction Island, which is the largest of the Keeling, or Cocos, group. The raider had four funnels, but the dummy one was so battered from being taken down and put up again that it deceived no one. . . . The shore radio operator was quick to send out S.O.S. calls. The *Emden* tried to jam the signals, but it was too late. This time, Müller's luck had failed.

The big convoy of Australian troop transports was sailing fifty-five miles north of the Cocos Islands just then, and the signals were picked up by the cruiser *Melbourne*. There were two other cruisers among the escort ships, the Australian *Sydney* and the Japanese *Ibuki*, each with more powerful armament than the *Emden*. Captain Silver of the *Melbourne*, who was in command of the escort ships, detached the less powerful of the two, the *Sydney*, deciding that the safety of the convoy came first and so preferring to retain as much strength as possible in case of attack. At seven in the morning Captain Glossop of the *Sydney* was ordered to proceed at full speed to the Cocos Islands, which had just sent out a call for help. The Japanese in the *Ibuki* were most envious. . . .

In the meantime, Müller did not seem to suspect any danger. He had sent Von Mücke ashore with fifty men to blow up the radio-station and cut the cables. The latter operation was proving long and laborious, for lack of proper tools, and only one cable had been cut when the *Emden* began to give signs of impatience. "Speed up the work!" The signal was shortly followed by hoots from the ship—and then she stood out to sea, leaving Von Mücke and his fifty men on dry land. The reason soon became obvious when her guns started firing.

It was nine in the morning, on that ninth day of November, 1914, when Müller signalled his shore party to return; and at a quarter past he quickly put to sea, the *Sydney* having been sighted fast approaching from the north-east. By 09.40 hours the *Sydney* was on the *Emden*'s port beam, and Captain Glossop turned on to a parallel course and opened fire at 10,500 yards. This was extreme range for the *Emden*'s 4-inch guns, but well within range for the *Sydney*'s 6-inch. Moreover, the *Sydney* had not been long at sea, whereas the *Emden*'s keel had only had the worst taken off at Diego Garcia, and even that was six weeks previously. The *Sydney* could thus do four or five knots more than the other, enabling Captain Glossop to regulate the distance as he wished.[1]

The *Emden*'s gunners, nevertheless, were the first on target. The Australians were a thousand yards over, due to an error in range-finding. It cost them a few men wounded and the destruction of the after control-turret, but that was the last damage caused by the *Emden*. As soon as the error had been corrected, the German cruiser began to suffer heavily. A lucky hit smashed the telemeter; and another hit damaged the helm, so that Müller was reduced to steering with his propellers. Then his forward funnel and the mainmast were brought down, several guns were put out of action, and fires broke out in many parts of the ship.

The *Sydney* closed to 5,500 yards and fired a torpedo, but it ran wide. Captain Glossop opened the range again, and the unequal fight continued with the two ships still on almost parallel courses. When it had lasted forty minutes, all the *Emden*'s funnels had gone, the gun-control turrets had been knocked out, and the fires aboard her were sending up such vast billows of smoke that at one moment observers in the *Sydney* could no longer see her and thought she had gone down. But she reappeared, heading east and still firing. Then she turned in a wide sweep; the *Sydney* imitated her movement, and both ships were heading towards North Keeling Island. Before the *Sydney* could race across to intercept the *Emden*, which was getting ever lower in the water, Müller had driven her aground. It was then twenty past eleven. The *Sydney* gave the stricken ship two more salvoes; then, being quite certain that the *Emden* would never get off, Captain Glossop turned away to deal with the supply ship *Buresk*. The German crew scuttled her at the cruiser's approach.

At four in the afternoon the *Sydney* returned to the *Emden*. Her colours were still flying. "Do you wish to surrender?" Glossop signalled. Müller replied in Morse that he did not understand that signal. A couple of salvoes added to the shambles on the wrecked deck of the German raider.

There were 115 dead and 56 badly wounded men in the *Emden*. Not a gun was still capable of being fired. His ship was aground on a lee shore. . . . Müller hauled down his flag.

Glossop was anxious to know of the situation on Direction Island, and to capture the demolition team left stranded there. But Von Mücke was not the kind of man to bow to adversity. There in the bay was the

---

[1] The comparative characteristics of the two cruisers were: the *Emden*—3,600 tons, 24 knots, ten 4-inch guns, two torpedo tubes, complement of 321; the *Sydney*—5,250 tons, 25 knots, eight 6-inch guns, two torpedo tubes, complement of 376.

schooner *Ayesha*, belonging to the owner of the island; Von Mücke did not hesitate to requisition her, and his men worked like mad to put stocks of food and water aboard her. At nightfall, they slipped away from the island in the schooner, escaping capture by only a few minutes, the *Sydney* having been delayed through rescuing a German sailor from the sea.

Von Mücke and his men reached Padang, on the coast of Sumatra, on November 24th. The Dutch authorities were highly suspicious of them, and refused permission to land. But Von Mücke again overcame his difficulties. There were three German cargo ships in the harbour, and he arranged for one of them, the *Choising*, to meet the schooner out at sea and take him and his men on board. After many misadventures, this was finally managed on December 14th, in the sheltered waters of a small island at the southern end of the Maldives. Three weeks later the *Choising* succeeded in evading British patrols off Aden and got through into the Red Sea during the night. The following day, Von Mücke and his men were put ashore at Hodeidah. Then they made their way overland, through Arabia, to Istanbul, having accomplished a journey that was in every way worthy of the cruise of the *Emden*.

PART TWO

Great Battles in World War Two

XXIV

THE SECOND WORLD WAR

On the night of September 3rd, 1939, the *U-30* commanded by Oberleutnant zur See Lemp was pursuing its stealthy way in the Atlantic, some two hundred miles west of the Hebrides. It had left its base at Wilhelmshaven a fortnight previously, like a score of other German submarines, to be on the prowl at the outbreak of hostilities. Now Germany had been at war with Great Britain since midday, and with France since five in the afternoon.

The Cunard White Star liner *Athenia* had sailed from Liverpool at four o'clock the previous afternoon, bound for Montreal with 1,100 passengers on board, including about 300 Americans. As fate would have it, the *Athenia* crossed the path of the *U-30*. . . .

The sinking of the *Athenia* stunned the whole world, and was the first blow in the long drawn-out Battle of the Atlantic. It also marked the beginning of world-wide naval warfare in which practically all the well-known fighting ships of the nations were to play a part. The war which started on September 1st, 1939, between Germany and Poland had spread to France and Great Britain two days later. On April 9th, 1940, it overtook Denmark and Norway, on May 10th Holland, Belgium, and Luxembourg; on June 10th Italy came into the war, then Rumania was drawn in at the beginning of August, and Greece on October 28th. The conflict spread to Bulgaria the following year, on March 1st; to Hungary on April 2nd, Yugoslavia on the 6th; and on June 22nd Russia and Finland, who had fought each other in the autumn of 1939, came in on opposite sides. Then came the turn of Persia, and a few months later the attack on Pearl Harbor announced Japan's entry into the arena—though she had been making war on China for the past four years. The United States then declared war. . . .

A mere half-dozen countries in Europe succeeded in remaining neutral—Eire, Portugal, Spain, Sweden, Switzerland, and Turkey. Elsewhere, even Brazil[1] took up arms, though there was no apparent reason why her soldiers should "die for Dantzig". But who, by that time, still thought of Dantzig as the excuse, if not the reason, for the Second World War?

Seamen fought and died in all the seven seas, and under a score of

---

[1] On August 22nd, 1942, Brazil declared war on Germany and Italy.

different flags. In naval communiques there appeared names of places which until then had only occurred in accounts of explorations. So great was the confusion and the clash of ideologies that almost over-night allies became enemies. Italy changed sides in 1943. Some countries became divided within themselves. Yuogoslavs fought each other, as did the French, alas. French sailors fought first against the Germans, then against the Italians, the British, the Siamese, Americans, and Japanese. They only just escaped fighting the Dutch;[1] and, worst of all, French merchantmen were torpedoed by Polish sailors—and France had entered the war to assist Poland!

It would be impossible to describe or even to enumerate all the naval battles of the war. The reader may feel that the best selection has not been made, and that what appear to be minor actions are dealt with, while far more important battles are hardly mentioned. But within the limits of this book, the guiding principle has been to concentrate on those naval actions which show sea warfare in all its different aspects, in which sailors of different nationalities took part, and above all which brought out the individual qualities of the participants. The Allied landings in the South of France in 1944, for instance, where success was assured by the overwhelming forces employed, have much less human interest—however great the impact on the course of the war—than some risky venture in which the skill and courage of a leader and his men turned the scale. Such was the Battle of the River Plate, with which I begin the final part of this book.

There is just one more observation I should like to make. In the Second World War men gradually became harnessed to increasingly complex machines and instruments; and in those six years, naval war-fare evolved more rapidly than in the whole of its history.

In olden days, battles were fought out on one plane—on the surface of the sea. The enemy was always within view, for distances were limited by the range of the weapons—first five, and never more than six hundred yards; and even at the beginning of the nineteenth century, boarding was normally the final phase of every action.

Nowadays, battles are fought under, on, and above the sea. Aided by elaborate instruments, sailors can aim far beyond their own vision, and weapons have a longer and longer range. Radar has made it possible for guns to be trained automatically on objectives which the human eye has not perceived. Asdic has enabled corvettes and de-stroyers to attack submarines without any sign of their presence having

[1] In September, 1941, the French gunboat *Amiral Charner* was escorting a convoy from Saigon to Madagascar. When in the Sunda Strait she had to threaten to fire on a Dutch patrol boat which wanted to take the convoy into an Allied port.

been noticed, because this listening instrument allows a specialist tucked away from sight of the sea to pick up the echoes made by a submerged submarine. Merely by the use of this instrument an attack can be made with precision; and sometimes only the cessation of those echoes has indicated that depth-charges have found their mark, and that the enemy has been destroyed without trace. Neither attacker nor attacked has seen the other, there was no human contact. Yet, after the war, German archives revealed that on such a day and in such a sector the *U-45*—to name but one—had suddenly ceased radio contact and had never returned to base.[1]

Even more remarkable was that the aeroplane made it possible for whole naval squadrons to fight without a sight of each other, and sometimes when several hundreds of miles apart. In May, 1942, at the Battle of the Coral Sea, for the first time in history two squadrons fought without ever having been visible to one another. In spite of this, five or six ships were sunk, including the American 30,000-ton carrier *Lexington* and the Japanese 12,000-ton *Shoho*.

But it is not enough to have instruments and machines. They increase efficiency and have greatly added to the possibilities of bringing the enemy to battle, but they make great demands on those who use them. The age-old skills still have to be mastered, and many more besides. The men aboard a destroyer which has just scored a victory over an enemy submarine, simply by the miracle of Asdic, have nevertheless been at action stations for days and nights on end, and have screwed up their eyes against the wind exactly as Nelson's sailors did when hunting Villeneuve in the Atlantic. They have had to sleep, eat, and work while their ship was pounded by the seas or battled her way through a gale. In short, these engineers and technicians and specialists of all kinds, more skilled in the use of delicate instruments than in taking in a reef, are still sailors for all that.

[1] The destroyer *Deptford*—as will be seen later—only learnt months afterwards, through a German communique, that she had destroyed the *U-567*. The French crew of the corvette *Lobélia* did not know until after the war that they had sunk the *U-609* in the Atlantic.

XXV

THE BATTLE OF THE RIVER PLATE

The German pocket-battleships—early successes of the Admiral Graf Spee—
the Deutschland *evades Allied patrols—Commodore Harwood anticipates
correctly—the Battle of the River Plate (December 13th, 1939)—the* Graf
Spee *is scuttled off Montevideo—her successors—the gallant sacrifice of the*
Jervis Bay—*convoys attacked by the* Scharnhorst and Gneisenau—*the
pursuit of the* Bismarck—*the last of the raiders.*

WHEN the Second World War broke out on September 3rd, 1939, the
situation of the German Navy was very different from what it had been
twenty-five years earlier. The aims of the Navy were much the same
as in the First World War, but the means of attaining them were considerably reduced. There could be no question of a full-scale battle
such as Jutland, for the Allied naval forces had overwhelming superiority. Nor was the employment of a squadron of commerce raiders
possible, for Germany had lost all her overseas possessions by the
Treaty of Versailles, and lacked the bases which had enabled Von
Spee to operate.

In 1914 it had been his squadron which had opened hostilities at sea.
In 1939 it was a ship bearing his name—the pocket-battleship *Admiral
Graf Spee*, the latest of the three 10,000-ton warships that Germany had
been allowed to build under the terms of the Versailles Treaty.

It was Great Britain who had insisted on this limitation to ships of
10,000 tons, which was the displacement of the heavy cruisers built in
considerable numbers by all the naval powers during the years between
the two World Wars. Germany scrupulously observed the limitation.
But when the first of the new type of warship came into service—the
Deutschland, in 1933—she was seen to have six 11-inch guns, whereas no
10,000-ton cruiser of any other power had guns larger than 8-inch; she
was armoured, whereas neither the French *Suffren* nor the British
London was; and her range of action greatly exceeded that of her
eventual enemies. The German technicians and shipbuilders had
achieved a real *tour de force*. These *Deutschland*-class warships had an
all-welded hull that did away with thousands of rivets, thus saving
several hundred tons in weight; they were driven by Diesel-engines of
54,000 horse-power that gave a nominal speed of twenty-six knots;
and they had two turrets of three 11-inch guns and eight 5·9-inch guns

mounted on their displacement of 10,000 tons. They were certainly remarkable ships—on paper; and the world was much impressed at the time by the ingenuity and skill of the German technicians.

The *Deutschland* was followed by the *Admiral Scheer*, and in 1936 the *Admiral Graf Spee* came into service. She was among the foreign ships at the Spithead Naval Review in honour of the Coronation of King George VI, and caused something of a sensation. Her end, four years later, was even more sensational.

The pocket-battleships had caused misgivings and much anxiety to other maritime powers. The French were the first to react, and laid down two 26,000-ton ships, the *Dunkerque* and the *Strasbourg*. These were the first capital ships to be built after the First World War, and were the only ones apart from the three British battle-cruisers *Hood*, *Repulse*, and *Renown*—nearly twenty years older—to have greater speed and firing-power than the *Deutschland*-class ships. With Germany rearming, and another World War looming on the horizon, Great Britain endeavoured to limit naval armament by concluding a new agreement with Germany. By the Anglo-German naval agreement of June 18th, 1935, the total tonnage of the German Fleet was not to exceed 35 per cent of the aggregate British forces in surface vessels, nor 45 per cent of the submarine tonnage. Germany speeded up her shipbuilding programme, and the other naval powers were obliged to follow suit.

However, when war was declared none of the new German ships was ready for service. Apart from the three pocket-battleships, and the two *Scharnhorst*-class battle-cruisers which had only just finished their trials, the Germany Navy was dependent on hopes. Grand-Admiral Raeder,[1] the commander-in-chief, had reported to Hitler on many occasions that the Navy would not be ready before 1944 or 1945, but the Fuhrer had taken no notice, being unable to realize that victory on the Continent would not be decisive while Great Britain was still undefeated. Raeder had accepted the task imposed on him, affirming that the navy would know how to go down fighting in an unequal combat in order to "prepare for future revival".[2]

The *Admiral Graf Spee*'s war really began on August 21st, 1939. On that day she sailed from Wilhelmshaven under the command of Captain zur See Langsdorf for "an unknown destination", well supplied with ammunition and fuel. Two days previously, the tanker

[1] He had been staff officer to Admiral Hipper in the battle-cruiser squadron at Jutland. (*Tr.*)
[2] Memorandum dated September 3rd, 1939.

Altmark had left Port Arthur (U.S.A.) with full tanks. She was to operate as the *Graf Spee*'s supply ship; and the raider's hunting-ground was to be the South Atlantic. The North Atlantic had been assigned to the *Deutschland*, which left home waters on August 25th; her supply ship was the *Westerwald*, which had sailed three days earlier with orders to make rendezvous in the empty waste to the east of Greenland.

Almost a month went by after the outbreak of war before the presence of the German raiders became known. The submarines had already made their presence felt—a score and more were on the prowl, and the sinking of the *Athenia* had been followed by that of many other ships. But at the beginning of October it was learnt that some thirty survivors from the British cargo ship *Clement* had been landed at Maceio, on the coast of Brazil. They said at first that their ship had been sunk by a German auxiliary cruiser, but more detailed questioning revealed that it had in fact been a pocket-battleship. A general alert followed.

The surprising thing was that no alert had occurred earlier. Not until after the war was the reason known, when the German naval archives came into the hands of the Allies.

When the *Graf Spee* had sailed from Wilhelmshaven, the invasion of Poland was already planned and the date fixed for August 26th. The troops were ready for the attack, and the warships which were to bombard the Polish coast were already at sea, when the invasion was suddenly postponed on the 25th. Hitler had been told that Britain and France would go to the support of Poland. Efforts to maintain peace were being made in many quarters. The German dictator hesitated, then his attitude hardened; he did not believe that the Western powers would really go to war. His troops crossed into Poland on September 1st; and on the 3rd Britain and France declared war on Germany.

Even then the Führer was not convinced, and the hesitant attitude of the Allies encouraged him in his false belief. When Poland had been overrun, the Germans began to put out peace feelers.

The pocket-battleships at sea had orders not to show themselves, to remain in areas far from the shipping routes. Each of them had taken an unfrequented route to reach her appointed area. The *Deutschland* had sailed up the Norwegian coast to the Arctic Circle and round the north of Iceland to cruise off Cape Farewell, the southern point of Greenland. The *Graf Spee* had reached the Western Atlantic by way of the Faroes and then steered due south; on September 10th she refuelled from the *Altmark* in mid-Atlantic, at a point about halfway between Brazil and the west coast of Africa, and had then spent the time avoiding any ship that appeared on the horizon—a rare occurrence in that part of the Ocean—while waiting to receive orders to commence operations.

But Hitler was still convinced that the Allies were bluffing, and he remained adamant—the two pocket-battleships were to remain away from shipping routes, and in particular no offensive action was to be taken against French ships. Admiral Raeder was not at all happy with the situation. If the orders were obeyed to the letter, a submarine would have to refrain from firing a torpedo at the *Dunkerque* or the *Strasbourg*, should one or the other be sighted—and they were two of the few Allied warships as powerful as the *Graf Spee*. Admiral Raeder pressed the Führer and finally obtained the consent he needed, on September 23rd. The peace overtures had not met with any success. On September 26th the *Graf Spee* and the *Deutschland* at last received their orders to proceed on their raiding missions.

The *Graf Spee* first moved towards the flow of shipping off the South American coast, and on September 30th sighted the British tramp S.S. *Clement*, of 5,000 tons, some sixty miles east of Pernambuco. The raider's plane flew off and forced the *Clement* to stop, and the crew were told to take to their boats. The *Graf Spee* fired a couple of torpedoes at the tramp but they both missed their mark, and Captain Langsdorf sank the ship by gunfire; he then informed the radio station at Pernambuco that the crew was adrift in the boats. Later the same day another ship was sighted, but she was found to be a Greek cargo vessel and so allowed to proceed. The raider then changed her area of operations, sailing east towards the shipping lanes between Freetown and the Cape of Good Hope.

On October 5th the *Newton Beach*, carrying 7,000 tons of maize, was captured and an armed guard put aboard her—a filthy ship, a German officer noted in his diary. She was made to accompany the raider, and two days later took aboard the crew of the *Ashlea*, of 4,200 tons, which was sunk by explosive charges along with her cargo of 7,000 tons of sugar. Then, the *Newton Beach* proving more of a hindrance than a help, the armed guard and the crews of the two British ships were transferred to the *Graf Spee*, and the prize was sunk on the afternoon of October 8th.

The next merchant ship to be captured, on October 10th, was the 2,000-ton *Huntsman*. She seemed more attractive than the *Newton Beach*, and this prolonged her life by a few days. The *Graf Spee* left her under guard on the 12th in order to refuel from the *Altmark*. Four days later the raider returned with her supply ship, and the two relieved the *Huntsman* of a quantity of useful goods—food, tea, skins, carpets, white slippers, sun-helmets. . . . The crew, chiefly Africans and Indians, then joined the other prisoners in the *Altmark*, and it was the turn of the *Huntsman* to disappear beneath the waves.

On October 22nd the *Trevanion* and her cargo of 6,000 tons of iron-ore were sunk. But she had at first refused to stop when ordered and, what was more serious, had radioed that she was being attacked. The time had come for the *Graf Spee* to disappear into the blue. For the next three weeks nothing more was heard of the raider.

It was already known that a German raider was operating in the South Atlantic. But five days after the sinking of the *Clement*, another British cargo ship, the *Stonegate*, was reported lost a few hundred miles east of Bermuda. On October 9th the American merchant ship *City of Flint* was captured in the same area, only a day before the *Huntsman* was taken more than 3,500 miles to the south. Before long, the Allies realized that not one but two raiders were at large. The one operating to the north was correctly identified as the *Deutschland*, but the other was taken to be the *Admiral Scheer*.

Scheer or *Spee*, it made no difference! The presence of the two pocket-battleships created a number of difficult problems for the British Admiralty. First, the escorts of the Atlantic convoys had to be strengthened. Then considerable forces were deployed to seek and destroy the raiders. Three battleships were allocated to protect the Halifax convoys; later, submarines accompanied the convoys, as it was realized that their presence would have a psychological effect upon the captains of the pocket-battleships which might well deter them. The battle-cruiser *Renown* and the aircraft-carrier *Ark Royal* were sent to the Freetown area, while the French based the battleship *Strasbourg* and three heavy cruisers on Dakar. The cruisers *Sussex* and *Shropshire* were patrolling south of the Cape of Good Hope. Commodore Harwood was at the Falkland Islands with the cruisers *Cumberland*, *Exeter*, *Ajax*, and *Achilles* under his command.

In those early days of the war there were very few long-range recon-naissance planes in service. The French Admiralty had the idea of using one of the four-engined planes built for the transatlantic airmail service and which Air France had on trial. The civilian crew of the plane—the *Camille Flammarion*—was retained so that it could make use of the air-bases in neutral South American countries; but a super-numerary was provided, as "engineer and technical advisor" and travelling on a civilian passport, in the person of Lieutenant-Commander Daillère—who a few months later dropped the first bombs on Berlin from a similar plane. The *Camille Flammarion* flew to and fro across the South Atlantic without sighting the German raider, but never mind—there can never be too many eyes for a hunt of this nature! In the search for the 10,000-ton pocket-battleship there were 270,000 tons of Allied naval shipping deployed; and that is counting only cruisers and larger warships.

The Atlantic was scoured by all these ships for several weeks without success. Then suddenly came the news that another victim had fallen to the raider, on November 15th, but in the Indian Ocean. It was the tanker *Africa Shell*, which had been sunk off Lourenço Marques. Now the convoys from Australia were being threatened. Two cruisers, the British *Kent* and the French *Suffren*, were sent to patrol the vulnerable area.

Meanwhile, the *Deutschland* had succeeded in evading the Allied patrols and had got back to Kiel on November 15th, after a somewhat disappointing cruise, having sunk only two ships of a total tonnage of less than 8,000. Moreover, her captain had the mistaken idea of bringing the ship he had captured, the American *City of Flint*, back to Germany; but the merchant ship had to be released at the demand of the Norwegian Government when the two reached the North Sea.

The *Graf Spee* was by then on her way back to the South Atlantic. At the same time, the German High Command created a diversion by sending the two battle-cruisers *Scharnhorst* and *Gneisenau* into northern waters. They left Wilhelmshaven on November 21st, and two days later were sighted to the south-east of Iceland by the *Rawalpindi*, one of the armed merchant cruisers of the Northern Patrol. The *Rawalpindi* went bravely into battle with her 6-inch guns against the 11-inch of the battle-cruisers. There could be only one end to such an unequal fight, but the *Rawalpindi* continued until she was ablaze fore and aft and her last gun was out of action. Then the two battle-cruisers disappeared into the northern wastes. Much of the Home Fleet was disposed to intercept them. Two cruisers sighted an enemy ship in the darkness, and took her for the *Deutschland*. From Brest to Scapa Flow, six battleships, two aircraft-carriers, a dozen cruisers, and scores of destroyers were sent to hunt for the enemy. But the elements came to the aid of the two battle-cruisers, and in heavy rainstorms and rough weather they succeeded in reaching their home port on November 27th.

The *Graf Spee* was not to be so fortunate. For ten days after leaving the Indian Ocean for the South Atlantic no success came the way of the raider. But on December 2nd she came upon the steamer *Doric Star* of the Blue Star Line off the west coast of Africa, and duly sank her. The following day it was the turn of the 8,000-ton *Tairoa*. The raider then transferred her attentions to another area, and on December 7th sank the *Streonshaln* and her 6,000 tons of Argentine frozen-meat, about

900 miles east of Rio de Janeiro. This was the *Graf Spee*'s last victim, for the net was already beginning to close.

The *Doric Star*, before being sunk, had been able to radio her position and report that she was being attacked by a battleship. And the *Tairoa*, too, had twice sent out a message giving her position and saying she was being attacked "by the German battleship *Admiral Scheer*". The radio operator was sending out the message for the third time when a shell from the *Graf Spee* put him and his transmitter out of action.

Some three thousand miles away, the messages had been picked up by Commodore Harwood's division, and when the two positions were plotted the line showing the direction being taken by the raider pointed towards the River Plate area. Harwood anticipated that the enemy's next objective would be the valuable flow of shipping off that coast, and that at a cruising speed of fifteen knots—the normal, most economical speed of capital ships at the time—the pocket-battleship was likely to be in the River Plate area by the afternoon of December 12th. He therefore proceeded to concentrate his immediately available force —the *Exeter*, *Ajax*, and *Achilles*—in that area.

Harwood had anticipated correctly. Langsdorf had been kept informed of shipping movements by German agents in Buenos Aires and Montevideo, and was indeed making for the River Plate area. In the early morning of December 13th his lookouts reported enemy ships approaching. A few minutes later he opened fire at a range of 19,500 yards. The time was then 06.16 hours.[1]

The *Graf Spee*'s chances were good. With her armour and six 11-inch guns she need have nothing to fear from the 8-inch cruiser *Exeter* and the two 6-inch cruisers *Ajax* and *Achilles*. Langsdorf had only to keep beyond their range and he could deal with them one after the other. Visibility was excellent, and his gunners were quite as good as their elders had been in the First World War.

But, as often happens in battle, the men—the British seamen—rose above the severe material disadvantages; and Commodore Harwood's tactical skill in attacking from widely different bearings caused the enemy to divide his fire. The *Graf Spee*'s gunners had to choose between three objectives, while the British could concentrate on the one.

The raider's fire was therefore uncertain at first, but after a few minutes all the 11-inch guns were turned on the *Exeter*, which was attacking from the south-east. At 06.24 hours, two direct hits destroyed the *Exeter*'s bridge and one turret and wrecked the steering communications. Further hits put her foremost turrets out of action; but Captain

[1] Local time, three hours behind G.M.T.

Bell and his men battled on with her one remaining turret, a chain of messengers being formed from the after-conning position.

Meanwhile the *Ajax* and the *Achilles* had pressed their attack from the north and gradually closed the range to 8,000 yards. Then the Graf Spee brought her main armament to bear on the *Ajax*, while varying her 5·9-inch guns from her to the *Achilles*. After an hour's fighting, with the *Graf Spee* on a westerly course, the *Ajax*'s after-turrets were knocked out by an 11-inch shell. The pocket-battleship then neglected the *Exeter* and drew nearer the *Achilles* and the *Ajax*; the latter fired her torpedoes, but the *Graf Spee* easily evaded them by altering course. At 07·38 the range was down to 7,000 yards, ammunition was getting short, and the battle had become hopelessly one-sided; Commodore Harwood therefore decided to break off the day battle and re-engage when night came on. But when he turned away to the east under cover of smoke the *Graf Spee* did not attempt to follow. Instead she steamed at high speed for the River Plate, and the two cruisers took up the chase; whenever they drew too near, the *Graf Spee* drove them off with her 11-inch guns. The *Exeter* had been ordered back to the Falklands for badly needed repairs.

At ten minutes to one on the morning of the 14th the *Graf Spee* dropped anchor in Montevideo harbour; and Harwood disposed his ships to watch the estuary. Reinforcements were on the way to him from several points. The *Cumberland* was the nearest, coming from the Falklands, and Harwood expected her to join him that evening. The *Ark Royal* and the *Renown*, as well as three cruisers, were speeding to the area, but the nearest would take at least five days. There were said to be even stronger forces closing in. . . . However, the fate of the *Graf Spee* was not being decided at sea but in offices.

Uruguay being a neutral country, the *Graf Spee* could not remain at Montevideo unless Captain Langsdorf proved there was urgent necessity serious damage that made his ship unseaworthy, badly wounded men in need of hospital care, shortage of food or fuel. If there were no damage to the ship, she had to leave within twenty-four hours. If repairs were essential, they had to be restricted to the minimum necessary to make the ship seaworthy. Otherwise, the Uruguayan Government would intern her.

The British were not too eager for the *Graf Spee* to sail straight away. So far as was known, she had not suffered any major damage, and she might well be still powerful enough to force a way past the *Ajax* and the *Achilles*. It was necessary to gain time until the arrival of reinforcements.

In Germany, the Marine Amt was worried and puzzled, and dismayed at the news that the *Graf Spee* had sought shelter in a harbour of a neutral but obviously unfriendly country. The situation would have been quite different at Buenos Aires, for Germany had strong links with Argentine. However, knowing Langsdorf as they did, the German Naval Staff had confidence in him; they knew he had made his decision as a last resort. But they were worried by a telegram from

The pocket-battleship *Admiral Graf Spee*

Langsdorf to the *Altmark*'s captain giving him liberty of movement. If the *Graf Spee* had dismissed her supply ship, it could only mean there was no hope of her continuing her raiding activities nor even of return-ing to Germany. The *Altmark* received orders from Berlin to remain in the vicinity for the time being.

But what else could be done to help Langsdorf? The chances of escape would diminish with each day that passed. Perhaps the *Graf Spee* could slip across the estuary, at the limit of territorial waters, to the more friendly shelter of Buenos Aires? In no event must she let herself be interned by Uruguay. It would be almost as bad as surrender-ing at an Allied naval base, for the Uruguayan Government would be unable to resist pressure from the British and the French. Admiral Dönitz was called in, and was asked whether it were possible to send a submarine pack to attack the Allied warships watching the River Plate estuary. And if so, when would the submarines reach the area? A look at the operational map was enough to see that they could not reach it at all without the help of surface supply ships. Even if that difficulty were overcome, the chief of the submarine service estimated that their earliest date of arrival would be . . . January 25th. The Uruguayan Government would never grant such a long respite.

On December 14th, at seven in the evening, a technical investiga-tion commission composed of a naval commander and an engineer, appointed by the Inspector-General of the Uruguayan Navy, went aboard the *Graf Spee*. Captain Langsdorf handed them a list of "damage affecting the ship's seaworthiness".

The Commission reported:

(*a*) There were twenty-seven holes from shells of various calibre.
(*b*) There was no sign of any gash or crack in the hull.

(c) The galleys had sustained some damage.

(d) The boiling-water tanks were intact, so the crew did not lack drinking water.

(e) The basic repairs could be carried out in three days.

The Uruguayan Government therefore granted a delay of seventy-two hours, in spite of the protests of the German chargé d'affaires, Herr Langman. He had requested permission for the *Graf Spee* to remain in harbour for at least a fortnight, basing this request on the report of a German technical expert who had been flown to Montevideo.

A crowd estimated at five thousand attended the funeral of the thirty-six members of the crew killed during the battle. Among the wreaths, mostly from the German colony in Montevideo, was one from the sixty British seamen who had been held prisoner in the *Graf Spee*; they had been released following representations from the Uruguayan Government. Their wreath bore the words: "In memory of brave sailors, from their comrades in the British Merchant Navy."

The diplomatic struggle continued for another forty-eight hours, during which time the Allied reinforcements drew ever nearer. Captain Langsdorf was kept informed by Berlin. The *Altmark*'s position had been discovered, and she had to move to another area.

By the 16th Captain Langsdorf realized that the approach of the *Ark Royal* and the *Renown* removed all chance of the *Graf Spee* regaining the open sea. He considered the possibility of taking his ship across to Buenos Aires; but if she were going to be interned, and unable to cause any further damage to the enemy, would it not be preferable to scuttle her?

At three a.m. on the 17th, Hitler sent the order to scuttle the *Graf Spee*.

The majority of the crew were transferred to the German tanker *Tacoma*, which was in the harbour, and that evening the remainder took the *Graf Spee* out into the river, watched by the huge crowd that had gathered. British warships were waiting outside the estuary, and their planes were patrolling above the limit of territorial waters; one of the planes suddenly reported thick smoke streaming from the pocket-battleship. Langsdorf had set off explosions to sink his ship about six miles south-west of Montevideo.

Captain Langsdorf was undoubtedly an officer of integrity and high standards. The British seamen made prisoner by him, and who were later transferred to the *Altmark*,[1] were unanimous in praising the fair treatment they had received from him. He was found dead in his hotel

[1] They were rescued by the destroyer *Cossack*, in February, 1940. The *Altmark* had taken shelter in a Norwegian fjord, but the *Cossack* went in and boarded her. (*Tr.*)

room, three days after scuttling his ship; he was lying on a German flag —not the Nazi flag with a swastika, but the old black, white, and red flag. He had left a letter for the German Ambassador: "The fate of an honourable captain is bound up with that of his ship. . . . I alone am responsible for the scuttling of the *Admiral Graf Spee*. I am happy for my death to wipe out anything that may have dishonoured the flag. . . ."

After little more than three months of war the activities of Germany's pocket-battleships seemed to have been brought to an end. The *Deutschland* had been forced to return to base. The *Graf Spee*'s career had come to a close not far from where Von Spee had gone down in the *Scharnhorst* twenty-five years previously. The commerce raiders were having no more success than in the First World War.

However, the fall of France a few months later gave the German Navy more favourable opportunities for renewing the activities of commerce raiders. By the summer of 1940 the Germans were in possession of the whole coastline from northern Norway to Spanish waters. The first raider to put to sea again was the pocket-battleship *Admiral Scheer*. Her cruise lasted five months, and in the course of it she sank or captured sixteen ships totalling almost 100,000 tons.

The *Admiral Scheer* sailed from Stavanger on October 23rd and escaped into the Atlantic, round the north of Iceland, in misty weather. On November 5th she was lying in wait for a large convoy of thirty-seven ships—the HX 84—which was known to have sailed from Halifax on October 27th. Aided by reports from her catapulted seaplane, the pocket-battleship sighted eight merchant ships and sank one, the *Mopan*, after taking off the crew. By then, the main body of the convoy was in sight. . . .

Fortunately for the convoy, the afternoon was already well advanced and darkness was not far off; moreover, the convoy was escorted by the armed merchant-cruiser *Jervis Bay*. She was armed only with 6-inch guns, but Captain Fegen, her commander, did not hesitate. He ordered the convoy to scatter and steered straight for the *Admiral Scheer*. There could only be one end, as Captain Fegen well knew. But it took the pocket-battleship nearly three hours to sink the *Jervis Bay*; and as a consequence only five of the convoy ships were destroyed, when all might well have been sunk but for the intrepid conduct of Captain Fegen and his crew.

The *Admiral Scheer* then moved south, made rendezvous with a supply ship, and after sinking several cargo vessels in the South Atlantic and Indian Ocean arrived back at Kiel in early April.

The heavy cruiser *Admiral Hipper* was the next raider to reach the Atlantic, sailing from the Elbe estuary on November 30th, 1940. She was followed a month later by the battle-cruisers *Scharnhorst* and *Gneisenau*, but they ran into foul weather and had to put back for repairs. They did not get to sea again until January 22nd. On February 7th the two sighted convoy HX 108, which had left Halifax a week previously. But, unfortunately for them, the convoy was being escorted by the 15-inch battleship *Ramillies*. Still, in view of their superior speed, the German battle-cruisers were in a favourable position; while one kept the *Ramillies* employed but remained out of range—which should not have been difficult, being ten knots the faster—the other could have destroyed the defenceless convoy. But Admiral Lütjens, commanding the two battle-cruisers, had express instructions not to engage a superior enemy force. The *Scharnhorst* and the *Gneisenau* therefore withdrew, to seek other opportunities. They found a good many, and by the time they entered harbour at Brest, on March 22nd, they had sunk twenty-two ships totalling 116,000 tons.

The *Admiral Hipper* had left Brest in February, and in the course of a short raiding cruise destroyed thirteen merchant ships.

These were the last successful operations of German capital ships in the Atlantic; and three months later the dramatic end of the *Bismarck* brought such raiding operations to a close.

The *Bismarck* was the newest ship of the German Navy, and its pride, being the most powerful warship in the world at that time. At least, no other had such an armament—eight 15-inch guns and twelve 6-inch, sixteen 4-inch anti-aircraft guns and sixteen smaller— and also her maximum speed of thirty knots. Only the battle-cruisers *Hood*, *Renown*, and *Repulse* had the speed and fire-power to take her on; and they dated from the end of the First World War, and were in several respects obsolete. The *Bismarck* escaped into the Atlantic from a fjord near Bergen, accompanied by the cruiser *Prinz Eugen*. They were intercepted by the *Hood* and the battleship *Prince of Wales* to the west of the Denmark Straits, on May 24th, 1941; a broadside from the *Bismarck* at 19,500 yards obtained a hit in one of the *Hood*'s magazines, and the battle-cruiser blew up and sank. The *Prince of Wales* also sustained damage in that short action, and the *Bismarck* was hit and at one time on fire. Only six days previously she had left Gdynia for her first cruise, with the object of making for Brest and operating from there—and on the sixth day of her active career the *Bismarck* had scored the greatest success at sea, by sinking the *Hood*, since the outbreak of the war. But three days later she was no more!

The pursuit and destruction of the *Bismarck* is the most celebrated episode of the war at sea during the Second World War, and has been described many times—how contact with her was lost for more than twenty-four hours, until sighted by a Coastal Command Catalina when only 500 miles from Brest; how she was attacked by torpedo-carrying aircraft from the *Ark Royal*, then by destroyers when night came. The following morning, the battleships *King George V* and *Rodney* opened up their broadsides on her. Hits were at once obtained, and the *Bismarck*'s fire was soon silenced. She was then finished off by torpedoes from the cruiser *Dorsetshire*, and disappeared at 10.36 hours on May 27th, 1941.[1] During the pursuit and action the *Bismarck* had been hit by nine torpedoes and several tons of explosive shells.

In order to bring the *Bismarck* to battle and destroy her, the Admiralty had deployed no less than two aircraft-carriers, three battle-cruisers, five battleships, fourteen cruisers, and twenty-one destroyers.

The *Bismarck* was the last warship of the German Navy to be used as a commerce raider, but there were still several disguised raiders—armed merchant-ships—operating in the Western Pacific and the Indian Ocean. And it was they who were the most successful. The *Atlantis* sank twenty-two Allied cargo vessels totalling 145,968 tons; the *Thor* also sank twenty-two ships, totalling 153,093 tons; and the *Michel* sank seventeen totalling 121,994 tons. The record was made by the *Pinguin*—thirty-three ships totalling 165,547 tons—which was finally caught and sunk off the Seychelles by the cruiser *Cornwall*, on May 8th, 1941.

Most of these raiders were eventually destroyed by Allied ships. The end of the *Kormoran* was extraordinary. She fought a duel with the cruiser *Sydney* off the coast of Australia, on November 19th, 1941, and took the cruiser down with her.

[1] According to a recently published account, the *Bismarck* only sank when she did because the crew opened the sea-cocks; all her guns had been put out of action, and it was feared that she would fall into the hands of the British.

XXVI

MATAPAN AND ALEXANDRIA: BRITISH VICTORY AND ITALIAN REVENGE

The Battle of the Mediterranean opens—weak situation of the British Fleet against the whole Italian Navy—successful attack on Taranto by aircraft from the Illustrious improves the situation—arrival of the Luftwaffe—the Battle of Matapan (March 28th, 1941)—aircraft from the carrier Formidable slow down the fleeing Italian ships—what the Valiant's radar screen revealed—destruction of the Italian cruisers—the changing fortunes of the war—the battleship Barham torpedoed—Italian piloted torpedoes attack the British ships in Alexandria harbour—six men put two battleships out of service for many months.

WHEN Mussolini plunged his country into war in June, 1940, the Italian Navy ranked fifth in the world, and was stronger than it had ever been in its whole history. Two new 15-inch battleships, *Littorio* and *Vittorio Veneto*, had joined the fleet in 1937, two more were being completed, and there were four battleships from the last war which had been recently reconstructed. There were nineteen modern cruisers, a hundred and twenty destroyers and torpedo-boats, and about a hundred submarines. The naval bases were in the centre of the Mediterranean, and although the navy had no aircraft-carriers—the Duce had stated that Italy herself was an unsinkable aircraft-carrier—a good Air Force could have co-operated with the fleet over almost the entire Mediterranean, using airfields in Italy, Sardinia, Sicily, and the Dodecanese.

The existence of this strong Italian fleet had caused the French to concentrate most of their naval forces in the Mediterranean in April, 1940. A French command was responsible for the area west of a line from Tunisia to Sicily; and in May a French squadron of three battleships, four cruisers, some destroyers, and submarines joined Admiral Cunningham's fleet at Alexandria. Two of the battleships were, however, withdrawn a few days later, when British reinforcements reached Alexandria.

The Allies took the offensive very soon after Italy entered the war. Genoa was shelled on June 14th by Admiral Duplat's squadron; Bardia, on the coast of Libya, received attention on the 21st from a British squadron which included the French battleship *Lorraine*. In both the East and West Mediterranean the Allies swept the seas without encountering any Italian warship. But the whole situation was changed almost overnight when France, overrun by the German Panzer Divisions, concluded an armistice with Germany and then with Italy. The British were left to defend the Mediterranean alone, with a small fleet that had little hope of being reinforced because of urgent needs elsewhere.

The Italian Navy, however, had responsibilities only in the Mediterranean, except for a small force of torpedo-boats, submarines, and gunboats in the Red Sea.

But the British Mediterranean Fleet was commanded by a man who, like Michiel De Ruyter, could be said to be worth an army. The name of Admiral Sir Andrew Browne Cunningham dominated this period of the war. By his aggressive policy he kept the supply channels open in the Mediterranean, and thus made possible the maintenance of large forces in Egypt and the Middle East.

Admiral Cunningham was a fine representative of the British naval commander with ten centuries of tradition behind him. His opponents, Admiral Campioni and later Admiral Iachino, were not without qualities, but the Italian Navy had expanded too quickly and lacked the solid foundations of the British. Its links with the maritime traditions of the Genoese and Venetian Republics had been broken too often and for too long. The Italians had good ships, brave and skilful crews, but no experience of strategy; and the High Command was handicapped by material deficiencies. The Italian Navy's finest hour was due to individual acts of heroism.

An additional complication to Admiral Cunningham's prosecution of the war against Italy was the presence of the French squadron at Alexandria. Its commander, Admiral Godfroy, had obeyed the Vichy Government's order to cease fire. If Admiral Cunningham had kept to the letter of his instructions from London he should either have destroyed or captured the French ships. But he was more fortunate than Admiral Somerville at Oran, in that he was able to avoid firing on his recent comrades-in-arms, and this will always be remembered by French sailors. On July 7th, 1940, he reached an agreement with Admiral Godfroy whereby the French ships were demilitarized for the duration; and that very evening Admiral Cunningham put to sea to seek out the enemy.

Two days later the first brush occurred between the British and Italian Fleets. Admiral Cunningham's flagship, the *Warspite*, engaged the two Italian battleships *Conte di Cavour* and *Giuglio Cesare*, supported by torpedo-carrying Swordfish from the *Eagle*. The *Warspite* obtained a hit on the *Giuglio Cesare*. Then the Italian Fleet retired behind a smoke-screen put up by its destroyers, leaving to shore-based aircraft the task of attacking the British ships on passage back to Alexandria. Thirty-seven attacks were made altogether, but not one British ship was hit.

Nevertheless, the Italian battleships were a constant threat to British convoys and to the Fleet's movements; they were together far more powerful than the three or four veterans of the last war—two had fought at Jutland!—which Admiral Cunningham had under his command. He had tried in vain to bring the enemy to battle. One form of attack remained to be exploited—attack by carrier aircraft on ships in harbour.

This was not a new idea. It had first been envisaged in 1935, when the League of Nations had voted sanctions against Italy at the time of the Abyssinian War, and for a while it had seemed Britain might be drawn into a conflict with Italy. Again, during the Munich crisis in 1938, Admiral Sir Dudley Pound, Commander-in-chief Mediterranean, had told Captain Lyster, commanding the aircraft-carrier *Glorious*, to prepare a plan of attack on the Italian naval base at Taranto, in the heel of Italy.

In the summer of 1940 Lyster, then a Rear-Admiral, arrived in the Mediterranean with the *Illustrious*. She was Britain's newest aircraft-carrier, with an armour-plated deck and fitted with radar, a device not then in general use in warships. She carried two flights of Sword-fish—already somewhat out of date, but well able to fulfil their function of firing torpedoes—and one flight of Fulmar fighters, which were new and armed with eight guns.

The *Eagle* was placed under Rear-Admiral Lyster's command too, and the plan of attack on Taranto was brought out of cold storage. Lyster had already studied it during the voyage out from Britain, and had discussed it in detail with the Fleet Air Arm crews aboard the *Illustrious*. When this ready-made plan was put up to Admiral Cunningham he was full of enthusiasm for it.

During the First World War Lyster, then a young Lieutenant, had been for a time liaison officer with the Italian squadron based at Taranto. He was thus well acquainted with the naval base, which consisted of an outer, or main, harbour, the Mar Grande, and a small inner harbour, the Mar Piccolo. The two were separated by a narrow tongue of land on which stood the town of Taranto, though a canal had been cut to enable ships to pass from one harbour to the other. The battleships were usually moored in the eastern part of the Mar Grande, and were protected by moles and nets.

However, this remained to be established. Aircraft from Malta was the obvious means of reconnaissance of Taranto. When Italy first came into the war, there were only three old Gladiators based on Malta —nicknamed by the garrison "Faith, Hope, and Charity". The Italian Command had let slip a fine opportunity by not attacking Malta at the very beginning, for the island was reinforced with American Glenn Martins flown direct from England and with Spitfires brought by aircraft-carriers to within range of the island.

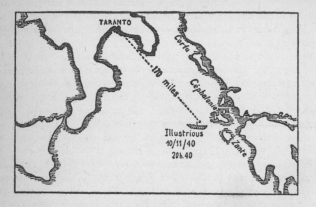

The first photographic reconnaissances of Taranto showed five battle-ships, eight cruisers, and twenty destroyers in harbour. There was plenty of choice for the striking force. The attack was planned for the night of October 21st, not so much because it was Trafalgar Day as because there would be a full moon. The aircraft would have little difficulty in finding their target, and take-off and landing on the flight-deck would be simplified. Night attacks by carrier aircraft were still something new.

Thirty Swordfish from the *Eagle* and the *Illustrious* were to make the attack. The two carriers were to be in position about forty miles west of the Greek island of Cephalonia, which is one hundred and seventy miles south-east of Taranto, at a time when the moon would have just risen in the eastern sky. The aircraft would approach the target from the west, so that the Italian battleships would be silhouetted against the moonlight. The guns were to be taken out of the planes and extra petrol tanks fitted, to enable the round flight to be made.

However, the attack had to be postponed and modified, due to several incidents in the meantime. A small fire broke out in the *Illustrious*, and a near-miss caused some damage to the *Eagle*. The attack finally went in on the night of November 10th, but with only twenty-one aircraft from the *Illustrious*. On that evening R.A.F. reconnaissance planes reported that another battleship had joined the five. The photographs also showed that there were now balloon-barrages protecting the ships.

On the night of the 10th the moon would be in its first quarter. So it was decided to divide the aircraft into two striking forces, one of twelve planes and the other of nine. Each force would have six planes carrying torpedoes, the rest would bomb the ships in the inner harbour and the oil-storage tanks; the fires caused would help the task of the torpedo-carrying planes.

Admiral Cunningham sailed from Alexandria with the fleet on November 6th. While he continued westwards with the battleships to escort a convoy on its way to Malta, Lyster and his squadron proceeded northwards into the Adriatic. Lyster had under his command the carrier *Illustrious*, Captain Boyd, the cruisers *Gloucester*, *Berwick*, *Glasgow*, and *York*, and the destroyers *Hyperion*, *Ilex*, *Hasty*, and *Havock*. By the evening of the 10th, after an uneventful passage, he was in position off the island of Cephalonia. The night was fine, but with so little wind that the *Illustrious* had to get up a speed of twenty-eight knots to enable the heavily laden aircraft to take off. The latest aerial photographs, which had been flown to the *Illustrious* from Malta, and reports sent by a Sunderland flying-boat, all confirmed that the six Italian battleships were still at Taranto.

The first striking force led by Lieutenant-Commander Williamson was airborne at 20.40 hours. The bombers and flare-droppers were over Taranto at 22.52 hours. The flares were released over the inner harbour, and the bombing-planes detailed to attack the ships succeeded in bombing the cruisers and destroyers, in spite of encountering very heavy fire, and setting fire to the seaplane base buildings. Meanwhile, the torpedo aircraft had gone in to attack the ships in the main harbour; Williamson had divided his force into two sub-flights, and they came down almost to sea-level to launch their torpedoes at either end of the line of moored battleships.

At that time the Italians had no radar and were therefore caught by surprise, but soon put up an intense anti-aircraft fire. The Swordfish, which were easy to handle but very slow—giving them time to take aim at their targets—had greater fears of being caught in searchlights and attacked by fighter-planes; but there was no manifestation from one or the other.

The second striking force, led by Lieutenant-Commander Hale, had flown off about three-quarters of an hour after the first. It numbered eight, not nine, planes. The ninth was delayed by mechanical trouble, but flew off an hour later on its solitary bombing mission.

Two planes of the first striking force were shot down, one being Williamson's; but all of Hale's returned safely. The last landed on the *Illustrious* at 02.30 hours. Three Italian seaplanes attempted to shadow the squadron as it returned to Alexandria, but they were soon chased off by fighter-planes from the carrier.

The attack on Taranto by aircraft from the *Illustrious*, November 10–11th, 1940

The gallant pilots could only report possible hits on the battleships, but the next day photographic reconnaissance by R.A.F. planes from Malta revealed the full extent of the damage. A battleship of the *Littorio* class—it was in fact the *Littorio* herself—had a heavy list to starboard and her forecastle was awash. She had been hit by three torpedoes, and repairs kept her out of service until March, 1941. One old *Cavour*-class battleship had been beached, and another was half awash. The *Caio Duilio* was out of service until May, 1941. The *Conte di Cavour* was not refloated until July, and was then towed to Trieste for repairs; she was still there when Italy asked for an armistice in September, 1943.

Half of the Italian Battle Fleet had been put out of action for some time by eleven aircraft torpedoes. Moreover, the Italian High Command feared another attack on Taranto and withdrew the remainder of the Fleet to Naples, a move which gave Admiral Cunningham far greater liberty of action in his support of General Wavell's victorious advance through Libya. But the special value of the successful attack on Taranto was that it came at a time when the fortunes of Britain were at a low ebb. . . .

Not long afterwards the Germans began to move some of their air squadrons to the Mediterranean, in response to Mussolini's appeals; for the Italian campaign against the Greeks was going badly, and the Italian army in Libya was in full retreat before the British Army of the Nile. One morning in January, 1941, Admiral Cunningham was escorting a Malta convoy with some of his forces when a large formation of enemy aircraft was sighted. Anyone who had been at Dunkirk in June, 1940, or on patrols in the Channel, would have quickly identified the approaching squadrons as Stuka dive-bombers. "We were too interested in these dive-bombing attacks, which were new to us, to have time to feel frightened . . ." Admiral Cunningham wrote later, "we could but admire their skill and precision."

The Stukas belonged to the Tenth Air Corps, recently arrived at bases on Sicily and Rhodes. Their main target in this attack was the carrier *Illustrious*. She was hit by six thousand-pounders; her flight-deck was wrecked, her steering-gear put out of action, and several fires were started. A squadron of her planes had been flown off just before the attack, and they shot down eight of the enemy during the day, continuing to fight by landing at Malta to refuel and re-ammunition. The Germans kept up a relentless attack on the *Illustrious*; but Captain Boyd, steering with the propellers, brought his ship into Malta harbour that night—a great achievement. The Luftwaffe repeatedly bombed her while in harbour there, but she was repaired and sailed to rejoin the fleet at Alexandria on January 24th.

German aid to Italy was not limited to air support. On February 11th a German general arrived at Tripoli to take command of the German–Italian army. Rommel had already made a reputation in France, and he was to make a much greater one at the head of his Afrika Korps. But the safeguarding of his supplies and reinforcements was the responsibility of the Italian Fleet; the Battle of the Mediterranean was entering a new phase, with the British trying to cut Rommel's supply lines between Italy and Tripolitania, and with the German aircraft trying to isolate Malta.

At this period, too, Mussolini had asked for German aid to defeat the Greeks; and the British had sent troops—that could ill be spared—from the Army of the Nile to give support to the Greeks. The task of safeguarding the flow of supplies and reinforcements to Greece was a further strain on Admiral Cunningham's fleet.

It was then that Admiral Riccardi, Chief of the Italian Naval Staff, put forward a plan to interfere with British communications with Greece, by a reconnaissance in force as far as the island of Gaudo, off the southern coast of Crete. This was the first time the Italian Navy had shown any initiative since entering the war. An important force was to be deployed, under Admiral Iachino, the commander-in-chief, and would operate in two battle-groups:

> Group One (Admiral Iachino): the *Vittorio Veneto* with a screen of four destroyers; the cruisers *Trieste*, *Trento*, and *Bolzano*, commanded by Admiral Sansonnetti; and three destroyers.
> Group Two (Admiral Cattaneo): the cruisers *Zara*, *Pola*, and *Fiume*, and four destroyers; the cruisers *Abruzzi* (Admiral Legnani) and *Garibaldi*, with two destroyers.

The naval force was homogeneous enough for the task, but the crews had little experience. The air support was problematical, for it was not placed under the immediate orders of Admiral Iachino. He had to make request to the Supermarina—the Naval High Command—for the Italian seaplanes, and to Luftwaffe liaison officers aboard his flagship for the German planes. In the event, this complicated chain-of-command resulted in the Italian ships being practically without air support when they were brought to battle.

The orders given to Admiral Iachino placed a very tight control over the movements of his force. His own group was to sail on March 26th and carry out an offensive reconnaissance to a position twenty miles south of Gaudo Island, while Admiral Cattaneo's group made a sweep some fifty miles to the north, into the Aegean Sea. They were then to return to base, having destroyed all the British convoys found proceeding to Greece.

The increase in the number of Italian reconnaissance planes appearing over Alexandria had warned the British that some enemy operation was impending. Moreover, it was expected that the Germans would press Mussolini to pursue a more active policy with his fleet, as part of their general offensive about to be launched in Greece and Africa. So when a Sunderland flying-boat from Malta reported on March 27th three Italian cruisers eighty miles east of Sicily and steering towards Crete, it came as no surprise. There was only one convoy on passage to Greece just then, and it was still south of Crete. The order was sent for it to return to Alexandria; and the convoys preparing to sail were told to delay their departure. There was thus little to worry about; the Italian sweep would find nothing in its path.

Nevertheless, Admiral Cunningham decided to put to sea when daylight began to fade, and to interpose his battleships between the enemy and the returning convoy. This was considered to be no more than a simple security measure, and that the enemy would not insist. . . .

The Japanese Consul at Alexandria at that period was known to be a keen golf player and an attentive observer of British fleet movements. Whether or not he had means of communicating information to his German and Italian friends, it was wiser to distrust him. So Admiral Cunningham decided to have a round of golf while waiting for evening to come. He arrived at the clubhouse with a small suitcase such as any sailor carries when intending to spend a night ashore, and he made certain that his presence was noticed by the Japanese Consul. After playing a round he returned to his flagship as discreetly as he had ostensibly gone ashore. At seven that evening he proceeded to sea with the battleships *Warspite*, *Barham*, and *Valiant*, the new aircraft-carrier *Formidable*,[1] and a screen of two destroyer flotillas. Admiral Pridham-Wippell had already been ordered to sail from the Piraeus with his four cruisers *Orion*, *Perth*, *Ajax*, and *Gloucester*, and four destroyers, and to rendezvous with the commander-in-chief at 06.30 hours next morning, thirty miles south of Gaudo Island. This was practically the same position as Admiral Iachino's orders would bring him to, and at about the same time.

The Sunderland's report of having sighted Italian cruisers proceeding towards Crete had been picked up and understood aboard the *Vittorio Veneto*, which had sailed from Naples on the evening of the 26th. Admiral Iachino therefore knew that all chance of coming upon a British convoy to Greece had practically vanished. There was no point in burning valuable fuel for nothing; far better return to base. But the decision did not lay with him; the Supermarina might well have had the same idea, but because of pressure from the Germans and for the sake of prestige in their eyes, it was decided that Iachino's battle-group, at least, would continue with the sweep as planned. Cattaneo, however, was ordered not to penetrate into the Aegean, but to rendezvous with his commander-in-chief at dawn on the 28th.

It was yet another instance of naval commanders being coldly sent to do battle, with little hope of winning, for reasons of high policy which had nothing to do with the principles of sea warfare!

At daybreak on the 28th Admiral Iachino was still unaware that the British battle fleet was at sea. He had almost reached the limit of his sweep and had no intention of proceeding any farther. Admiral

[1] She had been sent from England by way of the Cape as soon as the Admiralty learnt of the damage caused to the *Illustrious*.

Sansonnetti's outer screen of cruisers, seven miles ahead of the *Vittorio Veneto*, was given the order to turn about at 07.00 hours. At that moment Cattaneo's group was ten miles to the north. A seaplane was sent off from the *Vittorio Veneto* and another from the *Bolzano* to make reconnaissance flights over the area. At 06.42 the former reported four cruisers and four destroyers proceeding at eighteen knots on a southerly course fifty miles east of the Italian force. Admiral Iachino withdrew his previous order to Sansonnetti and instead ordered him to identify the ships and then to retire towards the flagship.

An hour later the *Formidable*'s reconnaissance aircraft reported three cruisers thirty miles south of Gaudo. They were thought at first to be Pridham-Wippell's; but that commander himself sighted these ships to the westward and reported them to Admiral Cunningham, adding that he was retiring towards the battleships in the hope that the enemy would follow. Admiral Cunningham was then about ninety miles to the south.

The Italian cruisers were of the 8-inch type, which could out-range and out-gun Admiral Pridham-Wippell's 6-inch light cruisers. The Italians had the speed of the British too, as the *Gloucester* could get no more than twenty-four knots out of her engines just then, and the other cruisers were obliged to reduce speed accordingly.

Admiral Sansonnetti pursued the British cruisers, instead of retiring as ordered, and at 08.12 hours opened fire at 22,500 yards. The rear ship, the *Gloucester*, was straddled three times, and this seemed to have a magical effect on her engines; for her speed increased to thirty knots, which was appreciated by the rest of the division. The Italian cruisers remained out of the range of the British, but continued to shell them for thirty-nine minutes, then turned away to rejoin Admiral Iachino. The latter then reported to the High Command that his whole force was returning to base on a north-westerly course.

Such were the opening moves in the action which became known as the Battle of Matapan, from the name of the headland at the southern extremity of the Peloponnese. Admiral Cunningham and his staff had felt a little uneasy about the light cruisers, and there was some relief on learning that the pursuing Italians had turned away. The *Warspite* could do no more than twenty-two knots, which meant she would have taken nearly four hours to reach a position to be of assistance to the cruisers.

However, when Pridham-Wippell saw that the Italians had turned away, he decided to follow them. At about eleven o'clock he sighted an enemy battleship to the northwards which opened fire at extreme range. She was the *Vittorio Veneto*, and some of her shots came unpleasantly close to the *Orion*, Pridham-Wippell's flagship. He ordered his destroyers to lay a smoke-screen; the *Vittorio Veneto*, with her speed of thirty-one knots, could easily knock out the four cruisers one by one, and still have time to retire before the British battleships arrived within range. Such seemed to be Admiral Iachino's intention—until the *Formidable*'s aircraft appeared on the scene.

Admiral Cunningham, although his career had been spent in surface ships, was certainly aware of the value of carrier aircraft. He had shown it by the attack on Taranto. However, they had not yet been used in strength against enemy ships at sea, and he was unable to judge their possibilities. He would have preferred not to attack with the *Formidable*'s aircraft until his battleships were within fifty miles of the enemy, and so able to bring him to battle once the aircraft had reduced the speed of his capital ships. But the danger that the cruisers were in from the *Vittorio Veneto* forced Admiral Cunningham's hand. The only quick means of assisting Pridham-Wippell was to send a striking force from the *Formidable* to attack the Italian battleship; and this was done at 11.15 hours. The disadvantage, as Admiral Cunningham well knew, was that he thereby lost all chance of bringing the enemy to battle before nightfall, as he was still sixty miles distant. The attack by the torpedo-carrying aircraft would reveal to Admiral Iachino the presence of a carrier less than one hundred miles away, and therefore of battleships too, and he would very likely retire on a north-westerly course instead of continuing eastwards towards Pridham-Wippell's cruisers.

That was exactly what did happen. When the striking force was sighted, at midday, the *Vittorio Veneto* swung round; she had already fired some eighty shots at the British cruisers with her 15-inch guns, and several had gone dangerously close. Other air attacks were launched on the Italian battleship without result, but at 15.30 a hit was obtained by a Swordfish piloted by Commander Stead, who pressed home his attack through a tremendous barrage of gunfire and was shot down a few seconds after firing his torpedo at close range.

The *Vittorio Veneto* was seen to be stopped. She got under way again at 16.00 hours, but her speed was much reduced. By 17.00 she had increased to nineteen knots, but the *Warspite* was then only forty-five miles away. One more attack was made before dark, by a striking force from the *Formidable* and a Swordfish from Crete. A hit was obtained on the 8-inch cruiser *Pola*, bringing her to a stop.

The British now had the upper hand. Although the battleship eventually reached Taranto safely, Admiral Cunningham succeeded in dealing a heavy blow against Admiral Cattaneo's division, which the Italian commander-in-chief sent to the help of the *Pola*—unaware that the British battle fleet was only thirty-five miles away.

Admiral Cunningham did not know the extent of the damage caused to the Italians by his aircraft, but had been informed they were steering west at about fifteen knots, the damaged battleship in the centre of the

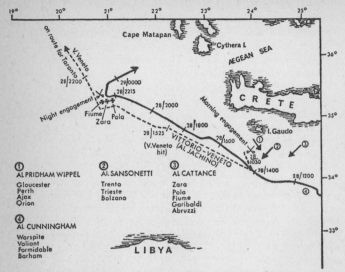

The Battle of Matapan, March 28th, 1941

formation. This report had been sent by Lieutenant-Commander Bolt, whose seaplane was catapulted from the *Warspite* at 17.45 hours. Admiral Cunningham ordered Pridham-Wippell to proceed at utmost speed and make contact with the retreating enemy, from whom he was only nine miles distant.

The British commander-in-chief now had to make a vital decision. By daylight the enemy could be in waters where he would be supported by land-based aircraft. The moment had come, thought Admiral Cunningham, to accept the hazards of night battle; but his staff officers showed some reserve. . . . "I gave the greatest consideration to their opinions, but as our discussions had brought us to dinnertime I said I would first go and eat, and see what I thought afterwards."[1]

There can be no doubt that the Admiral had a good appetite, and

[1] *A Sailor's Odyssey*, by Admiral Viscount Cunningham.

that he enjoyed his dinner! "My morale reasonably high when I returned to the bridge . . ." he then ordered the destroyers to attack. Two divisions proceeded at full speed to the estimated position of the enemy, only four destroyers being retained as a screen for the battleships.

It was obviously a risky move if the Italians were to carry out a similar attack, but there was little likelihood of that. Admiral Cunningham's decision was to have most fortunate consequences for the British.

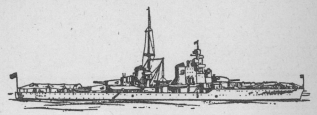

The Italian cruiser *Pola*

Soon after 21.00 hours Pridham-Wippell sent an unexpected item of information—the *Orion*'s radar had detected a large ship lying stopped about five miles to port. Pridham-Wippell thought she might be the *Vittorio Veneto*, and deemed it best to leave her to the attentions of the *Warspite*, which was not far off. There was much expectancy aboard the British battleships. The *Warspite* had no radar, but the *Valiant* had been equipped with it before leaving England the previous summer. And her screen, too, showed the blob of a large ship, estimated to be more than six hundred feet long, immobilized six miles away on the port bow.

The battleships turned forty degrees to port, towards the ship that everyone thought to be the *Vittorio Veneto*. With the aid of the *Valiant*'s radar, all three battleships already had their guns trained on the objective, before she was in sight. . . . This revolution in sea warfare, as important as the use of the aircraft-carrier, astounded the Italians when they knew of it.

Just before half past ten Admiral Cunningham's Chief-of-Staff, Commodore Edelsten, was scanning the sea through his binoculars when he announced in an unemotional voice that he could see two large cruisers and a smaller one on an opposite course about two miles away. One of the *Warspite*'s screening destroyers switched her searchlight on to the second ship and revealed an enemy cruiser with her guns trained fore and aft. The Italians had stumbled on the British battle fleet in the dark, evidently quite unaware of its presence. The two large cruisers were the 8-inch *Zara* and *Fiume* of Cattaneo's division, and were making towards the *Pola* to take her in tow; they had even left their destroyer screen astern. The first they knew of the enemy's presence was the scream of approaching shells.

The *Warspite* and the *Valiant* had at once fired their broadsides at 3,800 yards, almost point-blank range. "I shall never forget those few

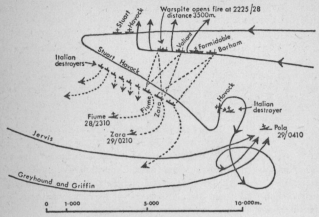

The destruction of the Italian cruisers

minutes," Admiral Cunningham writes in his autobiography. Standing directly behind the flight of the shells, he could see them speeding through the air. "Five out of the six made hits a few feet below the cruiser's upper deck, exploding in great bursts of flame."[1]

In a few seconds the *Zara* and the *Fiume* were literally blown to pieces. "Whole turrets and great masses of debris hurtled into the air and then crashed into the sea with an enormous splash. In a short space of time, the ships were nothing but flaming torches from stem to stern."

The Italian destroyers attempted to intervene, and the British battle-ships had to swing round to a northerly course to avoid their torpedoes. The British destroyers then dashed in, and for a time there was a general mêlée. The *Havock* only just escaped being hit by the *Warspite*'s guns; and the *Formidable* almost suffered from them, too—the night action had begun so quickly that the carrier had not been taken

[1] Admiral Cunningham, *op. cit.*, 15-inch shells are almost a yard long, and by standing in the axis of the gun it is quite possible to follow their flight with the eye.

out of the line of battleships. She was suddenly caught in one of the *Warspite*'s searchlights, and would have received a burst from the battleship's secondary armament if someone on the bridge had not recognized the carrier's outline and quickly gestured to the gunnery officer.

Admiral Cunningham deemed it advisable to steer northwards with his capital ships, and to leave his destroyers to finish off the blazing cruisers. The *Fiume* saved them the trouble, as she sank soon after eleven o'clock. The *Zara* was sent to the bottom with a torpedo from the *Jervis* about three hours later. Two Italian destroyers that intervened, the *Carducci* and the *Alfieri*, were also sunk.

There still remained the *Pola*—the cause of the night action. For she was the large ship which had been picked up on the *Orion*'s radar.

Shortly after midnight the *Havock*, which had pursued and sunk one of the enemy destroyers, came across a ship lying stopped. She was at first thought to be the *Vittorio Veneto*, but was later identified as the *Pola*. Lieutenant Watkins, the *Havock*'s commander, was faced with a strange situation. The *Pola* was apparently undamaged, her flag was still flying, but the greatest confusion reigned on board. Moreover, the *Havock* had used all her torpedoes, and could not sink the cruiser with just her 4-inch guns. But then other British destroyers arrived on the scene, and it was decided to take off the *Pola*'s crew by placing a destroyer alongside the cruiser. After this was done, she was sunk by a torpedo.

This was the final act, at 04.10 hours on March 29th in the Battle of Matapan. The *Vittorio Veneto* succeeded in reaching harbour, but the British fleet had sunk three 8-inch cruisers and two destroyers. Admiral Iachino was still in ignorance of his losses when he reached Taranto at three in the afternoon of the 29th; he only learnt of them the following evening in Rome, when the Chief of Naval Staff showed him the British communiqué!

Admiral Cunningham arrived back at Alexandria without loss, having fought off an attack on the *Formidable* by a squadron of Junkers 88. He had lost only two men—the gallant Commander Stead and his companion, who by their sacrifice had so largely contributed to the victory. The Italians, however, had lost 2,400 men, including Admiral Cattaneo. Even more would have been lost if British destroyers had not returned to the scene at dawn to pick up survivors. Unfortunately, German aircraft appeared while there were still several hundred Italian sailors struggling in the water, and showed every intention of attacking. The destroyers could not be exposed to heavy loss, even for such humane work. The operation was called off, but Admiral

Cunningham had a message radioed to the Italian Naval Command suggesting that it send a hospital ship to the scene. The *Gradisca* went and picked up 160 Italians. The British ships already had 900 on board as prisoners.

Matapan was the first big naval battle of the Second World War, and it marked the transition between actions fought with guns and torpedoes, such as the Battle of the River Plate, and those fought entirely by carrier aircraft, as was the case at the Battle of Midway. Matapan was also the first aero-naval battle in history, besides being the first in which radar was used—and with what success! For there can be little doubt that the Italian ships would have escaped if aircraft from the *Formidable* had not intervened, and that the British battle-ships would not have obtained such a complete surprise without the help of the *Valiant*'s radar.

Admiral Iachino, however, had received no support whatever from Italian or German aircraft, neither by reconnaissance planes nor fighter cover. Moreover, his crews had not been sufficiently trained. Once again it was shown—as every navy for centuries past had known—that crews get no experience from staying in harbour. In the eighteenth century the French had paid heavily for being cooped up by the blockading forces of Hawke and Cornwallis. Now the Italians had been kept in harbour by shortage of fuel. Even a short training exercise at sea involved great problems of supplies of fuel-oil, supplies for which the Italians were dependent on the Germans, who gave grudgingly—and gave even less after the Italian disaster at Matapan.

The Battle of the Mediterranean was still far from being won; there were many hard knocks in store for the British Fleet. For two years, the efforts to fight through supplies to Malta were often quite as desperate and dramatic as those of the convoys to Murmansk with supplies for the Russians. Moreover, the strategic situation in the Mediterranean, which was so favourable to the British after their victories at Taranto and Matapan, took a sudden turn for the worse towards the end of 1941; the Mediterranean fleet suffered a series of reverses, the most notable due to a mere handful of Italian seamen whose daring commands great admiration.

In April and May, 1941, Admiral Cunningham's fleet had severe losses from attacks by German aircraft during the evacuations of the army from Greece and Crete. Three cruisers and six destroyers were sunk during the Crete operations alone; while the battleships *Warspite* and *Barham*, the carrier *Formidable*, two cruisers, and two destroyers were all severely damaged.

On November 25th the battle fleet was off the coast of Cyrenaica, in support of the army, when the *U-335*, Lieutenant Tiesenhausen, succeeded in breaking through the destroyer screen and firing four torpedoes at the *Barham*. Three at least hit the battleship, between the funnel and No. 3 turret; she blew up and sank in less than ten minutes, throwing off a great cloud of yellow smoke. When this thinned, where the *Barham* had been was seen a large patch of oil scattered with debris and struggling men.

Three minutes before the torpedoes had struck, the destroyer *Jervis* made a contact on her Asdic; but it was a doubtful one, and the operators had logged it "non sub.". The *Valiant*, which was astern of the *Barham* when she blew up, went hard a-port. Fifty seconds later the *U-335*, lightened by having fired the torpedoes, broke surface about a hundred and fifty yards ahead of the *Valiant*, which steered straight for the submarine and tried to run her down. But the distance was too short. The submarine slid past the battleship with less than fifty yards between them, and submerged again before guns were brought to bear on her, and eventually got away.

The Malta cruiser squadron met with disaster less than a month later. The three cruisers and four destroyers were steaming to intercept one of Rommel's supply convoys bound for Tripoli, and during the night they ran into a minefield that the enemy had laid in deep water. The cruiser *Neptune* and the destroyer *Kandahar* were sunk, and the cruisers *Aurora* and *Penelope* were seriously damaged. But the heaviest blow of all was being delivered in the harbour of Alexandria almost at that same moment. In the early morning of December 19th, the battleships *Queen Elizabeth* and *Valiant* were attacked and put out of service for many months by Italian midget submarines.

If this success had been obtained at sea in the course of battle, then December 19th, 1941, would be remembered as the date of a great Italian naval victory. But because the attackers were so few—"A hundred men against a fleet", was an Italian description; only six in fact penetrated the harbour defences—and because the British hushed up the results of the attack, little was heard of it. Yet the immediate consequences were almost as serious as the destruction, a week previously, of the battleship *Prince of Wales* and the battle-cruiser *Repulse* by Japanese torpedo-carrying planes off Malaya. In any case, it was the first successful demonstration during the Second World War of what determined men could do to a fleet at its moorings.

Underwater assault was by no means new. The reader will remember that as early as the Battle of Sluys divers armed with lances tried to pierce the wooden hulls of enemy ships. Nearer our own times, during the First World War, two Italian seamen named Paolucci and Rossetti succeeded in fixing explosive charges under the Austrian battleship *Viribus Unitis* in harbour at Pola, during the night of October 31st, 1918, and she blew up and sank at dawn.

This exploit had not been forgotten in the Italian Navy, and from its ranks came the first exponents of the one-man and the two-men submarines.

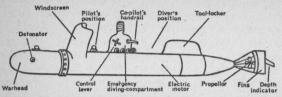

The *Maiale*, the Italian-manned underwater-charge

Early in 1940 a research team began work in a country house near the naval base of La Spezia, in close collaboration with the First Submarine Flotilla. This team formed the basis of what later became known as the Tenth Flotilla M.A.S., which built and experimented with various kinds of assault craft.[1] The first was the midget submarine C.A., based on a model dating from the First World War; this was intended to be carried near to its objective by a large submarine, and could be armed with torpedoes or with mines. It was followed by the *Maiale*—literally "pig"—or S.L.C. (*Siluro a lenta corsa*—slow-running torpedo), which could be compared to a midget submarine as a motor-bike to a Mini-car. It was, in fact, a manned underwater charge, a torpedo with two seats and a detachable warhead containing a delayed detonator. Several other types were developed from it: the San Bartolomeo torpedo, which was never tried out in actual war conditions; and the Barchino explosive motor-boat, whose one-man crew directed it at the objective and then dived overboard.

The attack on the British ships in harbour at Alexandria was made by *Maiale* craft. These underwater charges or propelled torpedoes had been tried out previously, the first attempt having been made in August, 1940. Four of them were put aboard the submarine *Iride*, which was to take them to the vicinity of Alexandria. But the submarine was sunk by R.A.F. planes on August 21st while still at her moorings at Bomba. In September, the *Gondar* suffered a similar fate. In the meantime, the *Scirè*, Lieutenant-Commander Prince Valerio Borghese, had made two unsuccessful attempts against warships at

---

[1] The letters M.A.S. stood for *Motoscafi anti sommergibili* (motor-torpedo-boats) and also for *Memento audere semper*, which was the motto of Gabriel D'Annunzio.

Gibraltar. The first success came on March 26th, 1941, when the cruiser *York* was severely damaged by a one-man "Barchino" in Suda Bay.[1] But then a third attempt by the *Scire* at Gibraltar ended disastrously for the *Maiale* crews; as did Major Tesei's attack with explosive motor-boats at Malta, on July 26th, 1941.

Nevertheless, the Tenth M.A.S. did not give up trying; and on September 21st the *Maiali* succeeded in sinking two ships at Gibraltar. Encouraged by this, another operation was mounted against the shipping in Alexandria harbour. The submarine *Scire* was again used to carry the piloted torpedoes to the harbour entrance. There were three teams taking part in the operation, the chief pilots being Lieutenant Durand de la Penne—who had participated in one of the attempts at Gibraltar—Captain Antonio Marceglia and Captain Vincenzo Martellotta, all naval officers. A reserve team was composed of Lieutenant Feltrinelli and Doctor Spaccarelli.

The *Scire* left La Spezia on December 3rd, 1941, ostensibly on an exercise. When out of sight of the coast, three new *Maiali* were taken on board—the S.L.C. Nos. 221, 222, and 223—and were stowed in special tubes on the submarine's deck. The *Scire* then made for the Dodecanese, and on December 9th arrived at the island of Leros, where the final preparations were carried out and the latest reports on the situation at Alexandria were awaited.

The operation had been planned with great care. Italian bombers were to attack the harbour as the *Scire* approached, in the hope of creating a diversion. The submarine would then send off the three *Maiali*, and when these reached their objectives the detachable warhead of each would be fixed to the keel with the aid of special clips; afterwards, the crews were to scatter small incendiary bombs about the waters of the harbour, the idea being that these would set fire to the fuel-oil escaping from the damaged ships. Another submarine, the *Topazio*, would lie off the Rosetta mouth of the Nile that night, and the following night, to pick up any survivors of this hazardous operation who managed to get out to her.

Rough weather caused Lieutenant-Commander Borghese to put back the operation twenty-four hours, from the night of the 17th. When his submarine surfaced at 18.40 hours the following evening, at about 2,400 yards north of the mole light, the weather was perfect for the attempt—a moonless night, with a calm sea and clear sky. The three manned torpedoes were launched and set off on their mission, while the *Scire* made her way back to Leros. Before she arrived,

[1] When the Germans occupied Crete they discovered the wrecked *York* and attributed the damage to the Luftwaffe.

Borghese received a message saying that reconnaissance planes reported that two battleships in Alexandria harbour had been severely damaged.

The events on the night of December 18th had been as follows:

The six men astride their "sea-pigs", wearing their breathing apparatus and with only their heads above water, reached the harbour entrance at a lucky moment—just as the boom had been opened for some destroyers returning from patrol. Lieutenant Durand de la Penne skirted the French squadron moored in the harbour,[1] and soon after two a.m. reached the *Valiant*. He then discovered that his co-pilot, Bianchi, had disappeared, and that his *Maiale* was sinking under him. He dived, caught hold of the torpedo and managed to haul it to a position on the harbour bed about ten feet below the keel of the battleship and halfway along its length. He switched on the delayed detonator and swam to the surface, exhausted by his efforts. He discarded his breathing apparatus, and the fresh air revived him; he was about to swim towards land when there came shouts from the *Valiant* and the sounds of men running along her decks. Searchlights swept the water, and then came a few bursts of machine-gun fire. Durand de la Penne scrambled on to the *Valiant*'s mooring, where to his surprise he found Bianchi installed.

A launch approached, and the two Italians were taken ashore and immediately interrogated. They produced their military identity papers, but quite properly refused to answer any further questions. Admiral Cunningham, who had been roused at four in the morning

---

[1] This was Admiral Godfroy's force which had been demilitarized after the French armistice. The log-book of the *Duquesne* had the following entries made in it that night:

02.00. The cruisers *Naiad* and *Euryalus* and several destroyers returned to harbour.
03.25. Two or three bursts of gunfire from the *Valiant*. Searchlights from the battleships swept the waters around them.
04.15. Whistlings, explosions.
04.20. All lights extinguished in the ships and along the quays. Searchlights playing; a launch patrolling the roadstead.
04.30. More whistlings and explosions, and a shock against the *Duquesne*'s hull. Explosions every five or six thousand yards.
05.25. Heavy shocks (depth-charges outside the harbour).
05.48. Heavy explosion followed by a great spout of water and smoke (about a hundred feet high) near the oil-storage tanks and on the *Queen Elizabeth*'s starboard quarter.
06.06. Heavy explosion and great spout of water and smoke on the *Valiant*'s port bow, a little forward of No. 1 turret.
06.15. Explosion similar to previous two on *Queen Elizabeth*'s port bow and right under her.
06.20. *Valiant* has a list to port and appears to be sinking by the bows. *Queen Elizabeth* listing to starboard.
07.00. Tugs arrived.

(N.B. The explosions logged at 05.48, 06.06, and 06.15 corresponded to the actions of the three *Maiali*.)

and informed of the incident, gave orders for the two to be taken aboard the *Valiant* and clamped in the bowels of the ship. If something serious were about to happen to the *Valiant* they might give the information in order to save their lives.

But they remained silent—until ten minutes to six. The explosion was set to take place at six. Lieutenant Durand de la Penne asked to be taken to the captain, and told him it would be advisable to abandon ship as she was due to blow up in ten minutes.

"Where are the charges placed?" Captain Morgan asked him.

The Italian officer refused to answer, and was taken below again. In the darkness he tried to cheer up Bianchi, but received no reply—for the very good reason that the other had succeeded in escaping from this dangerous situation. After a few more agonizing minutes, there came the expected explosion.

He was lucky enough to escape hurt, and a little later found himself on the after-deck where Captain Morgan was giving orders to the fire-fighting teams. A few cable-lengths away could be seen the *Queen Elizabeth*, with a number of the crew massed in the bows. Then she, too, was shaken by an explosion, and was distinctly seen to rise in the air. (Admiral Cunningham maintained that she rose five feet!) Debris and fuel were shooting out of her funnel.

This was the work of Captain Marceglia and his co-pilot, Schergat. Their attack had gone through almost exactly as planned. The warhead had been detached and suspended about three feet below the *Queen Elizabeth*'s keel by means of a length of cable. The two men had then surfaced and got astride their "sea-pig" and made for land. After sinking their craft—by setting the special mechanism—they hid for a while among some rocks. Eventually they reached Alexandria and took a train out to Rosetta. . . . But then their luck failed, and they never succeeded in getting out to the *Topazio*. Egyptian police captured them as they were going down to the beach.

The third team, Martellotta and Marino, had been given the carrier *Formidable* as its objective. They were almost run down by one of the destroyers while approaching the anchorage. Then they discovered that the aircraft-carrier was not at her moorings. So instead they fixed their warhead to the hull of a large tanker alongside the destroyer *Jervis*. The tanker blew up, and the *Jervis* was out of service for a month. The two Italians got as far as the dock gates before being captured.

A hundred Italian seamen—counting the crew of the submarine *Scire*—had inflicted the greatest damage since the beginning of the war to the British Mediterranean Fleet, and at the cost of six prisoners.

Great possibilities were thus offered to the Italian Naval Command, which at that time had three 35,000-ton battleships available, the *Vittorio Veneto* having been repaired and the new *Roma* having come into service; and three of the four old battleships were also in service. Six Italian battleships—and the British had none ready for sea.

However, the Italians did not venture to take the offensive, but concentrated their efforts upon the approaches to Malta and the *Rotta della morte*, as their sailors called the supply convoys to Rommel. Then the Allied landings in French North Africa, the surrender of the remnants of the Afrika Korps, and the assault on Sicily took the heart out of the Italians. With their mainland threatened, they sued for an armistice in the autumn of 1943, and the Italian Fleet sailed to Malta to surrender.

Nevertheless, the crews of the Italian "sea-pigs" had set an example —and their attacks had not ended at Alexandria, later attempts having been made at Gibraltar and then at Algiers.[1] The British were the most successful in the use of midget submarines, with their attacks in the Gironde and against the *Tirpitz* in a Norwegian fjord. But none equalled the men of the Tenth M.A.S. in tenacity, inventiveness, and resourcefulness. Where individual action was concerned, the Italian Navy showed itself as good as any.

---

[1] Lieutenant-Commander Borghese was planning to attack shipping in New York harbour with midget submarines which were to be carried across the Atlantic from Bordeaux by the Italian submarine *Leonardo da Vinci*; but the armistice on September 9th, 1943, brought the plans to a halt.

XXVII

GERMAN SUBMARINES AND THE BATTLE OF THE ATLANTIC

An ace submarine, the U-156—possession of the French Atlantic bases give the Germans great advantages in their submarine warfare—three of their ace-commanders lost in the space of ten days—the dramatic end of the U-574—campaign in the Caribbean of the U-156—her return to the Atlantic, and the Laconia tragedy—the U-156 attempts to save survivors—"I can't throw these people back into the water!"—a useless patrol and the end of the U-156.

PERHAPS the most famous of the eleven hundred German submarines built during the Second World War was the *U-156*. She was of the IX/C type, and had been laid down at Bremen towards the end of 1940. Her first commander, when she came into service in September, 1941, was Korvetten-Kapitan Werner Hartenstein, and he was still her commander when a United States flying-boat sank her in the Caribbean on March 8th, 1943.

The *U-156*, one of a hundred and forty of her type,[1] was 240 feet long, with a surface displacement of 1,120 tons, and 1,232 submerged, and a speed of 18 knots on the surface and 7 beneath. There was storage for 210 tons of diesel-oil, which gave the submarine a range of 11,000 miles at a speed of 12 knots on the surface. She carried twenty-two torpedoes, and had four bow tubes and two stern tubes. There was one 4-inch deck-gun and two anti-aircraft guns.

The *U-156* had a complement of six officers and forty-three ratings, all of whom shared in her many exploits and now lie eighteen hundred fathoms deep somewhere east of Barbados.

The *U-156*, like all new German submarines, did her trials with the Fourth Training Flotilla in the Baltic. This almost inland sea gave considerable advantage to the German Navy; not one British ship managed to penetrate it during the whole war. Russia had been at war for two months when the *U-156* started her trials, but by the end of September, 1941, Marshal von Leeb's army had pushed back the Russians under Voroshilov and reached the southern shore of the Gulf of Finland. As the Finns held the northern shore, the Russian naval

---

[1] During the war the Germans built about twenty different types of submarines—the I/A, II/B, II/C, etc. The IX/C was an ocean-going submarine.

base of Kronstadt was blocked. The Soviet Baltic Fleet could not get out, and new units and crews of the German Navy were able to train in safety. New submarines and warships finishing their refit passed through the Kiel Canal into the Baltic, where there were bases—Swinemünde, and Gotenhafen (formerly Polish Gdynia)—which were safe from R.A.F. attack.

Submarine crews were thus able to undergo a thorough training without fear of enemy intrusion. Old Norwegian destroyers—captured during the invasion of Norway in 1940—were used for target practice. The standard training was most comprehensive: firing torpedoes when submerged and on the surface, crash-diving, surfacing, and manning the deck-guns in record time, anti-aircraft practice. . . . Plenty of time was allowed for the training programme. However much in a hurry Admiral Dönitz was—for the *Befehlshaber des Unterseeboote* (the U-boat Command) always wanted more and more submarines in the Atlantic—he knew that to send out inexperienced crews was a sure means of increasing the already heavy losses. By the end of the war, Germany had lost 782 submarines out of a total of 1,135, and 30,000 men had gone to their deaths in them. Without the sound policy of exhaustive testing and training, the figures would have been even worse.[1]

Lieutenant-Commander Hartenstein had three and a half months in which to train his crew, and then on December 24th, 1941, the *U-156* left the Elbe estuary, gradually losing sight of the low-lying coastline of the German Bight—which her crew was never to see again.

During the First World War the Germans had been greatly handicapped by their lack of submarine bases within close reach of the Atlantic. The occupation of the Belgian coast gave them the use of Zeebrugge, nearer the Straits of Dover than the Jade or the Ems estuary, but it was only a slight advantage. The port of Brest was what the German Navy really needed to wage sea warfare against Britain; and early in the Second World War Germany got it—and other Atlantic ports besides. After the fall of France in June, 1940, the Todt organization was set to work to build reinforced-concrete submarine pens at Brest, Lorient, St. Nazaire, and La Pallice. So strong were they that in spite of the many R.A.F. bombing attacks on shipping and port installations at Brest and Lorient—which also wiped out much of the towns—not one of the submarine pens was demolished. This was not surprising. During R.A.F. raids on La Pallice in August, 1944, the roof

---

[1] The Schnorchel and the Walter apparatus which were great aids to submarine warfare were only incorporated into the XXI and XXIII types towards the end of the war.

of a submarine pen was hit almost in the same place by two 6-ton bombs within a day or two of each other. The only damage was a hole the size of a man's fist, through which the sky could be seen at the end of the funnel made in the concrete. The installations inside were damaged by the explosion, but the submarine was still intact and suffered little harm.

Admiral Dönitz transferred his H.Q. to Lorient at the end of 1940, then to Angers, and finally to Paris. Not only was it safer, but communications were better; besides, the B.d.U. had no need of a view of the sea. The submarine command headquarters was exceedingly well organized, particularly in its radio communications with submarines at sea and in monitoring enemy signals; it was most efficient in concentrating U-boat packs along the route of Allied convoys. By the end of the war, Dönitz's U-boats had sunk 20,000,000 tons of Allied shipping; the campaign was at its height in 1942, when 5,340,000 tons were sunk.

At the outbreak of war Commodore Dönitz—he was shortly afterwards promoted Rear-Admiral—only had 57 U-boats, 26 of which were capable of operating in the Atlantic. When 21 of them were got away to sea a few days before war was declared,[1] he had reached the limit of his possibilities.

The Allies could consider themselves fortunate that the rebuilding of the German submarine fleet, which had been forbidden by the Versailles Treaty, only began after the London Naval Agreement in June, 1935; and that Admiral Raeder, who did not imagine that war was so near, concentrated on the rebuilding of his surface fleet rather than his submarines. An immense naval programme, Plan Z, included six 45,000-ton battleships; but their construction was abandoned after September 3rd, 1939, so that the whole shipbuilding effort could be concentrated on U-boats. They were eventually coming off the stocks at a rate of two hundred a year.

However, that figure had not been reached on December 24th, 1941, when the U-156 left the Elbe estuary. The number in service had nevertheless reached a total of 249, in spite of the loss of 66 since the outbreak of war.

The expansion of the U-boat fleet was not so much a question of materials as the strain on personnel resources. Most of the experienced crews, those whose training had begun before the war, had been lost—either killed or captured—with the sinking of those 66 submarines.

[1] It was usual in wartime to reckon one submarine being repaired and one on passage for every one that was operational; so that to estimate the effective strength at any one time, the number of submarines in a navy should be divided by three.

Where among the new men were the successors to the ace-commanders? Commanders such as Gunther Prien, who had achieved great popularity by his master-stroke in sinking the *Royal Oak* in Scapa Flow, on October 13th, 1939; and Joachim Schepke and Otto Kretschmer, who between them had accounted for more than 500,000 tons of Allied shipping. In the space of ten days in March, 1941, all three disappeared from the scene, with their crews. Prien's *U-47* was sunk on March 8th; Schepke, in the *U-100*, was rammed by the destroyer *Vanoc* on the 17th; while Kretschmer was made prisoner after the sinking of the *U-99*, which had had a brilliant career.

The *U-99*—one of the VII/B type—had left the Germania shipyards at Kiel in April, 1940, at the same time as the *U-100*. After a training period in the Baltic, she went on her first patrol in June, in the North Sea. It was almost her last patrol too; for twenty-two hours on end the *U-99* was bombed and depth-charged, but eventually escaped with a twisted periscope and leaking oil tanks. Nevertheless, she had sunk 62,000 tons of shipping in ten days; and was able to make Bergen, then Wilhelmshaven, where she was repaired within a week.

On July 28th the *U-99* was off the south-west of Ireland and sank the 13,200-ton *Auckland Star*. The following day, and a hundred miles to the north, she torpedoed the 7,300-ton *Clan Menzies*; and on the 31st sank the 5,500-ton *Jamaica Progress* in the Notch Channel (at the northern end of the Irish Sea). Kretschmer then sighted a large westbound convoy escorted only by an old destroyer and a corvette. The convoy was pursuing a zig-zag course at a speed of eight knots; Kretschmer, having gained an attacking position, first torpedoed the 6,300-ton *Jersey City*, the third ship in the seventh column of the convoy. He was attacked with depth-charges for an hour and a half, but escaped unhurt. That night he torpedoed three cargo ships, all of which managed to make port. He tried to sink the third ship by surfacing and shelling her, but found himself up against a very determined skipper who returned his fire so effectively that he gave up the chase. He made for Lorient, arriving there on August 8th.

Three ships sunk and three damaged gained Kretschmer the award of the Iron Cross.

A fortnight later he was off again, and sank seven ships totalling 56,000 tons. Then, between the 10th and 24th of September, he took part with four other U-boats in an attack on convoy SC.7. Twenty of the ships were sunk, seven by the *U-99*.

On his fifth patrol Kretschmer sank three ships, two being armed merchant-cruisers. Having expended all his torpedoes, he returned to base on November 5th; and was awarded oak-leaves to his Iron Cross for having brought his total of shipping destroyed to 200,000 tons.

His sixth patrol was in December, when he had four more successes, one victim being another armed merchant-cruiser, the 16,400-ton *Forfar*, which went down in three minutes. After this patrol, Kretschmer was far ahead of other submarine commanders with 252,000 tons of shipping to his credit. But the *U-99*'s career was approaching its end.

It so happened that early in March, 1941, the three U-boat aces, Prien, Schepke, and Kretschmer, were operating together three hundred miles west of Scotland against a big, strongly escorted convoy. On March 6th, the *U-99*, the *U-47*, and two others were counter-attacked with depth-charges, but managed to escape. Prien even added a 20,000-ton Norwegian whaler, the *Terje Viken*, to his toll; though he had to share the credit with Kretschmer, who finished off the whaler just before sending to the bottom a 6,000-ton tanker. But at dawn the *U-99* was sighted on the surface by a destroyer and had to crash-dive. A prolonged attack with depth-charges followed. The *U-99*'s crew counted more than fifty; luckily for them, the depth mechanism had not been correctly set. It was during the attack on this convoy that Prien and the *U-47* succumbed to the destroyer *Wolverine*, on March 8th.

Schepke and Kretschmer had one more week to go. On the 16th, in company with the *U-557*—commanded by Lemp, who had sunk the *Athenia*—they were hunting convoy HX.112, which consisted of forty-one ships from Halifax with an escort of five destroyers and two corvettes. Kretschmer beat all his previous records that night by sinking the 6,600-ton British tanker *Fern* at 22.05 hours, the 5,700-ton *Venetia* five minutes later, the 9,300-ton French ship *Franche Comté* at 23.34, and two other merchant ships just before midnight—a total sinking of 59,000 tons,[1] which brought his aggregate for that patrol to 86,000 tons. He had no torpedoes left, so decided to return to Lorient.

Then the amazing luck which had held for nine months turned. The *U-99* was making off at all speed when she was sighted by the destroyer *Walker*. Schepke's *U-100* had just been rammed by the *Vanoc*, which was picking up survivors, and the *Walker* was guarding her sister destroyer. Now she chased towards the position where the *U-99* had dived, made a strong contact on her Asdic, and dropped depth-charges repeatedly. They damaged the U-boat, which was forced to surface. She reappeared between the two destroyers. This was

---

[1] The British announced 40,000 tons of shipping sunk that night—which was still a lot.

the end. Kretschmer gave orders to abandon ship and prepared to scuttle her. He stayed on deck, seeing that all his men jumped overboard, while the Engineer Officer, Gottfried Schroder, went below to open the valves. The U-boat went down so quickly that Schroder had no time to escape.

That week had been a costly one for the Allies. But the balance sheet was at least evened by the elimination of three U-boat commanders who had sunk between them almost 800,000 tons of shipping —338,000 by Kretschmer alone.

The Battle of the Atlantic was hardening. Although the worst was not yet over for the British, their anti-submarine defences were having increasing effect. The United States, though not then in the war, helped the situation by extending their neutrality zone, and the U.S. Navy began escorting convoys in the Western Atlantic. Radar was being brought into greater use, and Asdic had been improved so that its range of detection was extended. Convoy escorts were strengthened, and in September, 1941, aircraft-carriers were included for the first time. But before that date, the C.A.M. Ships had come into service, equipped with a Hurricane to chase off enemy reconnaissance aircraft; these ships were an attempt to solve the problem of air defence for convoys beyond the range of shore-based aircraft. And by December, 1941, destroyers were being fitted out with the "Hedgehog", which enabled two dozen depth-charges to be dropped at once, over a distance of two hundred yards.

One of the first convoys to have an aircraft-carrier among its escort was the HG.76. This consisted of thirty-two merchant ships that sailed from Gibraltar on December 14th, 1941, bound for Liverpool, and was escorted by two sloops, two destroyers, seven corvettes, and the carrier *Audacity*. The convoy was attacked by fifteen U-boats, and the battle raged for a week. Only four ships were lost, though one of them was the *Audacity*, torpedoed by the *U-751* on the sixth day out; but they cost the Germans four submarines. The *U-131* was sunk by the *Audacity*'s aircraft on the 17th. On the following day the *U-434* was destroyed by depth-charges and gunfire. On the 19th the *U-574* sank the destroyer *Stanley*, and after a long chase and gun duels was herself rammed and sunk. Finally, on the 21st, the *U-567* was sunk by the *Deptford*—which had her "kill" confirmed several months later, in a German communiqué.[1]

The end of the *U-574* was particularly dramatic. By the fifth day

[1] The *U-567*'s captain, Lt.-Commander Endrass, had been second-in-command to Prien, and was himself responsible for the sinking of over 200,000 tons of shipping.

out, the convoy had been driven far into the Atlantic by the running fight against the U-boat pack, and was nearly four hundred miles from the coast of Portugal and no farther north than the latitude of Lisbon. Since the evening of the 18th the *U-574*, Oberleutnant z. See Dietrich Gengelbach, had been lurking in the wake of the convoy. Once already she had been detected and pursued, but had got away in spite of the star-shells fired by the escort vessels in the hope of sighting her on the surface. She was still not far off, though. . . . At 03.45 hours on the 19th she surfaced quite close to the *Stanley* and the sloop *Stork*— so close that Gengelbach could see the flashes of a signal-lamp from the *Stanley*. He took advantage to fire three torpedoes into her. Flames three hundred feet high shot into the night sky; the destroyer blew up and sank, while the U-boat made off at full speed.

Gengelbach did not know it, but the *Stork*'s captain, Commander Walker, was renowned for his destruction of U-boats. Together with another sloop, he chased the *U-574* and forced her to dive. Depth-charges were at once dropped, and the explosions damaged the submarine considerably; her engines were stopped and water was coming in everywhere. She surfaced about two hundred yards on the *Stork*'s port bow, too near for the guns to be brought to bear on her. Commander Walker attempted to ram her, but Gengelbach had got his engines started again and turned in a tighter circle than the sloop. The U-boat was there at the mercy of the other, but for a few minutes that seemed an eternity all the British could do was shout curses at the enemy!

The *Stork* turned, and turned again . . . and finally rammed and sank the *U-574*, making sure of her by dropping depth-charges. Less than half an hour later, another U-boat avenged Gengelbach and his crew by sinking the leading merchant ship in the convoy. And that U-boat was not tracked down. . . .

A few days later the *U-156* left the Elbe estuary to reach her base at Lorient and begin her operational career. Like others, she took the long northern route round the British Isles. German submarines had used the Channel during the first few weeks of the war, but the Allies had soon laid extensive minefields between the Straits of Dover and the German Bight.[1] The *U-12* had struck a mine and blown up on October 8th, 1939, while passing through the Straits from the west, and five days later the *U-40* was destroyed in the same manner when attempting to pass down-Channel. On October 23rd the *U-16* had been detected and damaged by two British patrol vessels and went aground

[1] 8,565 mines were laid by the British, 1,429 by the French.

on the Goodwins. After that, the German U-boat Command stopped using the Channel, and did not return to that short route even after the occupation of the French coast.

So Lieutenant-Commander Hartenstein took the *U-156* the long way round, arriving at Lorient on January 10th, 1942. The voyage had been useful in revealing the various small deficiencies in a new vessel, and these were put right while she was being fitted out to operate in the tropics. On January 19th, fully equipped and supplied, Hartenstein took the *U-156* out to sea and set course for the Caribbean.

At that time, what has been called the golden age of the U-boats was just beginning. The entry of the United States into the war had presented the German U-boat Command with a new soft spot. The American shipping along the whole eastern seaboard, from Newfoundland to the West Indies, was without any organized defence against the German submarine campaign.[1] The U.S. Navy had made no preparations for a convoy system, and the American Merchant Navy had no defensive armament. Admiral Dönitz speedily sent a score of U-boats to the new area. But because of the distance from their bases on the French Atlantic coast—2,200 miles to Newfoundland, 3,600 to the Carolina capes, 4,000 to the West Indies and Florida—only U-boats of five hundred tons and upwards could operate, until a system of supply ships was organized.

Dönitz sent type VII U-boats to operate against shipping in the New York area and off Cape Hatteras, as they were smaller and had a shorter endurance than those of the *U-156* type. They found more opportunities, more targets for their torpedoes, than they could deal with; on average, there were 120 to 130 cargo vessels on passage every day. At the same time, five U-boats of the larger IX/C type were sent to attack the oil-storage tanks and the shipping in the Curaçoa area and in the Caribbean. The *U-156* was one of this group, named the Neuland Group, and the other four were the *U-67*, Lieutenant Gunther Mullec Stockheim, the *U-129*, Lieutenant Nicolai Clausen, the *U-161*, Lieutenant Albrecht Achilles, and the *U-502*, Lieutenant Jurgen Rosenstiel. They crossed the Atlantic separately, but their orders were to wait until all had arrived at the rendezvous and not to begin operations until February 16th. Then they were to sink all shipping seen in the vicinity of the port each was detailed to attack, and to surface at night—there would be a new moon—to shell the oil-storage tanks.

The five U-boats had each an uneventful crossing, and were at their

[1] It took months of discussion before the Navy Department succeeded in getting the neon-signs at Miami extinguished; they could be seen twenty-five miles out at sea.

respective stations on the date fixed. Hartenstein had been detailed to attack the Dutch island of Aruba, and on the 16th he sank two tankers in the vicinity. While waiting for night to fall he examined the oil-storage tanks through the periscope; they were near the shore and could be seen distinctly. A north-east trade-wind was blowing, and Hartenstein had every hope that a few well-aimed incendiary shells would start a blaze which would rapidly spread.

His orders, as already mentioned, were to shell shore installations during the hours of darkness, but some delay was caused by the preparations to surface, and dawn was breaking when the *U-156* emerged a short distance from the shore. However, this mattered little, for there was no danger.[1] The gun-crew leapt from the conning-tower and ran to the 4-inch deck-gun; but their officer, Sub-Lieutenant von dem Borne, who was examining the target through his binoculars, gestured to the men to hold their fire. He had noticed some people walking along the coast road towards a church—it was a Sunday morning—and he had not the heart to expose them to injury or death while on their way to early Mass. He waited until they had passed out of range, then gave the order to open fire.

But the incident had caused him to forget to inspect the gun; and the men, in their eagerness, had overlooked the fact that it was still sealed, being kept watertight while the submarine was submerged. The gun burst when fired; one of the crew was badly hurt, and Von dem Borne had his leg crushed by the recoil.

The U-boat carried no medical officer, and the unfortunate Sub-Lieutenant had to undergo an amputation by inexpert hands. Infection set in, and signs of gangrene appeared. Hartenstein reported the situation to the U-boat Command; and it caused a great stir at the Kriegsmarine, where the Sub-Lieutenant's father, Rear-Admiral Von dem Borne, was on the staff. What could be done? The one possibility near at hand was to land the two injured men at Fort de France, Martinique, where the French High Commissioner had supported the Vichy Government and a French squadron had remained since the armistice with Germany. The request was transmitted to the French Admiralty, through the Armistice Commission. In the meantime, Hartenstein had repaired his gun and used it to sink two more ships.

The French authorities at Martinique and Guadeloupe were having a difficult time just then. The American Press was demanding the occupation of the French islands, and the Navy Department was

---

[1] By agreement with the Dutch authorities, the United States had sent troops to Curaçoa and Aruba; but there were no naval forces, and coastal defences were still non-existent.

casting envious eyes on the harbour and roadstead of Fort de France—
"the finest naval and air base between Porto Rico and Trinidad", as
Samuel E. Morison bluntly wrote. And the shelling of Aruba and
Curaçao only a few days after United States troops had arrived in
those places caused a storm of indignant protests from the Press.
Obviously the French West Indies were serving as supply bases to
these cursed U-boats!

In short, it was hardly the right moment for a U-boat to call in at
Fort de France. Yet there were international conventions to be respected; a ship of a belligerent country has a right to enter a neutral

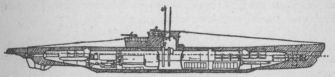

Submarine type IX C.—Longitudinal section.
Crew: 5 officers, 46 ratings. Maximum speed: surface—18 knots;
submerged—7 knots

Endurance: 60 days
Diving time: 45 seconds
Length: 240 feet

Width amidships: 22 feet
Periscope depth: 50 feet
Armaments: 4 torpedo-tubes forward,
2 aft (22 torpedoes carried);
1 deck-gun and 4 anti-aircraft

port in a case of urgent necessity. The Vichy Government therefore
raised no objection to the German request, but pointed out that the
U-boat should clearly identify herself and openly signal her reasons for
approaching the harbour, as it was by no means certain that instructions would reach the authorities at Fort de France in time.

However, when the *U-156* arrived off Fort de France on February
20th, at ten at night, the French High Commissioner, Admiral Robert,
had already been warned; and the patrol vessel *Esperanto* was waiting
for the submarine at the limit of territorial waters. Half an hour later,
having transferred the two injured men to the French vessel, the U-boat
was heading for the open sea.

There was a United States naval observer at Fort de France, and
Admiral Robert had informed him of the approach and mission of the
U-boat in order to avoid any misrepresentation. The naval officer
wanted to signal the U-boat's presence to the Commander of the U.S.
naval forces in the area, but his secretary had already left the office—
taking with him the keys of the safe containing the secret documents
and code-book. The secretary could not be found that night, and when
he arrived at the office the following morning it was too late to send

the information. The *U-156* had sped away on the surface, and might be anywhere in the Caribbean.

The Neuland Group had been remarkably successful. While the *U-129* was sinking tankers in the Curaçao area, Lieutenant Achilles had taken the *U-161* into the shallow waters of Port of Spain and sunk a tanker and a cargo ship. The *U-126* reached the Caribbean shortly afterwards, and soon distinguished herself by sinking nine ships. By the beginning of March it was time for the U-boats to return to base. The *U-156* was the first to make course for Lorient, arriving on March 17th. Meanwhile, the two injured members of her crew were recovering in hospital at Fort de France, where Sub-Lieutenant von dem Borne had to undergo another operation.

By an amazing coincidence, the U-boat which had been the cause of some embarrassment to the French in Martinique was also the cause of giving them an opportunity to show that their hospitality extended to both sides in the war. The *U-156* was back in the Caribbean three months later, and Hartenstein had orders to extend his efforts to the entrance to the Panama Canal. By then, in May, 1942, the situation had altered; tankers were sailing in escorted convoys, and their routing was frequently changed; United States planes were constantly on patrol. However, the German radio interception and monitoring services were most efficient and enabled Admiral Dönitz to redeploy his submarines farther south with telling effect.

Hartenstein received orders to make for Martinique. The situation there had become critical. The United States had demanded a stricter control over the French warships and merchant ships in harbour, but the Germans would not allow the French authorities to make any concessions. So ships of the U.S. Navy were exercising a tight blockade of Martinique, maintaining a constant patrol just beyond territorial waters. This seemed to Dönitz an admirable opportunity to send a pair of U-boats to attack the U.S. warships and any of the French which attempted to put to sea to join the Allies. The *U-156* and the *U-69* were detailed for the mission.

Hartenstein was lurking a few miles off Fort de France on May 22nd when the old American destroyer *Blakeley* appeared in his periscope. A well-directed torpedo smashed into her bows.

The *Blakeley* managed to keep afloat, but a number of the crew were seriously wounded and in need of urgent attention. It was her captain's turn to ask for assistance from the French; and the American destroyer was allowed into the harbour of Fort de France. She drew alongside the *Béarn*, the wounded men were transferred, and thence taken to hospital. The *Blakeley* then limped away towards an American naval base.

Hartenstein had in effect rendered a great service to the French. The help given to the *Blakeley* created a favourable impression, and the incident eased the situation between the United States and the French West Indies. The following year they rallied to the Allies.

This second patrol of the *U-156* in the Caribbean proved most exhausting for the crew. The 1X/C type of submarine had not been intended for operations in tropical waters, and in spite of some conversion conditions were very testing, especially when the submarine was submerged. And in one week while patrolling off Martinique, Hartenstein was forced to remain submerged for five days and nights. He could see that his men were nearing the limit of their endurance. But they were kept on patrol for another month, in the Trinidad area, before being recalled to base.

The *U-156* arrived back again at Lorient on July 7th, and Hartenstein and his crew had several weeks rest ashore. The Battle of the Atlantic was reaching its peak. The German submarine campaign had increased in fury during the first half of 1942, the number of U-boats operating having gone up from forty-two to sixty during the period. In the month of June alone, over half a million tons of Allied shipping was sunk. Even greater success seemed likely, if the Allies' countermeasures did not quickly prove effective.

On August 20th the *U-156* was off again, this time as part of the Eisbar Group, which consisted of three other U-boats and a "sea-cow" —as the crews called the supply ships, which had recently come into service. Hartenstein—still in command of the *U-156*—was not bound for the Caribbean, though, but for the Atlantic area south of the Cape Verde Islands.

Three weeks later, while on patrol some five hundred miles south of Freetown, the *U-156*'s radio operator picked up a message addressed to a British ship in the area. Hartenstein set out to look for her, and towards the end of the morning sighted smoke to the south-west. Closer inspection showed a liner heading north-west; she was larger than he had at first thought, and he decided to reach an attacking position and then wait until nightfall.

The ship was the 19,000-ton White Star liner *Laconia*, which was proceeding alone because of her high speed. She had left Suez, bound for England via the Cape, with 1,600 British troops, 250 sailors and airmen, some wives and children, and 1,800 Italians made prisoner after the battle of El Alamein; with the Polish detachment in charge of the prisoners, and the crew of 400, the *Laconia* had more than 4,000 people on board. She was due to put in at Freetown, but because of U-boat activity the naval authorities there had advised the captain to reduce speed and not to arrive until 48 hours later. This was the message that Hartenstein had picked up.

At 20.07 hours G.M.T. the *U-156* fired two torpedoes at the *Laconia*. Three minutes and ten seconds later the first one hit and exploded in No. 4 hold, which was crammed with Italian prisoners. The second torpedo struck the *Laconia* aft a few seconds later. She went down in fifty minutes, and there were scenes of horror and many tragic happenings. People were dancing in the lounge when the ship was hit. . . . The prisoners in the holds fought to get out, trampling on the Polish guards; some escaped through port-holes, others were killed or wounded by bayonets, and a good many went down with the ship.

The *U-156* had surfaced in order to identify her victim the better, and also to try and capture the captain and the chief engineer, in accordance with instructions. Hartenstein and his men heard shouts for help in the darkness, carried by the south-westerly breeze—shouts in Italian. The U-boat rescued some men from the water. They were Italians all right, allies of the Germans; and fifteen or eighteen hundred of them were said to have been held prisoner in the ship. What a catastrophe! And what could be done about it now? One could hardly abandon allies in peril, especially having been the cause of it. Hartenstein first sent off a report:

"Have sunk British *Laconia*, square FF 7721. Course 310. Unfortunately fifteen hundred Italian prisoners on board. Request instructions. Hartenstein."

Meanwhile, the numbers rescued from the sea were increasing aboard the submarine. Before a reply was received from the B.d.U., Hartenstein sent a message to the other U-boats of the Eisbar Group asking them to come to his aid:

"Join me at once square FF 7721. At full speed. Schacht (commanding *U-507*) and Wüdermann (*U-506*) report your positions. My vessel surrounded by rafts and wreckage swarming with Italians. Unable take any more, already have 193 on board. Absolute limit for submerging."

Admiral Dönitz, at his headquarters, frowned when this signal was shown to him. "All these messages made me most anxious," he said at the Nuremberg Trials, "for I knew it was bound to end badly." A submarine with so many extra people on board might well lose her stability, and be unable to dive quickly if aircraft approached. The B.d.U. asked Hartenstein if the *Laconia* had given her position when sending out S.O.S. The question was put to see whether there was any chance of a ship arriving on the scene to pick up survivors. Hartenstein replied in the affirmative, and added that the 193 survivors aboard his U-boat included 21 British. Hundreds were struggling to keep afloat, with only their lifebelts to help them. Hartenstein suggested that an attempt be made through diplomatic channels to neutralize the area; judging from radio signals that had been picked up, there was some ship in the vicinity which could then safely approach the scene of the sinking. Then, without waiting for permission from his superiors, Hartenstein sent out the following message in clear and in English:

"If any ship can come to the aid of the shipwrecked crew of the *Laconia*, I shall not attack her providing I am not attacked myself, neither by ship nor plane. I have picked up 193 men. Position 4 degrees 52 south, 11 degrees 26 west. A German submarine."

This appeal, one of the most unusual in the annals of submarine warfare—and made with every good intention, it must be said—did not produce the results hoped for by Hartenstein.

He next heard from the B.d.U. that an Italian submarine and the three U-boats of the Eisbar Group were on their way to him; then he was informed that the German Naval Command had requested the assistance of the French Navy, through the German Commission with the Vichy Government. The news was at once passed on to the survivors from the *Laconia*; and the crew of the *U-156* pulled some more out of the water, dried their clothes and gave them hot coffee, and then distributed them among the rafts and lifeboats.

When morning came, Hartenstein reckoned he could see 22 boats and a few rafts holding about 1,500 survivors. He had taken 400 on board altogether, then put 200 of them into the boats. No ship or plane had so far appeared on the scene; and none showed up that day. The following morning the *U-506* was sighted, and Hartenstein went to meet her; after he had transferred about half of the 263 Italians he then had aboard the *U-156*, the two submarines took some of the lifeboats in tow with the intention of making towards Abidjan, on the Ivory Coast.

One of the other two U-boats heading towards the scene had been attacked by a plane, and received orders to return to her base—Bergen—for repairs. The other, *U-507*, had been making utmost speed since the morning of the 13th to cover the seven hundred miles separating her from the scene of the sinking. On the 15th the crew sighted three boats filled with survivors, British, Italian, and Polish. They were all taken on board the submarine, though only the Italians were put below. Later in the day, nine more boats were found; when night fell, the U-boat took them in tow.

On the fourth day, September 16th, it was hoped that the French ships from Dakar and Konakry would arrive at any moment; but they had a long way to come. The *U-156*, after transferring some of the survivors aboard her to lifeboats, still had fifty-five Italians and as many British, four of the latter being women. In addition, the submarine was towing four boats.

Suddenly, a plane was heard approaching. It was a large, four-engined American bomber. Hartenstein had already spread a big Red Cross on the deck, and he tried to signal to the American pilot with a flash-lamp. It was all a waste of time. No response came from the plane, except that it turned away, then came back to fly low over the U-boat and drop two bombs.

"*Leinen los!*" cried Hartenstein. "Cast off the lifeboats!"

One of them had capsized. The bomber made another run, and a near-miss sent a great spout of water over the U-boat's conning-tower. Hartenstein had had more than enough. Diving-stations! The British must go overside—and the Italians too, for it was obvious that the U-boat could not dive with them aboard.

The horrible scene can be imagined. . . . The few survivors—half a dozen picked up that afternoon by the Italian submarine *Cappellini*—said that the Germans had to throw bodily into the sea those who hesitated to jump themselves. These few survivors had been found among a couple of hundred corpses floating in the water.

Yet the commander of the *U-156* had no alternative. He could not be expected to expose his vessel any longer to the plane's attacks, which had already caused damage. He dived, and set a westward course, not surfacing again until nightfall.

"Bombed five times by an American Liberator in good visibility when we were towing four boatloads of survivors, and in spite of a Red Cross four yards square showing distinctly on the deck. Have both periscopes damaged. Am abandoning rescue operations. On a westward course to effect repairs. Hartenstein. 23.04 hours. September 16th."

For the past three days Dönitz had been having a difficult time with Hitler, who wanted him to call off the rescue operations as being too dangerous for the U-boats. "I can't throw these people back into the water!" Dönitz had replied. Yet that had happened, because one of the enemy had not accepted the truce. One of the consequences of the *Laconia* tragedy was that Dönitz gave stricter orders to the U-boat commanders. After the war, the whole episode was brought up at the Nuremberg Trials, and the judges had to acknowledge that there was nothing in the conduct of the U-boat commanders concerned for which they could be reproached.

The end of it was that Hartenstein received orders never to take part again in such rescue operations, under no circumstances; and three days after being attacked by the Liberator he sank the cargo ship *Quebec City*—thus justifying to some extent the American bomber's action.

It was all in the book: "If you see a submarine, kill it." Even if it is rescuing survivors; and even if the survivors are allies, for who knows what it will attack when its rescue work has ended.

As for the rest of the survivors from the *Laconia*—the French cruiser *Gloire*, which had made full speed from Dakar, rescued 726, most of them British, from 14 boats on September 17th. The gunboat *Annamite* met the *U-507* and then the *U-506* at sea, and took off the 325 survivors which they had on board. Another French ship, the *Dumont d'Urville*, took 50 more from the Italian submarine *Cappellini*, and later picked up survivors from the cargo ship *Trevilley* which had been torpedoed on the night of the 13th by the *U-68*. The crew of the *Quebec City* was picked up by a British destroyer.

There were still two boatloads from the *Laconia* drifting in the Atlantic. One reached the coast of Liberia on October 10th, but only sixteen people were still alive of the sixty-eight who had got into it. The remaining boat was found on October 21st by the British ship *St. Wistan*; it had then been drifting for thirty-nine days, and contained four men in the last stages of exhaustion—all that were left of the fifty-one who had got away from the *Laconia*.

Of all the terrible episodes in the Battle of the Atlantic, some of which will never be known, it is doubtful if any was as tragic as that of the *Laconia*.

The fourth patrol of the *U-156* was her last. Commanded by Hartenstein, she set out in mid-January, 1943, in company with the *U-510*, Lieutenant-Commander Karl Neitzel. The latter submarine, incidentally, is at the present time a unit of the French Navy, with the name *Bouan*.[1]

The two U-boats first operated in the area south of the Cape Verde Islands; on February 8th they received orders to cross to the Caribbean, which they reached on the 26th. But that area was no longer a happy hunting ground for submarines. Nor were prospects any better farther south, off the coast of South America. Brazil had entered the war on August 22nd, 1942, and it was not a mere paper declaration; her warships were taking an active part in the anti-submarine campaign, and her air bases were being used by the United States Air Force.

[1] She returned to her base at St. Nazaire on April 24th, 1945, a fortnight before the German surrender, and was found intact when that strong-point was entered.

Hartenstein and Neitzel searched the sea in vain for an easy target for their torpedoes. There were no ships sailing independently, only convoys with a strong escort. And the crews of the U-boats were finding conditions in tropical waters difficult to bear. A useless patrol, in fact!

However, on March 8th, the *U-510* was some seventy miles off Cayenne when she sighted fifteen merchant-ships in convoy and making for Trinidad with only an air escort. Neitzel tried to contact Harten-stein, to call him to the area, but received no reply. The *U-156* had been destroyed that very day by planes of the U.S. 53rd Squadron.

The *U-510* was more fortunate. She dogged the convoy for three days, sank three of the ships and damaged five others; by April 16th she was back at her base. She was later sent to the Far East, and sur-vived to the end of the war.

The career of Hartenstein and the *U-156* was perhaps less brilliant than that of Kretschmer and the *U-99* or Prien and the *U-47*, yet it is a good example of the hard conditions on the German side in the Battle of the Atlantic.

XXVIII

THE MASSACRE OF CONVOY PQ.17

The convoys to Russia—Operation Rösselsprung—the German battleships put to sea—Convoy PQ.17 sails with strong cover—reported by the U-255—the first aerial attacks—the Admiralty recalls the convoy's cover force—Hitler orders the Tirpitz to return—the convoy scatters, and is attacked by U-boats and dive-bombers—fourteen ships sunk in one day—the Battle of the North Cape, and the end of the Scharnhorst (December 26th, 1943).

IN July, 1942, the military might of the Axis powers was everywhere triumphant. Tobruk had fallen on June 21st, and Rommel was advancing so rapidly on Alexandria that the Fleet was seriously considering evacuation. The Germans seemed likely to reach the Suez Canal. On the Russian front, Sebastopol, reputed to be the most impregnable stronghold in the world, fell on July 2nd after resisting stubbornly for twenty-five days. The German Army was building up the great summer offensive which carried it to Stalingrad and the Volga by the autumn.

At about the same time, the Germans achieved their most resounding victory at sea, sinking twenty-two of the thirty-three ships in a convoy to Russia. The PQ.17 was the largest of the convoys that had then been sent on that terrible run. It was given a very strong escort, and a battle fleet sailed from Scapa Flow to cover its passage. The German heavy ships also put to sea. Although there was no clash between the enemy capital ships—neither side appeared to want to risk them—the Germans obtained a tactical success just the same, for when the British Admiralty became aware that the German heavy ships were at sea, the convoy was ordered to scatter. The merchant ships were subjected to tremendous attacks by U-boats and aircraft, and many were lost.

The only possible route for the delivery of Anglo-American war material to Russia was by way of the Arctic, chiefly to Murmansk. As in the First World War, Russia was cut off from her allies by land. Both the Baltic and the Black Sea were blocked by the enemy. There remained a supply route overland from the Persian Gulf; but communications with Russia's industrial areas were under threat from the enemy (at least, until quite late in the war), and in any case were poor and very long. The same was true of communications from Vladivostock

The port of Archangel had been the main point of entry during the First World War. At that period, Murmansk was still only a fishing village. It owes its development as a port to the fact that it is free of ice all the year round; whereas Archangel, in the White Sea, is frozen over for more than half the year.

The first convoys were sent from Britain in the summer of 1941, and at first got through without difficulty. By March 1st, 1942, one hundred and eleven ships had reached Archangel or Murmansk, and seventy-eight had returned to Britain, all for the loss of only one merchant ship and one escort vessel. But German counter-measures were not long deferred.

In January, 1942, the German Naval Command had begun to move its heavy ships to fjords in Northern Norway. The new battleship *Tirpitz* showed herself for the first time on March 6th, when convoy PQ.12 was on its way to Murmansk and convoy PQ.8 was west-bound from Russia. It was only a fleeting appearance, and no engagement took place. One ship in the west-bound convoy, the Russian *Liora* which was straggling in the rear, was sunk by the *Frederick Ihn*, one of the *Tirpitz*'s destroyer screen. But it was a warning of what was in store for future convoys.

In April, five out of thirteen ships in convoy PQ.13 were lost through the combined operations of destroyers and dive-bombers based in Northern Norway. Then Admiral Donitz recalled some U-boats from the Atlantic, and during the long days of the northern summer the Russian convoys were exposed to attacks from the air, from surface ships and from submarines, with no cover of darkness to bring some respite.

In May, 1942, convoy PQ.16 was the object of simultaneous attacks by a pack of half a dozen U-boats and several squadrons of aircraft— more than three hundred planes in all. The U-boats were beaten off, but the planes sank seven merchant ships out of the thirty-four in the convoy.

Worse was to come. The German Naval Command planned to use all available strength against the next convoy. By June, the *Tirpitz* had been joined at Trondheim by the heavy cruiser *Admiral Hipper*, and the two pocket-battleships *Lützow* (formerly the *Deutschland*) and *Admiral Scheer* were based on Narvik. Together with half a dozen large destroyers, they formed the battle fleet.

The Eleventh U-boat Flotilla (about a dozen units) was based on Bergen; and the Fifth Luftflotte (Fleet Air Arm) with more than three hundred planes was at the air bases of Bardufoss, between Narvik and Tromsö, and Banak, a little east of the North Cape.

The combined operation of these forces was given the code-name Rösselsprung (the Knight's move in chess), and was placed under the command of Admiral Carls, who was responsible for the Northern theatre of operations and had his base headquarters at Kiel. He had every desire to gain a resounding victory which would be on a par with the Army's triumphs, and so raise the morale of the crews of the capital ships; for their inactivity had given them an inferiority complex with regard to the U-boat and air crews.

However, there were complications in the chain of command. The Luftflotte squadrons were not under the immediate orders of Admiral Carls. He had a liaison officer attached to the staff of Colonel-General Stumpf, the commander of the squadrons; but Stumpf came under Goering. Admiral Schniewind, commander of the naval forces in Norway, wearing his flag in the *Tirpitz*, was under Carls's orders; but above was Grand-Admiral Raeder—and Hitler.

Raeder was certainly not one to create difficulties in the use of surface vessels; nor Dönitz in the case of U-boats. But Adolf Hitler was commander-in-chief of all the German armed forces, and he continually hampered the naval effort throughout the war. The *Tirpitz* could not be moved a cable-length without his permission. He was responsible for the orders which could have turned Operation Rösselsprung into a complete fiasco; that the opposite was the case cannot be credited to the Führer's leadership.

Early in June Admiral Carls asked for increased air reconnaissance, but he failed to impress the Fifth Luftflotte with the importance of early warning of the sailing of a convoy. Stumpf's officers seemed so pleased with their success against the previous convoy that they wanted to hold their bombers in readiness for the attack. Carls therefore had to rely on U-boats for the information he needed. Three set out on June 10th to patrol the route usually taken by the convoys; two more followed on the 16th, and by the time convoy PQ.17 sailed from Iceland on June 27th there were quite ten U-boats lurking along its route.

The Admiralty was well aware of the gathering strength of the enemy forces based on Norway, and had provided powerful cover for convoy PQ.17. The close escort, under Commander Broome in the destroyer *Keppel*, consisted of six destroyers, two anti-aircraft ships, two submarines and eleven armed trawlers, minesweepers, and corvettes. Four heavy cruisers commanded by Rear-Admiral Dalrymple-Hamilton sailed one hundred miles ahead of the convoy as additional escort. On June 29th Admiral Tovey, Commander-in-Chief Home Fleet, sailed from Scapa Flow with the battleship *Duke of York*, the American battleship *Washington*, the aircraft-carrier *Victorious*, three cruisers and a number of destroyers. This force was to cover the passage of the convoy as far as Bear Island, ready to intervene should the German battle fleet put in an appearance. In addition, nine submarines (including the Free French *Minerve*) were on patrol north-west of the North Cape; and four or five Russian submarines were off the entrance to the fjords in which the German heavy ships were anchored. The total number of warships engaged in covering convoy PQ.17 was considerably greater than that of the merchant ships it contained. In view of the call on Allied resources by the Battle of the Atlantic, the struggle in the Mediterranean and the war in the Pacific, this was an amazing feat of organization.

Twenty-two of the ships in the convoy were American cargo vessels, and two were Russian tankers. There was one British tanker and three rescue ships. The convoy assembled off Iceland according to the usual procedure; some of the ships went round from Reykjavik and through the Denmark Strait towards Jan Mayen Island, while the others sailed from Seydisfjord on the east coast of Iceland and joined up forty-eight hours later.

Matters went badly from the beginning. One merchant ship ran aground while getting away from Reykjavik, and another was badly damaged by ice-floes in the Denmark Strait and had to return to port. So there were only thirty-three ships in the convoy when the commander of the *U-255*, Lieutenant Reinhard Reche, signalled that he had sighted the PQ.17 sixty miles east of Jan Mayen Island. The *U-408* confirmed the report shortly afterwards. No signals had been received from aircraft. Admiral Carls immediately ordered the U-boat pack to attack and to keep shadowing the convoy. This was on July 2nd, when the convoy was five days out. The weather was very bad, but the escort destroyers were fully on the alert and the U-boats had no success. Later in the day, at 18.15 hours, the first dive-bombers appeared. The Fifth Luftflotte kept up its attacks for an hour and a half, but all were beaten off by vigorous anti-aircraft fire.

The following day the convoy reached a position north-west of Bear Island, and turned on to an easterly course. This was always the most dangerous part of the run, for convoys were then at the nearest point to the German air bases. The ice-cap prevented the ships keeping more to the north.

It was particularly dangerous for convoy PQ.17, because the covering force was soon withdrawn. Admiral Tovey's ships were some distance from the convoy and could not be seen by the merchant ships, but their presence was known and was comforting.

The Admiralty's appreciation of the situation was that if the German heavy ships appeared while the convoy was still west of Bear Island the battle would be fought in favourable conditions, because the area was out of range of the German air bases. If, on the other hand, the German warships had not appeared, then Admiral Tovey would withdraw westwards in the hope that the German battle fleet would be drawn in pursuit. In either event, the convoy would escape attack by the German battleships; it would have the U-boats and the bombers to reckon with, but they were not the affair of Admiral Tovey's big ships.

As for Dalrymple-Hamilton's cruisers, their instructions were not to proceed farther than longitude 25 degrees east (that of the North Cape). If, contrary to expectations, the *Tirpitz* then showed up, the convoy would have to scatter and make for the coast of Novaya Zemlya or endeavour independently to reach Archangel. In the event, Dalrymple-Hamilton exceeded his instructions and proceeded as far east as longitude 30, before he was ordered to return. It was then that disaster came upon the convoy.

Meanwhile, on the German side, the two battleships and the two heavy cruisers had left their bases late on July 2nd to concentrate in Alten fjord, nearer to the North Cape. The *Lützow*, however, had scraped her bottom while making her way down the Tjelle-Sund in thick mist, and had to return to Narvik. A similar accident the following day damaged three destroyers in a fjord in the Lofoten Islands. The persistent fog was hampering the German plans. Air reconnaissance was impossible; and for thirty-six hours the convoy had been proceeding without interference. Nevertheless, the Germans did not believe that the Allies would allow their heavy ships within range of Stumpf's dive-bombers—a belief that was correct—and so the *Tirpitz* could put to sea and attack on July 4th or 5th without much risk to herself.

For Hitler would not tolerate losses! He had forbidden an attack by the *Tirpitz* if an enemy aircraft-carrier was in the vicinity, if superiority was not certain, if. . . . How was it possible to make war in such conditions?

The fog lifted on the morning of July 4th. The first air attack on the convoy came when it was north of Bear Island. A torpedo-bomber found a break in the cloud and obtained a hit on the 7,000-ton American cargo ship *Christopher Newport*, laden with tanks, and badly damaged her. A U-boat sank her later in the day.

The convoy continued unmolested until evening. There was low cloud, a calm sea, and no wind. When enemy aircraft next appeared, at 18.00 hours, they met with a hot reception. The U.S. destroyer *Wainwright*, in particular, positively spat fire, "with a gusto worthy of July 4th" (Independence Day). Two hours later, however, the convoy was attacked by twenty-five dive-bombers and three more ships were sunk. Four of the planes were shot down, one by the *Wainwright*, which certainly deserved this success. The three rescue ships did splendid work.

The German aircraft were so occupied with their attacks that they neglected to send back information about the convoy, for which Ad-

The *Tirpitz*

miral Schniewind in the *Tirpitz* was anxiously waiting. He was, however, aware that Admiral Tovey's force had turned westwards at 06·15 hours that morning. He had a report, too, from the air base in the Lofoten Islands that a patrol between longitude 14 and 26 had sighted nothing untoward.

This information was passed to Admiral Carls, who in turn asked permission from higher authority for the battle fleet to put to sea. Admiral Raeder referred it to the Führer. . . .

The convoy, meanwhile, was about to lose the cover provided by the cruisers too. So far, the U-boats had not been successful. The convoy would be liable to air attacks for another twenty-four hours, being within 250 miles of the German bases during that time. But the gunners in the cargo vessels and escort ships had shown great determination and tenacity, and there were hopes of reaching Archangel without further loss. Rear-Admiral Dalrymple-Hamilton remained in the area of the convoy until the evening of the 4th, but at 21.11 hours an Admiralty signal ordered him to return westwards at utmost speed; and twelve minutes later he received instructions to order the convoy to scatter.

At the time of greatest danger, the convoy ships thus found themselves deprived of all the strong cover that had been gathered in their defence. Only the few corvettes and armed trawlers remained in the area.

The reason for the order was that no news of the *Tirpitz* had been received for thirty-six hours; she was believed to be somewhere at sea. From midnight onwards the British heavy ships were expecting to do battle with the Germans.

Whereas, in fact, the *Tirpitz* was still in Alten fjord. Orders to sail were not received until 11.40 on July 5th, and it was one o'clock before the *Tirpitz* and the other warships were clearing the entrance to the fjord and shaping course north-east to intercept convoy PQ.17—by then dispersed all over the Barents Sea. There was no Allied heavy ship within four hundred miles of the North Cape.

However, Admiral Schniewind did not get very far with his squadron. Soon after the Führer had authorized the sailing he summoned Admiral Raeder and repeated that in no event was the *Tirpitz* to be exposed to danger—especially if an enemy aircraft-carrier was within range. . . . Some while later, at 17.00 hours that day, a radio signal was picked up repeating urgently in English the position and course of two enemy battleships and eight destroyers. It was the position of Admiral Schniewind's squadron at that time. So the *Tirpitz* had been sighted—and Admiral Tovey's battle group could be expected to wheel round and proceed at full speed towards the area . . . with the aircraft-carrier. So Hitler could no longer be assured that his fine new battleship was in no danger.

Admiral Raeder, sick at heart, called off the operation.

"On the bridge of the *Admiral Scheer*, the navigating officer, Admiral Kummetz and his Chief-of-Staff were discussing the situation, leaning over the map, when suddenly a signal was flown from the *Tirpitz* ordering the squadron to turn about. The time was 21.51 hours. The order appeared incomprehensible, and had to be repeated. . . ." [1]

At half past eleven the following morning, July 6th, the squadron dropped anchor in Kaa fjord. The crews were disappointed and dismayed.

The cause of it all was the commander of the Russian submarine *K-21*, Lieutenant Lunin. Shortly after four in the afternoon of July 5th he had sighted the *Tirpitz* and fired a torpedo at her, and thought it had found its mark. He later received the decoration of "Hero of the Soviet Union" for the exploit. Nobody in the *Tirpitz*, though, had been aware of the attack, let alone its success. But the effect of the *K-21*'s report of the *Tirpitz* was considerable. Admiral Tovey did in fact turn east again. He had no great hopes of bringing the German squadron to battle, for he was then four hundred and fifty miles away from it; but he believed, justifiably, that if his movements became known to the enemy they would at least deter him from proceeding. And, as the

[1] *Revue Maritime*, May, 1957, p. 582.

reader knows, the German interception of the warning signal was in itself sufficient for the squadron to be recalled.

Nevertheless, although the *Tirpitz* and her group never sighted the convoy, the mere threat of their intervention had had its effect. The convoy was now scattered and deprived of cover, and was soon subjected to a tremendous attack by U-boats and aircraft. Although the *Tirpitz* never fired a shot, she had indirectly contributed to a great German victory.

Fourteen of the convoy ships were sunk on July 5th alone! The first victim on that awful day was one of the faithful rescue ships, the *Zaafara*, which was sunk by dive-bombers. Her crew was saved by the *Zamalek*. Next was the *Carlton*, torpedoed by the *U-334*. Later, six merchant ships were sunk by aircraft, and six by U-boats; one of them was the *River Afton*, carrying the Commodore of the convoy. The American ship *Daniel Morgan*, in particular, put up a magnificent fight against the successive waves of aircraft, and her gunners shot down two of the bombers. They fought on for twenty-eight hours before the ship finally went down, and then the crew struggled and suffered for four days in the lifeboats, fighting against despair and snowstorms, and eventually reaching "the horrible icy realms of Novaya Zemlya", as a report put it.

Two more ships were sunk the following day, July 6th, one by aircraft and the other by a U-boat. Two more were sunk by U-boats on the 7th, and the *Olopana* was torpedoed on the 8th; her captain had refused to take the crew of a sinking ship aboard, three days previously, fearing there might not be room enough in the lifeboats for his own crew. Late on July 9th, bombers sank the U.S.S. *Hoosier* and the Panama ship *El Capitan* when they were within fifty miles of the White Sea and the crews were beginning to think themselves safe.

The first to reach Archangel was the rescue ship *Rathlin*, on July 9th, and was soon followed in by two merchant ships. The remaining ships, which had succeeded in gaining refuge along the desolate coast of Novaya Zemlya or in the Matoohkin Strait, arrived one after the other, the last getting in towards the end of the month. They totalled no more than eleven of the thirty-three which had sailed in the convoy. Of the 200,000 tons of war supplies being carried, only 70,000 reached Russia.

It was a great triumph for Germany, and a heavy blow to the Allies. An aggravating circumstance was that most of the merchant ships lost were American—fourteen out of the twenty-two. The cause of the disaster was undoubtedly the order to the convoy to scatter, which in the event proved to be misconceived. The German planes and submarines were able to operate freely, and had almost equal success. The *U-334* was, however, mistakenly attacked by a Junkers 88 and obliged to return to her base at Kirkenes. Her commander succeeded nevertheless in sinking the *Carlton* and taking the skipper prisoner.[1]

The cynical attitude of Stalin must have disgusted and disheartened the Allied seamen. The Russian leader refused to believe there had been thirty-three ships in convoy PQ.17—there were, he said, certainly not more than fifteen! Yet the courageous men of the Merchant Navy continued to take supplies to Russia through the dangerous, frozen wastes. Early in September a convoy of thirty-nine ships, the PQ.18, sailed from Iceland; in spite of being given a strong escort, including for the first time one of the new carriers with twelve fighters—the *Avenger*—twelve of the convoy were lost to aircraft and U-boat attacks.

For the next three months there were no convoys to Russia, as priority was being given to the requirements of the North Africa landings. But they were resumed in late December, and the Germans mounted an operation similar to Rösselsprung. Admiral Kummetz put to sea with the *Hipper* and the *Lützow* and some destroyers, but in a series of sharp engagements they were driven away from the convoy by destroyers and the two 6-inch cruisers *Jamaica* and *Sheffield*, commanded by Rear-Admiral Burnett. The convoy reached port without loss, much to Hitler's fury, as did the next convoy in January.

The *Scharnhorst* was sent in March, 1943, to join the Norway-based ships, but it was not until September that the German heavy ships again appeared in the Arctic Sea. The *Tirpitz* and the *Scharnhorst*, with a screen of ten destroyers, carried out a raid on the meteorological station at Spitzbergen. Soon after their return to Alten fjord, the *Tirpitz* was badly damaged as a result of a daring attack by British midget submarines, during the night of September 21st. Lieutenant Place, R.N., and Lieutenant Cameron, R.N.R., were awarded the Victoria Cross for this gallant exploit. The German battleship was repaired, but was attacked and again damaged by Fleet Air Arm planes in April, 1944, and was finally sunk on November 12th, when at Tromsoe, by R.A.F. Lancasters using very heavy bombs.

In late December the German Naval Command decided to risk the *Scharnhorst* in an attack on a convoy to Russia, the JW.55B, which had been sighted by the Luftwaffe. On the morning of December 26th, the

---

[1] The following U-boats took part in the attack on convoy PQ.17. *U-88*, Lieutenant Heino Bohman; *U-251*, Lt. Heinrich Timm; *U-253*, Lt. Adolf Friedrichs; *U-255*, Lt. Reinhart Reche; *U-334*, Lt. Hilmar Siemon; *U-376*, Lt. Friedrich Karl Marks; *U-408*, Lt. Reinhard von Hymmen; *U-456*, Lt. Max-Martin Teichert; *U-457*, Lt. Karl Brandenburg; *U-703*, Lt. Heinz Biefeld. They were ocean-going submarines of 750 tons, type VII/C. The majority belonged to the Eleventh U-boat Flotilla, commanded by Commander Hans Eduard Cohausz, based on Bergen.

Scharnhorst attempted to close the convoy but was driven off by the escorting cruisers commanded by Rear-Admiral Burnett. All that afternoon the battleship *Duke of York* was moving up at high speed to intercept; with the cruiser *Jamaica* and four destroyers, under the orders of Admiral Sir Bruce Fraser, she was providing distant cover for the convoy. The destroyers delivered a torpedo attack on the *Scharnhorst*, gallantly facing her powerful armament, and obtained hits which

reduced her speed. This enabled the *Duke of York* to close the range. The *Scharnhorst* fought a lone battle to the end, against the battleship, four cruisers, and eight destroyers. She was set on fire by the *Duke of York*'s heavy salvoes, and finally sunk by a torpedo fired by the cruiser *Jamaica*, going down by the bows just as her predecessor had done at the Battle of Falkland. She turned over, and the last seen of her were the three propellers, still turning.

The British ships found only 36 of the *Scharnhorst*'s crew of 1,900 to rescue from the icy, raging waters. Rear-Admiral Bey, Captain Hintze, and all her officers were among the missing.

"Auf einem Seemansgrab, da blühen keine Rosen. . . ."[1]

---

[1] "Roses do not flower on a sailor's grave"—a song of the German Navy. See *La Tragique Destinée du "Scharnhorst"*, by A. Vulliez and J. Mordal: Le Livre Contemporain, Paris.

XXIX

THE BATTLE OF MIDWAY, A TRIUMPH FOR AIRCRAFT-CARRIERS

Japanese carriers approach Pearl Harbor—"This is no exercise"—the U.S. battleships are destroyed, but the carriers remain intact—the Japanese advance across the Pacific and into the Indian Ocean—Australia is threatened—thirty seconds over Tokyo—the Japanese plan of attack on Midway Island—the Battle of the Coral Sea, the first between aircraft-carriers—Japanese advance halted—the Yorktown is repaired in two days, instead of the three months that was feared—overwhelming strength of the Japanese—the invasion force is sighted—diversionary attack on the Aleutians—the Glorious Fourth of June—unsuccessful attacks by aircraft from the "carrier" Midway—bombers from the Enterprise do better—four Japanese carriers sunk—"Operation Midway is called off"—the Japanese in retreat—alternating fortunes at Guadalcanal—steady progress of the U.S. Forces—the Battle of Leyte Gulf—Okinawa to Hiroshima.

THE coral atoll of Midway appears as a tiny speck on a map of the Pacific Ocean, a dot about halfway between the United States and Japan—hence its name. It consists of two islets, within its barrier-reef: Sandy Island and East Island, both less than two miles long. Midway was discovered in 1859 by a schooner from Hawaii, and has been an American possession since 1867. It forms an outpost 1,135 miles west of Pearl Harbor, and between the two is a line of stepping-stones, the atolls of Lisianski, Maro, Gardner Pinnacles, Necker Reef, Nihoa, Niihau. . . .

One of the most decisive battles of the world was fought near Midway Island on June 4th–6th, 1942. If not the biggest it was certainly the most important battle of the war in the Pacific. It brought to an end the run of Japanese victories, and also showed that henceforth the aircraft-carrier would be a decisive factor in sea warfare. At the Battle of Midway, Japan lost the war in the Pacific, and the battleship its place of "capital ship".

To understand the full significance of the American victory at Midway, a summary of the events in the Pacific following the Japanese attack on Pearl Harbor would be useful.

When the commander-in-chief of the Japanese Fleet, Admiral Iso-roku Yamamoto, realized that war with the United States would not be long in coming, he prepared a bold plan—to seize the two advanced bases of the U.S. Navy, Guam and Wake Island, and to destroy the U.S. Pacific Fleet based on Pearl Harbor, in the Hawaii Islands. It would have been even better to seize Pearl Harbor too, but that base was four thousand miles from Japan, and so an operation of considerable magnitude would have been necessary. Admiral Yamamoto decided that the required result could be obtained by a surprise attack on the U.S. Fleet, and in particular on the aircraft-carriers.

The Japanese High Command made these plans in January, 1941. During the eighteen months of the war in the West, aircraft-carriers had been in action but had not been employed to their full potential. Nevertheless, the attack on Taranto by aircraft from the *Illustrious* was a forerunner of the greater attack on Pearl Harbor a year later.

Although it was possible to wage an aero-naval war in the Mediterranean without carriers,[1] it was quite out of the question in the Pacific, where enormous distances separated the opposing sides. This Japan had realized long before the war, and had prepared accordingly. By December, 1941, she had twice as many carriers as her enemies.

The distance involved meant that the attacking force had to be well on its way before the actual declaration of war. The surprise attack on Pearl Harbor took place on December 7th, 1941, but the operational plan had been approved on November 3rd, and on the 10th the force began to assemble in Tankan Bay, in a remote part of the Kurile archipelago. At nine on the morning of the 26th the ships put to sea to begin their eleven days' crossing. The force consisted of 6 large carriers with a total of 450 planes, a considerable number for those days, and of an escort of 2 battleships and 9 destroyers. Its commander-in-chief was Vice-Admiral Nagumo, wearing his flag in the carrier *Akagi*.

Meanwhile, negotiations were still going on in Washington. The Japanese ambassador had handed a Note to the United States Government on November 20th, by which General Tojo, the Japanese Prime Minister, agreed to withdraw his troops from Indo-China if the United States raised the economic sanctions applied against Japan—the freezing of credits and an embargo on raw materials vital to the Japanese economy. Mr. Cordell Hull's reply, delivered on November 26th, was considered unsatisfactory by the Japanese military junta, which was openly pressing for war. The irrevocable step was taken on December 1st, and on the 3rd Admiral Yamamoto sent Nagumo a message containing just the three words "Niitaka Yama Nohore" (Climb Mount Niitaka), which was the order for the attack to go in as agreed, at sunrise on Monday, December 8th. This would be 07.50 hours by

[1] As was the case with Italy and Germany, though they lost it.

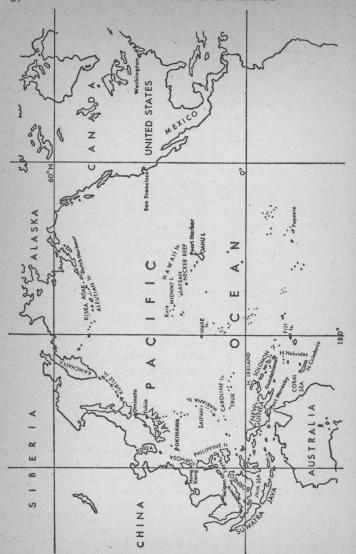

Japanese time, but in Washington it would be 13.20 on Sunday, December 7th.

With this difference of time in mind, the Japanese ambassador, Nomura, had asked to be received by Mr. Cordell Hull at 13.00 hours on December 7th, thus being able to inform the United States Government that a state of war existed with Japan just twenty minutes before the first bombs were to to be dropped on Pearl Harbor. But American Intelligence had managed to break the Japanese code, and it was known in Washington that at 13.00 hours Nomura would hand Cordell Hull something closely resembling a declaration of war; and an officer happened to remark that 13.00 hours in Washington was dawn at Pearl Harbor, a likely moment for a surprise attack. The Army Chief-of-Staff, General Marshall, could not be found; he had gone out riding, as he did every Sunday morning. It was 11.30 before he arrived at his office, and he, too, was convinced that something serious was afoot. A warning message was immediately despatched; but by then it was midday—06.30 by Honolulu time. The bombs had arrived first.

For various reasons the Japanese ambassador was not received until 14.20 hours. And by that time Mr. Cordell Hull had already been handed a message from the commander-in-chief, Pacific Fleet, which read: "Air attack on Pearl Harbor. This is no exercise."

It was so far from being an exercise that the main body of the Fleet had been annihilated. Of the battleships, the *Arizona* was sunk, the *Oklahoma* had capsized, the *California*, the *Nevada*, and the *West Virginia* were all aground; three of the heavy cruisers had been damaged, and 188 aircraft destroyed on the ground; 3,303 men were dead or missing, and 1,272 wounded.

After an uneventful passage, Nagumo had arrived unchallenged at the position from which he was to launch his attack, 175 miles north of Pearl Harbor. The 6 carriers turned into the wind and flew off their aircraft. H-Hour was at 07.50, and the first wave of 183 planes was over Pearl Harbor dead on time. The Americans were taken completely by surprise. But, to Nagumo's great

Admiral Chester W. Nimitz, commander-in-chief of the U.S. Pacific Fleet

disappointment, the two carriers *Lexington* and *Enterprise*, the king-pins of the Pacific Fleet, were not in harbour. By a great stroke of luck, the *Enterprise* was still on return passage from Wake Island, where she had taken a dozen Wildcat fighters as reinforcements; and the *Lexington* was on her way to Midway for a similar purpose. The *Saratoga* had only just left the United States to join the Pacific Fleet.[1]

Nagumo was well aware that by not destroying the carriers he had not inflicted the mortal blow that was intended. He had in fact hesitated when, the previous night, he had learnt of their absence. Events were to show that his disappointment was justified.

While the attack on Pearl Harbor was taking place, Guam was being bombed by Japanese aircraft based on Saipan, another of the Mariana Islands. After forty-eight hours of softening-up, troops were landed from ships under the command of Admiral Goto, and had little difficulty in capturing the island. Captain McMillin, of the U.S. Navy, had barely eight hundred men to defend Guam, and decided against a glorious, though useless, resistance.

It was not quite so easy at Wake Island. Although a heavy preliminary raid was carried out by the 24th Bombing Flotilla based at Kwadjalein in the Marshall Islands, the invasion forces commanded by Admiral Kajioka met with a hot reception on December 11th. After an hour and a half's fighting, six ships including a troop transport had been badly damaged by the shore batteries. Then a destroyer was sunk. Admiral Kajioka started to withdraw and lost another ship, sunk by one of the few remaining planes of those brought by the *Enterprise* a few days earlier.

The news of this determined defence raised morale at Pearl Harbour. Admiral Kimmel, still with three carriers under his command, decided to send the *Lexington* to make a show of force north of the Marshall Islands, to retain the *Enterprise* for the defence of Hawaii, and to send the *Saratoga* to Wake Island with more aircraft. She left on December 16th.

In the meantime, Kajioka sailed again from Kwadjalein, his force considerably strengthened by Admiral Goto's four heavy cruisers which had returned from Guam, and by two carriers which had been in Nagumo's task force. The attack on Wake Island was renewed on December 23rd, when the *Saratoga* was still 450 miles distant.

It was no doubt too late to save Wake. But the *Saratoga* was in a position where her aircraft could attack the Japanese ships; and both the

---

[1] The Japanese had also hoped to find the *Yorktown* and the *Hornet* at Pearl Harbor; but they were then in the Atlantic.

Lexington and the *Enterprise* could speed to support the attack. Such was Kimmel's plan; and it could have resulted in the first aircraft-carrier battle in history. An American victory at that moment would have abruptly changed the situation, by halting the Japanese advance in the Pacific in less than a fortnight. It might have had the same effect as the Battle of Midway, but six months earlier. The American attack might also have ended in disaster, and then the war in the Pacific would have been lost.

But Kimmel was no longer in command. Roosevelt had replaced him on December 17th by Admiral Chester Nimitz, who had still to arrive at Pearl Harbor. Admiral Pye, in temporary command, had not recovered from the loss of his battleships, which included his own flagship; he was in no position to risk losing the three aircraft-carriers. He recalled them, and Wake Island fell to the Japanese on December 23rd. One wonders whether it had been wise to change horses in midstream.

Meanwhile, events moved fast. The Japanese conquered the Philippines in little more than a fortnight; Manila fell on January 2nd, 1942.[1] A Japanese army had invaded Malaya on December 8th, and a few days later advanced on Singapore. The garrison of nearly one hundred thousand had to surrender unconditionally on February 15th. The battleship *Prince of Wales* and the battle-cruiser *Repulse* were sunk off Malaya by torpedo-carrying aircraft on December 10th. Hong Kong, which was also attacked on December 8th, surrendered on Christmas Day. On January 10th the Japanese invaded the Dutch East Indies; at the end of the month they were off New Guinea attacking the principal seaports, and early in February they invaded Burma. On February 27th began the disastrous Battle of the Java Sea, where the Allied forces under the Dutch Admiral Helfrich and commanded at sea by his compatriot Karl Doorman were destroyed after three days' fighting. This battle sealed the fate of the Dutch East Indies; Java capitulated on March 9th.

Australia was beginning to be alarmed. Japanese forces were landing at Kavieng in New Ireland, at Rabaul in New Britain, and on the northern coast of New Guinea. The Americans hastily sent reinforcements to New Caledonia, the last island barrier on the Japanese advance to Australia.

By the end of March, 1942, Nagumo was operating in the Bay of Bengal with all his carriers except the *Kaga*, which was being repaired. On April 5th he bombarded Ceylon, and on the same day sank the

[1] The gallant defence of the U.S. troops in the Bataan peninsula, which lasted until May 6th, 1942, made little difference to the situation.

cruisers *Dorsetshire* and *Cornwall*; on the 9th he sank the *Hermes*, the first carrier to be sunk by aircraft from another carrier. The small British carrier had not had a single plane on board, all her aircraft having already been destroyed on the ground at Trincomalee; and as everyone knows, there is nothing so sadly powerless as an aircraft-carrier without aircraft!

The Allies could not foretell which direction the enemy advance would take next. Even in Tokyo opinions were divided as to whether it should be to the south and Australia or to the east and Hawaii. Yamamoto was in favour of the latter, and advocated a diversion in the Aleutians and an attack on Midway Island. But there was a strong body of opinion for directing efforts southwards. As a preliminary to a direct assault on Australia, that continent would first be isolated by cutting the sea communications with America and by gaining air-supremacy over the northern waters, especially the Coral Sea, between Australia and New Guinea, the eastern Solomon Islands and New Caledonia.

While these projects were being studied, an incident took place on April 18th which had very slight effect at the time but was greatly indicative of things to come. That morning a small Japanese ship on patrol more than 700 miles east of Tokyo reported an enemy naval force proceeding at great speed in the direction of Japan. A general alarm was given. Vice-Admiral Kondo had just returned to Yokosuka with the Second Fleet after his victory in the Java Sea, and he at once put to sea again. Vice-Admiral Takasu sailed from Hiroshima with the First Fleet, which contained four battleships. Nagumo was off Formosa, on his way back from the India Ocean, and there was great excitement aboard his flagship, the *Akagi*. The enemy was too far off, though; and at one in the afternoon the reason for his presence became known—Tokyo had been bombed! It was the first counter-blow by the United States, the famous raid led by Lieutenant-Colonel Doolittle; the bombers had been brought within range by the carriers *Hornet* and *Enterprise*, commanded by Admiral Halsey. Thirty seconds over Tokyo—it was not long, and most of the population had not even known of the raid, but it was a distinct pointer. The enemy had begun to take the initiative; there was one way to put a stop to that—by pushing him back to the east, by capturing Midway. Yamamoto was "obsessed by the idea of preventing another air attack on Tokyo, and felt affronted by Doolittle's raid".[1] He was also anxious to gain a

---

[1] *Midway, the Battle that doomed Japan*, by Mitsuo Fuchida and Matasake Okumiya, U.S. Naval Institute, Annapolis.

dominating position before the industrial power of the United States could swing the balance of forces against Japan. This time he was able to make his ideas prevail.

Yamamoto was convinced that an invasion of Midway would bring out the U.S. Pacific Fleet, and that his superior strength in carriers would then enable him to gain a decisive victory. At the end of April, 1942, Japan had seven large and four small carriers in the Pacific, while all reports showed that the United States had only four.[1]

More than 200 ships were employed in the operation, including 11 battleships, 8 carriers, 22 cruisers, 65 destroyers, and 21 submarines. The number of aircraft was about 700. The commander-in-chief, Yamamoto, flew his flag in the *Yamato*, a new 65,000-ton battleship that was the largest and most powerful afloat. Vice-Admiral Nagumo was in command of the carrier force, Kondo of the invasion force, while Hosogaya directed the diversionary attack on the Aleutians. The full Order of Battle of both the Japanese and the United States Forces is shown on the following pages.

ORDER OF BATTLE AT MIDWAY

JAPANESE FORCES

I. *Battle Fleet (Admiral Isoroku Yamamoto)*
   Battleships *Yamato* (flagship), *Negato*, *Mutsu*.
   Light aircraft-carrier *Hosho*.
   Light cruiser *Sendai*, and nine destroyers.
   Seaplane-carriers *Chivoda* and *Nisshin*, transporting midget-submarines.
   Covering force (Vice-Admiral Shiro Takasu).
   Battleships *Hyuga* (flagship), *Ise*, *Fuso*, *Yamashiro*.
   Light cruisers *Oi*, *Kitakami*, and twelve destroyers.

II. *First Carrier Assault Group (Vice-Admiral Chuichi Nagumo)*
   1st Division—*Akagi* (flagship) and *Kaga*, one hundred and thirty-five aircraft.
   2nd Division—*Hiryu* (Rear-Admiral Tamon Yamaguchi) and *Soryu*, one hundred and twenty-six aircraft.
   Support group—heavy cruiser *Tone* (Rear-Admiral Hiroaki Abe), battleships *Haruna* and *Kirishima*, light cruiser *Chikuma*.

---

[1] The Japanese believed these to be the *Yorktown*, *Saratoga*, *Hornet*, and *Enterprise*. A Japanese submarine had torpedoed a carrier off Hawaii on January 11th and reported her to be the *Lexington*. In fact, she was the *Saratoga*, and had not been sunk but badly damaged. She was in the repair yards for some months, and was back in service when the attack on Midway began, but sailed from the U.S. too late to take part in the battle.

Screening force—light cruiser *Nagara* (Rear-Admiral Susumu Kimura) and eleven destroyers.

III. *Invasion Force (Vice-Admiral Nobukate Kondo)*
Heavy cruisers *Atago* (flagship), *Chokai*, *Myoko*, *Haguro*.
Battleships *Kongo*, *Hiei*.
Light aircraft-carrier *Zuiho*, twenty-four aircraft.
Light cruiser *Yura*, and eight destroyers.
Close-support group (Vice-Admiral Takeo Kurita).
Heavy cruisers *Kumano* (flagship), *Suzuya*, *Mikuma*, *Mogami*.
Two destroyers.
Transport Group (Rear-Admiral Raizo Tanaka).
Twelve troop transports (carrying 5,000 men) and three destroyers.
Light cruiser *Jintsu* (flagship) and ten destroyers.
Seaplane-carrier Group (Rear-Admiral Ruitaro Fujita).
Chitose and *Kamikawa Maru*, thirty-two planes.
One destroyer and a patrol vessel.
Minesweeper Group (Captain Sadatomo Miyamoto)
Four minesweepers. Three anti-submarine vessels.
One supply ship and two cargo vessels.

IV. *North Force (Aleutians) (Vice-Admiral Moshiro Hosogaya)*.
Heavy cruiser *Nachi* (flagship) and two destroyers.
Second Carrier Assault Group (Rear-Admiral Kakuji Kakuta).
Light carriers *Ryujo* (flagship) and *Junyo*, eighty aircraft.
Heavy cruisers *Maya* and *Takao*. Three destroyers.
Attu Invasion Force (Rear-Admiral Sentaro Omori).
Light cruiser *Abukuma* (flagship).
Four destroyers. One mine-layer. One troop transport (1,200 men).
Kisha Invasion Force (Captain Takeji Ono).
Light cruisers *Kiso* (flagship) and *Tama*.
Auxiliary cruiser *Asaka Maru*. Three destroyers.
Three minesweepers. Two troop transports (1,250 men).
Submarine Group (Rear-Admiral Shigeaki Yamazaki).
Submarines *I-9* (Yamazaki), *I-15*, *I-17*, *I-19*, *I-25*, *I-26*.

V. *Submarine-screen Group (Vice-Admiral Teruhisa Komatsu)*
Third Submarine Flotilla (Rear-Admiral Chimaki Kono, in Submarine Depot-ship *Yasukuni Maru* at Kwadjalein).
I-168, *I-169*, *I-171*, *I-174*, *I-175*.
Fifth Submarine Flotilla (Rear-Admiral Tadashige Daigo, in Submarine Depot-ship *Rio de Janeiro Maru* at Kwadjalein).

I-156, I-157, I-158, I-159, I-162, I-165, I-166.
Thirteenth Submarine Division (Captain Takeharu Miyazaki).
I-121, I-122, I-173.
Shore-based Aircraft (Vice-Admiral Nishizo Tsukahara)
Two hundred and sixteen aircraft based on Wale, Jaluit, Kwad-
jalein, Aur, and Wotje.

UNITED STATES FORCES

I. *Carrier Group (Rear-Admiral Fletcher)*[1]
    Task Force 17-2.
    Task Group 17-5: *Yorktown* (flagship), seventy-five aircraft.
    Task Group 17-2: cruisers *Astoria* and *Portland* (Rear-Admiral
    William W. Smith).
    Task Group 17-4: six destroyers.
    Task Force 16.
    Task Group 16-5: *Enterprise* (Rear-Admiral Raymond A. Spru-
    ance), seventy-nine aircraft, and *Hornet*, sixty-nine aircraft.
    Task Group 16-2: cruisers *New Oreleans, Minneapolis, Vincennes,
    Northampton, Pensacola, Atlanta* (Rear-Admiral Thomas C. Kin-
    kaid).
    Task Group 16-4: nine destroyers.

II. *Supply Group*
    Two tankers escorted by two destroyers.

III. *Submarine Group*
    Nineteen submarines under the orders of Rear-Admiral Robert H.
    English.

IV. *Aircraft Based on Midway*
    One hundred and nineteen aircraft, including thirty-two Catalina
    flying-boats and nineteen Flying Fortresses.

V.   *Garrisons and Units for the defence of Midway Island and the chain of
    atoll-outposts west of Pearl Harbour.*

VI. *North Pacific Force constituted on May 17th for the defence of the Aleutian
    Islands (Rear-Admiral Robert A. Theobald)*
    Heavy cruisers *Indianapolis* and *Louisville.*
    Light cruisers *Honolulu, St. Louis, Nashville.*
    Ten destroyers.

D-Day was fixed for June 7th. The various forces therefore put to
sea between May 26th and 29th:

[1] Vice-Admiral Halsey should have had the command, but was ill.

The North Force (Hosogaya) from Ominato, at the northern end of Honshu (the southern of the two main Japanese islands).

The Midway invasion force (except for Vice-Admiral Kondo's group) from Saipan and Guam, in the Marianas.

The groups under Yamamoto, Nagumo, and Kondo, from Harashima, on the Sea of Japan.

The first attacks were to be made against the Aleutian Islands, that being the diversion from the main attack on Midway. The time-table was therefore as follows:

D-Day minus three (June 4th)—bomb attack on the U.S. base of Dutch Harbour, in the eastern Aleutians, by carrier aircraft of Rear-Admiral Kakuta's Assault Group.

D-Day minus two—attack on Midway by carrier aircraft of Nagumo's group.

D-Day minus one—landings on Adak and Kiska in the Aleutians; occupation of Kure atoll (sixty miles west of Midway) by Fujita's seaplanes.

D-Day—landings on Midway.

But first there was the curtain-raiser to the overall plan of the Japanese—Plan MO. The idea of a southern advance towards Australia had not been entirely abandoned when Yamamoto's plan to attack Midway was accepted; and at the beginning of May the Fourth Fleet commanded by Admiral Shigeyoshi Inouye was given the mission of invading Tulagi Island in the eastern Solomons and Port Moresby on the southern coast of New Guinea.[1] Tulagi was occupied without any difficulty on May 3rd. The following day an invasion convoy sailed from Rabaul to attack Port Moresby; there were fourteen transports escorted by six destroyers. In support were the carrier *Shoho* and four cruisers which had left Truk, in the Carolines, on April 30th under the command of Admiral Goto, and two large carriers, the *Zuikaku* and the *Shokaku*, escorted by two heavy cruisers and six destroyers, this force being under the orders of Vice-Admiral Takeo Takagi.

The Japanese were unaware, however, that the Americans had broken their code and could read their messages like an open book. So Admiral Nimitz knew in advance their every move, and concentrated his available forces on meeting the threat to Port Moresby. He had little enough—the two carriers *Yorktown* and *Lexington*, and three

[1] The Japanese had already landed troops on the northern coast, but progress was terribly slow through the thick jungle and over the high mountain ranges.

cruisers, the American *Chicago* and the Australian *Hobart* and *Australia*. Halsey was not then back with the *Hornet* and the *Enterprise* from the raid on Tokyo.[1]

Rear-Admiral Fletcher was in the south-east area of the Coral Sea with the *Yorktown*. When informed of the Japanese landings on Tulagi, he at once sent a striking force against the enemy position. A few small Japanese craft were destroyed—after great expenditure of ammunition —and the presence of the *Yorktown* was revealed. Takagi's carriers moved in that direction. At dawn on May 7th his reconnaissance planes sighted the American squadron. The carriers flew off seventy-eight aircraft for the attack—but the reconnaissance planes had sighted a tanker and a destroyer, not the *Yorktown*. The seventy-eight aircraft sank the destroyer *Sims*, but failed to hit the tanker.

While the Japanese were thus occupied with a secondary target, the Americans had found a far more important one—the carrier *Shoho*. At eleven in the morning she was attacked by aircraft from the *Lexington*, and was sunk half an hour later by those from the *Yorktown*. Rear-Admiral Fletcher had scored a point; it was the first time that an American carrier had attacked a Japanese one. It was also the first American success of any note after five disastrous months.

But the Battle of the Coral Sea was not over. The next day, May 8th, there was reciprocal and almost simultaneous attack by aircraft of the carriers on either side. This time the Japanese had the advantage; although the *Shokaku* was hit three times and had to withdraw, the *Yorktown* was badly damaged and the *Lexington* so much that she had to be abandoned, and was eventually despatched by a U.S. destroyer. The American force was obliged to withdraw from the area. But it had inflicted damage enough for the attack on Port Moresby to be called off; the invasion convoy steamed away again. For the first time, Japanese plans had gone awry. In this battle between carriers—the first in which the opposing commanders had not been within a hundred miles of each other—the Japanese had marked a tactical success, but they had been halted in their triumphant advance. And the Battle of Midway was to begin the drive back.

The Japanese still lacked information on the latest situation of the U.S. Fleet at Hawaii. Their submarines were only able to send frag-mentary reports, and the distance was too great for their reconnaissance planes. Yamamoto's staff officers turned to a plan which had already been put into operation in March, when long-range flying-boats had been sent to bomb Oahu. A submarine had been waiting to

[1] They did not reach Pearl Harbor until April 25th.

refuel them along the route, at Necker Reef.[1] However, the Americans had in the meantime discovered how the flying-boats had been re-fuelled, and were using the lagoon for their own reconnaissance flights. When one of the Japanese supply submarines, the *I-123*, reached Necker Reef on May 30th its commander found two U.S. tenders already in possession. The reconnaissance over Hawaii had to be given up; and Yamamoto's intelligence on his opponent's dispositions was far less complete than the Americans' on his own.

The two Japanese carriers damaged during the Battle of the Coral Sea were not available for the Midway operation, but Admiral Nimitz was still outnumbered in carriers. The *Saratoga* was undergoing repairs on the West Coast, and the *Yorktown* had been reported as needing ninety days in dock for her repairs. It looked as though the *Hornet* and the *Enterprise* would be the only carriers available. Nimitz appealed to the engineers and ship-repairers; and they performed the first amazing feat in the Midway operation. The damaged *Yorktown* docked at Pearl Harbor on the afternoon of May 27th, and was at once taken over by an army of engineers, welders, and shipwrights—1,400 craftsmen who worked the clock round and got the carrier ready for sea again in forty-eight hours, instead of the three months envisaged. The *Yorktown* left dock on May 29th, took on supplies and aircraft, and was away to sea on the 30th, wearing the flag of Rear-Admiral Fletcher and making for the position assigned to her north-east of Midway.

Nevertheless, Admiral Nimitz's fleet was still greatly inferior in strength to the vast array that Yamamoto was about to deploy:

> Battleships, nil[2]—against 11.
> Carriers, 3—against 8.
> Cruisers, 13—against 22.
> Destroyers, 28—against 65.
> Submarines, 19—against 21.
> Aircraft, 338—against 700.

If the opposing battle fleets sighted each other, if the U.S. ships came within range of the powerful Japanese battleships, it would soon be over—Japan would have won the war in the Pacific.

Yet Nimitz had a trump or two in his hand. First, there was Midway itself—an aircraft-carrier that, although immobile, was unsinkable;

[1] These islets, Necker or French Frigates Reef, were discovered in 1786 by the French explorer Lapérouse, while on a voyage across the Pacific with the frigates *Boussole* and *Astrolabe*. They are situated 490 miles west of Pearl Harbor; even before the war, the lagoon had been marked as an emergency mooring for flying-boats.

[2] The battleships of the U.S. Pacific Fleet (Vice-Admiral Pye) which had escaped the disaster at Pearl Harbor were in any case too slow to sail with the carriers. After due consideration, Nimitz had sent them back to San Francisco.

and there were two excellent radars installed on the island. Secondly, he was kept well informed. As early as May 20th he knew the exact Japanese Order of Battle, though not that Yamamoto would be leading it in person aboard the *Yamato*. On May 23rd the commander of the aircraft based on Midway, Rear-Admiral Bellinger, had been able to make a very close appreciation of the enemy's intentions. There can be no doubt, as the naval historian, Samuel E. Morison, wrote,[1] that without the early and abundant information obtained, and the rapid and intelligent use made of it by Admiral Nimitz and his Staff, the U.S. Pacific Fleet would have had very little chance of gaining a victory.

Everything depended upon the constant air patrols which were maintained over a semi-circle 700 miles out from Midway. Rear-Admiral Spruance and Fletcher were with the carriers north-east of Midway, ready to inflict the greatest possible damage on the enemy as soon as he was reported.

The U.S. forces were fully alert this time. By putting to sea on May 26th the Japanese had already lost the major element of surprise.

The signal that sparked off this memorable battle was sent at 09.00 hours on June 3rd[2] by Lieutenant Jack Reid, who was on patrol in his Catalina some 700 miles west of Midway. He had already continued beyond the time when he should have started to return to base, and then sighted what he took to be the main enemy force about thirty miles away. It was in fact Rear-Admiral Tanaka's invasion convoy. The Catalina started to shadow it, while sending urgent reports.

A few hours later the first bombs fell, dropped by nine B.17s—Flying Fortresses—from Midway, which found the invasion convoy at 16 24 hours when it was 570 miles from the island. The attack was unsuccessful, though the optimistic aviators reported hits on two battleships and two troop transports. Tanaka had no battleships in his group. But it would not be the last mistake in identification, nor the last un successful bombing attack, in this battle which was destined to continue for three days.

The sketch-maps on the following pages, which are reproduced from the book on the Battle of Midway by Fuchida and Okumiya, show the approach on Midway and the Aleutian Islands by the Japanese Task Forces. It will be noticed that the routes taken extended over thirty degrees of latitude—which explains the varied weather met with by the different forces. It was poor weather on the whole. The ships

---

[1] *History of United States Naval Operations in World War II*, by Samuel E. Morison, Vol. IV, p. 80.
[2] Western Hemisphere date, 12 hours ahead of G.M.T.

ran into a belt of rain on the afternoon of May 30th, and the sea became so rough that Yamamoto was obliged to reduce speed to fourteen knots. Then the mist thickened; it was so bad in the area that Vice-Admiral Nagumo's carriers were passing through that the ships, five hundred yards apart, were barely visible to one another. In such conditions it was impossible to fly off patrols. The pilots passed the time

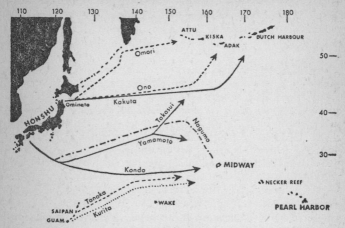

Battle of Midway, June 4th, 1942—the Japanese Fleet puts to sea

playing cards, while on the bridge of the *Akagi* their Vice-Admiral was wondering what the curtain of mist concealed. He knew nothing of the enemy dispositions, and could not communicate with the commander-in-chief because radio silence was still imposed. For that reason, Yamamoto, six hundred miles to the west, did not inform him of the sudden increase in enemy radio activity which was noted by the powerful receivers in the flagship. American "Urgent" signals were being picked up from many sectors—a sure indication that something was afoot, that very likely the U.S. Pacific Fleet had put to sea. Nothing of this was picked up by the *Akagi*'s radio operators; and Nagumo, who was the commander chiefly concerned, continued his advance like a blind man in a tunnel. The first he knew of the American activity was the report of the bomb attack on Tanaka's transports. It was a bitter disappointment; the Japanese had hoped to remain undetected until their first attack on Midway, and now they would obviously find the enemy on the alert. But it was too late to turn back; the die was cast.

Twelve hundred miles to the north, Vice-Admiral Hosogaya's invasion convoy had almost reached the position from where aircraft from the carriers *Ryujo* and *Junyo* were to fly off to raid Dutch Harbour. This, for the Japanese, was to be the opening of the whole operation. In that latitude, 52 degrees north, daybreak comes very early in June, and the first striking force was expected to fly off soon after 02.00 hours. But the weather was no better than in Nagumo's area; and when the planes were finally airborne, at 02.45, the ceiling was so low that

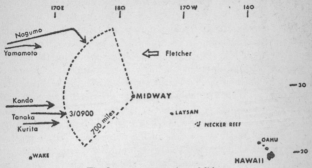

The Japanese approach on Midway

instead of flying in formation they had to make their way independently to the objective 180 miles distant. Hardly had they disappeared than U.S. aircraft were sighted over the Japanese carriers. So here, too, the enemy was expecting them!

The Japanese attack was nevertheless satisfactory. The pilots found the sky clear over Dutch Harbour, and considerable damage was caused to installations. The Japanese diversion might well have been taken for the main attack if Tanaka's transports had not been sighted heading towards Midway. As it was, Nimitz remained prepared for Nagumo's attack, and air patrols were searching the sea for the Japanese carriers; they were eventually sighted at 05.34 hours on June 4th by a Catalina pilot belonging to the same squadron as Lieutenant Reid.

The morning of June 4th was bright and clear, and it looked as though a fine day were in prospect for what the Japanese hoped to be a glorious date in their military annals, but which turned out to be a memorable one in the history of the United States. The sun was shining from a blue sky. There was a force three breeze from the south-east, and visibility was very good—35 to 40 miles. A little too good, in fact, for the commanders of aircraft-carriers, who preferred it less distinct. Rear-Admiral Fletcher had been steering south-west during the night to reach a position 200 miles north of Midway by dawn, being convinced that Nagumo's carriers would then be approaching from the north-west to attack the island that day. The Japanese commander was in fact 240 miles north-west of Midway when, at 04.30 hours, he flew off the first striking force.

At the beginning of this momentous day, Nagumo's four carriers were therefore opposed by four U.S. carriers—the *Yorktown, Hornet*, and *Enterprise*, which were 180 miles to the east, and the unsinkable Midway, 240 miles to the south-east. So that in spite of their overwhelming superiority initially, the Japanese opened the decisive battle without even the advantage in aircraft, having only 262 against the 338 of the Americans, and with only the two battleships and two heavy cruisers of Nagumo's group in close support of the carriers. After all the careful, detailed planning, the Japanese had begun the main battle with their huge forces dispersed, while the Americans had concentrated all their available strength at the right place and at the right time.

The first planes flown off the *Akagi* were 10 Zero fighters—thus called by U.S. airmen because the nose of the plane had a circle round it. They were followed by 18 Val dive-bombers carrying 500-pound bombs, commanded by Lieutenant Takehito Chihaya. The *Hiryu*, 4,000 yards to port of the *Akagi*, was flying off her aircraft at the same time; as were the *Kaga* and the *Soryu*, astern of the others. In all, the first striking force, which was airborne at 04.45, consisted of 108 aircraft—36 Val dive-bombers from the *Akagi* and the *Kaga*, 36 Kate torpedo-carrying bombers from the *Soryu* and the *Hiryu*, and 9 Zero fighters from each carrier.

The second striking force was similar, the dive-bombers coming from the *Soryu* and the *Hiryu* this time, and the torpedo-carrying aircraft from the other two carriers. But for the moment these remained on their respective flight-decks.

The Japanese formation was detected by radar on Midway at 05.53, when still 93 miles away. By 06.00 every U.S. plane was off the ground. The bombers and Catalinas were ordered to keep well away, while the fighter-planes gained altitude; but the latter became so occupied defending themselves against the Zeros that the Japanese bombers were hindered only by anti-aircraft fire. Much damage was caused, though less than the Japanese had hoped; the runway could still be used, and the Japanese air commander reported that another attack was needed. This was to be the cause of the Japanese disasters. In the meantime, the American fighter-planes had suffered heavily from the Zeros. A score of Buffaloes and half a dozen Wildcats had taken off to meet the attack, but only nine returned—and seven of those were badly shot-up. The Japanese had lost only six planes.

It was during this attack that the Catalina had sighted the Japanese carriers. Several other planes made individual attacks on them, but without success. Soon afterwards, at 06.15, the first raid by planes from Midway was made on them. The force was a small one—six torpedo-carrying Avengers and four Marauders, without any fighter-escort. They went in to the attack from both sides, but met with a hail of fire from the ships as well as being set on by Zeros; only three of the ten returned, and not one torpedo hit.[1]

The day was beginning badly for the Americans. But Nagumo then made a decision which was to have a disastrous effect for two of his carriers. He had received the report that another attack on Midway was needed to put the airfield out of action. But only the aircraft on the *Hiryu* and the *Soryu* had been loaded with bombs; the other planes on the *Akagi* and the *Kaga* were ready with torpedoes, and so orders were given for them to be taken down again to have the torpedoes replaced with bombs. It was a rush job; the mechanics and aircraftmen worked furiously.

Just then, the second American attack began. It was made by air-craft of the Marine Corps based on Midway, a squadron of Douglas Dauntless commanded by Major Lofton Henderson. They did no better than the first attack. Only eight of the sixteen got back to base, and six of those were only good for the scrap-heap. Fifteen Flying Fortresses attacked next, at 08.10 hours, each dropping about four tons of bombs from 20,000 feet but without obtaining a single hit on the Japanese ships. The Fortresses were followed ten minutes later by eleven Vindicators, which had no greater success with their bombs. Two of them were shot down, but all the Fortresses got safely back to Midway.

In the meantime, Nagumo had sent off air patrols to search for the U.S. Fleet to the east. The cruisers and battleships had flown off their seaplanes, and reconnaissance planes had taken off from the *Akagi* and the *Kaga*. At 07.28 the seaplane from the *Tone* had reported ten enemy ships 240 miles north of Midway and proceeding at twenty knots, course 150.

It was Fletcher! But the Japanese pilot had not sighted the carriers, at least not at first; and when he did report them, at 08.20, he was not quite certain. And this caused the more optimistic among Nagumo's staff officers to doubt the presence of the American carriers—otherwise, why had their aircraft not yet attacked?

---

[1] In addition to anti-aircraft fire, the battleships fired their main armament at the planes coming in at low level, so that great walls of water rose in front of them.

In any case, there was a large enough enemy force some 200 miles to the east that was worth attacking. But torpedoes rather than bombs were required, and Nagumo hesitated to change his orders a second time, and to send the planes now loaded with bombs on the flight-decks of the *Akagi* and the *Kaga* back to have torpedoes fitted again.

There was another problem, just then. The first striking force of 108 planes—or rather, the 102 which had returned from Midway—were wanting to land on their carriers: some were damaged, all were short of fuel. The flight-decks had to be cleared for them. But by flying off the planes waiting to make an attack, or by sending them below? Nagumo's second-in-command, Rear-Admiral Yamagachi, favoured the former solution, and signalled his opinion from the *Hiryu*. But Nagumo thought it dangerous to send off the bombers without fighter escort; the fate of the American bombers was a lesson in this respect. All the Japanese fighters, however, had just been used against the American attacks and were in need of fuel and ammunition.

It was a difficult choice to make. . . . But Nagumo decided that in order to receive the planes returning from Midway the bombers on the flight-decks were to be sent back below—and while they were there, the bombs could be replaced with torpedoes. Again, there was a hectic scene on the lower decks of the *Akagi* and the *Kaga*; and in their haste the mechanics unfortunately left the bombs lying about instead of stowing them away in their racks there and then.

The last plane landed at 09.18, and Nagumo at once speeded north at thirty knots to reduce the distance between himself and the American force, which he intended to attack at 10.30 with sixty torpedo-carrying aircraft.

Meanwhile, Rear-Admiral Fletcher, having received the reports that the enemy had been sighted, ordered Spruance to head south-west with

Vindicator, SB 2U-3 of the U.S. Marines

the *Hornet* and the *Enterprise*; he himself would follow with the *Yorktown* as soon as he had recovered the planes on patrol. Rear-Admiral Spruance reckoned on flying off the first striking force at about 09.00, when he would be one hundred miles or so from the enemy, supposing the latter had remained on the same course. But reports of the Japanese raid on Midway caused him to attack earlier; perhaps his planes would have the luck to come upon the enemy carriers while they were engaged in preparing a second raid, their flight-decks covered with aircraft. So at 07.00 he began flying off 116 aircraft—20 fighters, 67 dive-bombers, and 29 torpedo-carrying planes. And at 08.38 35 aircraft from the *Yorktown* were airborne too—17 Dauntless Douglas bombers, 12 torpedo-carrying planes, and 6 fighters.

But things went wrong. A formation of 35 bombers with fighter escort, commanded by Lieutenant-Commander Mitchell of the *Hornet*, was unable to find the Japanese carriers as they had altered course. Thirteen of the bombers had to land on Midway to refuel; and all the Wildcats ran out of fuel and had to make forced landings on the sea.

The first to find the enemy were the fifteen torpedo-carrying aircraft from the *Hornet* led by Lieutenant-Commander John C. Waldron. He sighted the Japanese carriers at 09.25 and went in to attack although without fighter escort. It was another massacre. The Zeros and the anti-aircraft fire made short work of the slow bombers, all of which pressed home their attack with determination. But no hit was obtained, and of the thirty men in the fifteen planes only one survived.[1]

A few minutes later the fourteen torpedo-carrying aircraft from the *Enterprise* attacked, also without fighter escort. All but four were shot down, and again no damage was caused to the enemy. Then the *Yorktown*'s planes went in; they had fighter cover—six planes which were almost at once destroyed by Zeros. Nevertheless, the leader of the squadron, Lieutenant-Commander Massey, bravely pressed home his attack on the *Soryu*. Six aircraft including his own were shot down in flames before they had even fired their torpedoes. The other six succeeded in getting within range, but all missed their target and only three of them returned.

It seemed hopeless. Apart from the lack of success of the planes based on Midway, less than fifty of the hundred-odd aircraft from the carriers had found their target, and only seven of them had returned. Were the Japanese unbeatable?

Hardly—since they were beaten eventually. But the Japanese pilots were undoubtedly the more skilful and had far more experience. Six months of uninterrupted success had its value, too. And the Americans had still much to learn. . . .

The Japanese fleet had re-formed after shaking off the attacks, and at 10.20 continued on its northward course in majestic array, the four carriers screened by the two battleships, three cruisers and eleven destroyers. The *Akagi* and the *Soryu* were five miles apart and were followed respectively by the *Kaga* and the *Hiryu*, 2,000 yards astern.

---

[1] Lt. George H. Gay was rescued from his rubber dinghy by a Catalina the following afternoon.

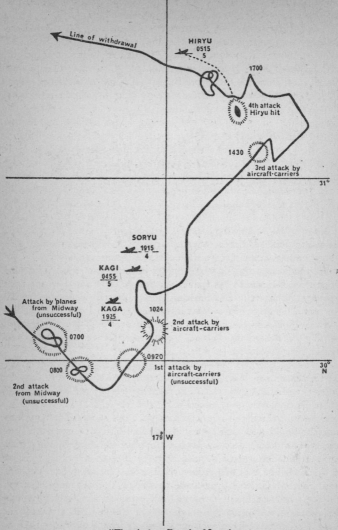

Line of withdrawal

HIRYU
0515
5

1700

4th attack
Hiryu hit

1430

3rd attack
by aircraft-carriers

31°

SORYU
1915
4

KAGI
0455
5

KAGA
1925
4

1024

2nd attack by
aircraft-carriers

Attack by planes
from Midway
(unsuccessful)

0700

0800

0920

1st attack by
aircraft-carriers
(unsuccessful)

30°
N

2nd attack
from Midway
(unsuccessful)

179° W

"The glorious Fourth of June"

On all their flight-decks were aircraft with engines turning, waiting to fly off for the attack scheduled for 10.30 hours.

It was then that the luck changed. . . . American dive-bombers were suddenly seen approaching. . . .

"Dark objects were already falling—bombs, and coming straight at me! Instinctively, I crouched and ran along the deck for the nearest shelter. . . . There came an explosion, a blinding flash from a direct hit, then a second explosion more violent than the first. I was badly

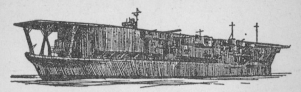

The U.S. carrier *Saratoga* of the same class as the *Lexington*

shaken by blast. Then there was an extraordinary silence. The crackle of ack-ack guns had ceased. I got to my feet and looked at the sky. The enemy planes were already out of sight. . . ."[1]

The *Akagi* had been hit three times. One bomb had smashed into the hangar amidships, another had split open the flight deck on the port quarter, and the third had burst among the aircraft waiting to fly off. No mortal hurt had been caused—except that, in the hangar, the bombs which had been left lying about began to explode one after the other. Then the fire spread to the loaded aircraft, and soon the whole hangar was ablaze.

It was the work of the squadron of Dauntless Douglas bombers led by Lieutenant-Commander McClusky of the *Enterprise*—"the big E", as the crew called her. McClusky and his thirty-three bombers had been airborne since 07.45, and should have turned back to their carrier long before sighting the target, if they were not to risk running out of fuel. But their leader had continued searching for the enemy, and as a just reward had sighted the Japanese carriers immediately after they had been attacked by the torpedo-carrying aircraft. In spite of the cost to the latter, their attack proved most useful; for when the bombers went in, the Japanese fighter-planes had not had time to regain height and were not in position to break up the attack. McClusky kept half the squadron with him against the *Akagi*, and the rest attacked the *Kaga*. The latter suffered even more heavily; the American air-crews

[1] Fuchida and Okubiya, *op. cit.*, Captain Fuchida was on Nagumo's Staff aboard the *Akagi*.

declared they had seen her deck "peel off like the skin of a banana". Everyone on the bridge was killed,[1] aircraft refuelling on the flight-deck caught fire, bombs began to explode, and soon the whole carrier was a mass of flames. She sank during the evening.

While the *Akagi* and the *Kaga* were being dealt these mortal blows, dive-bombers from the *Yorktown* attacked the *Soryu* and were as fortunate as those from "the big E" in finding the Japanese aircraft being

The Japanese carrier *Kaga*

got ready on the flight-deck and none in the air. The *Soryu*, too, was badly damaged and set on fire. And later, at 14.00, the U.S. submarine *Nautilus* fired three torpedoes into the blazing carrier. She went down at 19.13, a few minutes before the *Kaga* disappeared. The crippled *Akagi* was sunk by the Japanese during the night, on orders from Yamamoto, after Nagumo had shifted his flag to the cruiser *Nagara*.

There was still the *Hiryu*, in which Rear-Admiral Yamaguchi was flying his flag. While the destroyers were busy rescuing survivors from the other carriers,[2] he refused to be deterred from the task of flying off his aircraft to attack the U.S. carriers as ordered. Eighteen Vals and six Zeros were airborne at 10.40, commanded by Lieutenant Michio Kabayashi, a veteran who had taken part in all the battles since Pearl Harbor. His formation was guided to the target by the returning American planes. But the fighter cover shot down ten of the Japanese. Nevertheless, eight of them succeeded in attacking the *Yorktown*, which was damaged. Several fires broke out, but by 14.00 the situation was under control and the carrier was able to get up a speed of eighteen knots. Her radar and radio had been put out of service, and Rear-Admiral Fletcher shifted his flag to the cruiser *Astoria*.

Meanwhile, a plane from the *Soryu* which had been shadowing the U.S. fleet returned to the *Hiryu* with exact information about the composition of the enemy force; until then, the Japanese had only a general idea of it. Yamaguchi thus heard of the presence of the *Yorktown*, which

[1] Except the Captain, Ryusaku Yanagimoto, who refused to leave his ship and went down with her.

[2] 263 men were lost from the *Akagi*, 718 from the *Soryu*, and 800 from the *Kaga*.

the whole Japanese Navy believed to have been sunk at the Battle of the Coral Sea. Another attack was therefore prepared. All the available aircraft were flown off—ten torpedo-carrying bombers, including a survivor from the *Agaki*, and six Zeros, two of which had belonged to the *Kaga*. They were all airborne by 12.45, led by Lieutenant Joichi Tomonaga. Everyone on the *Hiryu*'s deck watched his plane with some emotion as it disappeared into the distance, knowing it had not enough fuel for the return flight. One of the petrol tanks had been smashed during the morning's attack on Midway, and there had not been time to repair it.

The *Yorktown* had just got under way again, and flown off fighter cover of eight Wildcats, when the second wave of Japanese planes was sighted. Their Zeros quickly disposed of the Wildcats, and the torpedo-carrying bombers went in at low level from all directions. Like the Japanese battleships earlier in the day, the American cruisers protecting the *Yorktown* fired their big guns at the sea to throw up great walls of water as the enemy planes approached. Four of them got through and launched their torpedoes at 500 yards. The *Yorktown* evaded two, but one hit her fuel tanks on the port side and the other struck her aft, putting the controls out of action. She drifted to a stop, and twenty minutes later had a list of 26 degrees. At three o'clock Captain Buckmaster gave the order to abandon ship.

It was lovely weather, with a calm sea, and the water was quite warm . . . ideal conditions for being shipwrecked. The sailors waiting to be picked up by the destroyers were making jests—"Taxi!" they cried, giving a jerk of the thumb, when a piece of wreckage or a raft went floating past. None of them is believed to have been drowned.[1]

Fletcher knew there was still one of the Japanese carriers untouched, and had sent off a patrol to report her position. The information was received at 14.45—just as the *Yorktown* was being attacked for the second time. A Japanese carrier, two battleships, three cruisers and four destroyers were on a northerly course, 110 miles W.N.W. of the *Yorktown*. Forty-five minutes later, the *Enterprise* turned into the wind to fly off four Douglas bombers for an attack on the remaining enemy carrier—without any fighter escort! The few Wildcats still available were needed as air cover for the fleet. McClusky—the hero of the day— was again in command, and his luck stayed with him; he certainly deserved it.

Everyone in the *Hiryu* was at the end of his resistance. The air-crews had all flown several missions since early morning. The ship's crew

---

[1] Morison, *op. cit.*, 2,270 men from the *Yorktown* were picked up by destroyers in two hours.

were exhausted. Altogether, attacks by 79 planes had been beaten off, 26 torpedoes and 70 bombs had missed the carrier. But those of McClusky and his handful of men did not miss, in spite of the frantic efforts of the anti-aircraft gunners, and although the carrier's commander, Captain Kaku, sent her surging through the water at thirty knots. The first bombs fell harmlessly into the sea, but then four hits in swift succession were obtained. The flight-deck was split open and aircraft were set on fire; the engine-room was damaged and cut off by fire from the rest of the ship. The *Hiryu* lost speed. Soon after nine she was lying stopped with a list of 15 degrees. It became evident that she could not be saved, and half past two in the morning Nagumo ordered her to be sunk. The destroyers *Kazagumo* and *Yugumo* torpedoed her at 05.40 hours; but it was 08.20 before the *Hiryu* finally disappeared, taking 416 men down with her—nearly all the engine-room personnel, who had been cut off by the flames. Both Yamaguchi and his flag-captain, Kaku, shared the fate of their ship.

With the last Japanese carrier eliminated, the American aircraft turned their attention to the battleships and cruisers. But all the bombs aimed at the *Haruna* missed her; the cruiser *Tone* beat off three attacks in the space of an hour, and so did the *Chikuma*. Nearly all these attacks were made by planes based on Midway, and they had no better luck than in the morning.

Nagumo, who had been directing the battle from the light cruiser

Nagara since eleven-thirty in the morning, realized that the situation was hopeless after the *Hiryu* had been put out of action. At one moment he considered concentrating his ships for a night attack, then decided to withdraw on a north-westerly course.

While these dramatic events had been fought out, Admiral Yamamoto and his battle fleet were ploughing through thick mist, and the reports he received from Nagumo did not make the outlook any clearer. He was 350 miles from the scene of action, and all he could do

Admiral Nagumo

was to head eastwards through the mist as fast as possible. He looked at the positions of his other forces on the operations map: the nearest to Nagumo was Vice-Admiral Kondo's invasion group—160 miles away —which had two battleships and four heavy cruisers but only one small aircraft-carrier; Rear-Admiral Kakuta had two carriers with him, but he was far away, 120 miles from Dutch Harbour—and was due to refuel from tankers on the morning of the 6th. In other words, he could not reach the scene with the two carriers until June 8th.

Yamamoto was still considering the possibilities when, during the evening, he was informed that the *Hiryu* had been put out of action. After some hesitation, at 02.55 on July 5th, he sent out the order which admitted the Japanese defeat. It began with the words: "Operation Midway is called off. . . ." But the curtain had not yet come down.

By the evening of June 4th Admiral Nimitz could breathe more freely. Three or four of the large enemy carriers were already out of action—the loss of the *Hiryu* was only confirmed later; while on the American side the losses were relatively slight, especially as the fate of the *Yorktown* was still in the balance. The order had been given to abandon ship, but she was still afloat and the list had not increased. If an ocean-going tug had been with the American Fleet it might have been possible to tow the *Yorktown* to Pearl Harbor. American pilots who flew over her at dawn on the 5th thought she looked almost intact. At the same time, Lieutenant-Commander Ramsey, whose destroyer had been detailed to keep watch on the carrier and to torpedo her should she seem likely to fall into enemy hands, reported that in his opinion she might still be saved. Ramsey had just rescued two men who had been left for dead in the sick-bay when the *Yorktown* was abandoned; one of them, with a badly gashed head, had managed to crawl up to the deck and fire a machine-gun to attract attention.

The incident had led Ramsey to put a few men aboard the carrier. At noon the mine-sweeper *Vireo* arrived and got a tow aboard the *Yorktown*, but was hardly powerful enough to hold her against the wind. It was late on the night of June 5th before the destroyer *Hammann* was able to put Catain Buckmaster and 170 men back on board the carrier. Everyone set to work. The *Hammann* had come alongside to give the necessary power for correcting the list and for putting out the few remaining fires. Five other destroyers were patrolling in the vicinity, on the watch for enemy submarines.

Yet the *I-168*, Lieutenant-Commander Yahachi Tanabe, slipped through the screen.[1] Yamamoto had directed Tanabe to the area, and after twenty-four hours' searching he had found the *Yorktown* soon after noon on the 6th. At 13.30 he fired four torpedoes at her. One missed,

[1] The *I-168* had shelled Midway during the night of June 4th.

two others passed under the *Hammann* and exploded against the carrier, while the fourth blew the destroyer in half.

Still the *Yorktown* did not sink. She stayed afloat all that night, but at daybreak her list suddenly increased, and just before six o'clock on June 7th she went down to join the four Japanese carriers which she had helped send to the bottom.

Throughout June 5th American aircraft had been harrying Vice-Admiral Kurita's cruisers, which were approaching Midway with the intention of shelling the island that night. Two of them, the *Mogami* and the *Mikuma*, had collided; their position was reported by the submarine *Tambor*, and they were attacked at dawn on June 5th by aircraft from Midway. But ill-luck still dogged the Americans. Not one hit would have been scored had it not been for the misfortune of Captain Richard E. Fleming of the Marines, whose aircraft got out of control and crashed on the after-turret of the *Mikuma*.

In the afternoon, bombers from the *Hornet* and the *Enterprise* searched in vain for the remainder of Kurita's ships. All they could find was a spiteful destroyer, and they failed to sink even that. The *Tanikaze* not only evaded about fifty dive-bombers, but to add insult to injury shot one down! However, the American pilots, returning long after sunset, were able to congratulate themselves on accomplishing the first successful deck landings at night in time of war.

At dawn on the 6th they found the two damaged cruisers, and sank the *Mikuma*; but the *Mogami* escaped, though unable to do more than sixteen knots. However, she spent the next two years in the repair yards.

A tail-piece to the battle is recounted by S. E. Morison. Among the aircraft sent to bomb the retreating Japanese were Flying Fortresses recently arrived on Midway, and whose crews made up for their lack of experience by their tremendous gusto. On the evening of the 6th, the crews of half a dozen of them returned overjoyed. They had found one of the enemy cruisers and sunk it in the record time of fifteen seconds!

One man who was not impressed by this feat was Lieutenant-Commander Olsen of the submarine *Grayling*. When he reached Midway a few days later he was fuming with rage and demanding to know who those damned B.17 crews were who had showered him with bombs and made him crash-dive—at the exact place and time that the supposed Japanese cruiser had been sunk in record time.

The Battle of Midway ended in a crushing defeat for the Japanese on June 6th, the day they had intended to be D-Day minus one. The Americans had been lucky, very lucky in fact. They had indeed done all they could to deserve this victory, but it must be admitted that they had been greatly helped by their opponents' mistakes. The Japanese had been too sure of themselves, had under-estimated the enemy and spread their forces over too wide an area; their adversaries had never despaired, but had fought on with determination, inexperienced yet persevering, and extremely well informed—this was the best card in their hand—and in the end were favoured by Fortune.

The Battle of Midway marked not only the first Japanese naval defeat in 350 years, but also a change in naval warfare. Midway tolled the knell of the battleship and ushered in the aircraft-carrier as the capital ship of the future. For although the Japanese had eleven battleships and the Americans none, they were not able to employ any of them effectively in the battle, except once or twice against enemy aircraft.

However, Yamamoto had not deployed his battleships to the best advantage. If he had grouped them with his carriers, their great anti-aircraft fire-power might have saved the *Kaga* and the *Akagi* during those fateful five minutes. The Americans kept their carriers and battleships in close association, during the remainder of the Pacific campaign, and results justified their tactics.

Nevertheless, after the Battle of Midway the Japanese still had numerical superiority, even in aircraft-carriers. But they had received a setback in their offensive, and the Americans proceeded to exploit that advantage tentatively at first, until the new ships on the stocks came into service, then with ever greater assurance.

On August 7th, 1942, two months after Midway, a division of Marines landed on Guadalcanal, in the Solomons, to try to dislodge the Japanese. Admiral Mikawa reacted swiftly; on the night of the 8th his cruisers attacked the Allied covering force off Savo Island, and in a matter of minutes torpedoed three American cruisers—the *Vincennes*, *Astoria*, and *Quincy*—and one Australian, the *Canberra*. The channel in which they were sunk became known by the appropriate name of "Ironbottom Sound". But this was only the beginning of a long drawn-out struggle for the possession of Guadalcanal, which was costly to both sides. On August 23rd, during the battle for the eastern Solomons, the Americans sank the *Ryujo* and destroyed ninety aircraft. Then on October 11th, off Cape Hope, Rear-Admiral Scott succeeded in crossing the T to the Japanese force and sank a cruiser and a destroyer. Unfortunately, an American destroyer was sunk through coming under cross-fire.

A fortnight later the scales turned in favour of the Japanese at the Battle of Santa Cruz, where the *Hornet* was lost and the *Enterprise* was badly damaged. But at the naval Battle of Guadalcanal on November 14th, "one of the fiercest actions ever known", to quote Admiral Halsey, the battleship *Washington*, though fighting against the whole Japanese squadron at one period, so badly damaged the enemy battleship *Kirishima* that Admiral Kondo had to order her to be scuttled.

Then, in the course of a night action known as the Battle of Tassafaronga, on November 30th, eight Japanese destroyers torpedoed four U.S. cruisers—one of which sank—for the cost of only one destroyer. This battle, which can be considered a model of a destroyer torpedo-action against superior forces, was the last important naval battle in the struggle for Guadalcanal. Two months later, on February 9th, 1943, the Americans found themselves in undisputed possession of the island; the Japanese had evacuated their remaining troops during the previous three nights, sending in fast destroyers to take them off—an operation which the American sailors called "the Tokyo Express".

All through 1943 and 1944 the American—and Australian—operations made steady progress in the South-West Pacific. In the space of fifteen months the Allied forces captured the Gilbert and then the Marshall Islands, expelled the Japanese from New Guinea, and on June 15th, 1944, American marines and infantry landed on Saipan Island in the Marianas, the key position of the Japanese defences. Four days later, the aircraft of the rival fleets met in a fierce battle.

There was a day's indecisive fighting between aircraft of the 58th Task Force (Admiral Mitscher) and those of Admiral Ozawa's carriers; then, that evening, the U.S. submarines *Albacore* and *Cavalla* succeeded in penetrating the Japanese destroyer screen and sinking the *Taiho* and the *Shokaku* in a torpedo attack. Ozawa withdrew westwards, and Mitscher spent most of the following day (June 20th) trying to locate the enemy. He was hampered in his pursuit by a fresh easterly wind, which obliged his carriers to turn about each time their aircraft took off or landed. So modern carriers were as dependent upon the wind as sailing-ships had been.[1]

Finally, at 15.30 hours, the enemy was sighted far to the west speeding at twenty knots and only just within range of the American carrier-aircraft. Mitscher hesitated whether to send his planes on what would undoubtedly be a hazardous and costly enterprise. But the decision was made, and they flew off; and the first reports of victory were received at 19.00 hours—the carrier *Chiyoda* had been set on fire, and the *Hiyo* was sinking.

There was no moon that night, and the returning planes had to land in the dark; they had hardly any fuel left, and so were unable to circle their carrier and wait for permission to land. They landed as best they

[1] Except that the sailing-ships tried to get to windward, whereas the carriers have to turn into the wind.

could, on the first carrier they sighted, and there were many serious accidents. One light carrier eventually had twice its complement of planes on the flight-deck, and the damaged ones were pushed overside to make room for planes still in the air. The sea became studded with signal-lights, where pilots had made forced landings. Throughout the night, destroyers and aircraft searched the waters, and altogether picked up 150 of the 209 airmen.

A powerful U.S. force landed in the Philippines on October 20th, and between the 23rd and 28th a series of major naval actions—the Battle of Leyte Gulf, as they have been named—ended in the total defeat of the Japanese Fleet attempting to interfere with the landings. The battles involved every type of ship from battleship to motor-torpedo-boat. The Japanese lost three battleships, four carriers, ten cruisers, and nine destroyers, and the cost to the Americans was only two small carriers and three destroyers. It was during these battles that the Kamikazes, the Japanese suicide-pilots, first put in an appearance; they caused the destruction of the carrier *St. Lô*.

In spite of this decisive blow to the Japanese Fleet, the war in the Pacific continued for another ten months. In February, 1945, the Americans captured IwoJima after fierce fighting. On April 1st their Navy launched an amphibious offensive to capture Okinawa, 350 miles south of Japan; not until mid-June was the island finally conquered, so desperate was the Japanese defence. Plans to land Allied forces on the main Japanese islands were being prepared, when in August came the devastating explosion of the Atom-bomb over Hiroshima. Japan surrendered on August 15th.

The triumph of the aircraft-carrier has been acknowledged in all the many books on the navies in the Second World War. Yet battleships were brought into use by the Americans during the Korean War. The prestige of the carrier received a blow when the U.S. Government cancelled the order for 60,000-ton *Forrestal*-class carriers. But three years later work began again on them. The guided missile seemed to make bombers unnecessary; yet it was soon discovered to have little chance of hitting a fleet at sea. The nuclear submarine is thought to have transformed sea warfare, but no one is very sure . . .

One fact is certain—while air freight is so costly, there will always be ships to carry the millions of tons of cargoes every year. And while there are ships, there will be seamen to sail them. . . . The eternal problems of sea warfare will always exist, in changing form no doubt, but bounded by the same laws which have held good over the past twenty-five centuries—if it is only Archimedes's principle.

CHIEF DATES IN SEA WARFARE

CHIEF DATES IN SEA WARFARE

	B.C.
Salamis	480
Mycale	479
Mylae	260
Mount Ecnome	256
Drepanum (Trapani)	249
Egadian Islands	241
Syracuse	212
Coryce	191
Myonnese	190
Lemnos	73
Nauloque	35
Actium	31

	A.D.
Sinnigallia	551
Bravalla	735
Paris	885
Beirut	June 7th, 1191
Constantinople	July 17th, 1203
„	April 22nd, 1204
Damme	May 31st, 1213
South Foreland	August 24th, 1217
Portsmouth	March 24th, 1338
Arnemuiden	September 23rd, 1338
Southampton	October 6th, 1338
Sluys	June 24th, 1340
Constantinople	1453
Famagusta	1571
Lepanto	October 7th, 1571
Spanish Armada (Plymouth—Gravelines)	July 21st–29th, 1588
Dover	May 29th, 1652
Plymouth	August 26th, 1652
Kentish Knock	October 8th, 1652
Dungeness	December 10th, 1652
Portsmouth	February 28th, 1653
North Foreland	June 11th, 1653
Scheveningen	August 10th, 1653
Lowestoft	June 13th, 1665
The "Four Days' Battle"	June 11th–14th, 1666
Thames Estuary	June 17th–22nd, 1667
Sole Bay	June 7th, 1672
Schoneveldt	June 14th, 1673
Texel	August 21st, 1673
Alicuri	January 8th, 1676

Augusta	April 22nd, 1676
Palermo	June 2nd, 1676
Bantry	May 9th, 1689
Beachy Head	July 10th, 1690
Barfleur	May 27th, 1692
La Hougue	June 2nd, 1692
Lagos	June 27th, 1693
Texel	June 29th, 1694
Cadiz	August 22nd, 1702
Vigo Bay	October 22nd, 1702
Gibraltar	August 4th, 1704
Velez-Malaga	August 22nd, 1704
Toulon	1707
Beachy Head	May 13th, 1707
The Lizard	October 21st, 1707
Toulon	February 11th, 1744
Finisterre	May 14th, 1747
St. Cast	September 4th, 1758
Quiberon Bay	November 20th, 1759
Tchesme	July 5th–7th, 1770
The *Belle Poule* and the *Arethusa*	June 17th, 1778
Ushant	July 23rd, 1778
Grenada	June 30th, 1779
The *Serapis* and the *Poor Richard*	September 23rd, 1779
The *Surveillante* and the *Quebec*	October 6th, 1779
Dominica	April 17th, 1780
La Praya	April 16th, 1781
Dogger Bank	August 3rd, 1781
Chesapeake Bay	September 5th, 1781
The Saints	April 12th, 1782
Viborg	June 3rd, 1790
Svenksund	July 9th, 1790
The "Glorious First of June"	May 28th–June 1st, 1794
Cape St. Vincent	February 14th, 1797
The Nile	August 1st, 1798
Malta	March 30th, 1800
Copenhagen	April 2nd, 1801
The "Fifteen-Twenty"	July 22nd, 1805
Trafalgar	October 21st, 1805
Finisterre	November 4th, 1805
Copenhagen	September 2nd–5th, 1807
Navarino	October 20th, 1827
San Juan d'Ulloa	November 27th, 1838
Sinope	November 30th, 1853
Hampton Roads	March 8th–9th, 1862
Heligoland	May 9th, 1864
The *Alabama* and the *Kearsarge*	June 19th, 1864
Lissa	July 20th, 1866
Danube Estuary	May 25th, 1877
Batoum	January 20th, 1878

Foochow	August 23rd, 1884
Yellow River	September 17th, 1894
Manila	April 30th, 1898
Santiago, Cuba	July 3rd, 1898
Port Arthur	February 8th, 1904
Yellow Sea	August 10th, 1904
Tsou-Shima	May 27th, 1905
Penang	October 28th, 1914
Coronel	November 1st, 1914
Cocos Islands	November 9th, 1914
Falkland Islands	December 8th, 1914
Dogger Bank	January 24th, 1915
Jutland	May 31st, 1916
River Plate	December 13th, 1939
Calabria	July 9th, 1940
Taranto	November 11th, 1940
Matapan	March 28th, 1941
Pursuit of the *Bismarck*	May 24th–27th, 1941
Pearl Harbor	December 7th, 1941
Kuantan	December 10th, 1941
Alexandria	December 19th, 1941.
Java Sea	February 27th, 1942
Coral Sea	May 6th–8th, 1942
Midway Island	June 4th–6th, 1942
Convoy PQ.17	July 1st–7th, 1942
Savo Island	August 8th, 1942
Eastern Solomons	August 23rd, 1942
Cape Hope	October 11th, 1942
Santa Cruz	October 26th, 1942
Tassafaronga	November 30th, 1942
Guadalcanal	November 14th, 1942
North Cape	December 26th, 1943
Philippines	June 19th–20th, 1944
Leyte Gulf	October 23rd–28th, 1944
IwoJima	February, 1945
Okinawa	April–June, 1945

GENERAL INDEX

INDEX OF SHIPS

INDEX OF SHIPS

NOTE: Except where otherwise indicated, ships are British. Aus = Austrian; Aust = Australian; Da = Danish; Du = Dutch; F = French; G = German; It = Italian; Jap = Japanese; R = Russian; Sp = Spanish; US = American